What Blood Won't Tell

What Blood Won't Tell

A HISTORY OF RACE ON TRIAL IN AMERICA

Ariela J. Gross

HARVARD UNIVERSITY PRESS

Cambridge, Massachusetts

London, England

First Harvard University Press paperback edition, 2010

Library of Congress Cataloging-in-Publication Data

Gross, Ariela Julie.
What blood won't tell : a history of race on trial in America / Ariela J. Gross.
p. cm.
Includes bibliographical references and index.
ISBN 978-0-674-03130-2 (cloth : alk. paper)
ISBN 978-0-674-04798-3 (pbk.)
1. Race discrimination—Law and legislation—United States.   2. Minorities—Legal status, laws,
etc.—United States.   3. United States—Race relations.   I. Title.

KF4755.G76 2008
305.800973—dc22   2008011271

For Raphaela and Sophia

Contents

A Note on Terminology

This history traces a moving target, talking about "race" in relation to "nation," "culture," "character," and "citizenship," although these concepts were themselves in flux. Americans used the word "race" in a variety of ways, sometimes to refer to the "african and caucasian races," which they considered the grand divisions of "mankind," and sometimes to refer to much smaller groupings of people, the "mediterranean" or "iberic" or "Italian" races. Regardless of the actual genetic basis for the racial categories "black," "white," or "Indian," Americans have organized their society and polity around these categories, and we can learn what *they* thought race was, in practical terms, by the way they sorted individuals into identities.

For particular racial identities I have employed conventional terminology for the most part, using the terms "black" and "African American" interchangeably, as well as "white" and "Indian" to describe people who identified themselves or were recognized socially as such. I prefer "Indian" to "Native American" because in early America as well as today, most Indians have identified themselves that way. When possible and appropriate I refer to people as members of their particular tribe or nation. I use terms such as "black" and "white" not to invest them with any essential meaning but to explore the meanings Americans endowed them with over the course of the past two centuries.

Talking about racial "mixture" is even more problematic than talking about race itself, because the metaphor of mixing suggests the plausibility of race as "blood." The term "mixed race" evokes "mixed blood," an important historical concept but not a phrase to be accepted and used uncrit-ically. I have tried to avoid terms like "mixed race," "interracial," "racial mixture," and even "multiracial," because they imply that race is an inter-nal essence, like blood, that can be mixed, two parts this and three parts that. "Mixture," however, can describe the social interaction, marriage, and sex among peoples thought to have been distinct by contemporary ob-servers. The phrase "mixed ancestry" can describe, as neutrally as possi-ble, those individuals whose parents and grandparents held differing iden-tities, regardless of the bases of those identities. That is, a woman whose mother was a citizen of the Paiute Indian tribe in Arizona and whose fa-ther identified as "negro" (regardless of the variety of their ancestry, and even if both her parents shared the same fraction of "Indian" and "negro blood") could be meaningfully described as "of mixed ancestry." At the same time, many people who might fall into the rubric of "mixed ancestry" did not have a settled identity. I refer to these individuals and communi-ties—people who were not recognized by contemporary society as fitting into the categories of "black" or "white"—as "racially ambiguous"; a vari-ety of geographic metaphors, such as "borderlands" and "middle grounds," also describe people who confounded racial categories. The unexpected persistence of the challenges they posed is the subject of this book.

What Blood Won't Tell

Introduction

IN 1857 ALEXINA MORRISON, a slave in Jefferson Parish, Louisiana, ran away from her master and surrendered herself to the parish jail for protection. She told her jailer, William Dennison, that she was white and had been kidnapped into slavery in Arkansas. Dennison believed Alexina, who had "blue eyes and flaxen hair," took her home with him to the town of Carrollton, and introduced her into white society, eventually taking her to balls and other amusements with his family. With the help of Dennison and other white citizens, she sued her master, James White, for her freedom in parish court. Alexina had won over the white people of the town of Carrollton to such a degree that when James White came to file his answer at the courthouse, he "was surrounded and threatened by a lawless mob" who wanted to lynch him for keeping poor Alexina as a slave.[1]

Morrison v. White went through three trials in Jefferson Parish Court. At the first trial, Alexina's lawyers asked the jurors to trust the evidence of their senses: to look at her for themselves, and to believe the testimony of neighbors like them. Alexina's witnesses assured the jury that she had fit in perfectly at their balls, that she had slept in their beds with their daughters, and that they surely would have known if she had a drop of African blood. White's lawyers instead tried to show that race was something one could not discover through appearances, something that required expertise to discern. White's witnesses used the language of science to declare Alexina Morrison "colored," and White introduced documents to prove that she and her mother before her had been slaves of the Morrison family

1

in Arkansas and Texas. The trial ended in a hung jury. After the mob attack, White won a change of venue for the second trial, claiming that the citizens of Carrollton were biased against him.[2]

At the second trial Alexina brought more white witnesses who swore their certainty that she was white, arguing that a true Louisiana native could "always detect in a person whether that person is of African origin," just as "the alligator . . . knows three days in advance that a storm is brewing." Several doctors testified on her behalf that the shape of her hair follicles and the arches of her feet proved her whiteness. James White, by contrast, tried to prove her "negro blood" by calling her sexual virtue into doubt, accusing her jailer of having fathered her child, and questioning her witnesses about her behavior at public balls. Yet the second jury found in Alexina Morrison's favor. White won a new trial in the Louisiana Supreme Court, but the third trial, in January 1862, ended in another hung jury, with ten votes for Morrison and two against. Although White appealed again, the Supreme Court shut its doors in February of that year as the Union Army occupied New Orleans. There the documentary trail ends. We don't know what happened to Alexina Morrison, although almost certainly, one way or the other, she found her freedom in 1862 or 1863.[3]

All of the jurors in Alexina's three trials were white men. None of those whose histories we can learn were slaveholders; they included a German butcher, an Irish railroad worker, and a steamboat captain from Alabama. They were people whose deepest commitment to the system of slavery arose from their belief in white supremacy. Yet as wage workers in a slave society, they knew that their whiteness was not completely secure. They themselves were vulnerable to a form of enslavement, laboring for wealthy industrialists and planters who seemed socially and economically alien.[4]

In the process of determining her identity, the white men in the courtroom treated Alexina Morrison in ways a white woman of the time—even a dancing girl or prostitute—would never have been treated, publicly disrobing her and touching her body, enacting the rituals of the slave market. Yet these white men upheld Alexina's claims to whiteness. While it is impossible to know whether they truly believed her claims, it is apparent that her case raised troubling questions for white workingmen about the relationship between whiteness and enslavement. Indeed they may even have found in her favor because they empathized with the specter she raised of "white slavery."

Alexina's story suggests both the power and limits of individual action in the history of race and racism. This enslaved woman might be thought to be the most powerless of victims. Whether she was kidnapped into slavery, as she claimed, or born to the whip and chain, she was at the mercy of her master and other white men. Yet she fled enslavement, persuaded her jailer to free her and crusade on her behalf, performed the role of a white woman, and convinced others of her moral worthiness. In newspapers and fugitive slave narratives, Alexina Morrison's story entered into the larger debate in which Southerners and Northerners argued about the significance of race for citizenship and equality before the law. Her story was at once a buttress to the ideology of white supremacy and a weapon in the war against slavery.

Alexina Morrison was undoubtedly a slave, and almost certainly had some African ancestry, yet she repeatedly won over white jurors, who believed that she should have her freedom. Her racial identity should have been obvious to everyone—certainly to Southerners who insisted they knew race as alligators knew when a storm was coming. But race was not obvious. Nor did legal rules about "negro" identity, formulated in terms of ancestry (such as "one great-grandfather an African"), decide the question. More persuasive to the witnesses and jurors at trial were stories about the hidden marks of race as interpreted by experts, and stories about Alexina's behavior—her dancing at white balls, her mingling with white families, her love affairs with white men. While racial identity might inhere in her blood, how would blood make itself known? The participants in her trial believed that they had to read not only bodies but also actions, demeanor, character, all the ways in which Alexina might *perform* her identity. Alexina may have had a "negro" grandfather, and she certainly had an enslaved mother, but she exhibited whiteness in a way that convinced neighbors and jurors that she was white.

Alexina's story turns on the racial identity trial that became a local cause célèbre. Today the very idea of a racial identity trial may seem bizarre. Trials involving racial identity, however, were common occurrences in local American courts from their beginnings in the late eighteenth century well into the twentieth century, encompassing people of European, African, Asian, Mexican, and Native American ancestry, from the Deep South to the industrial North to the far West.

In the pre–Civil War South, slaves like Alexina sued their masters for their freedom, claiming they were really white and were being wrongly held in slavery. "People of color" who had attained their freedom in one way or another still faced a host of criminal restrictions: they were not allowed to carry handguns, to gather in groups, to dance at night, to speak insolently to a white person, to travel without a pass, or to mingle with slaves. Individuals prosecuted for such crimes sometimes claimed whiteness to avoid prosecution. In these cases it was the individuals themselves who put their own racial identity at issue. Much more often other people challenged an individual's racial identity. For example, "free people of color" were barred from testifying against a white person in every Southern state, so defendants in criminal and civil cases alike tried to have witnesses disqualified on the basis of "colored blood."

Although these trials did not directly put slave status at issue the way freedom suits did, the ultimate point of these cases was to draw the boundary between slaves and free people. Individuals of ambiguous racial identity, especially free people of color, challenged Southerners' equation of slavery with blackness and freedom with whiteness. This came to seem especially important as white Southerners developed a race-based ideology of slavery as a positive good. During the colonial era, and even in the early republic, race had rarely provided the explicit justification for slavery. The founders of the republic perceived slavery as a necessary evil that they professed hope would wither away.

This began to change in the first decades of the nineteenth century. In early America courts framed race in relation to nationhood; in contrast to the Indians, who were members of their own nations, Africans became "negroes," a degraded race uniquely suited for slavery. As the institution of slavery came under increasing attack in the 1830s from Northern abolitionists as well as from insurgent slaves, Southern white ideologues, including judges and lawyers, developed a more explicitly racial justification for slavery. Because blacks were incapable of self-government, slavery was the best possible institution to allow them to flourish. This ideology made it increasingly important to align the slave/free boundary with black and white, giving rise to more hotly contested trials of racial identity.

After the institution of slavery came to an end in a bloody civil war, white Southerners redoubled their efforts to maintain white supremacy in political and social life through violence, law, and a variety of social practices that together became known as the system of "Jim Crow." Northerners and Westerners, too, sought to exclude African Americans and other people of color from public life, and even to expel them from the towns and cities where they lived. As part of the new effort to enforce racial separation, strict legal limitations on sex and marriage across the color line in nearly every state led to continued trials of racial identity long after the end of slavery, throughout the United States. Family members tried to have heirs disinherited by alleging that they were of mixed race and therefore the product of an illegitimate marriage. Marriage bans gave rise to criminal prosecutions against husbands and wives who defended themselves by claiming that the state had mistaken their racial identities. And sometimes husbands sought to avoid the obligations of marriage by claiming they had been tricked into an interracial union. These cases arose in the context not only of black-white marriages but also of relationships involving Indians, Asians, and Mexicans, until the Supreme Court invalidated anti-miscegenation laws in 1967.

Until the mid-twentieth century, racially segregated "Jim Crow" schools meant that some children of contested racial identity would be excluded from white schools. These exclusions resulted in trials when parents brought individual claims asserting that their own children were actually white, or when advocates for excluded groups argued that an entire community or nationality should count as white. Throughout the nineteenth and twentieth centuries, in small towns and mountain hollows, when neighbors feuded, one of the most effective weapons against an enemy was to call him a "negro." For those who lived in the borderlands between black and white, all it took for a family's children to be barred from the white school was for one neighbor to charge another with having "negro blood." Such accusations of "negro blood" might end up in court in suits for slander as well.

Native Americans presented their own unique set of issues regarding racial identity. While courts drew a distinction between membership in an Indian tribe and identification as a "race"—a distinction that corresponded to the difference between "nation" and race"—not all Indians were members of recognized nations. Many tribes in the Northeast and Southeast mixed with other "free people of color" as well as with whites, and some Southeastern tribes held slaves of African descent just as their white neighbors did. Some Indian groups mixed with people of European and African ancestry to form entire communities of racially ambiguous identity which became known by colorful names such as the Melungeons, Brass Ankles, Red Bones, and Croatans. Over the course of the nineteenth

century, the nationhood once accorded to native peoples gradually became subsumed into a racial identity. Particularly after the Civil War, the
new regime of Jim Crow segregation pressured people of multiple, contested, or ambiguous racial identities to come down on the white or black
side of the color line. Ultimately, to attain full citizenship, both individuals
and native groups had to distance themselves from blackness.

Administrative commissions, legislatures, and courts all became involved
in attempting to draw the line between "Indian" and "negro" in the post–
Civil War period. These adjudications of Indian/black identity became especially frequent—and had immediate consequences—at the turn of the
twentieth century, when the federal government began to draw up rolls of
Indians in order to implement its policy of "land allotment," breaking up
tribal lands and governments and apportioning small plots to individual
Indians. The agencies in charge of allotment carried out a segregated process of enrolling Indian citizens, separating "Indians" and "negroes." This
Jim Crow process made a multiracial Indian identity impossible. Thus, the
substantial historical connections between blacks and Indians were covered over and erased from the history of both the South and the West.
Even as far away as Hawai'i, where there were no people of African descent, land allotment introduced the first efforts to define native identity
in racial terms, through fractions of "blood."

Native Hawai'ians, Indians who took up land allotments, Melungeons
who passed as white, and African Americans were all formally U.S. citizens, although they were to different degrees excluded from full participation in social and political life. In the early twentieth century, however, large numbers of new immigrants faced a significant legal barrier
to formal citizenship. Until 1952 the Immigration and Naturalization Act
required that immigrants applying for naturalization to citizenship prove
that they were "free white persons." After the Civil War, when the Fourteenth Amendment to the Constitution finally made citizens of the freed
slaves, the Immigration Act was amended to allow people of "African
nativity" to be eligible for citizenship, but it left all other nonwhites ineligible.

As immigrants from China, Japan, India, and the Near East applied for
citizenship, federal courts had to determine whether they were white.
While Mexican Americans who were in the Southwest at the time of the
Mexican American War attained citizenship automatically by virtue of the
Treaty of Guadalupe Hidalgo—and that presumption of citizenship was

extended to new Mexican immigrants as well—their white status was hardly clear or uncontested. Mexican Americans in Texas and California were excluded from white schools, political institutions, and public accommodations, much as blacks were in the South, and they protested that exclusion by bringing civil rights suits arguing both that the "Mexican race" had suffered discrimination and that Mexican Americans were white and should not be excluded. To the extent, however, that state officials recognized Mexican Americans as white, it was a "Caucasian cloak" that they threw over Jim Crow segregation so they could maintain that Mexican Americans were represented on juries and in schools by "other whites."

To some extent immigrants faced the same strategic issues as Indians about identifying as "people of color" or claiming whiteness. This history reveals the close ties between whiteness and citizenship in this country. People who were not able to win a claim of whiteness found themselves shut out of full participation in the public sphere, and sometimes even excluded from U.S. borders. In recent years historians have focused attention on the racial identity of numerous nationalities of European immigrants to the United States, arguing that Irish, Italians, and Jews in the mid-nineteenth century were not considered white, but through the racial politics of American cities they became white over time. My story emphasizes the extent to which European Americans were always white before the law.

Trials contesting racial identity illustrate the ways that racial categories have come into being over the course of U.S. history. Through them we can observe the changing meanings of race throughout our history, and the changes and continuities in racism itself, from its roots in a slave society up through the twentieth century. Drawing lines between "races" determined not only who could be free but also who could be capable of citizenship. Thus trials of racial identity became trials about the attributes of citizenship for the men and women who were their subjects.

Formal citizenship was the first step to becoming an American. Before the Civil War one could be a citizen of one's home state, but there was no such thing as national citizenship. Some residents of the United States were excluded completely from citizenship; the Constitution of 1787 created a category of "Indians not taxed" who would not be enumerated in the census or counted for taxation or representation; and slaves would famously be counted as three-fifths of a person for the purposes of representation. The doors were open to immigration without restriction, but only "free white persons" could naturalize to citizenship. Nor was it clear what rights went with formal citizenship. While native-born white women were assuredly citizens, in most states they could not vote or hold office, and married women lost many civil rights in addition, such as the ability to form contracts or bring suit in court. Free people of color, despite their free status, faced numerous restrictions on their ability to participate in society: restrictions on freedom of movement, the ability to vote, sit on juries, or hold public office, and even the right to form contracts or testify in court.

Therefore it makes sense to think about citizenship in two dimensions: first, formal legal citizenship, and second, full social and political citizenship. Race was central not only to formal legal citizenship—who could naturalize, and who was counted in the census—but also to the larger sense of membership in the polity. Women were excluded from citizenship in this second, larger sense, and so were people of color. In most states before the Civil War, only white men were eligible to vote, to sit on juries, or to muster in the militia. Even after the Civil War, when the Reconstruction Amendments guaranteed to freed slaves the right to vote, and the Supreme Court declared that blacks could not be barred from jury service, people of color were excluded by law from white schools, primary elections, and a host of "public accommodations," including rail cars, hotels, and swimming pools. Furthermore, state officials kept blacks, Mexican Americans, and Asian Americans from voting or sitting on juries even when no state statute or constitutional provision justified their action. In the broad sense of participation in political and social life, only white people could become—and were seen as *capable* of becoming—citizens.

Like the witnesses and jurors in Alexina's case, we tend to believe that race is a fact of nature, a property of blood, and like them, we are certain that we ought to know it when we see it. But as Alexina's trial makes painfully clear, race may not be objectively observed. Instead it is a powerful ideology, which came into being and changed forms at particular moments in history as the product of social, economic, and psychological conditions. Fundamental to race is a hierarchy of power. Despite the language of racial *difference,* and the neutrality of terms like racial *categories* and *bound-*

aries, central to racial thinking is not only the notion that the categories of white, black, brown, yellow, and red mark meaningful distinctions among human beings but also that they reflect inferiority and superiority, a human Chain of Being, with *white* at the top and *black* on the bottom. Determining racial identity was about raising some people up that chain to put others down; enslaving some people to free others; taking land from some people to give it to others; robbing people of their dignity to give others a sense of supremacy.

Despite Americans' belief that race should be self-evident, a matter of common sense, we have never reached a consensus about what race means or how to discover it. Legislators passed rules about racial identity primarily on the basis of physical appearance and ancestry. Color created legal presumptions of slave or free status: white people were presumed free and black people presumed slaves. Yet decision makers always worried that looks could deceive. Ancestry might define race, most often by reference to the origins of a grandparent or great-grandparent, but ancestry was hard to discover. Status—whether one was slave or free, married or single—could be proven by documentation, but race could not. Early on, courts drew a distinction between membership in an Indian nation or tribe, which could be proved only by documented evidence of descent from an Indian in the maternal line, and race or "pedigree," which could be proved by reputation evidence—the testimony of neighbors as to how a person held himself out, how he was treated by his neighbors, and how he performed in social and civil life. The distinction was between a political identification and the lived experience of race.

Race came to be known very differently from nation. It could be based, at different times, on appearance, ancestry, performance, reputation, associations, science, national citizenship, and cultural practice. In the middle decades of the nineteenth century, both the science and the performance of race became increasingly important to the determination of racial status. Medical experts in the courtroom claimed to read signs that ordinary people could not decipher: "hollow" arches meant whiteness; oval hair follicles meant blackness. Yet just as often, trials turned on the testimony of lay witnesses giving reputation evidence. Doing the things a white man or woman did—attending white churches or dances, sitting on juries and voting (for men), exhibiting sexual purity (for women)—became the law's working definition of what it meant to be white. After the Civil War and Reconstruction, trials of racial identity continued to center on both medi-

cal expertise about race and community observation and retelling of racial performances. This understanding of race as both a scientific fact
of nature and something that we perform makes up our "common sense"
of race.

Beginning in the antebellum period, doctors presented themselves to
courts as experts on racial identity, claiming a monopoly on scientific racial
knowledge. Yet trials always returned to common sense and community
understandings, often by casting ordinary people as racial experts. Lo-
cating expertise in the community was not always a good thing: neighbors
wielded their racial knowledge as a weapon against enemies; and danger
and violence often resulted from community action. But it reminds us of
the power of local law and local culture in creating the ideas and norms
that shape our lives. Race was not something imposed from above, imagined by experts and acquiesced in by ordinary people; race was created
and re-created every day through the workings of community institutions
and individuals in daily life.

The fact that courts gave effect to communities' racial knowledge meant
that communities trying to reshape their racial order used trials to reimagine the future by reinventing their pasts. After the Civil War, individuals in the courtroom increasingly emphasized race as association, an understanding of the concept that could make sense only in a segregated
world, in which people associated only with those of their own race.

In the early twentieth century, the new science of cultural anthropology challenged nineteenth-century phrenology and physical anthropology.
Cultural anthropologists argued that differences among groups of people
heretofore designated as races could best be explained by culture rather
than biology. Scientific experts in the courtroom, professors rather than local doctors, began to offer a variety of cultural explanations of race, at
times arguing that race was a cultural category that was biologically inde-
terminable, at other times that racial differences were merely physical
with no cultural significance. While litigants continued to turn to science
for answers about who was white, when science offered contradictory or
counterintuitive answers, courts always returned to racial common sense,
with the U.S. Supreme Court referring to what the "common man" would
understand to be a white person.

One metaphor of racial identity has held particular sway with respect to
the rights and citizenship of native peoples: race as blood. The concept of
"blood quantum," that fractions of Indian identity can be measured out in

blood, did not become meaningful in U.S. law and culture until the early twentieth century. Individual Indians attained U.S. citizenship, and allotments of land, at the price of their national identity. New laws defined Indians and native Hawai'ians according to fractions of "blood" and defined Indians with African ancestry as "freedmen," a separate category ultimately excluded from citizenship in Indian nations. This idea of race as blood has had enormous consequences for Indians today.

At first it may seem nonsensical to suggest that racial identity could be such a source of conflict when for so many people racial identity seems obvious, unquestionable. A slave with very dark skin and African features was unlikely to be the subject of racial identity litigation. But why was this so? In the case of the black slave, her identity went unremarked most likely because appearance, ancestry, reputation, slave status, and associations all came together to make her a "negro" many times over. A social scientist would say that her identity was "overdetermined."

Yet litigating the identity of the smaller number of people who were not clearly marked "white" or "negro" mattered tremendously in the history of race and racism for two reasons. First, because the margins were bigger than we have thought. Since the earliest days of the republic, there have been a significant number of people whose identity was not fixed by appearance, or even by a confluence of appearance, status, ancestry, and associations. Second, because the margins of a category create the core. People revealed what race meant to them only when they needed to adjudicate its boundaries. And in drawing those boundaries, they were creating race.

Individuals and communities who inhabited the borderlands of race often managed to survive for years with an ambiguous or shifting racial status. But anything could happen to upset their precarious position—a crackdown by government officials, a vendetta by a neighbor, the decision by a slave owner to exercise more control, a campaign to enroll all members of the community according to Indian blood quantum—and then they would find their identities on trial. Sometimes they achieved an intermediate status between black and white, as did the Croatan Indians of North Carolina, who fought for a third, separate school system under Jim Crow. Others functioned with a hybrid identity, treated legally as both races and nations, as did many Indian tribes. Sometimes they were considered white for some purposes but not others, as many Mexican Americans found themselves in the Southwest. But almost always, these people on the margins have created periodic crises and conflicts over racial identity—for themselves and their neighbors—many of which have ended up in court.

Of course, what happened in the courtroom is not a faithful mirror of people's internal beliefs, their self-understandings, or even their interactions in the social world beyond the courtroom. In court, people told stories about racial identity strategically—in order to win their cases, in order to put themselves in a favorable light, in order to constitute their communities in a certain way and to ostracize outsiders. Nevertheless, law has been a crucial institution in the process of creating racial meaning at every level. And by reading trial transcripts critically, it is possible to catch glimpses of ordinary people's, as well as lower-level legal actors', understandings of legal and racial categories and of their own places in the racial hierarchy. Trials brought to the surface conflicting understandings of identity latent in the culture, and brought into confrontation everyday ways of understanding race with definitions that fit into the official, well-articulated racial ideology that supported the maintenance of slavery and postwar racial hierarchy. Legal rules passed by high courts and legislatures had to be translated into practical action on the ground. Witnesses, lawyers, and litigants learned to tell stories that resonated with juries or with government officials. At the intersection of law and local culture, we can see the day-to-day creation of race.

The stakes were high in these cases because personal freedom, property, marriages, children's education, and community status hung in the balance. The stories people told in the courtroom setting took on life, not only in future cases but in lessons learned as well by the neighbors who participated as witnesses, jurors, and audience members, and those that traveled through gossip, newspaper accounts, and literary narratives. The courtroom conclusions about how to decide a person's racial identity reverberated through American culture because of the importance of the courtroom as a cultural arena.

And while many cultural institutions participate in the creation of racial meanings, legal institutions often had the final word. A legal case could fix the identity of an individual or an entire national group with a conclusiveness that was hard to overturn. Over the course of U.S. history, the possibility of mixed, intermediate, and hybrid identities has narrowed. For many Indian tribes this has happened by their adopting blood quantum as a marker of identity. Citizenship in many tribes depends on the fraction, or quantum, of "blood" one can trace to ancestors on early-twentieth-century Indian rolls. For example, a person with one great-great-grandfather and one great-great-great-grandmother on the 1906 Cherokee Dawes Roll has three-thirty-seconds "Cherokee blood." Making blood quantum, as determined by reference to these early-twentieth-century rolls, the sine qua non of tribal citizenship has helped to turn national identities into racial ones in the eyes of the law as well as in the eyes of tribal members themselves. Other groups and individuals have been pushed into—or have fought to achieve—the status of "white" or "black."

This gradual narrowing has not been a linear process. There has been more contestation of racial categories than one would expect. Whites in Rhode Island were lamenting that the Narragansett Indians were disappearing through mixture with "negroes" as early as the eighteenth century, yet in the 1870s the Narragansett were still there, fighting against detribalization while acknowledging that they had mixed with African Americans. Laws that appeared to narrow the available racial categories have also had sometimes surprising results. For example, new "one drop of blood" rules in the early twentieth century, meant to make it more difficult for mixed-race individuals to pass as white, in some cases actually created more possibilities for individuals by making it harder to prove that a grandparent was African. And communities continued to experience a great deal of disagreement and conflict about particular individuals' identities. There were always a few people who were able to use racial indeterminacy to advantage, whether to gain freedom or access to schools or land, or to exclude others from access.

While in some respects this book is a story of continuity—the persistence of many bases for racial knowledge, and in particular of science and performance—it is not a static history. Rather there were key moments in American history at which the determination of racial identity became particularly fraught. One such moment was the decade or so leading up to the Civil War, as the nation struggled over the future of racial slavery. During that era racial identity trials shifted from more routine adjudications of ancestry to intense contests about science and performance. The second such moment was the turn of the twentieth century, which marked the beginning of the American adventure with imperialism, as well as the beginnings of immigration restriction in the United States and efforts to define the boundaries of citizenship racially. At the same time, the U.S. government began to implement a new policy toward its own indigenous people, a policy of forced assimilation, tribal enrollment, and land allotment, which tied the administrative determination of identity to the destruction of Indian nations and the creation of U.S. citizens through individual land ownership.

Across time as well, the determination of racial identity has moved into different forums. Whereas the local courthouse was a key arena throughout the nineteenth century for struggles over identity, other legal institutions became important in the twentieth century. Federal courts made the decisions about naturalization to citizenship, administrative agencies such as the Commission to the Five Civilized Tribes decided Indian citizenship, and legislatures also debated identity. Administrative and legislative hearings differ in important ways from local trials, but all of them involved the testimony of local witnesses and the strategic efforts of lawyers and litigants. The most important difference among these adjudications was the identity of the decision maker: whether a jury of neighbors or a national official would make the final determination. Another significant difference in the later cases was that they no longer concerned primarily the status of an individual but rather the status of an entire group—not whether this individual is or is not a white person, but whether all Armenians, for example, should be considered white.

By the mid-twentieth century another important factor entered the mix. Beginning in the 1930s, for the first time self-conscious civil rights litigators were attempting to use the courts to achieve racial equality. When Mexican American whiteness was on trial at this time, it was in part because Mexican American civil rights lawyers had placed it front and center as a matter of litigation strategy. In civil rights cases involving jury selection and school desegregation, racial identity was a matter not only of community ascription or self-identification but of strategic use as well. These cases too regarded the status of all Mexican Americans, not just the individual who stood before the court. Finally, the U.S. Census has been used to enumerate individuals by race for two centuries, but only recently has it become the focus of aspirational identity politics, as a new multiracial movement argued for changing racial identity categories in the 2000 census.

Ultimately we have to ask why communities and legal institutions invested so much time and effort in determining racial boundaries. Why did people care so much about whether an individual or group counted as "white," "negro," "Indian," or something else? A lot was at stake in these cases: personal freedom or enslavement, a good education for one's children, the right to marry the person of one's choice, the right to be a citizen. In every one of these cases, racial line-drawing served to uphold white privilege: the enslavement of African Americans, the appropriation of Indian lands, the exclusion at U.S. borders of those deemed unworthy of citizenship. Even in conflicts over the line between Indian and "negro," legal institutions sought not simply to control the decision making, diminishing Indian sovereignty, but almost always to narrow the resources available to the group.

Today race and racism are still with us. If it were true that racism in the past was based only on a now discredited biological understanding of race, it would have been comparatively easy to eradicate racism with "color-blind" policies in the late twentieth century. Yet despite the hard-won victories of civil rights struggles in the twentieth century, racism has survived, and it has done so in part because its bases are shifting and mobile. For so long as many still believe that differing life chances do and should correlate with one's performance of identity, one's ability to achieve citizenship through "blood," or one's practices of culture, racism will persist.

CHAPTER ONE

The Common Sense of Race

TWO CONTRADICTORY NOTIONS—race as clear-cut identity (with the ever-present possibility of deception) versus race as ever-shifting category (with the ever-present possibility of confusion)—together make up our contemporary "common sense" of race: what we know without being aware that we know it. Indeed this racial common sense now appears so self-evident to most Americans—whether we consider ourselves white, black, or "other"—that it is virtually impossible to imagine a world in which people thought about race in any other way.

Yet our notions of race were forged over several centuries of interaction among blacks, whites, and Indians, and then refined in the face of immigration from Asia, Latin America, and Europe. The first ideas of race in America were hammered out by European colonial elites in response to two non-European groups, the native peoples who were the primarily free and often hostile occupants of North American territories, and the Africans who were primarily enslaved (though the legal status of this enslavement also took more than half a century to work out). Modern racial categories came about to justify the enslavement of Africans for their labor, and to prevent indentured, propertyless, and other non-slaveholding whites from making common cause with Africans and Indians against the slaveholders. Before 1830 the primary concern of the colonial and Republican slaveholding class was to prevent solidarity across lines of color. Lawmakers gradually clarified the distinction between white indenture and black enslavement and created a body of law that established "white" and "black" as two separate legal categories. Over time, a variety of social, economic, and political pressures created the need for a clearer, sharper, and more fundamental distinction between black and white. The creation of "black" and "white" was a slow, gradual, and vexed process. On the one hand, race was supposed to be immutable and clear; on the other hand, it was shifting and hard to define; either way, it was central to people's identities and a crucial factor in determining their social lives, their economic opportunities, and the way they were perceived by others.

In the earliest days of American colonization, when slavery was introduced, "race" had yet to become a vitally important means of categorizing humanity. Before the mid-eighteenth century, most English speakers used "races," "nations," and "peoples" interchangeably to describe groupings of individuals who shared a common language and geographic origins— Englishmen, Irishmen, Indians, Moors. Although Europe in the sixteenth and seventeenth centuries was marked by a striking xenophobia (one has only to look at how Shakespeare portrayed the French and the Welsh), and though this xenophobia frequently included Africans (think of *Othello*), blackness was not necessarily associated with weakness, inferiority, or slave-like qualities. Indeed, medieval and Renaissance-era justifications of slavery had often focused on the inferior qualities of *white* people; the original slaves were Slavs, the derivation of the term. Europeans often viewed black people not as degraded and servile but as powerful and warlike: "Before the Atlantic slave trade began, racism justifying slavery in medieval Spain and Portugal was aimed at people with light skin . . . [while] dark-skinned people were often identified as conquerors and rulers rather than as slaves."[1]

The early colonies functioned without clear definitions of race—and they likewise featured a great deal of racial mixing. In fact, social divisions in the first North American colonies—British, French, and Dutch—were far less likely to reflect color than class. Africans, Indians, Irish, and other Europeans worked alongside one another as servants, whether indentured or enslaved, and it did not become clear until the late seventeenth century that Africans and not whites would be slaves for life.

In British North America the first Africans were introduced into Virginia as "servants." Many of them became free after some years of service, not unlike the indentured servants brought from England and Ireland. In the mid-seventeenth century, some Africans (but no whites) were being held in bondage for life. Still, as many as 30 percent of the people of color in the Chesapeake were free people of African descent in the middle decades of the 1600s.[2]

Virginia saw a continual series of alliances formed among white, black, and Indian workers. Most famously, Nathaniel Bacon in 1676 led a "motley army of small holders and indentured servants, black and white," in rebellion against the planters. In reaction against this workers' uprising, planters began to import slaves rather than indentured servants to work on their plantations, and passed new laws as well declaring that "all Indians taken in war be held and accounted slaves during life." Indians, however, because of their dwindling populations, could not satisfy the demand for labor, so the planters turned increasingly to the African slave trade. Historians of early British North America suggest that the real question regarding the turn to slavery in Virginia is "Why did they wait so long?"—and that the answer lies in the mortality rate for servants of all origins: until servants began to survive longer than a few years in the New World, it did not make sense to pay more money for a slave who would not live very long.[3]

Not only did Indians, Africans, and English servants form political alliances, but they also married and bore children. For most of the seventeenth century there were no laws against interracial sex or marriage, and "fornication" was treated the same way by law no matter who the protagonists were. Beginning in 1662 the first statutes distinguishing fornication between "negroes" and "Christians" were passed, and not until 1691 were all interracial sexual acts criminalized in Virginia. Most states did not pass bans on intermarriage between whites and "negroes," "mulattoes," and Indians until the eighteenth century: for example, North Carolina in 1715 and again in 1741; Massachusetts in 1786. Other states prohibited white-Indian intermarriage, as Rhode Island did in 1798, followed by Maine and Tennessee in 1821. Perhaps ironically, these laws had the effect of encouraging marriages between blacks and Indians, laying the groundwork for black-Indian alliances that the elites also came to fear. These alliances not only posed a possible military threat but also enabled slaves of mixed ancestry to claim freedom on the grounds of their "Indian" identity, and provided a safe haven in Indian territory for runaway slaves. Some even set up "maroon" (runaway slave) communities within Indian national boundaries.[4]

By the late eighteenth century, a significant number of people, slave and free, traced their roots to both Indian and African ancestors—a fact that many slaves employed in their claims to freedom. In Virginia, late-eighteenth-century newspapers were filled with advertisements for runaway slaves who had insisted on their free Indian ancestry. In October

1772, for example, Paul Michaux advertised for "a Mulatto Man named Jim, who is a Slave, but pretends to have a Right to his Freedom." Jim was the son of an Indian man and had "long black hair resembling an Indian's"; Michaux suspected that "he was gone to the General Court to seek his freedom." Likewise, William Cuszens complained that his "Mulatto Slave" David, who "sa[id] he [wa]s of the Indian breed," had gone "down to the General Court, as I imagined, to sue for his freedom."[5]

Many of these Virginia "free people of color," such as John Geaween, or Gowen, a "negro servant" freed in March 1641, migrated to the Carolinas, and some continued to migrate along the Appalachians into eastern Tennessee in the seventeenth and eighteenth centuries. Families with names such as Goins, Chavis, Bass, and Bunch were sometimes counted on tax rolls as "white," sometimes as Indian, and sometimes as "mulatto." As they settled along this path, they formed entire communities of racially ambiguous people which became known to anthropologists in the twentieth century as "racial islands" or "tri-racial isolates." Their neighbors gave them colorful and mysterious names like "Melungeons," "Brass Ankles," and "Red Bones."[6]

Likewise, despite the attempts of whites to keep Africans and Indians apart, New England saw a significant number of marriages between Indian women and African American men, especially after the Revolution. Men of African-Indian descent worked the whaling boat crews of Nantucket and other ports along the Eastern seaboard. Certain Indian tribes along the coast, such as the Mashpee and the Narragansett, became well known as "various and mixt." At the same time, Spain granted asylum to runaway African American slaves from the Carolinas, who created "maroon communities" in Florida, striking up alliances with the Seminoles to ward off slave catchers. There African Americans and Native Americans intermingled, so that by the late eighteenth century, some African Americans were already known as "Seminole Negroes" or "estelusti."[7]

Whites viewed the intermingling of free black people and Indians with increasing alarm, particularly in such "black-majority" regions as colonial South Carolina. Slaveholding whites in these areas were particularly concerned to enlist Indians as allies in catching runaway slaves, or at least to prevent Indians from aiding runaways. They employed a number of "divide and rule" tactics to foster anti-Indian feelings among blacks and anti-black feelings among Indians so as to preclude cooperation.[8]

By the time the United States became a republic, slavery had long been exclusively African, and views about Indian difference were beginning to justify policies of expropriation of Indian lands and subjugation of native people. But a modern ideology of race had not yet emerged. Out of a colonial background of extensive racial mixing and indeterminacy, and growing white elite fears of interracial alliances, colonial and republican elites began to feel increasing urgency about defining slave and free status in terms of race. Only during the Revolutionary era did "race" come to denote broad divisions of humankind, marked by physiological difference. The racial category crystallized in contrast to the new sense of "nation" as the unit of political organization, a people with a state. In the American context, the "negro" came to stand for "race," a race fit for servitude, by contrast to the "Indian" as a member of a nation inferior in civilization but capable of improvement. Drawing the contrast between blacks and Indians served to divide and conquer two groups who threatened the new slave societies being built in the American republic.[9]

"Black Race" versus "Indian Nation"

In the antebellum era, American law was lurching toward two binary categories of race: a "blackness" that was identical with absolute chattel slavery and a "whiteness" that served to mobilize poor and non-slaveholding whites on the side of wealthy planters and slaveholders. These categories were powerful—and they still are—even though they never really reflected the complexity of the American experience.

Only in late-eighteenth-century Europe and America did "races" come to indicate broad divisions of humankind marked by physiological difference and color, and organized hierarchically into a chain of being: white, brown, yellow, red, black. Within this system, whites, blacks, and Indians came to be viewed very differently. Africans were frequently contrasted with Indians, who at this point were citizens of sovereign nations with a formidable degree of military power. Africans, by contrast, became "negroes"—members of a degraded, enslaved race who were frequently, unfavorably contrasted with "noble Indian nations."

In 1753 Benjamin Franklin praised the Indian residents of North America and disparaged "attempt[s] to civilize our American Indians," arguing that their "present way of living" was more natural to all humans; "almost all their Wants are supplied by the spontaneous Productions of Nature, with the addition of very little labour . . . [T]hey are not deficient in natural understanding and yet they have never shewn any Inclination to change their manner of life for ours, or to learn any of our Arts." Franklin noted that Indians raised among the English always returned to their people, given the chance, whereas white men raised among Indians refused to leave. Thirty years later he commented, "Savages we call them, because their manners differ from ours, which we think the Perfection of Civility; they think the same of theirs." Indians might have strange customs, but these customs were not necessarily inferior and might even be superior to those of the colonists.[10]

Thomas Jefferson likewise praised Indians—to the explicit disadvantage of blacks. In *Notes on the State of Virginia,* Jefferson claimed that Indians with no education "astonish you with strokes of the most sublime oratory; such as prove their reason and sentiment strong, their imagination glowing and elevated. But never yet could I find that a black had uttered a thought above the level of plain narration . . . Among the blacks is misery enough, God knows, but no poetry." Elsewhere Jefferson wrote that "the Indian [is] in body and mind equal to the white man." Like Franklin, Jefferson respected the strange but admirable Indian, even as he held the degraded African in contempt.[11]

Indians in colonial America and the early republic were viewed in terms of their organized tribal nations—not surprisingly, in view of their ongoing military challenges to American settlers and their possession of huge amounts of territory. The U.S.-British treaty that ended the American Revolution put the new nation's western boundary at the Mississippi River, but most U.S. citizens still lived east of the Appalachians. The remaining "U.S." territories of the Mississippi Valley were filled with native peoples, some of whom had fought for the British and others who were barely aware of the colonists. In the South, the five nations which white Americans called the "Five Civilized Tribes" occupied much of what later became Mississippi, Alabama, Georgia, and Tennessee. Across New England and the Middle Atlantic states, numerous Indian communities dotted the landscape: many separate nations—and many potential military threats. The federal government's concern with wresting control of relations with Indian tribes away from the states lent force to the view that Indian tribes were foreign nations, placing them firmly within the purview of the national government. Under the Constitution, "Indians not taxed" made up their own category of inhabitants, excluded from census enumeration and political representation. And for the first half of the nineteenth century, while treaties with Indians were broken, abrogated, forced, or signed by trickery, the U.S. government continued to treat Indian tribes as nations, at least in name, through the treaty process. Indian tribes were "domestic dependent nations," Chief Justice John Marshall explained in 1831, and they had the power to decide their own membership. This gave Indian identity a political status distinct from race.

Enslaved Africans, by contrast, had become America's primary source of labor; their treatment as racialized property was the foundation of the colonial and U.S. economies. Instead of being viewed as Africans— much less as Coromantee, Wolof, or Igbo—they were viewed simply as "negro." Here again we see a double consciousness operating beneath the protective cover of "common sense." African nationhood was recognized as a practical matter by the slave owners and slave traders who sought particular nationalities for various purposes (e.g., gold mining and rice growing) and who noted national characteristics including language and "country marks" in their ads for runaways. Yet the appellation "negro" erased national difference to create the notion of race, even as the words "slave" and "negro" began to be used interchangeably. By contrast, Indians were still perceived as nations—the Narragansett, the Cherokee, the Mashpee—particularly when being compared to blacks.

It was no mistake that the U.S. Supreme Court spoke most respectfully of Indian nationhood, calling Indians "a free and independent people, associated together in nations or tribes, and governed by their own laws . . . regarded and treated as foreign Governments, as much so as if an ocean had separated the red man from the white," in the most infamous case regarding race in American history, the *Dred Scott* case. In deciding that free blacks were not U.S. citizens, Chief Justice Roger Taney wrote that the position of blacks was "altogether unlike" that of Indians. The "negro" was "degraded," while Indians were "a free and independent people." Indians received no such respect from the Supreme Court when it was deciding the title to Indian lands. In cases about Indian land title and Indian sovereignty, the Supreme Court disparaged Indian nationhood, establishing U.S. supremacy through the right of "discovery." It was in contrast to the "negro" that the Indian came to represent a nation.[12]

For white elites, the idea of "negroes" as a degraded race helped to justify the anomaly of chattel slavery in a republic that was otherwise devoted to liberty. Black chattel slaves would never be free; nor would their children—an extreme form of slavery that had existed nowhere in the world prior to the colonization of the Americas. For the first time in history, one category of humanity was ruled out of the "human race" and into a separate subgroup that was to remain enslaved for generations in perpetuity. What could possibly justify this type of slavery except a special category of person—or subhuman—to occupy it?

Thus it is no surprise that Americans' first efforts to determine racial identity in a courtroom involved both the question of who could be legally enslaved and the effort to draw the line between black and Indian. Indians—except for those few living in Virginia in the immediate aftermath of Bacon's Rebellion—could not legally be held as slaves. Any slave who could prove Indian maternal ancestry might make good a claim to freedom. And so the first and most important lesson of the early racial identity trials was simple: only a "negro" could be a slave.

The most important rules regarding racial and slave status were laid down in the 1806 case of *Hudgins v. Wright,* in which the slave Hannah sued for her freedom, claiming that her mother, a woman known as Butterwood Nan, had been not black but Indian. Hannah brought in a wide variety of evidence to defend her claim. Her witnesses agreed that Hannah appeared white, though that alone was not enough to free her. Witnesses also testified that Hannah's father had been an Indian, but that was not enough to free her either: the system of chattel slavery depended on the premise that every child of an enslaved mother would be enslaved as well.[13]

In theory, Hannah's owners could keep Hannah in legal slavery simply by proving that she had been born either to a black mother or to a mother descended from a legally enslaved Indian. For Hannah to win her freedom, she had only to show that she was the descendant of free Indians. And indeed witnesses did testify that Hannah's mother, Butterwood Nan, was "called an Indian." Although Nan was in fact a slave, witnesses claimed that she could have had her freedom had she wanted it. Hannah's putative owners argued that despite Nan's Indian reputation, Nan's mother could well have been black; or possibly she was an Indian who had been enslaved during that period of legal Indian slavery. Either way, they pointed out, Hannah would have been born to a legally enslaved mother and would therefore be legally a slave herself.[14]

In the end, no one was able to prove whether Nan was really an Indian or only reputed to be one. Nor could anyone prove that Nan was—or was not—descended from Indians who had been legally enslaved. Yet the court's decision makes clear the early American tendency to consider Indians citizens of free nations—while insisting that Africans were a degraded race of slaves. Because of Hannah's "red complexion," the court ruled, she enjoyed a legal presumption of freedom. In other words, if she looked like an Indian, she was an Indian—and therefore free, unless her owners could offer any affirmative evidence that she belonged in slavery. By contrast, a person who appeared "negro" would be presumed a slave, unless affirmative evidence could prove that she was free. Indians were by default citizens of a free nation; Africans were by default members of an enslaved race.[15]

This contrast between race and nation extended even to different modes of fact-finding. Indian identity was equated with membership in an Indian nation, and so was considered by Hannah's judges to be a straightforward matter of proving one's citizenship, if not with a piece of paper, then by tracing one's female ancestry according to the rules of the tribe. But race—or "pedigree," as it was sometimes called—was a far more slippery category. Race went far beyond citizenship papers toward a type of identity about which people might have widely varying opinions. Racial knowledge resided not in documents but in communities, and it required reputation evidence to determine. And so when racial identity trials began to admit and even to center on reputation evidence, the new common sense of race was born. The rare freedom suit to be appealed all the way to the U.S. Supreme Court, *Negro John Davis v. Wood,* in 1816, established the rule that hearsay and reputation evidence would be allowed only to establish "pedigree" (that is, race) and not, for example, one's status as slave or free. Community members might testify as to their understanding of a person's race, and the jury could rule on that race accordingly. To determine "slave" or "free," however, the jury would require firsthand evidence, documentation, or something more persuasive than hearsay.

Some years later the Virginia Supreme Court ruled that the same distinction held between litigating Indian identity and one's status as "black." Just as Hannah had done, the slave James Baugh sued his Chesterfield County owner for his freedom, claiming that his mother's mother was an Indian woman entitled to her freedom, though apparently enslaved. Twice James won his freedom, and twice his owner appealed the case to the Supreme Court. At the second trial James had submitted the deposition of an eighty-three-year-old witness talking about his grandmother's Indian identity. The Virginia Supreme Court ruled that this hearsay testimony about Indian tribal status was inadmissible—in striking contrast, as the dissent pointed out, to the general rule about the admissibility of reputation evidence regarding "pedigree," that is, racial status. The community could decide on the basis of its own understanding who was black—but not who was a citizen of an Indian nation, nor who was legally owned as a slave. Race was something everyone could—and should—recognize on sight, whereas membership in an Indian nation or one's status as property required more sophisticated and objective evidence.[16]

In trials drawing the line between black and white, courts routinely allowed every kind of hearsay or reputation evidence, no matter how remote, to be heard by the jury, on the grounds that reputation was often the only way to know someone's race. But Indian identity was not yet conceptualized legally in racial terms. Hence the court sharply distinguished "the country, nation or tribe, of [James Baugh's] ancestor" from her "[race or] pedigree." Although the dissenting justices pointed out that documentary proof would not be forthcoming in this case, since few Indians could provide such written documentation, the majority of the Virginia Supreme Court remained unmoved. They wanted a clear distinction between the type of fact-finding used to identify Indians (citizens of a nation) and that used to identify "negroes" (members of a race). Indian citizenship required hard proof, but "race" was a matter for community consensus—for common sense—something any white man with eyes in his head ought to be able to determine.[17]

Because of the race/nation distinction, freedom suits before 1830 that turned on the identity of an Indian grandmother, like Hannah's and James's, did not blow up into major battles over racial identity. Even hard-fought cases in which passions were inflamed did not become contests over whiteness and blackness. No experts were called in to testify about racial identity; no neighbors bore witness to their own common sense notions of race. The story of Phoebe and her sons Davy and Tom, a freedom suit litigated in Tennessee over a period of six years in the 1820s, reveals one of the last moments in American history when a contest over slave status did not explode into a contest over racial knowledge.

Phoebe's case begins in 1822, when Abraham Vaughan, a Revolutionary soldier who had settled in Tennessee in the early nineteenth century, brought two young men of color before two magistrates at a neighbor's house. Enraged, Vaughn accused the youths—known as Davy and Tom— of various crimes, in particular of running away. Davy and Tom were the

sons of Phoebe, an enslaved woman whom Vaughan had bought from a
Virginian named Thomas Hardaway when she was a young woman. The
magistrates eventually acquitted Davy and Tom, but according to several
white witnesses, Vaughan nevertheless whipped them both so severely
that most of the other white observers left the room in disgust or distress,
and Davy lost most of the flesh on his back.[18]

With the assistance of John Bonner, a member of the Methodist and
Quaker Humane Society who had also been a Revolutionary Minuteman,
Davy and Tom sued for their freedom and also sued Vaughan for assault
and battery. Phoebe later joined them in their suit. Determined to retain
his rights to the three people whom he saw as his legal property, Vaughan
not only fought the suit but swore before witnesses as well that he would
"have Davy's hide" and "kill him or his arm would rot off." He considered
the suit a particular betrayal by Phoebe, a woman whom Vaughan's family
had known as "moms" and whom his children had called "mother."[19]

The claim to freedom was based on Phoebe's descent from an Indian
woman named Beck. Although Beck had been raised in slavery in Virginia,
her sister and some other relatives had won their freedom in a Virginia
court by proving that they were Indians wrongly enslaved after 1691,
when Virginia law put an end to the enslavement of Indians. By claiming
descent from Beck, Phoebe suggested that she was descended from a
wrongly enslaved Indian—and thus entitled to the benefits of freedom.

Ironically, Vaughan had said in the company of many witnesses that all
men of all colors should be free—a declaration that, only a few years later,
would be inconceivable in a Southern court. At this point Vaughan had
only to attest that while he believed in freedom in a general way, he did
not think the principle applied to his own slaves and had never acknowledged their specific right to be free. Furthermore, he explained, he had
been drinking and "in a passion" when he had proclaimed slaves' abstract
right to freedom.[20]

Yet neither Vaughan's views on slavery nor Phoebe's racial status per se
was the focus of the courtroom testimony, which centered exclusively on
Phoebe's relationship to Beck, Beck's status, and the status of Indian slavery in Virginia. If Beck was rightfully enslaved, then Phoebe was a slave,
regardless of her Indian or black ancestry. If Beck had been wrongly enslaved, then Phoebe was free—though she might still be "Black."

John Bonner went to Virginia to take depositions from witnesses who
remembered Beck as the slave of Thomas Hardaway, while Vaughan called
witnesses who claimed that Phoebe had been bought not from Thomas

Hardaway but from another man, and that she had never claimed her freedom. Although witnesses for Phoebe mentioned her "copper complexion," suggesting Indian descent, and witnesses for Vaughan talked about her as "tolerably bright and freckled when young," Phoebe's appearance did not become a central issue in the case. No experts testified as to Phoebe's "Indian-ness" or blackness, nor did neighbors suggest that her associations or behavior marked her as one or the other. Indeed there was little discussion of whether Phoebe and her sons *were* "Indian" or "negro." Nor did Vaughan, despite his professed belief in freedom for all, seem overly concerned that an Indian might have been held in slavery—only with whether the Indian had been enslaved during the brief period when such enslavement was legal. On the whole, the attitude of the defense witnesses seemed to be that if Phoebe was a slave and had been a slave when brought to Tennessee, then she must be a "negro."[21]

Phoebe's suit was tried before Judge Thomas Stewart in neighboring Sumner County, just north of Wilson County. Most of the jurors and witnesses in Phoebe's case were farmers who owned a handful of slaves. Nevertheless, they gave a verdict for Phoebe's freedom, suggesting that even slaveholders were concerned with the principle that only "true" slaves should remain in bondage.[22]

Only a few years later, racial identity trials would proceed very differently. Legal status and documentation would fade in importance beside notions of reputation, behavior, and racial common sense. Phoebe's story is a remarkable example of how racial identity issues appeared in the United States before our modern notions of racial common sense were fully formed.

Race as Essential Identity

With a few exceptions, race in America before the 1830s was viewed as a more or less straightforward aspect of status. Depending on what race you were born into, where you lived, and when you were born, you might find yourself either slave or free. In antebellum America, however, race became an essential category, an all-encompassing definition of who you were and where you belonged in the social sphere. What caused the transition from race as documented ancestry to race as essential identity? To understand this shift, we have to look at the changing ideology of slavery itself.

Until the 1830s defenders of slavery primarily portrayed it as a necessary evil, a part of the Southern economy that would doubtless wither away as America developed. After all, tobacco production in the Upper South was failing. With many seasons of tobacco growing having depleted the soil, planters in Virginia, Maryland, Delaware, and North Carolina found themselves with more slaves than they could afford to feed. They hoped to sell these slaves to rice planters in Georgia and South Carolina before the slavery system collapsed under its own weight.

The invention of the cotton gin, and the newly profitable cotton crop, changed all that, as did the expansion of U.S. territory westward with the Louisiana Purchase. Far from being a dying system, slavery now looked as though it could have a lucrative future. By the 1830s pro-slavery advocates had moved from defending the institution as a necessary evil to promoting it as a positive good—an institution that reflected the unbridgeable barrier between "black" and "white." Thomas Reade Cobb, author of a treatise on the law of slavery, explained that "a state of bondage, so far from doing violence to the law of [the African's] nature, develops and perfects it; and that, in that state, he enjoys the greatest amount of happiness, and arrives at the greatest degree of perfection of which his nature is capable."[23]

This vision of race spoke directly to the anxieties of antebellum slaveholders. They faced continual resistance from their own human property—people who refused to work to capacity, broke tools, fought back, ran away; people who might secretly poison their masters or openly rise up in outright insurrection. In 1831 "free Negro" preacher Nat Turner had led the largest slave revolt in U.S. history, overseeing the killing of nearly sixty whites. Images of this violence put all slave owners on notice that the institution of slavery was insecure. At the same time, a more militant Northern abolitionism was beginning to emerge, spearheaded by the 1839 publication of *Appeal to the Colored Citizens of the World,* in which the African American abolitionist David Walker called for blacks to take up arms against slavery. Two years later William Lloyd Garrison put out the first issue of his newspaper *The Liberator,* the first publication by a white author to demand immediate abolition of slavery rather than gradual emancipation.

White Southerners, too, offered a potential challenge to the slavery system. The vast majority of white Southerners were poor and middling farmers, artisans, and small business owners, most of whom did not own slaves and never would. In 1860 only one-quarter of all white Southerners belonged to families owning slaves, and just 4 percent of the total white population owned more than twenty slaves. Slavery drove up the price of labor, while large plantations tended to squeeze out small farmers. How could the planters retain non- and small slaveholders' loyalty to a system that was not necessarily in their economic interests? The key to upholding slavery in the face of these multiple challenges was race.

Racial theorists were working hard to define two distinct categories of race: black and white. Yet they had to recognize the reality of a large number of people living in the racial borderlands between black and white, slave and free. There were two exceptional groups who occupied this space in the early republic, distinct but overlapping: free people of color, and people of mixed African and European ancestry. The Northern states had all abolished slavery in the wake of the American Revolution, but most did so gradually, so that there were small slave populations in the mid-Atlantic and New England states into the 1820s, and growing populations of freed slaves. In the South, the Revolution gave rise to some individual manumissions of slaves but provoked no mass effort at emancipation. Free people of color were concentrated in a band across the Upper South, and in a few cities of the Deep South with long histories of free mulatto elites—New Orleans, Louisiana, and Charleston, South Carolina, in particular.

In the Upper South, the proportion of African Americans who were free steadily grew over the course of the antebellum period, ending up at 12.8 percent on the eve of the Civil War. Many of these were slaves freed in the Revolutionary era by their masters, and the children of these freed slaves. The Upper South also had a relatively large population of mulattoes, many of whom were free and most of whom were poor. In the Lower South, the share of free people of color in the total population dropped from 3.5 percent in 1820 to 1.5 percent in 1860 as the internal slave trade shifted more slaves to the region. In that year more than one-third of free people of color lived in cities or towns, compared to only 5 percent of slaves. Some of these were the children of slave masters, freed by their fathers, but a significant number were the children of white women and black men. Yet while the Lower South did have a small, wealthy free mulatto elite concentrated in Charleston and New Orleans, there was a much larger group of enslaved mulattoes. These light-skinned free people of color and the mulatto slaves challenged any attempt at a clear-cut definition of race or a notion that blacks were inevitably destined for slavery while only white people could enjoy freedom.[24]

Southern states initially tried to reinforce black people's *essential* identity as slaves by tightening their manumission laws and making it increasingly difficult for owners to set slaves free. They imposed new restrictions on free blacks' freedom of movement and other civil rights, culminating in the self-enslavement laws of the 1850s, which gave free blacks a choice between leaving the state or enslaving themselves to a master of their choice. But even as lawmakers tried to make slave status more congruent with blackness and freedom more congruent with whiteness, people of all colors continued to cross racial boundaries—and the law's efforts to prevent it were uneven. Although most states in both the North and the South had bans on interracial marriage and fornication before the Civil War, Alabama had no barrier to interracial marriage until 1852, and Mississippi's statute provided only that ministers and officials were authorized to celebrate marriages between free whites. Interracial unions were a kind of blank spot in the law, neither permitted nor forbidden. In prewar Tennessee, interracial marriage was punishable only by a fine. (Compare that mild censure with the 1870 law making such unions a felony for which one could be imprisoned for five years.)[25]

For the most part, though, white Southerners responded with increasing apprehension to what they perceived as a rapidly growing number of mulattoes. Their unease was further fueled by the dramatic degree of geographic mobility among people of all colors, as white people sought new opportunities in the frontier states, while the domestic slave trade forcibly transferred millions of black people from the Upper to the Lower South. White Southerners could no longer count on personal acquaintance or community tradition to establish a person's whiteness or blackness. There were simply too many new people, of indeterminate appearance and untraceable background—people whose racial identities ought to have been clear but often were not. In this climate of anxiety, even non-slaveholding white people came to believe with increasing urgency that they needed to know race when they saw it—that race had to become a matter not of documents and ancestry but of straightforward common sense. It was in this inflammatory climate that the case of Abby Guy was brought to trial.

Abby Guy's Story

In 1850 Ashley County, Arkansas, was on the frontier of the slave South, its rural population half white and half slave. According to the U.S. Census, only one family lived outside these categories, neither white nor slave, but rather "free people of color." Ten years later the census counted everyone as either "white" or "slave." What happened to the one free colored family of Ashley County?

Abby Guy told Judge Theodrick Sorrels one version of the story in her 1855 complaint to the circuit court that William Daniel had falsely imprisoned her as a slave. Then and later, Abby claimed that her mother was a poor white orphan girl kidnapped into slavery in Virginia by "negro traders" who brought her to Alabama and sold her to William Daniel's father. Although her family had lived as slaves of the Daniel family for some years, William Daniel's brother Nathaniel had arranged for their freedom after his death to right the injustice of white slavery. Abby Guy and her children had been living free since the two families moved to Arkansas in 1844 and would have continued living in peace forever, according to Abby, had William Daniel not captured them and reduced them again to slave status.[26]

Abby Guy's case made its way through a jury trial in the neighboring county and two appeals to the Arkansas Supreme Court. The proceedings drew crowds to local courthouses to watch Guy and her children display themselves for inspection, to hear a reading of the will and documents of sale, to listen to the opinions of medical experts, and to witness testimony from several counties about Abby's appearance, conduct, self-presentation, reception in society, and inherited status.

The main issue in each trial was Abby Guy's racial identity. Unlike Phoebe's case, which focused on documenting her ancestor's legal status, Abby's claim rested on establishing her own whiteness by showing that she had behaved as a white woman would and had been treated as white by people who ought to know. The details of her (probably specious) story of being kidnapped were quickly left behind during both trials, as was William Daniel's evidence that Abby Guy and her mother had been his slaves and had inherited that status legally. Instead, evidence about Abby's behavior came to predominate: Had she properly played the role of a white woman, and had her performance been accepted by the white community? With Abby Guy's suit, racial identity became a question of performance, reputation, and common sense. It was no longer a matter of documentation but rather a complicated system of contradictory cues, something that respectable white people were nevertheless supposed to recognize at first sight.

Witnesses in the courtroom reinforced this notion of race as common sense by testifying that there was an ineffable something that made someone white—a "something" that any Southerner could discern. A drop of African blood would make itself known for certain, and a Southerner could sense it "as the alligator . . . knows three days in advance that a storm is brewing." Witnesses in racial identity trials often insisted that they did not need to know the finer points of physiology or craniology to know "the distinction between the caucasian and african races": they just *knew*. Yet freedom suits like Abby Guy's, which required a jury to determine racial identity, revealed not consensus but conflict, not only over whether a litigant was black or white but also over how to decide what a person's "race" was at all.[27]

Abby Guy's story follows as many twists and turns as the bayous on which she made her living. Until 1854 she and her four children lived down on Bayou Bartholomew, a murky channel of the Arkansas River meandering along the western edge of the Arkansas delta into Louisiana, while her nominal master William Daniel and his family lived up in the hills. Although most of the white witnesses in her freedom trials described the bayou as a country of white families, at least one section of Bayou Bartholomew was known in southeastern Arkansas as "Free Nigger Bend." The bottom lands were good for cotton but also for mosquitoes, and promoters had to fight the reputation of the area as malarial. The ambiguous legacy of the bayou mirrors Abby's paradoxical status—tallied by the census as a free person of color at the same time neighbors recalled her "living white."[28]

Tennessee-born William Daniel, one of the earliest settlers in sparsely populated Ashley County, had come from Alabama ten years before with his large family and a number of slaves. Even in 1854 railroads were decades away from reaching this remote county, and the main form of transportation was by boat on the Marie Saline River. Daniel cut a large figure in the tiny county seat of Hamburg as justice of the peace, postmaster, the area's first notary public, one of its largest landholders, and one of only four men in the county who owned more than ten slaves of taxable age. In a more established area his fifteen slaves and 240 acres would have been a very modest estate, but in Ashley County he was a leading citizen.[29]

William Daniel's father, James, had bought Abby's mother, Polly (also known as "Pal"), from slave traders in Alabama. Abby herself was born in 1812, apparently to a white father. Although he never acknowledged paternity, James Daniel was of the right age, power, and opportunity to be

Abby's father, and all the members of the Daniel family agreed that James treated Polly and Abby as "most favored" slaves. Many a slaveholder freed a favored sexual partner and her children upon his death. But when James Daniel died in 1821, he willed nine-year-old Abby to his adult daughter Betsey, separating the little girl from her mother, who remained with Daniel's wife. Four years later William bought Abby from Betsey's husband and kept her for ten or twelve years, during which time Abby gave birth to her first daughter, Frances, and possibly also to a second daughter, Elizabeth.[30]

Between 1835 and 1837 William executed a document of sale transferring Abby to his brother Nathaniel, although no money changed hands. At some point Abby gave birth to a third daughter, Mary. In 1842 Nathaniel returned Abby and her three daughters to William, canceling his debt for the purchase price, never paid. Such transfer of slaves among family members was common at the time; with the price of slaves continually going up, families often did everything they could to avoid selling them, using their human property as a kind of currency.

Abby claimed to have gone straight from James Daniel's home to Nathaniel's, so it is possible that during the entire period 1825–1842 she and her children simply lived with Nathaniel, regardless of whom she nominally belonged to. All three daughters appear to have had white fathers—most likely, William and/or Nathaniel. Certainly all family members agreed that, just as Nathaniel's father had done a generation earlier, Nathaniel treated Abby and her children as "most favored" slaves.

When William Daniel and his family moved to Arkansas in 1844, Abby and her children began to live on their own; in fact, according to the first judge to review her freedom suit, much evidence suggested that "she and her children were treated in the neighborhood as white persons." When Nathaniel died in Alabama one year later, his will did not mention Abby, although he had apparently given her reason to believe that he was going to arrange for her freedom and her support.[31]

For some years in the 1840s Abby lived with a white man named Guy, who died around 1850; during that time she "passed as Mrs. Guy," as a friendly trial witness put it. She gave birth to more children, several of whom bore the Guy name and were likely fathered by him. By 1850 Abby owned considerable property—forty acres of land, farm implements, and livestock—and she supported her family on her farm, producing corn, potatoes, peas, beans, butter, and one bale of cotton to sell for other goods.[32]

Abby Guy's quasi-free status may not have pleased everyone. In 1849, in

William Daniel's only brush with the wrong side of the law, the county court cited him for giving his slaves too much freedom, "to the annoyance of the neighborhood." Abby Guy and her children would have been well known to the two thousand or so inhabitants of this small county. Yet they continued to live somewhere between slavery and freedom—somewhere between black and white—for several more years. Indeed it was only when Abby tried to move with her children to Louisiana that William Daniel decided to assert his right of ownership.[33]

Perhaps being on the frontier actually worked to Abby's benefit. A community struggling to establish itself might be more likely to allow people to live on the margins of social orders that were still emerging. And Abby would have been only one of many people on the move, seeking to reshape their identities—and in her case, to reinvent her race. Such pockets of the South retained a peculiar place for light-skinned young women of mixed race. In the 1850 census Abby's eldest daughter, Frances, was described under the occupational category as "Belle of Hamburg Dance." Despite her well-known slave origins, Frances apparently found social acceptance in Ashley County—even if that acceptance was tinged with forbidden sexuality. Down the river in Louisiana, light-skinned women were highly prized companions for elite white men, and the "quadroon balls" where they met were part of an elaborate system of *plaçage*, whereby white men were able to conduct relationships across the color line. Was Frances the "Belle" of the dance in the small town of Hamburg, Arkansas, because white men there sought similar forbidden fruit? It was highly unusual for a census taker to mark one's "occupation" as anything other than "farmer," "merchant," or some kind of artisan, and women rarely had any occupation listed other than "teacher." Frances may have been the belle of the ball because she passed as white, or because she was known to have some "black blood," but she was certainly well known.[34]

In April 1855 Abby Guy and her children petitioned the court of Ashley County for their freedom and asked to be allowed to sue William Daniel as paupers, who would not have to pay court costs and would be awarded court-appointed counsel. The judge required Daniel to post bond and adjured him not to take Guy and her children out of the court's jurisdiction or subject them to any severity. During the time of the suit, Daniel was not allowed to keep Abby Guy or her children in his house. He had to hire them out to the highest bidder, and was not to bid at their hiring "or in anywise molest them."[35]

In May, Abby Guy, her children, William Daniel, and all of their witnesses gathered at the brand-new Ashley County Courthouse in Hamburg for its first session of the circuit court. Until that year circuit courts in Ashley County had been held in a private home. During Court Week in a rural Southern county, people from all walks of life came to town to attend court, gossip, and sell their wares; Ashley County's establishment of its very own courthouse was doubtless considered a significant development in the frontier community. So a large audience probably crowded the new courthouse to hear the case of *Abby Guy v. William Daniel,* to see Abby and her children display themselves for the jury's "inspection," to hear the testimony of medical experts and neighbors, and to decide for themselves whether she was black or white, and therefore slave or free.

Abby's lawyers evoked the image of Abby's mother as "a poor destitute orphan child . . . without any friend or home and living from place to place." This poor orphan, however, was white, and so her condition was the most feared of all—white slavery. The travesty had continued for so long, Abby's lawyers argued, because Daniel's father and brother had treated the family well, as "more favored than . . . an ordinary slave," so Abby and her mother had "submitted during [Nathaniel's] life, to that condition." Still, Abby claimed, Nathaniel had willed her manumission. She further asserted that this provision was not even the gift of a new status but rather an "admission of [her] previous Right" to freedom. The villain of her tale was William Daniel, who "tore [Abby and her children] from their home and . . . reduced them . . . to a state of slavery."[36]

Abby's construction of her white slavery story revealed much about antebellum notions of race. If whiteness equaled freedom, then the white slave represented an error of tragic proportions. Her hidden whiteness made her unfit for slavery, just as hidden blackness was supposed to make a light-skinned "African" unfit for freedom. But clearly these essences *could* be concealed, raising new anxieties among whites throughout America.

By the mid-nineteenth century, white slavery stories reverberated throughout the North and South. They began as trial transcripts, were repeated in fugitive slave narratives, were invoked by abolitionist literature, and finally appeared in novels. Abolitionists hoped that once white Northerners imagined themselves or their loved ones in bondage, they might extend their sympathy to black slaves, or at least look with horror upon an institution that wrongly enslaved white people. Pro-slavery Southerners too were fascinated by the notion of white slavery, but they used the term in quite a different way. The same issue of the *Arkansas State Gazette and*

Democrat that reported the Arkansas Supreme Court's decision on Abby Guy's case featured a separate story titled "White Slavery in Connecticut." That story reprinted an advertisement from the 1764 issue of the New Haven *Connecticut Gazette: "Just imported from Dublin,* in the Brig Darby, a parcel of *Irish servants,* both men and women, *to be sold cheap,* by Israel Boardman at Stamford." "So," commented the Arkansas editors, "it seems that less than 100 years ago, men and women were brought from Ireland, and sold as slaves, in the State of Connecticut." Apparently it was Northerners, not Southerners, who were prone to enslaving whites.[37]

But Southerners could also use stories of Southern white slavery to justify the slave system. Newspapers routinely printed stories about the freeing of "white slaves" like Abby Guy in an effort to demonstrate that the system could correct its own mistakes. Thus on May 30, 1851, the *Gazette* reported that "Clarissa, a mulatto woman," had won her suit for freedom—a "practical and conclusive refutation of [Northern editors'] teachings." Because whiteness was unmistakable, the *Gazette* implied, no white person could remain a slave for long. This notion that whiteness would prevail and "white slaves" would be freed retained considerable power long after slavery had ended. Writing in 1956, white Arkansan Y. W. Etheridge emphasized the fairness of Abby Guy's trial, the lengths to which Southerners went to ensure the equitable administration of slavery, and "the horror of placing anyone under the system unless it was shown without a doubt that this under the law must be done."[38]

White Northerners may have been horrified by the idea of enslaved whites, but white Southerners were more concerned about the opposite possibility: What if people of African descent were lurking unknown in their midst, enjoying all the privileges of whiteness despite their hidden black essence? Worse, what if race were simply unknowable? How many people of "negro blood" might even now be passing as white, turning those who accepted them into fools?

The greatest blow to a white man's honor was to be deceived into bestowing the privileges of whiteness on a "negro," and judicial rhetoric warned against the dangers of believing one's own eyes about race. As late as 1864, Judge Joseph Henry Lumpkin of Georgia told the following anecdote:

A man, at the beginning of this war, dropped into a village of one of our counties in Middle Georgia, and becoming rather famous for his pugilism, he was chosen as an officer in one of the volunteer companies enlisting for the military service. His *status* was never questioned, until, accosted rather familiarly by his *fellow-servant* . . . [,] an investigation was had, and Sambo was returned to his owner. Which of us has not narrowly escaped petting one of the pretty little mulattoes belonging to our neighbors as one of the family?

Of course, as Judge Lumpkin well knew, those "pretty little mulattoes" most likely *were* "one of the family." But the fiction was to be preserved at all costs that slaves were black and white people were free—and that "we" could always eventually tell which was which.[39]

Abby's proceedings turned upon the community's deeper worries about the very nature of racial identity. Her lay witnesses focused on Abby's social identity, her associations with white people, and her performances— the extent to which she did the things that white people do. Her neighbor Richard Stanley testified that Abby "visited among white folks, and went to church parties, etc." He noted that Frances "boarded out" at a school in the town of Birch Creek.[40]

Keightly Saunders, a fifty-seven-year-old farmer who in 1850 owned four slaves, one a mulatto, testified that Abby "visited among the whites as an equal." Saunders was "locally known as quite a character," a drinker and storyteller, free with "curse words which flowed in his conversation like water from a spring." Nevertheless, he commanded respect in the neighborhood, and was friends with Judge Hawkins, considered the leader of the bar in the region. Saunders's speaking for Abby must have carried considerable weight.[41]

Jeremiah Oats, a farm laborer with no slaves or land of his own in 1850, had done work for Abby, and testified that she had been competent to contract and pay her bills herself. Such competence was apparently beyond the power of a black woman; moreover, Oats's willingness to work for Abby indicated that he had recognized her as white. Meanwhile, William M. Drucker, sheriff of Ashley County, himself a slaveholder, explained that he "never thought of taxing Abby because the law exempts widows"—not because she was a person of color, who would normally be exempt from taxation. Drucker went on to explain how assessments of slave property worked, and testified that William Daniel had never included Abby's family on his slave lists for tax assessment.[42]

"A. Bull," who may have been Ambrose Bull (foreman of the jury), had heard William Daniel say in court in another matter that "no person except himself could prove that Abbey had a drop of Negro blood in her and that he could only do so by reference to his papers and perhaps not even then." Apparently even Daniel himself recognized that Abby Guy did not fit well within the boundaries of blackness.[43]

The courts in Abby Guy's proceedings were far less concerned with establishing her provenance than they were with analyzing her behavior. As in the case of Alexina Morrison, Southern anxieties were in full flower. Who counted as white, who might counterfeit whiteness, and who might live up to the high standards of white Southern womanhood were questions far more important to judge, jury, and community than any documents William Daniel might muster to show that he had legally owned Abby and her mother.

As Abby's proceedings revealed, juries needed to believe that they could rely on their own common sense. But the notion of expertise was becoming increasingly important by the mid-nineteenth century. Phrenologists like George Combe and Samuel George Morton were increasingly preoccupied with how racial difference might be read in such physiological characteristics as the size of the cranium and the shape of the foot, as well as with attempts to link physiological, moral, and intellectual difference. The most famous texts of the period include page after page of measurements comparing African and European skulls and other body parts and seeking to link physical and mental differences among the "Negroid," "Caucasoid," and "Mongoloid" races.

These antecedents of physical anthropology were seized upon by Southern medical writers such as Josiah Nott and Samuel Cartwright, who developed "scientific" racial theories specifically intended to support slavery. Cartwright, a doctor practicing in Louisiana and Mississippi, argued that African Americans suffered from unique "negro diseases," including "drapetomania," the disease of running away from one's master; and "dysaesthesia ethiopica," or "what overseers call Rascality," characterized by unreasonable surliness, work slowdowns, and the breaking of tools—a disease that could only be treated by whipping and hard physical labor. Such racial theories were well known to Southern physicians, who often quoted them in the courtroom.[44]

Scientific experts were invoked at a time when doctors, lawyers, and other professionals were beginning to stake their claims to expert knowledge. The result was a tug of war between judge and jury, expert and lay witnesses, creating bitter arguments among those claiming to know racial identity scientifically and those claiming to know it experientially. So-called expert knowledge was countered with "common sense" arguments. That is, while medical experts relied on racial "science," juries used common sense to make visual inspections and hear testimony about reputation. Sometimes, however, lay witnesses spoke in the language of science and expertise, and often doctors resorted to notions of common sense. Scientific and "performance" evidence could work together, as they did for Abby Guy; or they could be opposed to each other, as in the trial of Alexina Morrison.

Abby Guy's attorney called two experts. One was Dr. Isaac Newton—an elderly local physician who owned substantial landholdings as well as a young mulatto woman slave with two children; he apparently qualified as an expert because he "had read Physiology." Dr. Newton testified that curly hair and flat noses "[remain] observable for several descents [from the negro]," implying that Abby Guy, without these features, must have been far removed from any black origins. Another local doctor, M. C. Comer, who owned thirty slaves, corroborated his colleague's testimony. Meanwhile, lay witnesses who had highlighted the same aspects of Abby's physical appearance were asked to put their testimony in "scientific" terms or were quizzed about whether they had studied "Physiology or the Distinction of the races."[45]

Asserting one's expertise was important—even if that expertise was based on grounds other than formal study. While some judges believed that doctors' testimony should weigh more heavily than that of laypeople, lawyers routinely asked witnesses who were to testify about someone's racial identity whether they owned slaves themselves, suggesting that mastery—ownership—conferred an expertise of its own. Likewise, witnesses laid claim to expertise by referring to their status as slave owners. As Judge William Horn Battle of North Carolina explained: "[It does not] . . . require a distinguished comparative anatomist to detect the admixture of the African or Indian with the pure blood of the white race. Any person of ordinary intelligence, who, for a sufficient length of time will devote his attention to the subject, will be able to discover with almost unerring certainty the adulteration of the Caucasian with the negro or Indian blood." He went on to approve the expert qualification of a slave owner to testify as to whether the defendant, indicted as a "free negro" for carrying firearms, was of African descent.[46]

Similarly, in the case of Alexina Morrison, Alexina's lay witnesses were asked on cross-examination to explain the "characteristic difference be-

tween the white Race and the black," and one who "did not understand
the question first put to him" quickly amended, on reexamination, that
"now he knows the difference." The lay witnesses for Alexina's owner used
the language of science to declare Alexina Morrison colored: one planter
who possessed many slaves judged that she "ha[d] African blood . . . from
the shape of her cheek Bones and the conformation of the lower part of
her mouth." A witness named B. Preston saw African blood in "something
between the eyes and cheeks [and] also something in the lips, the pecu-
liarity of the eyes and a darke [sic] shade of the teeth which are characteristic with quadroons."[47]

In Alexina's second trial, a doctor testifying on her behalf proved his racial bona fides on cross-examination by asserting that he did "not believe
in the unity of the human race" and by detailing the racial differences he
had found. A merchant seaman testified that he had thoroughly examined
Morrison and found her to have several "characteristics of the whites," including a "double cartilage" and a "hollow foot." This merchant testified
that he had studied as a surgeon and made a detailed comparison of black
and white sailors in Massachusetts in 1840 or 1841. He explained that he
had undertaken this study "before [Massachusetts] legislated itself out of
the Union," in other words, before Massachusetts had passed strong "personal liberty" laws protecting fugitive slaves.[48]

At the same time, witnesses on either side of Alexina's case insisted on
the power of common sense in knowing race. A Creole planter (in this
case a white member of the French community born in Louisiana), P. C.
Perret, in answer to a question by the court, testified that "from natural
[instinct] he would say she was white, why he feels this to be so he cannot
explain . . . because a creole of this place, being among colored persons of
so many different shades of color from snowy white to jet black and the
constant intermingling of races the creole can always detect in a person
whether that person is of African origin."[49]

The notion that Southerners knew racial identity by instinct was supported by the custom of allowing juries to view the contested individuals
in court. Abby Guy and her children "were personally presented in Court"
for visual inspection midway through the testimony, and Judge Sorrels instructed the jury to "treat their observation and inspection of plaintiffs'
persons as evidence," applying their own "knowledge of the distinction between the negro and the white races" and whatever rules might apply for
discerning "negro blood." Likewise the Mississippi Supreme Court ruled

in 1876 that one's identity as a "colored person" was "susceptible of proof by ocular demonstration," because sometimes "jurors may use their eyes as well as their ears."[50]

In 1876 a North Carolina court noted that "the eyes of the members of the jury must be presumed to be as good as those of medical men," thus reinforcing the notion that race was immediately apparent. Litigants seeking to prove a person's whiteness almost always sought to exhibit him or her to the jury. And witnesses' descriptions of appearance—skin color, hair, eyes, and features—were ubiquitous in racial identity trials, even if the person being described was a long-dead ancestor. In *State v. Chavers* the defendant objected that the trial judge had allowed a witness to assert "that the defendant's father was a man of dark colour, and had kinky hair, that he was a shade darker, than the defendant himself, and his hair was about as much kinked." The state responded by reiterating the importance of appearance: "As a negro is almost entirely known by his external marks, for example, his colour, his kinky hair, his thick lips . . . the nearer the defendant approached the appearance of a negro in these marks he was consequently by so much the farther from a white person." Yet even when jurors could see a person with their own eyes, they still had to worry about being fooled. Witnesses often called attention to features that might be deceptive or have gone unnoticed. In *Williamson v. Norton* several witnesses mentioned the way Robert, allegedly a runaway slave, dressed to make himself look whiter. In *State v. Jacobs,* a North Carolina criminal case, the state introduced a witness to testify that "the Defendant was of yellow complexion had kinky hair though his hair on the day of the trial was much straighter than usual."[51]

Although appearance was supposed to speak for itself, the language of court proceedings reveals at every turn white Southerners' awareness of how deceptive it might be. Hair might be dyed or straightened. Clothing might be carefully chosen. Often witnesses appeared to see the same person quite differently, or they insisted that the person had made himself look different on prior occasions. A whiteness that was supposed to be inherent and unchangeable might be cleverly counterfeited—and by a black person whose slave-like essence was thereby concealed even from the most perceptive white observer.

Since appearance, behavior, and reputation were all in Abby Guy's favor, William Daniel fell back on documentary evidence of Abby's slave origins to prove his case, trying valiantly to demonstrate that he was indeed her legal owner. He produced his father's will, which, he pointed out, did not free Abby but rather left her to William's brother-in-law, as well as his receipt for Abby from that new owner. He tried to relate Abby's supposed white performance not to a hidden white essence but to her poor showing as a slave: because Abby had been of little value to him, he claimed, he had "permitted her to go when and where she pleased, for several years past." His lack of regard for her usefulness, however, did not mean that he forfeited his claims of ownership: when she left the state of Arkansas for Louisiana, he brought her and her children home and reasserted his rights. In effect, he argued that since Abby's legal status was clearly that of a slave—his father had owned her and no one had freed her—she must be black, because only blacks were slaves.[52]

William further claimed that he should not have to prove Abby's racial identity; her status as a slave should be enough. Once he had demonstrated that she was rightly his slave, she should not be free, whatever her degree of blood or racial identity. Thus he called to the stand Thomas S. Thompson, a relatively wealthy local farmer who owned six slaves. Thompson told the jury that he had known both Abby and her mother, Polly, as slaves, although they were both "bright mulatto." Thompson betrayed some confusion over how exactly to define their race: Polly "was a yellow woman, darker than white . . . Could not say whether Polly was of African or Indian extraction. I have seen some only of half blood who would provably [sic] be as white as Polly was." But if he could not determine Polly's racial identity, he could be confident of her and Abby's slave status: Polly "always held herself as a slave and acted as such. She and Abby always labored and conducted themselves as slaves in the family, with the exception that they took more care of themselves perhaps than others."[53]

On cross-examination Thompson acknowledged that he was Daniel's brother-in-law and that he "had never studied Physiology nor the distinction of races." He also admitted that he had seen white persons who worked in the fields become as dark as Abby and her mother, and had seen white persons with hair as curly as theirs. When confronted with an alleged lock of Polly's hair, Thompson said, "I do not know whether she had any negro blood in her veins, only inferred so from her being treated as a slave, and from her dark color." Several more of Daniel's witnesses likewise acknowledged the difficulty of defining Abby's and Polly's race, even as they insisted on the women's slave status. As William's nephew James

Barnett noted, he "had seen persons *recognized as white,* who were as dark as Polly." Light or dark, however, Polly was still his uncle's slave. Significantly, Daniel's witnesses explicitly acknowledged that people of ambiguous appearance fell on both sides of the line between white and "negro." What mattered, in their view, was not race but status—or rather, once Abby's slave status was determined, she must, ipso facto, be black.[54]

Clearly, if Abby Guy had had a piece of paper certifying her free status, she would have relied on it. Having no such documentation of "that previous Right [to freedom]," she was forced to make her case in her own person. Her success at trial—like that of Alexina Morrison and many other litigants—rested on her ability to shift the ground of argument from legal documentation to the question of performance, an argument that cleverly relied on prevailing antebellum notions of race as self-evident, clear-cut, and binary. Ironically, both Abby and her putative owner made the same argument: Did the jury really want to live in a world where local white residents could be grievously mistaken for slaves?[55]

After the testimony closed, lawyers on both sides proposed instructions for Judge Sorrels to give the jury. The judge gave all of the instructions drafted by Abby Guy's lawyers, which charged the jury to follow a "one-fourth rule" but with one wrinkle: Guy and her children could be proved slaves only if they had more than one-fourth "negro blood" *or* if they were descended in the maternal line from a slave who was one-fourth negro or more. Furthermore, "every presumption, consistent with reason, should be indulged in favor of freedom." The judge refused to give most of William Daniel's proposed instructions, including an instruction to ignore "all evidence on Physiology, [which] is irrelevant," and several to the effect that evidence that Abby had been held in slavery should be evidence of her status as a slave.[56]

Although the jury list for *Guy v. Daniel* no longer exists, we know that the foreman was Ambrose Bull, a forty-nine-year-old farmer who owned six slaves and property worth $1,000 in 1850. We also know that everyone on the jury was white and male, and we can assume that at least one or two other slaveholders would have served alongside Ambrose Bull. This was the jury that voted to free Abby Guy and her children. As in the case of Alexina Morrison and so many other light-skinned women, an all-white pro-slavery jury had disregarded substantial documentary evidence to rely on their own sense of whiteness.[57]

Daniel appealed to the Arkansas Supreme Court, which ruled in his favor, rejecting the one-fourth rule propounded by the trial court in favor of maternal descent: if Daniel could show that Abby was descended from a maternal line of slaves, she legally belonged to him. In effect, the Supreme Court was invoking a "one drop of blood" rule, considering Abby "negro" with even a tiny fraction of African ancestry—so long as it passed through the maternal line. In this, however, Arkansas was extremely unusual. Despite the popular notion of a "one-drop rule," most states did not define race this way until late in the nineteenth century, as part of a post–Civil War effort to implement Jim Crow legislation. Far more common was the requirement of one-fourth, or sometimes one-eighth, African ancestry, enabling people who clearly had black forebears to be legally considered white.

Even where the one-drop rule was invoked, it rarely decided actual cases. Because blood could not be scientifically evaluated nor ancestry known for certain, juries determined race on the basis of other types of evidence. And race was nearly always a matter for the jury. Indeed courts consistently held that juries should be allowed to see and hear the widest array of evidence and should have great discretion in finding the "facts" of race, a clear assertion of the community's role in determining and policing racial identity. Particularly in the antebellum period, the realms of "law" and "fact" were far from distinct; although the nineteenth-century trend was toward greater power for the judge, vigorous popular efforts to limit judicial power and strong customary traditions of juries deciding "law" questions meant that the battle was far from won. Juries received instructions about the legal definition of "negro" and "mulatto" in these trials, but such instructions rarely settled the matter. In some cases the judge did not specify a definition of "negro" or "white" but only explained to the jury that if they found the person to be "negro," it would lead to one result, and if they found her to be white, it would lead to another. In other cases the judge simply instructed the jury about the kinds of evidence they were allowed to consider. In still other cases the jury instructions specified some fraction of African ancestry as the definition of "negro" or "mulatto"—but even then, court testimony often traveled far afield from questions of ancestry.[58]

William Daniel succeeded in having the jury's verdict overturned, and the case was sent back to Ashley County for a new trial. Daniel then won a motion to remove the case to Ashley County's northern neighbor, Drew County, where he thought he would find a more sympathetic jury. Like

Ashley, Drew County had built its courthouse in 1851, and its county seat, Monticello, had been incorporated in 1852. Only one lawyer made his home there, but the town included three slave dealers, and a third of its population was enslaved. Court proceedings in Drew County were informal. According to one lawyer's reminiscences about the early days of Drew County Court, when attorney J. S. Winter presented himself at court, "armed with Blackstone and Greenleaf," and "read from his authorities," the court "ordered the jury to pay no attention to Mr. Winter's 'furren' books, as they had nothing to do with justice in Arkansas." Perhaps under similar instructions, Daniel's suit in Drew County ended in a verdict for Abby.[59]

Once again Daniel appealed the verdict, this time on the ground that the jury had based their verdict on an improper exhibition of Abby's feet, which had required her to remove her shoes and stockings in court, as well as on the more general ground that "there was a total want of evidence to support the verdict." The high court was not persuaded. When Daniel's counsel objected, "with much warmth of expression," to the exhibition of Abby Guy's naked feet as inappropriate to the decorum of the courtroom, Chief Justice Elbert English rejected his appeal, noting that it did not take an expert to recognize the value of such an inspection in a case of racial status: "The experience of every intelligent observer of the race . . . will doubtless attest the truth . . . No one, who is familiar with the peculiar formation of the *negro foot*, can doubt, but that an inspection of that member would ordinarily afford some indication of the race." Furthermore, the justice emphasized, it was the "province of the jury to pass upon the weight of the evidence." Here again we see the merging of common sense and contemporary scientific theory, which posited important differences among feet.[60]

In his final opinion in Abby's case, Chief Justice English expressed his own skepticism about the jury's decision, remarking that "it is possible that the jury found against the preponderance of evidence, through reluctance to sanction the enslaving of persons, who, to all appearance, were of the white race, and, for many years before suit, had acted as free persons and been treated as such." Nevertheless, he affirmed the trial verdict in *Daniel v. Guy*. On the eve of the Civil War, the Supreme Court of Arkansas set Abby and her children free.[61]

What mattered to the Arkansas Supreme Court in Abby Guy's case was not what made the difference to the witnesses and jurors. At trial, racial

identity was disputed on the grounds of physical appearance, social acceptance and reputation "as an equal," and exercise of the rights of free persons. Abby Guy may have won because the jury was reluctant to remove
rights to which she had a "prescriptive" claim by virtue of having exercised
them for some years. She may have won because the jury believed from
their own observation that she was white, regardless of her ancestry. Perhaps the jury feared the horror of "white slavery." Or perhaps Abby Guy's
medical experts and other witnesses were simply more credible than those
of William Daniel. Almost certainly, though, the jury outcome did not depend on a determination of a precise fraction of the "African blood" in
Abby Guy's veins.

Modern observers might expect that physical markers of race would
dominate any racial identity trial, if not documentary evidence of a person's legal status. Yet these supposedly solid ways of knowing race were
surprisingly indeterminate and unreliable, particularly within a society
where race was such a crucial aspect of identity. Despite the visual power
of exhibition, not all candidates for whiteness were paraded before the
jury, and even when they were, jurors were given many reasons not to
believe their own eyes. Only twenty of sixty-eight case records from the
nineteenth-century South referred explicitly to inspections. Only two of
the twenty relied solely on physical appearance, and only one case relied
on physical appearance plus a single other type of evidence.[62]

As for Abby Guy, she never spoke to another census taker, so we do not
know for certain whether she lived the remainder of her life as white, colored, or something in between. Yet other records show that she remained
in Ashley County, even after an 1859 law banished all free people of color
from the state. She married another white man named Roper and continued to fight for her rights. In June 1863, six months after the Emancipation Proclamation, she sued William Daniel to recover the horses, oxen,
and cart he had taken from her when he brought her back from the bayou
eight years earlier. Daniel responded that Abby Guy could not sue him—
because she was a slave. Yet his fellow white men of Ashley and Drew
counties had preferred to free Abby and her daughter, the "Belle of Hamburg Dance," rather than to ratify Daniel's mastery over these women who
had survived on the middle ground for so long.[63]

In Abby Guy's day, white Southerners and Northerners alike read tales
of white slavery and heard stories about black folks passing, and they

shuddered to think that racial identity could be so easily counterfeited. Their anxiety rested at least in part on the precarious nature of slavery itself: any system that requires the forced labor of large numbers of people—who might at any time rebel overtly or covertly—is bound to produce a certain uneasiness among those whose wealth, privilege, and security depends on that system. Non-slaveholding whites, having bought into the notion that their citizenship was racially defined—effectively allying them with wealthy planters and industrialists—likewise felt a great deal of anxiety over the stability of their status. If their whiteness was their most prized possession—the only thing distinguishing them from the one class lower than themselves—what did it mean that this supposedly unique attribute could be counterfeited by members of a degraded race?

The trial of Abby Guy, unlike that of Phoebe and her sons, had turned away from documented proof of Abby's status toward the testimony of medical experts and of local neighbors about her racial identity. While medical experts taught the participants in the courtroom that there were scientific distinctions between the "african and caucasian races," laypeople also learned to speak about those distinctions, basing their expertise on their experience in a slave society. This common sense of race kept the power to decide racial identity in local communities, and it meant that local decision making would continue to trump the rules handed down by legal institutions in distant state capitals.

CHAPTER TWO

Performing Whiteness

RACIAL IDENTITY TRIALS were based on a series of contradictions. On the one hand, whites in antebellum America believed that racial identity was obvious, something that any white person should be able recognize on sight. And indeed, with regard to people whose features were obviously African or northern European, this belief remained largely unchallenged, especially as society moved to tighten the associations between whiteness and freedom, blackness and slavery. On the other hand, antebellum America understood that racial identity was a troubling enigma, something that could be read only with difficulty—if at all—for those men and women who lived in the racial borderlands between slave and free, whose appearance was ambiguous, and whose personal histories were unknown. Over the course of the antebellum era, two ways of knowing race became increasingly important: science and performance.[1]

Performing White Manhood

During the 1850s and 1860s perhaps the greatest contradiction in Southern white culture was the effort to combine the aristocratic ideal of honor with the republican notion of white man's democracy. Southern gentlemen were expected to adhere to a code of conduct that prescribed unique ways of interacting with social inferiors, peers, and superiors—customs meant to distinguish them from the vast majority of common folk. Yet Southern politics depended on a belief that all white men were equals, that only blacks constituted the "mudsill" class. As sectional conflicts sharpened, the need to mobilize ordinary white people under the planters' banner became ever more urgent.

Hence, honor in the South was democratized, and some aspects of it became available to all white men, especially acts of citizenship: sitting on a jury, voting, and mustering in the militia. In racial identity trials—and particularly at the appellate level—judges gave special weight to the civic performance of white manhood.[2]

Thus the very first case to deny citizenship to "free people of color" equated white identity with civic acts. *Bryan v. Walton* traveled up and down the judicial system to the Georgia Supreme Court three times in the 1850s and early 1860s and set a precedent for the infamous U.S. Supreme Court case *Dred Scott v. Sandford,* which found that even free black people could never be U.S. citizens. Yet *Bryan* focused little direct attention on how state or constitutional law defined either slavery or citizenship. Instead the case turned on whether the men of the Nunez family were black or white.[3]

Joseph Nunez was the son of Lucy, a white woman. He died without descendants, having sold six slaves to Seaborn Bryan, a white man. His white administrator, Hughes Walton, sued Bryan to recover the human property, claiming that Nunez was a man of color and so was legally barred from conveying slaves.

At the first trial in 1848 the jury found for Walton on the basis of instructions that simply assumed Joseph Nunez's identity as a person of color without explaining how the jury should determine that "fact." Bryan appealed. Because of problems with the way wills had been introduced as evidence, the Georgia Supreme Court remanded the case for a new trial.

In his opinion Judge Lumpkin agreed entirely with Hughes Walton: Nunez was a man of color and so had no right to convey slaves. Lumpkin elaborated on his decision with a long disquisition on the "social and civil degradation, resulting from the taint of blood, [that] adheres to the descendants of Ham in this country, like the poisoned tunic of Nessus." Although the judge claimed to "forego the temptation" to "sketch hastily the history of African slavery in this country" in order that "the present status of free persons of color could the more clearly be ascertained and defined," he did manage to fill eight pages before concluding that a free person of color had no right to convey property because "he resides among us, and yet is a stranger. A *native* even, and yet not a citizen. Though not a *slave,* yet is he not free . . . The prejudice, if it can be called so, of caste, is unconquerable."[4]

As the case went forward, there was no doubt that only as a white man did Joseph Nunez have the right to do what he wished with his property. Thus did racial identity become the focus of the second trial. Since witnesses on both sides agreed that Joseph's mother was white, attention turned to Joseph's father, James.[5]

Bryan mobilized a number of witnesses to testify to James's whiteness. They essentially agreed that James had a dark complexion: some thought he might be Indian; others considered him Portuguese. No one suggested that an Indian background removed James from the white race; on the contrary, it offered a rationale for his color that explained away his "blackness." Witnesses seemed to accept Mary Rogers's physical description of James: "straight long nose, thin lips, straight and very black hair, rather a narrow, long face and of a red complexion; he was not a large man, walked trim and nice."[6]

Rogers went beyond appearance to report on "Jim" Nunez's behavior and reputation: "[He] was always treated and regarded in the neighborhood as not a negro, or having any negro blood in his veins, but as a respectable Indian and white blooded man." She noted that "Jim was always among respectable white people in the neighborhood in their dances, parties, &c. and was received by them as on a footing with whites."[7] Rogers further explained that she had always considered Jim's son Joseph to be "of color" yet "never regarded that color as arising from negro blood" but rather from "Indian and white." Likewise Harriett Kilpatrick, who had stayed in the home of Joseph's mother, reiterated that "neither Jim or Joe Nunez were regarded as free negroes, nor did either regard himself as such or act as such." Mary Rogers agreed that Joseph associated with free "negroes," though she thought "it was because Joe had a negro for his wife."[8]

Stephen Newman and Mary Harrel testified not only that Jim Nunez looked more Indian than negro but also that "his action and movements were as genteel as any man witnesses have known; there was no clumsiness about him. Witnesses well remembered Jim Nunez's dancing, which was very graceful; many persons tried to catch his step, and nearly all admired its style." (Contrary to modern stereotypes, this evidence of being a good dancer went to prove Jim's whiteness.) Mary Harrel testified that Jim

Nunez "never kept low, trifling or rakish company; he associated with respectable whites in the neighborhood; was often at their balls and parties,
assemblies and little gatherings, where no free negro was allowed to associate with the whites, and dined with the whites just the same as any gentleman would have done."[9]

Bryan had offered a persuasive explanation of the Nunez men's appearance and had amassed a great deal of testimony about their behavior as
white men. There was only one hole in his argument: no one presented
any evidence of Nunez's exercising either political or legal rights. Indeed
Harriet Kilpatrick testified that as far as she knew, "neither Jim or Joe
Nunez ever voted or exercised any of the rights of citizenship."[10]

On the opposite side of the courtroom, Walton's Burke County witnesses testified that James Nunez was a mulatto. Charles Cosnahan
claimed that the Nunezes "passed in the neighborhood as free colored
persons," although he allowed that he did "not know what their blood
was." Cosnahan gave as evidence of their race their appearance ("tolerable
kinky hair[,] . . . did not have a fair complexion"), their reputation ("they
passed in the neighborhood as free colored persons"), and his belief that
neither Jim nor Joseph "voted or performed military duty"; he believed
that "they exercised no other rights than those of free negroes."[11]

Joseph Cosnahan agreed that the Nunezes were mulattoes. He first
mentioned their appearance: "They had hair which curled, does not recol-
lect their features, but their general appearance indicated them as mulattoes." Then he discussed their social and civic performances, explaining
that he "never knew of their exercising the usual rights of white citizens;
they considered themselves as mulattoes; James Nunez was an educated
man and mixed sometimes with white men; they were regarded in the
neighborhood as mulattoes; the white citizens associated with them and
regarded them as mulattoes." Several other witnesses corroborated this
version of Joseph's and James's racial identity. The jury at the second trial
apparently found this testimony persuasive, awarding a verdict to Walton
for the full amount he had claimed.[12]

Not content with the result, Seaborn Bryan moved for a third trial,
where several witnesses continued to give much the same testimony, corroborated by the new witnesses who were called. William C. Bates, supporting the notion that James Nunez was white, testified that he had
straight black hair, that "his features were more of the Portuguese or
Spaniard than any other, unless Indian; his race or blood was either Span-

ish, Indian or Portuguese, or a mixture of the three races." Despite this
mixture, James Nunez "was treated by his neighbors as a gentleman,
recognized as a gentleman, and enjoyed the privileges of a gentleman
and a free citizen; he was recognized as a free white man."[13] Yet on cross-
examination Bates explained that he "was too young, when I knew James
Nunez, to answer whether he voted, mustered, or served on juries." James
Nunez had never been seen performing the specific acts of white manhood—a serious omission.[14]

Only one witness gave testimony showing James Nunez's exercise of his
civic rights. The deposition of South Carolinian Matthew Alexander suggested that before James had moved to Georgia, he had been a "fine
dancer—quite a gentleman in manners and appearance," with long straight
black hair. More important, "he enjoyed all the privileges of a free man . . .
James Nunez voted, mustered, and did jury duty, and exercised the usual
privileges and duties of free white citizens."[15]

Walton, for his part, found three new witnesses to testify to Joseph
Nunez's "Negro blood." One thought Joseph had "combined the White,
Indian, and Negro race, with a preponderance of Negro blood"; the second thought he was "of the White and Negro race . . . composed equally of
each," and the third that he was "mostly of the Negro blood." But all three
asserted that Joseph "was not received and treated as a white man, and he
did not associate with free white citizens, and was not allowed to eat at the
tables with free white citizens, neither did he sleep on the beds with
them," and "he did not seek to do so."[16]

Significantly, on cross-examination these witnesses had to swear to their
own whiteness, asserting "that they and their parents are as white as most
white people, and especially as white as their interrogator, and that they
are not advocating a free negro cause." Apparently in response to his questions suggesting that they themselves might have "colored blood," the witnesses asserted "that their hair is not kinky or curly, or straight, and one of
them has little or no hair on his head . . . We have no negro veins, you old
rake, and advise you to amend yourself." Unlike in Phoebe's case, in which
even the slaveholder himself admitted anti-slavery beliefs, these witnesses
had to choose sides in the sectional battle over slavery in order to be taken
seriously as white men who were qualified to give opinions about an individual's racial identity.[17]

By the end of the third trial, juries had heard conflicting testimony on
every aspect of Joseph Nunez's white identity—appearance, self-presentation,

reputation and acceptance among blacks and whites, white ancestry, white conduct, white character—and on his failure to exercise the rights and privileges of whiteness. While no one could agree whether James and Joseph had straight or curly hair, almost everyone agreed on this point: they had not performed the civic duties of white manhood. The jury was persuaded. They found for Hughes Walton.

Judge Lumpkin, for the Supreme Court of Georgia, sought to set the matter to rest at the case's final disposition in 1864. Lumpkin disparaged all testimony in favor of Nunez's whiteness as given by dupes who had been fooled by appearances. (Here was where he made his reference to "pretty little mulattoes.") Keen to avoid being fooled himself, Lumpkin dismissed all of the evidence of appearance and performance—the "common sense" of the community—as unreliable. Instead the judge relied on old-fashioned legal documentation of ancestry: the will of Moses Nunez, James's father, leaving his possessions to his wife, "Mulatto Rose." Lumpkin characterized Moses Nunez as "a Portuguese . . . from a left hand marriage with a mulatto by the name of Rose." Then, he explained, "from this connection sprang James Nunez . . . [who] emigrated to a then distant part of the country[,] . . . acquired some notoriety at dances for the grace and agility with which 'he tripped the light fantastic toe'; . . . intermarried with a very pretty white woman," and that was "the origin and blood of this mongrel family." Judge Lumpkin's rhetoric of fraud and deceit suggests the dangers he perceived lurking in the world of racial performance.[18]

We may never know who Joseph and James Nunez really were. It is quite likely that Moses Nunez was Jewish, the descendant of a Portuguese Jew named Samuel Nunez who arrived in Georgia in 1733 by way of England. Nunez's sons "ate and slept with Indians, blacks, and Christians." They became fur merchants. By the nineteenth century, the Nunezes of Georgia were a well-known Jewish family, though the question of religion was never raised at trial.[19]

Yet despite the community's disagreement over the Nunezes' identity, they did agree on one point: the Nunezes' race could be known through their performances. Race was not only something Joseph and James *were*, it was something they *did*. Who was a white man? A civic being who voted, served on juries, and mustered in the militia. Degraded black men were not capable of such things, while honorable white men could not keep from doing them.

Thus we can see that the law—the public sphere—was involved not merely in recognizing race but in creating it; the state itself—through its legal and military institutions—helped make people white. In allowing men of low social status to create their whiteness by voting, serving on juries, and mustering in the militia, the state welcomed every white man into symbolic equality with the wealthy Southern slaveholder.

This definition of whiteness may appear to modern observers as a kind of circular argument: in order to be a citizen, one must be white; in order to be (recognized as) white, one must act like a citizen.

Yet contemporary participants in the Southern system did not view these arguments as circular; rather they saw them as self-evident. In part, witnesses and jurors thought that testimony about civic acts was one more form of reputation evidence: if a man was allowed to vote, at least some people must have recognized him as white. In part, too, courts may have been deferring to earlier administrative determinations of the individual's identity. If one branch of government allowed a man to vote or to enlist in the militia, the courts were included to support that determination.

But when appellate judges articulated the grounds for their decisions, they often gave other kinds of explanations. In effect they were relying on the antebellum notion that whiteness and blackness were self-evident qualities. Having demonstrated citizenship, a man must be white. The argument was less circular than self-reinforcing, since a person who was *not* white was presumably incapable of performing the acts of civic participation that white men performed.

The clearest judicial statement of white manhood as civic performance came from South Carolina, which significantly had no antebellum law defining "negro" according to ancestry. Instead South Carolinians preferred to define race entirely through behavior, reputation, and social status. Thus in 1835 Judge William Harper of the South Carolina Court of Appeals found to be white several witnesses whose "maternal grand father[,] . . . although of a dark complexion, had been recognized as a white man, received into society, and exercised political privileges as such." The people in question were now "respectable . . . [O]ne of them is a militia officer, and their caste has never been questioned until now." For a person of ambiguous appearance, Judge Harper ruled, evidence of reception in society and exercise of legal and political rights could overcome evidence of negro ancestry, or even determine an ambiguous racial identity: "It may be well and proper that a man of worth, honesty, industry and respectability, should have the rank of a white man, while a vagabond of the same degree

of blood should be confined to the inferior caste . . . It is hardly necessary
to say that a slave cannot be a white man."[20]

A slave cannot be a white man. Here was the clearest possible statement that racial identity was neither a scientific fact nor a mere matter of
documentation but rather a socially and legally defined status that rested
on a deeper ideological commitment to race, in which white equaled free
(civic, responsible, manly) and black equaled slave (degraded, irresponsi-
ble, unfit for manly duties).

The South Carolina Court of Appeals continued to make similar pronouncements throughout the next two decades. In 1842 Justice John
Belton O'Neall, riding circuit in South Carolina, sat before the spring term
of the circuit court in Walterborough. The three Johnson brothers had
sued the parish tax collector, claiming that they should be exempt from the
"free negro" head tax. Judge O'Neall found two of the brothers "on inspection . . . very passable white men" with "excellent characters." They
proved at trial that they "had been raised as white, and had been so received in society, and had exercised all the privileges of white people, such
as mustering and voting." By contrast, the state's witnesses claimed that
the three brothers were "considered as colored people" and that "they associated with white persons, but never without question." One brother
had voted once, but then the voting official "took his vote out of the box,
and scratched his name off the list." O'Neall instructed the jury to take
into account "color, blood, and reception in society," and the jury "very
properly found the relators to be free white men."[21]

In *White v. Tax Collector,* sons of Elijah Bass claimed that they were
white and should be exempt from payment of the capitation tax on "free
negroes." The tax collector argued that Elijah Bass was "a man of some
property, but was never admitted to any of the privileges of a white man,"
whereas the plaintiffs gave evidence that their father had been a witness in
the Court of Common Pleas at Camden with free white persons as parties.
Although the plaintiffs lost at trial, the trial judge reported: "I wish the
court may be able to find some ground to give a new trial. For if any people tinged with African blood are worthy to be rated as white," it was these
plaintiffs. On appeal they presented evidence that although Elijah Bass
was not "a clear-blood white man," nevertheless he had "always been
treated by his neighbors as a free white man," ate with them at their tables, was "honest and industrious[,] . . . respected by his neighbors and all
who know him, for his good character[,] . . . and has never, to our knowl-

edge, been refused any of the rights and privileges of a free white man."
For all of these reasons, they argued, the members of the family, "with the
consent and approbation of society and the acquiescence of the State,
have established their case." The judges of the Court of Appeals split three
to two against the plaintiffs; the majority decided not to disturb the jury
verdict on the ground that the question of racial status was a matter for the
jury and "must partake more of a political than a legal character."[22]

These cases were decided in South Carolina, the state with the most
"aristocratic," caste-based social structure in the Deep South, and one un-
burdened with "blood"-based statutory rules of racial definition in this period. Yet it is possible to find similar statements in judicial opinions from
all over the South, regardless of the statutory definition of "negro." In
1854 the Mississippi High Court of Errors and Appeals, in finding Augus-
tine Krebs to be mulatto, considered it determinative that he had "married
a slave, that he did not claim or exercise the right to vote at elections, to
act as a juror in court, or to testify against white men in court . . . though
several witnesses testify that he was considered to be a white man." In the
1847 case of *Dean v. Commonwealth*, the Virginia Supreme Court, in considering whether trial witnesses were mulattoes, found it significant that
"their grandfather, David Ross, who was spoken of as a respectable man,
though probably a mulatto, was a soldier in the revolution and died in the
service." Again and again courts singled out evidence of the exercise of
rights and privileges as particularly strong markers of white manhood.[23]

One important dimension of these opinions is the notion of a *prescriptive* right to whiteness. "Prescriptive" has several meanings, but in its
strictest legal sense a prescriptive right means that one might acquire a
right to property after a *prescribed* number of years by virtue of having
used the property and treated it as one's own for those years without challenge. Thus Judge Harper of South Carolina suggested that it would be
unwise—indeed, he wrote, "very cruel and mischievous"—to disturb the
racial identity of a man "whose caste has never been questioned until
now." He went on to make the connection between this gentleman's prescriptive right to be considered white and other rights in property: "Shall
time and prescription, which secure and consecrate all other rights, have
no effect in fixing the civil condition of an individual?"[24]

Reading this, we might draw the conclusion that the prescriptive aspect
of whiteness was simply the result of judicial reluctance to disturb the conclusions of the community. Yet as we have seen, communities were by no

means decided about the racial status of marginal individuals. Furthermore, people in the community themselves spoke of the prescriptive aspects of whiteness in both senses of the word: the way in which identity was formed by an accretion of acceptances by and associations with other white people over a *prescribed* period of time; and the way in which identity was formed through performance, by doing the *prescribed* things white people do.

The significance of civic performance, then, is the extent to which it reveals the *creation* of racial categories, the way that public and private actions combine to develop ongoing ideologies of race. It is tempting—but incorrect—to view racial definitions as something the participants had ready in their minds before the trial began. Rather, jurors and judges struggled over these definitions, creating and re-creating racial categories with every decision. How much should voting weigh versus being accepted at a ball or dinner table? Could a white man *really* be white if he had never voted? Was a gentlemanly mulatto more "gentleman" than "mulatto"—and if so, how could he *not* be white, despite the African ancestry that could easily be read in his features and complexion? Nagging questions like these arose at virtually every racial identity trial, a testament to how slippery and problematic racial identities can be.

Today, too, we like to think that we understand race, that the categories of "black man" and "white man" are self-evident, essences that common sense can immediately discern. Yet our own definitions are often just as fragmented, uncertain, and provisional as those of the antebellum era. For example, the police practice of racial profiling rests on a set of beliefs about racial common sense and performance, marking as nonwhite—and therefore dangerous—men who fit certain criteria of appearance, clothing, and behavior. Devon Carbado, a black law professor from England, has written movingly about how he "became American"—and African American—by being stopped by the police. The experience of being profiled and targeted, despite his English accent, expensive clothing, and other markers of education and wealth, helped to produce a racialized identity for Carbado. From the point of view of the police, they were responding to a set of obvious cues—visual markers such as color—and then proceeding to a set of assumptions about what black men were likely to do (commit crimes, resist arrest, pose a threat to the community). Had Carbado objected to their actions, he might have been charged with resisting arrest—and he would then have had a criminal record. The equation of "black man" and "criminal" would thus have been entirely produced by police assumptions and actions; yet to many in white society, the association would seem natural and as obvious as the visible color of Carbado's skin.[25]

Performing White Womanhood

Like the claims of white manhood, women's claims of whiteness also rested on honor, but of a very different kind. Most obviously, a white woman's honor lay in the purity of her sexuality, in stark contrast to the degraded sexuality of a black "Jezebel." Thus for a woman, performing whiteness meant acting out purity and moral virtue. Although women—even white women—could not fulfill the same civic and political roles as men, their purity and moral virtue did have legal significance, for these were the same qualities—and the same performances—required of them in the legal arena in many other cases, such as those involving divorce, rape, and even inheritance. Performing pure white womanhood was therefore the feminine equivalent of performing white male citizenship.

Performing white womanhood was actually even more central to racial identity trials than the male equivalent, since the most frequent—and most dramatic—suits involving racial determination were freedom suits brought by women, nearly all of which were successful. Of sixteen manumission suits, twelve were initiated by women, of which eleven were won by the plaintiffs and one ended in a hung jury. Although these women could not vote, serve on juries, or muster in the militia, they could dazzle their neighbors and jurors with their beauty and goodness. In at least three famous cases—those of Abby Guy, Alexina Morrison, and Sally Miller—the documentation was on the side of black ancestry, or at least slave status. Yet these women won their cases by creating campaigns to demonstrate their feminine whiteness in the public eye and in the popular press, at a time when newspapers studiously avoided the subject of miscegenation and almost never commented on a civil case.

One of the most notorious whiteness cases ever prosecuted was that of Sally Miller. Her story reveals the extent to which Southern communities needed to see white women as frail, virtuous, and sexually pure, for that was the identity she claimed—contrary to all the facts—and that was the identity that enabled her to win her freedom.

In 1844 Sally Miller sued her owner, Louis Belmonti, claiming to be a German Redemptioner who had been separated from her family off the boat from Holland and then sold or bound to service in Attakapas Parish, Louisiana, to John F. Miller. Miller had then sold her to Louis Belmonti at a public auction in New Orleans. According to her story, Sally had been orphaned on the treacherous journey. Unable to defend herself, she was therefore kidnapped into slavery at the age of four. She knew nothing of her past until one day, aged about sixteen and working as a servant in Belmonti's New Orleans café, she was recognized by a German compatriot named Madame Karl Rouff, who had seen the four-year-old child on the transatlantic voyage. This fateful meeting set in motion the train of events that led to Miller's lawsuit.

Following the new antebellum ideology, Belmonti's witnesses testified that Miller possessed an ineffable quality that revealed her "colored" blood. One explained that "persons who live in countries where there are many colored persons acquire an instinctive means of judging that cannot be well explained" and that "he judges she was of mixed blood." This witness, like many others, admitted that there were "many white persons of dark complexion and many colored persons of light complexion" and that he had seen people "whom experienced men would have taken for white but whom he knew to be colored." Another witness "considered [Sally] a quatroon," and a third "took her for a colored girl"; all of them agreed that "she is as white as most persons," and yet they had "always thought [she] had something resembling the colored race" about her, although it might have been that she associated with colored people and was treated as a slave.[26]

Belmonti's case rested on the notion that Sally Miller's hidden essence was "negro," and that people who thought her white had been deceived. Despite her white appearance, he argued, Sally's actions revealed her hidden blackness. Sally Miller, by contrast, introduced a number of German witnesses who claimed not only that she was white but also that they could identify her as the long-lost Salomé Muller. Several claimed that she was their cousin or neighbor, testifying that they remembered from her girlhood the birthmarks on her thighs.

This powerful testimony was, however, problematic. There were discrepancies, for example, in the ages of the lost Salomé Muller and the "rediscovered" Sally Miller. Yet as we might expect, the chief argument of Sally's attorney depended not on age or birthmarks but rather on a moral argument: Sally's sterling performance of white womanhood. Although

Sally's fellow German Redemptioners were "well off, many of them really affluent," and Sally was poor, her moral behavior revealed her hidden whiteness:

> The perseverance, the uniform good conduct, the quiet and constant industry, which are found in those she claims as relatives, have always been found in her, and however polluted and degraded her person may have been, these traits have yet left her worthy of the relatives who ask her at your hands—*and these traits prove her white nature* . . . [B]oth morally and physically, she shows before the Court that there is nothing of the African about her.

The fact that public opinion was on Sally's side, her lawyer argued, was one of the surest proofs of her whiteness, which could be read in Sally's

> *moral power, and weight, and influence. An influence, which I contend no one but a white woman could possibly raise up and control—an influence as inconsistent with the nature of an African, as it would be with the nature of a Yahoo* . . . I contend that the moral traits of the Quartronne, the moral features of the African are far more difficult to be erased, and are far more easily traced, than are the distinctions and differences of physical conformation. The Quartronne is idle, reckless and extravagant, this woman is industrious, careful and prudent—the Quartronne is fond of dress, of finery and display—this woman is neat in her person, simple in her array, and with no ornament upon her, not even a ring on her fingers.

Miller's case was so well known that newspapers referred to it as "the celebrated Miller case," or simply "Sally Miller's case," as though everyone in the city of New Orleans would know whom they meant. Most of the coverage was sympathetic to Sally. The *Daily Picayune,* for example, reported before the trial that she *alleged* to have "suffered the hardships and privations imposed only on the African race," but by the time of the trial the newspaper was recounting her allegations as fact. The *Picayune* described Sally as "a woman of some 33 years of age or thereabouts; has a dark olive complexion, and when young must have been pretty good looking."[27]

In response to the negative publicity, John Miller wrote to the *New Orleans Picayune* to plead his side of the matter on May 31, 1844; his letter was reprinted in the *New Orleans Bee* the following day. He argued that the Sally Miller who was lost to her family in 1817 or 1818 in Attakapas was a different person from the slave he sold to Louis Belmonti; the latter was a mulatto slave named Bridget, brought from Mobile. But he also argued his own bona fides: "I can say that I have never in my life had a German—man, woman or child—bound to me, either as redemptioner or apprentice. For the last thirty-six years I have been well known as a resident of New Orleans. I think the position I have ever occupied is such that no person who has ever known me can believe that I could be capable, knowingly, of attempting to convert a white apprentice into a slave for life." John Miller obviously felt that his own honor was at stake: "Numerous publications in the papers have repeated the rather romantic pretensions of the plaintiff in a manner to give rise to injurious imputations upon my character."[28]

Sally Miller's story also became grist for fugitive slave narratives purveyed to Northern audiences by abolitionists, with Sally as a real-life version of the stock character of "tragic octoroon." In this classic plot, a very light-skinned young woman grows up free, or nearly free, often in the household of her white father; because of some tragic event such as her owner/father's bankruptcy, she is then sold into true slavery. Literary critic James Kinney has argued that when abolitionists used this plot, it was in an "attempt to appeal to a common humanity" with white readers, along with "a bit of reverse racism anchored in the idea that a nearly white person enslaved was more pitiable than a pure African similarly situated." But the tragic octoroon story also appealed to Northern readers because it fed their sense of moral superiority to Southern slaveholders, even as middle-class women readers empathized with the "sudden, horrible reversal of the tragic octoroon's fortunes"; their own dependency on fathers or husbands made them similarly vulnerable.[29]

Black authors, by contrast, used the quadroon or octoroon to call into question the stability and validity of racial categories. The abolitionist and former slave William Wells Brown, in his novel *Clotel or the President's Daughter,* based on the Sally Hemings story, devotes a chapter to the story of "Salomé Miller," titled "A Free Woman Reduced to Slavery."[30] Brown introduces Salomé Miller as a hired servant in the Morton family home, where his slave heroine, Althesa, lives. Salomé, he writes, "was perfectly white; so much so, that Mrs. Morton had expressed her apprehensions to her husband, when the woman first came, that she was not born a slave." Salomé is very unhappy and weeps at her work. When Mrs. Morton expresses sympathy, Salomé reveals that she was born in Germany, that she became separated from her mother, and that her father had died. One day, while she was visiting with a former employer, "two men came into the room and told me that they had bought me, and that I was their slave. I was bound and taken to prison, and that night put on a steamboat and taken up the Yazoo river, and set to work on a farm. I was forced to take up with a Negro, and by him had three children."

"Unhappy woman," whispers Althea. "Why did you not tell me this before?" Salomé explains that she was afraid because she "was once severely flogged for telling a stranger that I was not born a slave." And indeed Salomé is removed from this home, too, when Mr. Morton learns her story. Finally, a German woman who had crossed the Atlantic on the same ship with her happens to recognize her: "The poor woman [Salomé] was raised from the ground by Mrs. Marshall, and placed upon the door step that she had a moment before been cleaning. 'I will do my utmost to rescue you from the horrid life of a slave,' exclaimed the lady."

Fugitive slaves William and Ellen Craft also used Sally Miller's story as the framing tale of their own groundbreaking narrative, *Running a Thousand Miles for Freedom.* There they gave even more details, in addition to quoting the *Law Reporter*'s account of the case. According to the Crafts: "There was no trace of African descent in any feature of Salomé Muller. She had long, straight, black hair, hazel eyes, thin lips, and a Roman nose. The complexion of her face and neck was as dark as that of the darkest brunette." Although so many years under the hot Louisiana sun had darkened her exposed skin, "those parts of her person which had been shielded from the sun were comparatively white." This and other stories of free children sold into slavery provided the Crafts with evidence of the moral depravity to which the institution of slavery had reduced white men.[31]

Like Brown, the Crafts used Miller's story in an effort to destabilize racial categories, warning that a slaveholder's inhumanity might easily extend to other victims: "He who has the power, and is inhuman enough to trample upon the sacred rights of the weak, cares nothing for race or colour . . . It may be remembered that slavery in America is not at all confined to persons of any particular complexion; there are a very large number of slaves as white as any one." Given the inadmissibility of a slave's testimony against that of a free white person, however, whites unjustly held in slavery had little chance of regaining their freedom—just as, by implication, black slaves had little chance of achieving justice.[32]

In the end, both the jury and the Louisiana Supreme Court affirmed

Sally Miller's freedom. Judge Henry Adams Bullard was impressed not only with her "complexion" but also with the fact that Sally "did not seek this controversy, and was apparently contented with her condition."[33]

Decades after the Civil War, Sally Miller's legend survived in the popular stories of the racial liberal George Washington Cable, who in 1889 included "Salomé Muller, The White Slave" in his *Strange True Stories of Louisiana.* And in our own time, lawyer and author John Bailey has written *The Lost German Slave Girl: The Extraordinary True Story of Sally Miller and Her Fight for Freedom in Old New Orleans.* Published by the reputable Atlantic Monthly Press in 2005 and chosen as a History Book Club selection, Bailey's book suggests that fears of white slavery led to an incorrect verdict; in all likelihood the woman who became known as Sally Miller had indeed been born into slavery with at least some African parentage and is unlikely to have been the long-lost German child. Yet the jacket copy suggests that we are still prey to the binary equation of whiteness with freedom and moral virtue, even as blackness somehow legitimizes enslavement and indicates moral degradation: "Had a defenseless European orphan been callously and illegally enslaved, or was she an imposter? . . . Was Sally Miller's licentious lifestyle proof that she was part African, as the defense argued? Or was she the victim of a terrible injustice?"

The contemporary fascination with Miller's case—and with the notion of white slaves—suggests our ongoing difficulty with transcending antebellum notions of racial essences. We still have not abandoned the associations of blackness with sexuality that animated her appeal, nor have we lost the sense that a white Sally Miller would have been somehow more pitiable than the rest of the million young women enslaved in the South in the 1850s. When Orlando Patterson opined in the pages of the *New York Times* in 1991 that black women expect sexual banter like Clarence Thomas's "There's a pubic hair on my Coke," or when Don Imus referred to the Rutgers women's basketball team as "nappy-headed ho's" in 2007, they drew on the same associations of blackness with sexuality and whiteness with moral virtue that played out in Sally Miller's case.

Performing Melungeon Identity

So far we have considered racial identity trials in the form of freedom suits (Alexina Morrison, Abby Guy, and Sally Miller) and inheritance suits (the

Nunezes). The third major type of racial identity case was the slander suit, in which a person sued someone who had called him "a negro." A number of these cases involved members of "tri-racial communities," such as the Melungeons, who had moved beyond their home counties. The "Melungeons" of Newman's Ridge in East Tennessee, like many "free people of color" in the South, claimed Portuguese ancestry when their identities were challenged. Over time they developed more elaborate origin myths, some tracing back to the Portuguese-Spanish captain Juan Pardo's sixteenth-century expedition to the New World; others include descent from early Carthaginian or Phoenician seamen, from survivors of the "Lost Colony" at Roanoke Island who intermarried with Native Americans, or from the Welsh explorer "Madoc." It is likely, however, that the Melungeons were indeed "tri-racial" amalgamations of Africans, Portuguese (including Portuguese-Africans), Indians, English, and others, who came into the hill country of the Carolinas and Tennessee in the eighteenth century.[34]

During the pre–Civil War era the Melungeons appear to have attained a precarious status, sometimes white and sometimes not white, in part depending on their relations with their neighbors. The first U.S. Census to classify the people of what later became Hancock County, Tennessee, tallied the Melungeons as "FPC," meaning "free people of color," in 1830. That census taker also noted "melungeon" or "malungeon" in the margins after some of the family names. The new Tennessee Constitution of 1834 imposed additional legal disabilities on free people of color, disqualifying them from voting, sitting on juries, and bearing witness in court against white persons. It is perhaps not surprising that in the 1840 census many of the same families who had been denoted "FPC" in 1830 were reclassified as "white." Yet at least some "Melungeons" did not find it so simple to pass over to the "white" side of the color line, because a number of them found their whiteness on trial in East Tennessee courtrooms after 1840. At least eight were charged with illegally voting as "free persons of color" in 1846 and 1847, and seven went to trial in 1848. In two of the cases the juries acquitted the defendant, and following these acquittals, the state attorney general declined to prosecute the remaining cases. Only one defendant entered a guilty plea and served a three-month jail term. According to a local doctor who wrote about Melungeons for the *American Anthropologist* in 1889: "The question was decided by an examination of the feet. One was found sufficiently flat-footed to be regarded 'a free person of color' hence not allowed to vote, while the others were determined to have enough white blood to permit them suffrage." This story has become famous in Melungeon lore and is still cited today, although no trial records have survived. But what we do know is that Melungeons' claims to whiteness *were* contested. On the one hand, there is evidence that they continued to own and convey property, vote, and sit on juries. On the other hand, the state did try to prohibit at least some of them from voting.[35]

While Melungeons lived as a separate "racial island" in Hancock, Tennessee, they often blended into white society after they moved. If ever they made someone "mad," however, that was when the trouble began. Then a Melungeon became vulnerable to a neighbor's accusation of having "negro blood." This neighbor might even go so far as to travel hundreds of miles to gather evidence for his vendetta, and take his evidence to the school board, to the church, or to other community institutions, trying to have the deceiving "black man" banned; but the dispute entered the courtroom only when his victim fought back.

One of the most fascinating racial identity slander suits in antebellum America was brought by Jacob Perkins, an East Tennessean of a Melungeon family who, in Carter County, Tennessee, in July 1855, attempted to win damages from John White for the accusation that he had "negro blood." The conflict evoked the hysteria of an entire community, including a chilling ceremony to determine whether or not the Perkins family had souls. Yet once the case reached the courtroom, the testimony was all about jury service and militia duty, just as it had been in the case of Joseph Nunez.

Jacob Perkins's story reveals the degree to which borderland communities could become hysterical about race—particularly poor white communities that ostensibly had nothing to gain by supporting slavery and racial bias. The Perkins case also shows the calming effect of the law, in which state power was mobilized to soothe community anxieties and restore order. On the one hand, slaveholders benefited from poor and middle-class white people's passion to defend whiteness. Yet on the other, too much passion could disrupt an entire community and raise troubling questions about the extent to which race was truly knowable. On the eve of the Civil War the law both inflamed these tensions and helped to resolve them.

The case of *Perkins v. White* ostensibly began when Perkins refused to allow White's slaves on his property—at least, that was how White's wife told it. Angered, she had "said they should come when they please one negrow had previlidges to go where others was and her negrows should come there and she dare him to whip them." When Perkins ignored her, "White came rushing up with his gun," and Perkins apparently decided to take the matter to court.[36]

Most of Perkins's witnesses testified that members of the Perkins family were "always called Portuguese"—a "white" nationality that nonetheless could be used to cover a world of racial ambiguity. Portuguese people were understood to be dark, and a man who "looked Portuguese" might easily have some African heritage. Moreover, slaveholders in colonial America commonly held as slaves "Spanish negroes" and "Portuguese negroes"—African sailors on Iberian vessels who claimed to be free in Europe but who appeared to be slaves to colonial Americans.[37]

Nevertheless, to call the Perkinses Portuguese in the 1850s was to assert the family's right to be treated as white. Yet some witnesses who testified that they "never heard them called any thing but Portuguese" also remembered rumors and accusations of other origins: "I heard Joshua Perkins' [Jacob's father's] uncle's daughter say they need not throw up negro to them they were Portuguese."[38]

On White's side, witnesses gave depositions testifying to the Perkinses' reputation as "mulatto" or "negro." John Nave testified that "some called Jacob a Portuguese & some a negro." According to Perkins's lawyers' notes, Dicey Whaley testified that her mother "would not let me go there [to the Perkinses' home] as they were colored . . . When people mad, called them Negroes—Not mad, [they called them] dark skinned." Indeed, the Perkinses' status to a large extent seemed to depend on whom they had made "mad." Whenever they got on someone's bad side, they became vulnerable to the "negro" accusation.[39]

The bases for racial determination in *Perkins v. White* included both the Perkinses' bodies and their civic participation. Interestingly, the evidence of physical racial difference that many witnesses considered fundamental seems to have derived from the most intimate shared experiences. For example, Dicey Whaley's mention of the Perkinses' "negro smell" referred to times when she "smelt them by being with their wives in having children. Lay with Evelina & smelt her." Other defense witnesses' testimony about smell referred to time spent washing clothes together, eating together, or sharing a bed (a common practice in nineteenth-century America).[40]

Several witnesses described the religious ritual that a man called Jim

Dugger created to determine the Perkinses' racial identity. According to Alfred Greenwill, Dugger "intended to put all the Perkins by their oath— and if he succeeded as he whish to he would indict them every court for living with their wives." (Greenwill also made the only mention of Indian identity in the case, reporting that Dugger "said what made their hare strate was the Indian in them.") Also referring to the ritual, Isaac Moody testified that Dugger planned "to have a speaking at the forge to see if the Perkins had souls or no and if it was apertained that they had no souls he would take his gun and go down and asked me if I would go, with my best impression that he said he would go down and kill them." Dugger further told John Moody that "he intended to put the children by at the next court if he could he said they were going to have a speaking at the forge to see if the Perkins had souls or not if not he allowed to take his gun and go down and kill a passel of them he said they were like mules—mules was don breeding and these molotters when mix that far had no souls."[41]

Jim Dugger, who did not appear on Carter County census rolls during this period, seems to have played the role of racial detective in this community, blending religious, legal, and "scientific" theories of racial determination in one continuous flow of invective. Dugger apparently did not testify in the case, and Perkins chose not to sue Dugger directly (perhaps because he was, as the lawyers say, "judgment-proof"—too poor to pay damages). Yet he was a central figure in the Perkins case who, provoked by Perkins's suit, apparently took it upon himself to cast out this deceptive family from enjoying the privileges of whiteness.

But, as in so many cases litigating male whiteness in the antebellum South, most testimony turned on whether Jacob and his father, Joshua Perkins, had voted, sat on juries, testified in court, or acted as the legal administrator of an estate. Perkins's lawyer, T. A. R. Nelson, made lists in his notes of the best evidence for his client:

> As to Joshua Perkins Voting
> As to Joshua serving on Juries
> As to Joshua being a judge & clerk at an election
> 4. As to Joshua being a witness
> 5. As to his being an administrator
> 6. As to his being an overseer.

As in the other cases we have considered, each side appealed to different principles. In this case White defended himself against the charge of

racial slander by arguing that the Perkinses were in fact "negro." Thus
Perkins's lawyer observed in his notes that the evidence against the family
was "all about color."[42]

Perkins, by contrast, based his case on settled principles of law, as his attorney also observed in his notes. The lawyer's notes reveal the extent to
which even Southern professionals heavily invested in antebellum notions
of race understood that color was unreliable: "Color no test because the
tawny races fill three fourths of the earth. Shades of color among whites.
Impossibility of defining color. Mulattoes whiter than French Spanish or
Indian or Chinese." The lawyer's notes reiterate that the Perkins family had
a "Portuguese reputation before difficulties," by which he seems to have
meant the growing political conflict between North and South and the im-
pending sectional battle over slavery. He also attributes the case to "political & personal excitement," suggesting that both personal enmities and
sectional conflict had forced the question of the Perkinses' racial identity.[43]

Certainly the question of slavery was keenly felt on the eve of the Civil
War, as was the question of race. It is striking, given the community's poverty, how invested it was in protecting the privileges of whiteness, since
in Carter County even the most privileged white person could rarely afford to own slaves. At the time of the lawsuit, fewer than fifteen county
residents held more than ten slaves, and most slaveholders held three
or fewer. Nor was Carter County home to a large "ambiguous" population of free blacks: census takers counted only thirty-two "free colored" in
1850 and twenty-two in 1860. Apparently, for the non-slaveholding and
small slaveholding yeoman farmers of Carter County, whiteness was less
about distinguishing themselves from "colored" neighbors than about laying claim to citizenship itself. Thus Jacob Perkins, in notes to his lawyer,
specified what he considered so damaging about the accusation of "negro
blood":

> 1st The words impute that we are liable to be indicted = liable to be
> whipped = liable to be fined; They bastardize our children; They disqual-
> ify us from serving on a jury—from being a witness—from merchandizing;
> 2. These words worse than theft or murder; 3. They are slander upon the
> plaintiff and his ancestors who are dead.[44]

Although some plaintiffs in slander suits were primarily concerned with
the economic repercussions of being called a "negro," Perkins was more
upset about the "imputation" that he and his family members (even the

dead ones) did not have the legal status of full citizens. Both he and his neighbors seem to have agreed with the prevailing opinion in the antebellum South that full citizenship could belong only to white people. For people who possessed little else, this particular white privilege was particularly important.[45]

The judge appears to have shared the community's concern. Fearing the logic of prescriptive whiteness, which assigned white privilege to those who might not "really" deserve it, he focused in his instructions to the jury on the meaning of the state's "one-eighth negro blood" rule. If Jacob Perkins's great-grandfather, old Jock Perkins, had been a "full-blood negro," the judge explained, that would make Jacob one-eighth "negro." If, however, Jock Perkins were less than "full-blood," that would make Jacob less than one-eighth, "unless he may have derived a sufficiency of indian or negro blood from some of his other ancestors either of the paternal or maternal line to make up the deficit."[46]

But the judge was not content to rely on some abstract notion of blood quantum to determine the Perkinses' race; like his contemporaries, he too was concerned with the proper performance of whiteness. So he went on to instruct jurors to consider all the evidence about the "privileges of the citizen which the pl[ainti]ff and his ancestors had enjoyed as voters jurors witnesses, public offices and marrying and giving in marriage with white persons, and the like, and the length of time that these high privileges had been so enjoyed." Still, as Judge Lumpkin had once pointed out, these privileges might—for a time at least—be enjoyed by the wrong people. If the jurors were satisfied by the balance of the evidence that Perkins was indeed a person of color, then "these privileges no matter how long enjoyed by him and his ancestors would not *constitute* him a citizen."[47]

Unfortunately there is no record of the verdict in this suit, so we do not know how the jury weighed the evidence. But records do survive of another racial slander suit brought by a Melungeon in the same period. In 1858 Elijah Goin won fifty dollars in damages from Sterling Mayser for accusing Goin of having "negro blood"; fifty dollars may have been a settlement that split the difference in a community divided over the status of the plaintiff.[48]

Goin's witness testified that Mayser "had a negro 'ditty' which he had sung to Elijah Goin . . . 'Elijah Goin being a little blacker, he run up and down the creek like a damn mulatto,'" and that Mayser had "said his children should call" the Goin family mulatto "& he would protect them in it."

As White had done in Perkins's case, Mayser defended himself with a number of witnesses who testified "that it was generally reported and believed that [Goin] was a man of mixed blood." Peter Mareum and William Murphy both stated that they were well acquainted with Goin's grandfather, and "he was reputed to be distantly mixed blooded," although they also testified "that he voted, served on jurys, and was examined as a witness between white men never heard him questioned or denied." Goin, by contrast, invoked the codes for performing white manhood by bringing in evidence that he, his father, and grandfather had voted, sat on juries, and acted as witnesses in courts of law.[49]

Goin's lawyer, John Netherland, is an interesting figure whose personal history suggests many of the contradictions of the antebellum South. An attorney of some renown, Netherland had won much of his reputation as a defender of the rights of Melungeons and of "free people of color." Some histories report that in 1859 Netherland secured the Melungeons' right to vote in state and federal elections, although no records remain of such a voting case in that year. A "slaveholder of high social standing," Netherland nonetheless supported the Union before the Civil War; later he counseled leniency toward ex-Confederates. When Tennessee cracked down on "free people of color" in the 1830s, limiting the rights of slaves to be freed and then requiring freed slaves to leave the state, Netherland apparently tried to ameliorate the new laws. A Democratic Party circular from the 1840s excoriated Netherland for his efforts to "repeal so much of the act of 1831, concerning free persons of color, as requires the emancipator of slaves to remove them without the limits of the State." Despite the fact that his opponents tried to use his reputation as a friend of the Melungeons against him, Netherland remained a successful lawyer and legislator.[50]

Until the Civil War it appears that Melungeons and other "mixed" individuals lived a precarious existence in the borderlands between black and white, an existence that seemed to have depended on whether they had made someone "mad" or not. Their success in surviving in these borderlands rested on the ways they performed whiteness.

The Legacy of Race as Performance

Sally Miller and Alexina Morrison performed white womanhood by showing their beauty and whiteness in court and by demonstrating purity and moral goodness to their neighbors. In a world that characterized white womanhood as a state of legal disability, so that women required the protection of honorable gentlemen, women of ambiguous racial identity found ways to call upon the state's protection by convincing the court that they, too, fit this feminine ideal. White manhood, by contrast, required the exercise of legal and political rights. By this definition Elijah Goin and possibly Jacob Perkins successfully performed white manhood, whereas James and Joseph Nunez failed to do so.

In both cases, as well as in the trials of Abby Guy, witnesses and jurors observed or heard about performances and believed that they were considering *evidence* of these individuals' *essential nature*. From our modern vantage point, we can more easily see that performance and racial essence do not necessarily correspond. What is harder for us to grasp—and to reject—is the assumption that underlay antebellum reliance on performance. The practical effect of valuing such performances was to make white identity equal to a set of moral and civic virtues.

In the antebellum South, racial ideology insisted that such virtues could be performed only by white people. What black man could vote or bear arms? What black woman could be pure and refined? Today, while we accept in theory the notion that people of color are equally capable of fulfilling civic duties or upholding moral virtues, it is worth noting how color-coded our values have remained. Thus African Americans who are able to succeed professionally or socially are considered to be "acting white" as they perform codes of whiteness that have changed remarkably little over the past 150 years. Certain styles of dress, music, speech, social behavior, and decorum remain defined as "white virtues," and for people of color to be accepted by the larger society—as political candidates, officers in the armed forces, corporate executives, professionals—they must perform their whiteness even if their blackness can be read in their skin, hair, and features. Indeed the strains of performing whiteness have been extensively chronicled by many African American writers, even as the world of rap music insists on its stars' performing "blackness," which is defined as criminality, irresponsibility, hypersexuality, and rebelliousness. White rappers are expected to perform blackness just as black professionals are expected to perform whiteness—cultural constructs that have proven remarkably durable.

Today most people recognize discrimination on the basis of ancestry or a discredited racial "science" as racism. Coaches are fired for making comments about the "natural" talents or abilities of black people; we recognize that making assumptions about social groups on the basis of biology is an unacceptable form of racial stereotyping. Yet we still invoke experts as well as common sense to distinguish among people on the basis of the way they perform their identities, and the law still does not define it as race discrimination if employers hire or fire people on that basis.

Our complex notions of race and performance may seem very modern to us. At first glance they appear to be the artifacts of our post–civil rights society, in which slavery was abolished 150 years ago, and equal protection under the law has been a legal fact for at least half a century. Yet if we look more closely at the racial identity trials of the antebellum era—a time when racialized slavery was still the dominant national economic system— we can see the roots of our own attitudes, ambivalences, and anxieties in our common past.

Certainly much has changed politically and socially for America's people of color. For those who would argue otherwise, it is worth pointing out that before the Civil War, the equation of whiteness with citizenship was firmly entrenched in American law. When Justice Roger B. Taney declared in the infamous *Dred Scott* decision that black people had no rights that the law was bound to recognize, his holding was controversial, but his assumption that whiteness uniquely suited one for citizenship was by then a commonplace. It took a civil war to create a new constitution guaranteeing U.S. citizenship for the first time to all African Americans. But what actually happened in America's postbellum courtrooms suggests that the equation of whiteness with citizenship died hard.

CHAPTER THREE

Race as Association

IN 1865 SLAVERY—the economic and social system that had dominated American life from the first European presence in the New World—was officially ended. A cruel and horrific system, it had brought most slaves into frequent and intimate contact with masters, overseers, and other whites. Domestic slaves nursed their owners' children, brushed their mistresses' hair, and helped their masters dress. Among the households possessing fewer than twenty slaves—which constituted the overwhelming majority—the enslaved worked side by side with their owners in fields, kitchens, and workshops, sharing a lifetime of backbreaking labor. Slavery was a form of intimate domination in the South.

Slavery often included sexual relations that ran the gamut from coercive to consensual. Free people of color—most of whom had some European ancestry—were visible and constant reminders of the race mixing that was an inevitable part of this intimate domination of master over slave. Racial hierarchy had institutionalized forms of domination, and they were maintained not so much by racial separation as by a vast network of laws mandating racial difference. Free women of color in New Orleans, for example, were legally required to wear *tignons,* or head kerchiefs, so that they might never be mistaken for the white women they often resembled. Yet they were not legally barred from living in "white" neighborhoods, and an entire system called *plaçage* gave them legal protection in their sexual relationships with white men. Women of color could not legally marry white men in Louisiana, but they could enter into contracts requiring the men to supply them with specified income, property, and other benefits derived from their sexual liaison.[1]

This degree of "race mixing"—socially, sexually, and economically—became inconceivable by the end of the nineteenth century. Just as American colonial elites had earlier felt compelled to disrupt potential interracial alliances by legally distinguishing between white indentured servitude and black slavery, so did post–Civil War elites find it necessary to drive a wedge between poor and middle-income white people and the newly emancipated black slaves. Populations that were not necessarily hostile to one another in the immediate wake of the war, that had experienced decades of interracial intimacy—cruel, violent, and unequal, though it often was—mandated a system that would, in slavery's absence, prevent any possible form of interracial alliance.

The implementation of racial separation was not simply a response to the legal end of slavery and the constitutional elimination of the "badges and incidents of servitude." It was also a reaction to former slaves entering into the political, economic, and social life of a free citizenry in the era of Reconstruction. No longer could "white" be assumed to indicate "free," while "black" no longer denoted either "slave" or "slave-like." Now black men were running for office, voting, and engaging in all those civic duties that had been the very essence of white manhood, while black men and women together were establishing their own farms, workshops, and households as best they could.

Free people of color and newly freed slaves were at the forefront of this radical change, and they had a valuable ally in the Republican Party, which pushed through Congress both the constitutional amendments and the civil rights legislation that called for full equality of all male citizens without regard to race. The Civil Rights Act of 1875—still the basis of much of the civil rights legislation we rely on today—called for the "full and equal enjoyment of the accommodations, advantages, facilities, and privileges of inns, public conveyances on land or water, theaters, and other places of public amusement" for all persons, without regard to race, color, or previous condition of servitude, and guaranteed as well to male citizens of all races the right to serve on juries. While the Supreme Court struck down the act eight short years later, opining that it was time for the "negro" to cease being the "special favorite of the laws," the legislation was radical while it lasted, anticipating the far-reaching provisions of 1960s civil rights legislation almost a century later.[2]

Significantly, the word "miscegenation"—a term that describes a mixing of "kinds," that is, "races"—was coined in 1864 by Democrats seeking to mock the Republicans for their association with blacks. Fear of intimacy with former slaves spurred Southern white Democrats to pursue new legal means to separate the races and erect new barriers to guarantee it. Attacks on association—specifically on sexual association—became the means for making race an instrument of division among people who might otherwise have found common ground.

During and after Reconstruction, white Southerners waged political and legal campaigns to reduce ex-slaves to their prewar status of subjugation. Since the institution of slavery could no longer be relied on to maintain white supremacy, new practices such as vigilantism, terror, and lynching arose in an attempt to keep African Americans in a subordinate position, with a particular focus on efforts to abolish "race mixing," especially sex and marriage between white women and black men. As Southern legislatures produced a plethora of laws prohibiting interracial marriage and fornication, so did Northern and Western states add new bans on marriages between whites and a growing list of other "races." This gave rise to a novel national consensus on interracial relations. To already existing bans were added harsher penalties, including stiff fines and long years of imprisonment. These postwar statutes carried a heavy burden for Southern blacks who could not afford the fines and so faced years of hard labor either on a prison chain gang or leased to work in the mines or on the railroad. The Ku Klux Klan, founded in 1866 in Tennessee and spreading quickly throughout the South and Midwest, took the law into its own hands in order to ensure racial separation. Klan members routinely intimidated, beat, and killed men and women whom they suspected of crossing racial lines.

Despite such legal and illegal obstacles to achieving freedom, African Americans in the South made many striking gains during the brief era of Reconstruction. Most notably, they elected legislators, local officials, and delegates to state constitutional conventions, thereby participating in the political life of the state. They established churches and schools in their communities to teach their young and to minister to their spiritual needs. And they achieved a striking measure of political and economic success. Although integration was not the rule, there was nevertheless interracial political activity in the Republican Party and among Farmers' Alliances, as well as increased social interaction as blacks migrated to urban areas in the South as well as in the West and North.

These gains, however modest, were more than many white citizens

could bear. Economic and political power seemed to presage more racial
mixing. The vast majority of violent racial incidents that transpired during Reconstruction were directed against men who had threatened to
achieve some economic or political status. Ida B. Wells-Barnett, an African American anti-lynching activist in the early twentieth century, collected many stories of black men falsely accused of rape. These individuals
were targeted because of their assertiveness or achievements. Sexual accusations were tacked on relatively late, often completely without basis.
Many whites assumed that an "uppity" or "forward" man who had claimed
his rights to citizenship might also demand his right to intimacy with a
white woman. It is no surprise, then, that lynching peaked in the 1890s, at
precisely the moment when the Populist movement seemed likely to offer
genuine opportunities for black sharecroppers to ally with white tenant
farmers. Once again, white elites sought to protect their economic interests and labor costs by dividing poor farmers along racial lines.

Reconstruction came to an official end with the "Compromise of 1877."
This informal bargain between Republican and Democratic leaders to resolve the contested presidential election had two clear results: Republican
Rutherford Hayes became president, and Southern blacks were abandoned to their fate by the federal government. When Hayes took office, he
promptly pulled out the last of the federal troops that had supported Reconstruction governments in the South. Without federal military support
for these fledgling interracial governments, their survival rate was nil. The
men who came to power in their stead were known as "Redeemers,"
Democrats who promised to "redeem" the South through white supremacy and segregation. A rapprochement with Northern industrial interests
resulted in a longstanding accommodation to Southern white Democrats
and their political goals. The result was Jim Crow legislation that segregated every aspect of daily life and excluded African Americans from every
political institution. By the early twentieth century, Southern states could
truly claim a "lily-white" electorate with no black political presence at all.
In the North and West, in both formerly integrated areas and regions with
new black populations, whites also fought to drive blacks away. They employed a violence that amounted to a form of "ethnic cleansing" of not just
African Americans but Chinese and other minorities, as well as legal ordinances, restrictive covenants, and repression by local police officials.

The federal government increasingly turned a blind eye to these illegal
and discriminatory actions. In the North, the Republican Party had be-

come so preoccupied with commercial development and labor activism that it had little time for racial issues. Eager to reconcile with the South, Republicans joined with Southern conservative "Redeemers" in political coalitions that would have been anathema a decade earlier but now signaled national reunion and the mutual benefits of economic prosperity. As Reconstruction came to an end, so did the promise of full citizenship for the freed slaves. North and South reunited in a shared commitment to white supremacy. Despite variations in Jim Crow legislation in different regions, America was united in its use of racial segregation and racial violence to maintain white dominance.

Just as racial identity trials had helped to establish the "slave/black" and "free/white" equivalences of the slavery era, so now they became a key arena for working out and enforcing post-emancipation efforts to separate the races. Many racial identity trials after the Civil War concerned black-white marriages, either as criminal prosecutions for miscegenation or as inheritance disputes in which "negro blood" was raised as a justification for disinheriting an heir and/or delegitimating a marriage. Interracial marriage cases often became opportunities to rewrite history: instead of acknowledging the actual race mixing and intimacy that occurred, plaintiffs or defendants sought to impose postwar notions of segregation onto prewar life. As white elites' efforts to re-create their racial order after the war captured the imagination of lower-income whites, poor white farmers found ways to tell new stories about the old racial order, remembering themselves as having formed communities completely separate from their black neighbors.

In the Jim Crow era that succeeded Reconstruction, racial identity trials often turned into debates about the nature of race relations under slavery. What did it mean, for example, that an individual had earlier associated with white people? Did that necessarily mean that he or she *was* white? That would be the case in the newly segregated South, because black people's associations with white people were severely curtailed. But in the antebellum era, race mixing had been common—an inconvenient fact that whites sought to forget in their attempt to legitimize segregation. By telling stories about the way blacks and whites had interacted in the past, witnesses at trials helped create a revised past in which black and white were separate in every way and always had been.

Yet people whose racial identity was challenged still won their cases—only now, juries granted their whiteness by overlooking signs of their mixed identity. Whiteness had to be portrayed as clear-cut and unquestionable. As in slavery days, white people seemed less concerned with excluding potentially "unfit" candidates from the benefits of whiteness than they were preoccupied with establishing that whiteness *could* be clearly defined and immediately recognized. Under slavery, performance of civic virtue (for men) or sexual purity (for women) had been the key to establishing a white identity. Under Reconstruction and Jim Crow, separation became the key to whiteness. People who had associated with whites must be white themselves, just as people who had associated with blacks had to be black. Once a black man could become a citizen and even a landholder, whites had to find another means of racial definition. They found it in racial segregation.

In the post–Civil War period, African Americans participated actively in racial identity trials for the first time, and in doing so they joined in the debate about racial relations in the past. Slaves had not been allowed to testify in court, but now ex-slaves offered their own observations and opinions of racial identity and even gave explosive evidence about interracial sex. Time and time again, participants in Jim Crow–era trials described a world of extensive race mixing even as whites sought to demonstrate that race mixing had never occurred. The trials were a significant part of the process by which segregation was established as natural and the only possible way in which the races could coexist—indeed, the only way in which they had *ever* coexisted. White society wanted to forget its own intimate past with blacks, even as that past reemerged again and again, confronting the new Jim Crow system with all its distortions and contradictions.

"The Celebrated Melungeon Case"

One of the most significant racial identity trials of the Reconstruction era became known as "the celebrated Melungeon case"—the story of a young Melungeon woman who returned to Tennessee from Illinois to claim her inheritance. The trial that was held in Chattanooga ostensibly turned on the racial identity of the young woman's grandfather, who had frequently associated with "negroes." In fact the trial asked a question that before the Civil War would have been meaningless: Did this association, by its very nature, establish the man's racial identity; was someone who associated with "negroes" by definition a "negro" himself?

By the time of the Civil War the Melungeons were already facing increasing challenges to their whiteness in their home territory of Hancock and Hawkins counties, even as people known as "melungeon" or "Goins" could be found throughout the Appalachians. The Melungeons probably shared European, African, and Indian heritage, and had been variously viewed as members of all three groups or of an unspecified "other" group. Throughout their history, in fact, Melungeon identity had proved a touchstone for America's confusion over how to define race and how to assign importance to racial definitions.

The case, however, is celebrated precisely because it seemed to establish once and for all the Melungeons' whiteness. The Chattanooga case known as *Jack v. Foust* is still cited by proponents of a new Melungeon identity movement today as evidence that Melungeons are free of the taint of "negro blood." The actual records of the case had remained buried for so long that accounts had relied exclusively on the lawyer Lewis Shepherd's 1913 memoirs. Shepherd told the story of an injustice done to a beautiful young heiress, an injustice based on scurrilous rumors about the racial identity of the people known as Melungeons. The wrong was quickly righted, Shepherd claimed, when the young woman's aunt submitted as evidence a lock of wavy hair—"good" hair that proved the woman's whiteness, as her lawyer explained the mysterious (non-African) origins of the Melungeons. The discovery of the actual trial records of the case in the Tennessee State Archives in 2002, however, reveal a far more complicated story that can now be told.[3]

A few years before the Civil War, a young man of some estate, Jerome Simmerman, married a beautiful young woman, Jemima Bolton, the daughter of one of his farm tenants who was commonly known as a Melungeon. When Jemima died in childbirth, her daughter, Martha, was sent north to live with her aunt Betsy Bolton, where she could pass as white. Several years after the war, at the height of Reconstruction, when many whites felt their world had been turned upside down, the girl returned south to claim her inheritance after her father's death. Although the young girl had been raised as white, she was not necessarily white in the townspeople's eyes. The Simmerman family, who had opposed the marriage in the first place, now argued that it had never been valid because of Jerome's mental state and because of the bride's race. The lawsuit they brought against Martha's claim to an inheritance became a contest over the past, in which the litigants and witnesses told stories of how things "really" had been before the war. At a time when white Southerners were first implementing the new

Jim Crow order, they remembered a past that would underwrite the new
way of segregation. They asked themselves, Would we have allowed such a
marriage? And in their memories the response was, No, we would not.
Did whites mix with blacks in social and political life? The plaintiffs said,
No, we did not. Their vision of the past, and of every intricacy of daily life
in it, was brought into line with their present.

The origins of the case lay in Simmerman's mental health, which in his
later years had degenerated to the point where he was considered a "lunatic" and put under the legal guardianship of one W. H. Foust. In 1874
Jerome's half-sister, Elizabeth Jack, joined with other relatives to bring suit
against Foust for mismanagement of the estate and to ask the court to declare them the heirs apparent of the estate. They probably expected their
efforts to be uncontested. But a friend of the family, Samuel Williams, had
kept in touch with Martha's aunt Betsy and maintained an interest in Martha's welfare. He contacted the aunt and arranged for Martha to file a
cross-claim to the estate. The trial proceeded on the issue of whether
Martha was Jerome Simmerman's rightful heir. Simmerman's half-sisters
contended that their brother's marriage to Jemima had been illegitimate
·because she was a person of color, and therefore Martha could not inherit his estate. Martha and her lawyer argued instead that she was a
Melungeon, "not even remotely allied to the negroes." From this argument came a bitterly contested trial that eventually produced some five
hundred pages of testimony regarding Jerome's mental state at the time of
the marriage, the marital relationship of Jerome and Jemima, and especially the racial identity of Jemima, her father, and her grandfather, "old
man Bolton," who had lived in Tennessee and South Carolina.[4]

The trial was one of the first to take place in the new Hamilton County
Courthouse in Chattanooga, Tennessee, which had just become the county
seat. Chattanooga was a young and growing city, having escaped the worst
ravages of war and much of the turmoil of Reconstruction because of its
early readmission to the Union. The city had been home to a regiment of
black soldiers, which became a magnet for runaway slaves in what was
known as "Camp Contraband." (As property that no longer belonged to its
rightful owner, runaways were called "contraband.") As such, in the aftermath of the war, the site of the trial threatened to become overrun with assertive and armed black men.[5]

Because the case concerned the disposition of property, it was brought
into a court of equity and heard before a chancellor rather than a jury. Eq-

uity, or chancery, courts still exist today in some states, but they are far less prevalent than they were in the nineteenth century, when the common law divided jurisdiction between courts of law, which dealt with matters such as contract disputes in which money damages were assigned, as well as criminal cases; and courts of equity, which dealt with matters of individual justice, or equity, including disputes over property and inheritance. As was common at the time, many witnesses, rather than appearing in person before the chancellor, answered a set of written questions in depositions, which were then read into testimony.

The first depositions in the case were taken in 1874. They suggested that the marriage of Jerome and Jemima in Hill's Valley, Georgia, had been controversial because it violated racial boundaries. Hiram Davis explained that he had gone with the couple to marry out of state because "[Jerome's] folks were not willing for him to marry her." They were married by Squire Clark, standing in the road outside his house. Samuel Williams claimed that "they were to have been married . . . the Christmas before they were, but were in some way prevented by the interference of Tom Foust and Jane Simmerman." James and Elizabeth Jack portrayed the marriage as fraudulent and void because Jemima was a "person of mixed blood." As they saw it, the marriage was "all a mere pretense," as a person of color could not legally marry a white person.[6]

Trying to play down the racial angle, Lewis Shepherd claimed that it was Jerome's mother and half-sisters who opposed the engagement, not because of race but because "if he married their prospects of some time falling heir to his property would be destroyed." Shepherd portrayed the out-of-state marriage as a romantic elopement: "Our hero . . . was a young man of resources . . . He took his bride-elect and crossed over the river and secured the aid of [two friends], both of whom were young men, and they entered joyfully into the plot." Squire Clark himself remembered the afternoon of the marriage and "saw nothing unusual" in it.[7]

Some of the testimony regarded Jerome's mental state at the time of the marriage. If he had been mad when he married Jemima, perhaps he had not realized that she was black; whereas if he had been of sound mind when he married her, surely he would only have chosen a white woman. Accordingly, witnesses for Martha portrayed Jerome's mental state as good with the exception of occasional "spells." They mentioned his "shrewd" trades and in particular an 1858 sale of a slave to A. C. Carroll for $1,200 as evidence of his ability to manage his own affairs sanely and capably

when he was not having a "crazy spell." These witnesses argued that
Jerome only became a lunatic after the Civil War. Witnesses for the Jacks,
by contrast, claimed that Jerome had been crazy since before his marriage
to Jemima as further indication that Jemima might be black.[8]

Most of the testimony turned on Jemima's racial identity. Here most of
the evidence concerned her father, Solomon Bolton, who had lived in
South Carolina before moving to Marion County, Tennessee. As in pre–
Civil War cases, witnesses disagreed about whether Solomon Bolton had
effectively acted like a white man, particularly in the civic dimensions of
white manhood. Jemima's sister claimed that Solomon was of Spanish and
German descent, that he was "a citizen and voted in the elections," and
that although his hair, eyes, and skin were dark, his skin was only "tolerable dark but not to hurt." On cross-examination she was pressed, "In what
election do you know of your father voting?" She could not give an example. Yet she insisted that "he voted in all . . . and he always mustered [in
the militia] until he got too old."[9]

Other witnesses for Martha also claimed that her father, Solomon, had
voted and had testified in court against white men, which seemed to be a
clear indication that he was white. Being recognized as white in a court of
law and performing as white men did demonstrated that a man *was* white;
otherwise this racially defined society had to accept the unpalatable possibility that a black man had counterfeited civic virtue well enough to fool
white citizens. Local citizen Arch Brown remembered a case tried in
Marion County, Tennessee, in 1849 or 1850 in which Solomon Bolton had
prosecuted William Broomley, a white man charged with child murder.
On cross-examination it came out that Bolton's whiteness had been challenged in that case. Eventually, though, his identity as "a Portugese" had
been accepted in the case and his testimony had been admitted. Brown
had played the role of racial investigator in the Broomley prosecution,
traveling to Bolton's previous residence in South Carolina to ask his former neighbors "if [Bolton] was not a colored man." Brown reported that
"they told me he was not, but was a Portugese [sic]. They told me that he
was a member of Baptist Church there in good standing and was received
in good society."[10]

On cross-examination Brown reiterated the definition of race by association. He rebuffed such questions as "Do you not know that negroes did
visit the house of Solomon Bolton and associate with him and his family[?]
. . . Do you know that one or more negroes married into the family of Solo-

mon Bolton[?]" As part of his argument that Bolton had to be white, Brown asserted that Bolton had never associated with "negroes," nor had "negroes" married into his family. As further evidence of Bolton's white civic virtue, Brown gave particulars of the elections in which Bolton had voted, even naming the clerks and judges. Following the same line of argument, another witness testified that Bolton had applied to the pension office for bounty land because he had served in the War of 1812.[11]

Still other witnesses on behalf of Martha remembered that not only had the Boltons lived among whites and exercised the privileges of whiteness, but also they had survived successive challenges to their white status. Mrs. Malinda White asserted that in South Carolina the Boltons "were never called or treated as negroes. They mustered with white people, visited and associated with white people . . . They voted in elections just as other citizens." She went on to explain: "They were not white men, but were never regarded and treated as free negroes. The old man belonged to the church with white people. I have seen him take sacrament in the church with white people." Mrs. White thus managed to argue that Bolton both was and was not white. She may have considered the Boltons to be members of a race that was neither white nor "negro"—the Melungeons, who were accorded the social and political privileges of white people without actually being considered completely white. Yet often, being given the privileges of whiteness was enough to make someone white—for only a white person could exercise these privileges. Another possibility is that Mrs. White referred only to the color of their skin when she said they were "not white men": in other words, they were dark-skinned white men. Here again the confusion of racial identity with color in a society where such categories were supposed to be binary and clear-cut is glossed over; performance—in this case of civic virtue—and association together trumped appearance.[12]

Mrs. White remembered Bolton's children going to school with white students and his daughters marrying white men. She noted that "sometimes children would throw up to old man Bolton's children about being negroes and it made them very mad to be accused of being negroes." In her testimony and that of many others, the Boltons' anger at being called "negro" was a clear indication that the accusation of "negro blood" lurked in the Boltons' lives. Yet they had successfully turned back these challenges, convincing neighbors of their whiteness by the strength of their response.[13]

On cross-examination of a witness named A. Kelley who testified that Solomon Bolton had always voted, the lawyer for Elizabeth Jack tried to insinuate that Bolton had been admitted to vote only because he was a Whig in a strong Whig district in the William Henry Harrison election. Kelley answered that "I have heard [Bolton] brag a heap of times that his father was in the old Revolutionary War, was a Whig, and that he stood in his shoes." When asked about "negroes" visiting Bolton's house, Kelley answered: "Yes, but those times negroes would go to most houses. People were not so particular then as now." Kelley, in making explicit the shift in social mores, was in sharp contrast with other witnesses who spoke as if the post–Civil War brand of racial segregation had always existed.[14]

Another witness for the defense, the tax collector of Spartanburg District, South Carolina, recalled that he had investigated Bolton's "blood" in order to decide whether to levy the "free negro" tax on him and had decided not to, whereas he had levied it on another person who claimed to be Portuguese. Clearly, the witness implied, he could not be fooled by a false claim to Portuguese identity; he could tell the difference between a "negro" and a white person like Bolton, regardless of how a "negro" might attempt to muddy the waters.[15]

The plaintiffs, for their part, argued that the Portuguese were not white. Thus Elizabeth Jack's witnesses asserted that "Solomon Bolton never claimed to be a white person. He claimed to be a Portuguese himself, but his neighbors considered him to be a part negro." Other witnesses testified that Bolton, Perkins, and other people of the same community called themselves "Portuguese" or "Spaniards" but were considered "free negro." When asked what Bolton's racial identity was and "with what race of people did he eat, drink and sleep?" W. L. Dugger answered: "He was a mixture. I can't tell what race he was of. He was called part negro. He never denied it to me." As for Bolton's associations, he knew only about steamboat life, in which "blacks would sometimes eat [by] themselves and the whites [by] themselves and sometimes all together." During this era of Reconstruction, whites did not find it so easy to argue retrospectively that the two races had never associated.[16]

As in other post–Civil War racial identity litigation, ex-slaves had a voice in the courtroom for the first time. Former slaves had a chance to testify about their own perceptions of an individual's racial identity and about their own practices of racial knowledge and association. Jefferson Simmerman, an ex-slave of Jerome's brother James Simmerman, testified that "we were slaves and [Bolton] was counted a free negro and we all associated together pretty much. Bolton and family eat with negroes or colored people." Bolton would have "dances or frolicks" at his house for "negroes," until "the people put out patrols, and stopped us colored folks going there and that stopped the frolicks at Boltons." Jefferson also testified that Jemima Bolton was a "lewd woman" who gave birth to Martha only three or four months after her marriage to Jerome. While other witnesses alluded to this fact, only the ex-slave referred directly to Jemima's sexuality. This accusation almost certainly operated to impugn her claim to whiteness. How could a white woman be so impure?[17]

Kittie, the wife of Samuel Williams, testified for the defense but undercut her own testimony when she reported on her slaves' perceptions of Bolton. She claimed that during the time Solomon Bolton lived in her family's neighborhood, "he was treated and recognized . . . as a Spaniard" and ate at the table with her white family. Her husband owned "a considerable number of negro slaves" and never allowed "a negro or person of mixed negro blood" to eat at the table, she claimed. Clearly, in her testimony, association was a strong racial definition and sure evidence of Bolton's whiteness. She also acknowledged, however, that "our negroes complained that we were letting Bolton eat at the table" because he was a "negro" with "kinky hair at the back of his neck." Determined to investigate for herself, she walked behind him to examine his hair and satisfied herself that it was straight. On cross-examination she was asked, "Did you take hold of his hair, and look through it to see whether it kinked or not, or did you just look at it from behind him?" She admitted that she had not looked at the underside of his hair, thus somewhat discrediting her testimony. As in pre–Civil War trials, whites' anxieties over the deceptiveness of appearance plainly continued to have an impact.[18]

Indeed anxiety marked much of the physical testimony in the Melungeon trial, and other factors—both the familiar performance and reputation evidence and the new race-as-association argument—were invoked to support the witnesses' claims that they could read Solomon Bolton's physical appearance and thereby know his race. Thus John Godsey testified that he knew Solomon Bolton was "not a negro" and was "confident that he was not a mulatto," either, because "he had none of the negro brogue—had well formed features, a good countenance. His foot had as much hollow as most any white man." Godsey considered him "Spanish" and claimed that Bolton was "always admitted to the table with white families." Bolton's hair was curly but not very curly, "not kinky"; his daughters married white men, "and I think certainly I would have heard of it if there had been any talk of that kind." Asked on cross-examination if he had any doubts, Godsey reasserted that he did not believe Bolton "had negro blood in him," but he did have "something in his blood besides white blood." To support his expertise in racial science, Godsey was asked about his acquaintance with "the distinguishing characteristics between negroes or mulatoes and white people"; he answered that he had "worked among the negroes all my life."[19]

As in pre–Civil War trials, the court relied on the presumed ability of the ordinary white man to recognize racial identity. John Divine considered Solomon Bolton "Portugese"—for Divine, this meant he was white—and for effect, compared him to the other white men in the courtroom. Bolton, he said, was "a man of rather medium size—about the size of Samuel Williams," and he had "a large Roman nose—something like Lew Shepherd's. At any rate his nose was not flat." Furthermore, "he was rather a trim made, well formed man physically." The court asserted that witnesses could give their opinions about racial identity, suggesting that it remained ideologically important that race be seen as something easily and universally recognized rather than as a legal or scientific matter.[20]

In pre–Civil War Tennessee, white people, slaves, and free people of color had frequently attended corn shuckings together. Accordingly, Shepherd tried to elicit testimony that Bolton had associated with people of color only in the manner in which all white people did, when shucking corn. Lawyers for the other side tried to portray these gatherings instead as "negro frolics," events that only "negroes" would have attended. Witnesses for Elizabeth Jack's family denied that there had ever been any interracial socializing in the community, whereas Martha's witnesses portrayed a world of relative fluidity in which a prominent white man—one who voted and played a role in court proceedings—could also shuck corn with local "negroes." To some extent, all the witnesses, even those arguing for Bolton's "negro" identity, had to acknowledge a certain amount of mixing, even if they disagreed about its nature and about Bolton's relationship to it. William Rogers stated that Bolton "was among white folks in shucking corn &c. like other Negroes, but when the eating time came he did not eat with the white folks." By contrast, Augustus Evans affirmed the frolics at Bolton's house, saying, "I have known of negroes having corn shuckings on the place, but in the same way they would have had them at any other white persons house in the country."[21]

The people of color who testified at the trial painted a picture of prewar racial hierarchy that included a great deal of interracial socializing. Jack Williams, a man of color, remembered dancing at Bolton's corn shuckings. "Both white and black danced together," he testified. Lewis Shepherd cross-examined him: "Did not all farms in the country have corn shuckins and invite in the negroes from the neighboring farms to assist in shuckings? And did they not generally wind up with dances among the hands?" Williams answered, "They did." Shepherd asked, "Was there any thing about the shuckings at Bolton's which made them peculiar or different from the shuckings at other white farmers?" Williams: "Nothing more than that the women folks would dance, and white women didn't." Another ex-slave remembered that the Boltons had "said they were Spaniards" but associated "generally with black [people]."[22]

It was in defense attorney Shepherd's interest to show that Bolton's mixing with colored folks did not make him black. Yet when he tried to get Williams to admit that Solomon Bolton sometimes ate meals at his master's table with the white people, although "negroes" were not allowed to "sit at his table," his strategy backfired. On reexamination by Elizabeth Jack's lawyer, Williams clarified that his master did not always allow Bolton "to eat at his table with white folks when company was there." At those times Bolton "generally went back home" rather than eat with the "negroes." So Williams's testimony was inconclusive: Was Bolton not allowed to eat with the company because he was *not* white, or did he refuse to eat with the "negroes" because he *was* white?[23]

For the first half of the trial, racial debates proceeded with no mention of the Melungeons, until local resident A. B. Beeson introduced the term: "[Bolton] was called a Malungeon [*sic*] . . . His general association was with the Malungeons—his own people. I never saw him associate with whites except when he had business." Although Melungeon identity as black, white, or "other" had long been contested, Beeson clearly considered the "Malungeons" to be nonwhite. The lawyer for Elizabeth Jack then asked, "How many different families in this County or adjoining Counties did you know of the same race or character of people—name them?" Beeson named several "Malungeon" families, including the Perkinses and the Goins. He also cast doubt on Bolton's whiteness by explaining that he had administered the elections for sixteen years and that Bolton "never offered to vote when I held the election." As for testifying in court, the only time he knew of Bolton's appearing at a trial was in a "nigger suit . . . the result of a drunken spree," in which "the parties were

all negroes": Bolton had been the plaintiff and the Perkinses—other "Malungeons"—were defendants.[24]

Shepherd tried to recoup his losses by establishing that "Malungeons"
were, if not exactly white, then not quite black either. On cross-examination
he asked Beeson what he understood by "Malungeon," and Beeson answered, "I think it is a term applied to mixed blooded people." Other witnesses also referred to the Perkins family as "dark colored people." William McGill characterized Solomon Bolton as "a mixed blooded man in
some way, that was his character. We generally called them Malungeons
when we talked about the Goins & them—the Goins that were mixed
blooded." "Mixed blood" at this point in time was still a fluid identity; the
one-drop rule was a Jim Crow invention precisely intended to support the
revisionist efforts suggesting that the races had always been separate. For
a society interested in keeping the races apart, intermediate groups had to
be defined as black in order to preserve the notion of pure whiteness.[25]

This purity, however, was a fiction. Here at the celebrated Melungeon
trial, many witnesses invoked such intermediate groups as Spanish and
Portuguese, who might be white, colored, or neither. Elizabeth Bolton,
the "Aunt Betsy" who had raised Martha Simmerman, testified that her father was of Spanish descent, and that the family had associated "with the
white people—generally poor people." In an effort to establish Jemima's
white female virtue, she asserted that in terms of character, Jemima was
"just as good as any other poor girl." Bolton apparently believed that Elizabeth's appearance was also testament to her own whiteness, for when she
was asked to attach to her deposition a lock of her own hair, she did. According to Lewis Shepherd's memoirs, this piece of physical evidence
helped clinch the case. The fact that a white woman—whose racial purity could be read in her "good" hair—had raised Martha Simmerman was
enough to satisfy Chancellor William Bradford that Martha's mother had
been white. Shepherd also waxed romantic about Jemima Bolton's physical beauty, including her hair. In his memoirs, and presumably in his closing statement, he described her as a girl who was "most beautiful of face,
and had a rich black eye, in whose depths the sunbeams seemed to gather.
When she loosed her locks, they fell almost reaching the ground, and
shone in the sunlight, or quivered like the glamour which a full moon
throws on the placid water." That a "negro" would have such hair, or that a
white woman would raise a black child as her own niece, was unthinkable.[26]

The cornerstone of Shepherd's closing argument, as detailed in his memoirs, was the racial identity of the Melungeons. At trial, he had explained that

> these people belonged to a peculiar race, which settled in East Tennessee at an early day . . . known as "Melungeons." It was proven by the tradition amongst these people that they were descendants of the ancient Carthagenians; they were Phoenicians, who after Carthage was conquered by the Romans, and became a Roman province, emigrated across the Straits of Gibraltar, and settled in Portugal . . . About the time of our revolutionary war, a considerable body of these people crossed the Atlantic and settled on the coast of South Carolina, near the North Carolina line.[27]

When South Carolinians "began to suspect that they were mulattoes or free negroes, and denied them the privileges usually accorded to white people," the Melungeons left South Carolina and wandered into Tennessee. Shepherd also claimed that the Melungeons "do not miscegenate or blend in color," whereas "a mulatto is always half white and half black." Shepherd was writing in 1913, by which time the Jim Crow notion of separate races had taken firm hold. He claimed that "our Southern high-bred people will never tolerate on equal terms any person who is even remotely tainted with negro blood, but they do not make the same objection to other brown or dark-skinned people, like the Spanish, the Cubans, the Italians, etc." From the high point of the Jim Crow era, it seemed impossible even to Shepherd, whose case had depended on portraying an earlier world less organized by racial separation than by racial hierarchy, that Solomon and Jemima Simmerman could ever have lived among whites had they not been recognized as white.[28]

And so, on November 16, 1875, Chancellor Bradford found in favor of W. H. Foust and Martha Simmerman, declaring that Jerome Simmerman and Jemima Bolton had been lawfully and legally married on June 14, 1856, and that Martha Simmerman was "entitled to be supported, maintained, and provided for, clothed and educated" out of Jerome's estate. Several months later Elizabeth Bolton, Martha's aunt, sued W. H. Foust, the guardian of Jerome's estate, for all the expenses of raising her, and won that case as well.[29]

Martha had won her whiteness claim in part by rewriting the past. The testimony revealed a world in which Melungeons lived on the margins of free white and enslaved black societies as "free people of color"—sometimes admitted into the privileges of whiteness, sometimes associating with other people of color, always precarious and often challenged, but apparently accepted among the "poorer classes." After the Civil War, as the institution of slavery gave way to the institution of Jim Crow, people recast the social order through stories of the past told in terms of clear lines separating white and black worlds. Lewis Shepherd argued that Melungeons were white because they had been accepted into the white world; those attacking Martha's claim argued that Melungeons must have been black because they would never have mingled with blacks to they extent they did were they anything else. Evidence about social associations and civic performances in the past had become a way to legitimize racial identity in the present.

Telling Stories about Race and Marriage

Just as former slaves had a chance to testify in court about the identity of Solomon Bolton, calling into question the whiteness of someone they may have seen as a traitor to their people, other Reconstruction-era lawsuits led to dramatic confrontations between the free and the formerly unfree. In these confrontations, stories about interracial sex and marriage became the narratives in which people on both sides could express their anxieties about the possibilities for a future in which ex-slaves and ex-masters would live side by side.

A decade after the Civil War, ex-slave Lawson Carpenter took the stand in a North Carolina courtroom to tell the judge that he had "repeatedly had sexual intercourse" with his former master's wife while his master was fighting in the Confederate Army. Ostensibly, the case in which Carpenter testified, *Warlick v. White*, concerned property, not sex: distant relatives were challenging the right of the master's daughter to inherit his estate. If in fact she had been born of Carpenter's illicit union with Naomi White, then the girl, Sarah, was an illegitimate mulatto who could not inherit. But although money and property were important to the parties in the suit, sex was what mattered to the jury and the community at large.[30]

The twelve white men on the jury weighed testimony about the relationship of the ex-slave and his alleged mistress, now a widow. The child was then "subjected to medical examination" by experts from both sides, but as had often happened in pre–Civil War trials, the experts "differed in their opinion as to whether the child was mixed blooded or not." Regardless, the jury did not accept the "scientific" argument that she had mixed blood. Nor were the jurors persuaded by the experts on the other side; rather, the community members appear to have relied on testimony about the widow's reputation. As they cast their verdict for Naomi White, who had successfully argued that she could not possibly have allowed herself to be sullied by a connection with a black man, they chose to believe her and thus reinforce the ideal of pure white womanhood.[31]

In antebellum proceedings such as those of Alexina Morrison and Sally Miller, the idea that white women had had sexual relations with black men was never openly raised at trial, though such liaisons were perhaps the unspoken horror behind the figure of the wrongfully enslaved white woman. After the Civil War, however, such fears were made explicit, and the possibility of interracial sex—the horrific specter of miscegenation, the threat of the alleged black rapist who sought white victims—was openly discussed. The difference underscores the new status of African American men: now that they were free and supported by the Fourteenth Amendment, they were theoretically able to claim equal citizenship and economic opportunity with white men. White people's fears of black equality (and white elites' fears of interracial alliances) were expressed not in political or economic terms so much as sexual ones: if black men claimed equality with white men in every other sphere, might they not also seek it in the sexual sphere?

When the plaintiffs' lawyer put Lawson Carpenter on the stand, he was asking the jury to recall a world where a white woman had willingly had sex with her black slave. Though presumably such liaisons were common during the antebellum and Civil War eras and were presumably known to adult white men in Southern communities, the jury refused to acknowledge them. Instead they chose to accept Naomi White's assertion of virtuous white womanhood and the segregated worldview it implied, a history of race relations in which consensual sex between white women and black men was literally unthinkable.

The Jim Crow era saw numerous cases involving marriages between white men and women of color, in which the men sought to absolve themselves of responsibility for their ex-wives after a divorce on the grounds that the women were "negro." Sexual relationships between white men and black women never gave rise to the kind of hysteria—and certainly not to the violence—that relationships between white women and black men did. Significantly, in nearly all of these cases of white men and women alleged to be of color, the men failed to convince either a jury or judge that they bore no responsibility toward their former wives because of race. Instead they seemed all too willing to believe that white men would indeed knowingly enter into sexual relations with black women. Indeed some of these cases amounted to referenda on the practice of "concubinage" by wealthy white men in the antebellum South.

In *Dillon v. Dillon,* a Georgia case in 1877, the trial turned on the relationship between a wealthy white Savannah businessman, David Dillon, and a woman of color, Rachel Verdury, who had begun to live together sometime before 1854. Although the couple were never officially married, David had had the Georgia legislature pass an act in 1857 guaranteeing property rights to Rachel and their children. Between 1854 and 1868 Rachel gave birth to nineteen children, five of whom survived. According to David, "knowing what [their children] were," he sent them away to Europe and "never intend[ed] them to come back to the United States." Several of the children did return and, again according to David, tried to kill him. (The incident may have become the basis for a well-known short story by Langston Hughes, "Father and Son," in which a returning black son of a white master actually does kill his father.) At trial David claimed that he had never married Rachel, and that she could not have been his common-law wife because she was a woman of color. As he explained it, he had begun sneaking into Rachel's window at night when he was still a teenager, and would "take a shot when I wanted to." Although Rachel moved into his house after his mother died, he never called her his wife, never introduced her to anyone as his wife, and kept her away from company.[32]

The testimony centered on Rachel's racial identity and the status of the marriage. David's case relied on scientific testimony. Several physicians testified confidently about her "negro blood." James B. Read, the family doctor, recalled: "[Defendant] asked me if I could tell the distinction between the races. I told him that I could if he would give me a piece of the hair and fifty dollars." Replying to the judge, he explained that "it was impossible to give an opinion as to race by merely observing an individual, the color of the hair, etc.; that it required a critical examination; and one of the tests was the smell." Another physician, Dr. J. D. Fish, explained that it was possible to determine degree of blood "with the aid of the scientific knowledge of the present day" and "close and critical examination." Dr. John Mayer was more cautious. He opined that it was not possible by "science alone" to determine the "exact proportion of either the African or Caucasian blood" but that one could achieve something "very near this result." His studies in anatomy, as well as his living "in the midst of the two races for years" and "look[ing] at [Rachel] very closely while feeling her pulse, etc.," enabled him to form an opinion.[33]

The jury could not agree unanimously whether Rachel Dillon had "one eighth or more of African or negro blood in her veins." They rendered Rachel's racial identity irrelevant, however, by answering two questions in the affirmative: they said that if Rachel was white, she was David's wife, and if she was a "negro," she was also his wife. They refused to allow David Dillon to escape financial responsibility for Rachel with the fiction that her racial identity made it impossible for them to have had a long-lasting relationship.[34]

When the case reached the Georgia Supreme Court, Judge Logan Bleckley agreed that the jury knew best whether the relationship was "concubinage or matrimony." But more than that, he insisted that Rachel Dillon should have the benefit of the doubt as to her racial identity. First, he found, she was "not black, but of a complexion approximating that of many white persons of pure blood." Science rather than mere inspection would be required to determine her race. "It is thus not an open, bald case of the intermarriage of an African with a Caucasian," the judge concluded, and therefore, "can the husband (after marrying her, living with her as his wife for many, many years, rearing by her a family of children, some of them to the age of manhood and womanhood) institute a narrow search into her pedigree, that he may deny to her the full measure of support in her declining years to which, if she is truly and legally his wife, the law entitles her?" For some purposes Rachel's racial identity might be open to question, the judge agreed—but not for this purpose.[35]

Even if white men's sexual relationships with black women were far less controversial than the reverse, Southern courts still seemed reluctant to focus on the racial differences that were being bridged in such associations. Instead they behaved as though a white man's decision to associate with a black woman conferred upon her a kind of whiteness, or at the very least a benefit of the doubt—surely a way of acknowledging the well-known prevalence of white male relationships with black women while denying at the same time that they constituted the "race mixing" that the Jim Crow era was so eager not simply to avoid but, further, to render unthinkable.

In order to prove race through association, a prosecutor had to paint a picture of a world in which racial groups did not mix at all. Even under Jim Crow this was a difficult case to make, especially with regard to antebellum times, and so miscegenation prosecutions often foundered. Such portrayals were particularly confounded by testimony about people who lived in racial borderlands. Thus in a 1914 Missouri case a husband tried to have his marriage annulled on the grounds that his wife's brother had forced him into it, and that she was in fact a "negro." Only two or three witnesses besides the husband testified regarding the woman's racial identity, and the Missouri Court of Appeals dismissed their testimony as "neighborhood gossip—talk."[36]

The wife, by contrast, presented a picture of a family that associated with whites, but not exclusively. She had attended a Catholic school for girls that did not accept blacks, but "she and her family were enrolled as Indians." The family had lived in Mexico, two of her sisters had married white men, and "their associates are with white people, not with negroes, although they had a few friends who are negroes." The husband was therefore not able to prove that she was black, both because the wife seemed to be claiming a racial "middle ground" (Indian, Mexican) and because a certain amount of racial mixing had to be acknowledged.[37]

Similarly, in a Kentucky case, Lillian Theophanis won a divorce from her husband, George, including alimony; he cross-appealed to annul on the basis of fraud, claiming that he had not known his wife was mulatto. Evidence from this trial suggests that Lillian's mother's mother, "Mary Jane," may have been a woman of color—but maybe not. Some of her children "married colored people and some married white people." Some court proceedings treated her and her children as "colored people." But even if she was "colored," the Kentucky court ruled, she was not "of pure negro blood," so Lillian was not a mulatto. The court also found that her husband knew of the rumors about her "blood" before he married her. Once again the court seemed to accept a certain amount of race mixing even while denying it, a double move that undermined the husband's attempts to prove race by association. The court also acknowledged the racial borderlands in which a woman could be "mixed" and so, if not quite white, not quite colored either—at least, not colored enough to nullify a marriage. To allow the racial definition of such women as black was to acknowledge far too publicly and irrevocably that many white men indeed chose to associate intimately with black women. This type of interracial liaison may have been an accepted—if disapproved—form of race mixing under slavery, but it was apparently far too dangerous to be acknowledged under Jim Crow.[38]

In general, courts were reluctant to allow husbands to avoid alimony or annul marriages with the claim that their wives were women of color, perhaps because it seemed dishonorable for a white man to behave that way to a woman he had once treated as white, and because judges preferred to see these upstanding white citizens as cads rather than as dupes. As one North Carolina court admonished a husband trying to avoid alimony and dower, the man seemed willing to "consign [his former wife] to the association of the colored race, which he so affects to despise." It may also have been the case that even courts committed to white supremacy were willing to discipline one white man who violated the norms of his class in order to buttress the power of white men in general to control the sexuality of white women and people of color.[39]

Racial identity trials involving interracial marriage were not limited to the South. As more states passed bans on mixed marriages, more cases came to trial in which husbands sought to leave their wives on the legal ground of "negro blood." Indeed, many of these trials became causes célèbres in Northern cities. For example, in 1908 the executor of an Illinois husband's estate sued to enforce a premarital agreement. While normally the agreement would have been set aside for depriving the widow of her "dower" rights to one-third of her husband's estate, the executor argued that in this case the contract should be enforced because the widow was "of negro descent," and therefore the marriage was invalid. Four thousand pages of testimony in the case covered a number of legal points, only one of which was the racial identity of the wife, Isabella Warner, and her father, Stephen Robinson, sometimes known as "Black Robinson." Yet racial identity was ultimately at the heart of the case, for both parties agreed that had Isabella been "negro," she would not have been entitled to one-third of the marital estate.[40]

At trial, numerous witnesses testified that they had heard rumors about Stephen Robinson's reputation for having "colored blood," and even that Robinson's "colored blood" was "conceded" in the neighborhood. Yet at the same time, many testified that the daughters were respectable and well liked, and associated with whites, a contradiction that seems to have baffled this Jim Crow–era community. G. W. Coit, a sixty-three-year-old farmer, was first asked "what the reputation was of Stephen Robinson in that community with reference to whether or not he had or had not some admixture of African blood." Coit expressed his reluctance to rely on rumor and reputation in answering: "Of course, I can only say. I have not the family record. The way I trace breeding stock, I should want the papers . . . I demand the papers." Otherwise the only thing that "denoted" Robinson's "African blood" to Coit was his "head of hair." Coit further emphasized that he had never heard anything "talked about in the neighborhood as to the effect of the talk or understanding with reference to African blood upon their standing in the community." When Isabella had married her husband, all the talk was about her having "struck a bonanza" in marrying such a rich man—nothing about race.[41]

Other witnesses testified about Stephen Robinson's black identity. Warren Severance heard and saw "colored blood" in Robinson's voice and gait: "There was a sort of jingle to [his voice] . . . [T]here was something in the tone that was common in that class of people. His gait that suggested to me that he had colored blood in his veins was a kind of loose-jointed shacking way of walking." Barnett Roe saw colored blood in Robinson's "expression, peculiarities in dress, and there was something suggestive about his voice, that is all." On cross-examination he added that "it is one of the characteristics of the colored race, in my judgment, to associate with and talk with younger persons than themselves." Dr. D. H. Young saw "African blood" in "the character of the hair, his voice, and walk . . . He had a walk peculiar to people with flat feet and rather peculiar shape, without any arch . . . His voice had that peculiar loudness and coarseness that goes with mixed races." Isabella and her sister, however, were "fine girls, "industrious girls . . . modest and dignified in their conduct" and "highly respected."[42]

In the end the jury found for the widow, and the Illinois Supreme Court upheld the verdict, finding that whether or not "Black Robinson" "had a trace of negro blood in his veins," his children "associated on equal terms with the other people of that [white] community" and "married white people." In other words, race by association—the children's ability to socialize with and marry white people—trumped any other sort of physical or documentary evidence. Just as racial performance had been key under slavery, a time when white supremacy required a clear delineation between the capacities and "natures" of whites and blacks, so was racial association key under Jim Crow, when white dominance required an entire society to believe the manifest lie that an interracial world was unthinkable.[43]

Likewise, a New York annulment case that filled the city newspapers in

1925 focused public attention on the racial associations and behavior of Alice Jones, who had married the wealthy New York socialite Leonard Rhinelander. The case captivated New Yorkers, playing to large courtroom audiences and the burgeoning tabloid press. Although Alice Jones admitted that she had some "negro blood," her racial identity remained front and center in the court case. Had Alice acted as a white woman in such a way that Leonard could have been duped into believing she was white when she was not? This question was difficult to answer because Alice's racial associations and performances sent mixed signals, indicating how difficult it was to map reality onto the fictional segregated and hierarchical world of Jim Crow.[44]

Alice had worked in homes where her employers had expressed a preference for hiring "colored help" only, but she did not frequent black churches, clubs, or other community organizations. She had become friendly with both white and black co-workers—a social fact that Jim Crow ideology would have deemed impossible. She had apparently dated a black man but had ended the relationship when she told him she was white and would have nothing further to do with him—an unthinkable action for a "pure white woman," but equally so for a black woman, who ought not to have been able to counterfeit whiteness successfully, even to a person of color. Neighbors reported that Alice's family was "generally known" as "colored" but that she and her sisters did not "associate with Negroes"—again, a statement that Jim Crow ideology would have had to view as an oxymoron. Alice's parents were from England and attended the exclusive Christ's Church, which would seem to make her white, while her schoolmates remembered Alice as an exquisite dresser and thought she was Spanish. Her teacher, though, thought she was "colored."[45]

Even more than in antebellum America, such racial confusion ought to have been impossible in the post–Civil War era. Race was supposed to be knowable, and known, and no person of color ought to be able to associate successfully with white people, just as no white person ought to be willing to associate with blacks. Whatever her race, Alice's checkered history gave the lie to the racial notions that underlay Jim Crow segregation; yet the very testimony at the trial suggests that many if not most people, both black and white, knew that reality was often very different from what it was supposed to be. Just as antebellum slave owners *both* recognized Africans' national origins in their ads for runaways or their requests for particular purchases *and* insisted that Africans were only one large, undif-

ferentiated racial mass, so did Jim Crow whites understand that their supposedly segregated world actually included quite a bit of racial mixing, not
to say racial counterfeiting that was able to fool even the most perceptive
white man. The whole notion of segregation was based on a profound
sense of incompatibility between "white" and "colored," not to mention a
bedrock belief in black inferiority. Passing and all types of racial confusion
suggested that neither of these fundamental Jim Crow assumptions was
true—and moreover, that everyone suspected or at least worried about
this possibility.

At trial Leonard Rhinelander insisted that he had indeed been fooled
about Alice's true racial identity, claiming that she had told him she was
Spanish, despite Alice's insistence that she had told him of her "colored
blood." Unlike other racial identity trials, then, the Rhinelander case turned
not on whether Alice was *actually* white or colored, but on whether an intelligent upper-class white man could have been fooled by her performance of whiteness. More explicitly than any other Jim Crow trial, this
case was a referendum on racial common sense. What *should* "everybody"
know about race, and what *did* everybody know?[46]

The cross-examination of Leonard centered on whether he had basic
"color vision"—that is, was he equipped with the racial common sense
people expected of all whites? Significantly, at this point even the lawyer
for an African American woman could invoke this argument, and so Alice's
lawyer asked Leonard, "Was your brain working?" and then again, "Eye-
sight good?" When Leonard did not answer, the lawyer asked: "How is
your eye-sight—are you color-blind? Can you tell black from white—
brown from white?" According to the *New Rochelle Standard Star,* Leonard answered "feebly . . . 'Yes.'"[47]

Alice's lawyer was playing on the jury's wish to know race when they saw
it—and on their belief that they did know, and so, too, Leonard must have
known. By disbelieving Leonard's story that Alice and her father had
fooled him, the jurors reasserted their own belief in the self-evidence of
"negro blood." Although when Alice disrobed in court, most newspapers
interpreted it as a test of her actual racial identity, it was in fact a test not
of who she was but of what Leonard would have seen. The jury was being
asked to reassure themselves that they *could* tell that Alice was black.[48]

The jury deliberated on four specific questions: whether Alice had concealed her "colored blood"; whether she had represented to Leonard that
she was not of "colored blood"; whether she had done so in order to in-

duce him to marry her; and whether he would have married her if he had known the truth. The jury answered the first three questions in the negative and the final one affirmatively; in other words, they believed that Leonard must have known that Alice was "colored" and married her anyway. Like the Southern women accused by husbands of racial fraud, Alice Jones benefited from the community's wish to see race as knowable and so she won her case, although she paid a steep price in public humiliation, having to disrobe in court as Alexina Morrison had done sixty years before. As the black newspaper the *Amsterdam News* commented, "Few women of any race would have paid so dear a price."[49]

The Rhinelander case drew wide public commentary in New York. W. E. B. Du Bois commented: "If Rhinelander had used this girl as concubine or prostitute, white America would have raised no word of protest . . . It is when he legally and decently marries the girl that Hell breaks loose and literally tears the pair apart." White author U. S. Poson used the case to show the inevitability of miscegenation. "America is a melting pot, and in the process of melting it is only natural for the colored race to become part of the process." But the most enduring significance of the Rhinelander case is the evidence it provides that even in the Northeast, racial "common sense" required constant shoring up. The reassurance whites sought that race could be known by association could not be achieved without acknowledging that interracial intimacy did take place even in the era of Jim Crow.[50]

In all of these cases in which racial fraud was at issue in a marriage, white men presented evidence of their wives' or ex-wives' "negro blood" through racial science, reputation, and performance. Their claim, in most of the cases, was that their wives had appeared and acted white enough to fool them, even as the women's (hidden) blood in fact made them "negro" or "mulatto." The wives, however, presented evidence of associations and performances that made their identities at least ambiguous, often revealing ancestors who had lived on middle ground between black and white, perhaps making it easier for their children to "pass." They benefited on technical grounds from the "degree of blood" rules that shifted the trial focus to a grandfather or great-grandfather who, if he could be proven to be other than "pure" negro, would render her white. Yet juries and judges also exhibited surprising reluctance to allow husbands to rewrite history by denying their marriages. Ultimately, perhaps, the deep need to believe in racial common sense—that we can know race when we see it—led juries and judges to believe that white men could not have been fooled by a "ne-gro" woman pretending to be white. They may have shown poor judgment in marrying a woman of color, but not such "color-blindness" as to have lived and slept and borne children with such a woman believing she was white. True white womanhood could not be so counterfeited.

Degree of Blood, Associations, and Performance

Jim Crow was not just an ideology; it was also a set of laws. From the end of Reconstruction through the first decade of the twentieth century, Southern and Western states imposed a series of restrictions on black civil rights that collectively made up the legal system known as Jim Crow: seg-regating school systems and public accommodations, restricting voting rights to guarantee a "lily-white" electorate, and criminalizing marriage across racial lines. Each law contained definitions of the "negro" and "mu-latto" to be segregated, excluded, or criminalized. Just as racial segrega-tion was a gradual process that required erasing an earlier history of race mixing, so did racial definitions become increasingly narrow and rigid even as they denied an earlier understanding of race as more fluid, variable, and mixed. Whereas most states before the Civil War had defined "negro" as one-eighth African ancestry, twentieth-century definitions diminished the fraction of "negro blood" to one-sixteenth, one-thirty-second, or even "any visible admixture."

Probably the pinnacle of this fever for purifying the white race was reached when Virginia passed the Racial Integrity Act of 1924. This legis-lation put into place a new state bureaucracy to track people from birth, prohibiting whites from marrying persons of any other race, strictly defin-ing white racial "integrity," and enforcing traditional gender roles. Racial definitions had come a long way since South Carolina's Supreme Court de-clared that a man of "worth, honesty, industry, and respectability should have the rank of a white man" even if his "degree of blood" would have consigned him to "the inferior caste."[51]

These new laws, meant to create greater certainty, actually introduced greater doubt about a person's claims to whiteness. Very commonly, courts applied "one-sixteenth" rules by taking testimony regarding the racial iden-tity of a great-grandparent of the individual in question, and if this per-son could not be shown to be a "pure negro," then the individual did not have one-sixteenth "negro blood." Courts struggled with the question of whether the great-grandparent—often the only "colored" ancestor—could be proven "negro" by the usual testimony of reputation or performance, or whether there had to be some kind of definitive proof that the great-grandparent was a "pure negro." Intended to restrict whiteness more narrowly, degree of blood rules actually made a "negro identity" more difficult to prove, while implicitly giving more weight to testimony about the living individual's performance and associations.

Defendants who were able to introduce conflicting testimony about an ancestor's identity could thus escape prosecution for miscegenation. In a 1918 Kentucky case, the children of Thomas Shelby and Mary Scott were alleged to be illegitimate on the basis of miscegenation. Shelby was white, Mary perhaps not. Mary's grandfather could have been either Joe Scott, a "negro," or Casselberry, a white man. Joe Scott was perhaps of mixed race, but some said he "lived as a white man; mixed and mingled with the white people at the dances and gatherings and danced with them, and that he preached in the churches of the white people." Others said "that while Joe Scott was of mixed blood, he was not a negro but was mixed up with some other kind of nation, perhaps of Indian mixture." The jury upheld the children's claim, and the higher court affirmed the verdict.[52]

Similarly, in 1910 Frank Ferrall sought a divorce from Susie Ferrall on the grounds that she had "negro blood." Frank claimed that he had just discovered her racial identity, while she responded that she had repeatedly told him about the "strain of Indian or Portuguese blood" in her veins and the rumors of a "strain of negro blood" as well. The jury found that Susie's great-grandfather was not a "pure negro," so Susie was not "of negro descent within the third generation." Frank Ferrall's lawyer, on appeal, made the argument that the question whether or not the great-grandfather was a "real negro" should be judged by his associations and performances. The Supreme Court, however, insisted that while such evidence could show that he was "negro," it could not prove that he was "pure African"; the jury's verdict was upheld.[53]

As in the antebellum era, courts continued to insist that racial identity was a question for a jury, and that the jury should have as much leeway as possible in considering different kinds of evidence. Numerous cases established that the jury had a right to view the individual and evaluate her appearance. The only limitation on a witness's testimony was that some courts distinguished between testifying about reputation, associations, and appearance as opposed to testifying about the (nonexpert) witness's own conclusions regarding the individual's "degree of blood." In other words, witnesses were not allowed to present their nonexpert opinions about race per se, but juries were still empowered to use their racial common sense and to base their decisions on reputation, associations, and appearance.

Thus in an 1890 North Carolina land dispute a nephew of Nash Booth sued Nash's wife, Ann Bowers, and her children, alleging that Ann was "of negro blood," which would render her marriage invalid and her children illegitimate. Apparently Ann's mother, Lydia, had also been Nash's lover, so Ann claimed title to the land both as Nash Booth's widow and also as the heir of Lydia Bowers. According to Ann, her mother had deeded her house and land to Nash Booth on her deathbed. Ann had been ready to challenge Nash's title by charging that he had exercised undue influence on Lydia, but he "prevailed upon her not to bring suit," saying that "if she would marry him it would secure the land to both."[54]

At trial H. R. Lloyd testified that although Nash and Ann had "lived together and cohabited as man and wife for ten to twelve years," he believed "from their appearance" that Ann and her daughter were "mixed blooded." Although Lloyd testified that he thought Ann was "a colored person," the court did not allow him to give his opinion about her "degree of african descent" because he was not qualified as an expert. He was allowed to offer evidence about performance, association, and appearance, but not to present his own conclusions about racial identity. Likewise, several other witnesses testified that Nash Booth "was a white man, though dark skined," but that Ann appeared to be of mixed blood. The plaintiffs then exhibited Ann and her children to the jury "and called attention to their skin, their hair &c. &c." They also called attention to her six-month-old child, "begotten and born since the death of Nash Booth," and the infant's relative whiteness.[55]

Customarily, in the nineteenth-century courtroom, litigants were not allowed to testify in their own cases. Ann's lawyer, however, argued that by being exhibited to the jury, Ann and her children had been made in effect witnesses for the plaintiff, so he was allowed to cross-examine her. She then testified in court, as did one of her daughters, about her marriage to Nash and his paternity of their children, and she exhibited her six-month-old baby again to the jury. No other witnesses testified for Ann, so when the jury rendered a verdict in her favor, the plaintiffs were able to appeal successfully on the technical ground that Ann and her daughter should not have been allowed to testify to "transactions" between them and Nash, even if it was acceptable for them to be exhibited. At the second trial,

Nash's heir brought new witnesses to talk about Ann's "mixed blood" and her associations with black people. The second jury went the other way from the first, finding Ann and her children to be "negro" on the basis of this testimony. Once again racial common sense determined the outcome of a jury trial, resting on the society's need to believe in the ability of nonexpert white male citizens to know black from white when they saw it.[56]

Similarly, in *Weaver v. State,* a 1928 Alabama case in which a woman recognized as white and an allegedly "negro" man were criminally convicted of miscegenation, lay witnesses for the state who remembered the husband's grandfather were allowed to describe his appearance, behavior, and associations, including his "kinky hair," although they were not permitted to draw conclusions about his "degree of blood." The Alabama Supreme Court explained that one could "prove a man's race by his admissions, either verbally or by his acts; i.e., if he says he is a negro, such declaration may be proven. If he associates with negroes, in his social intercourse, attending negro churches, sending his children to negro schools, and otherwise voluntarily living upon terms of equality socially, such are acts which may be taken as admission." This way of understanding racial associations and performances as "admissions" seemed to be a way of trying to accommodate racial identity trials to the new emphasis on "degree of blood" even as performance, association, and appearance remained powerful bases for testimony.[57]

In cases about intimate relations, associations continued to trump ancestry as proof of racial identity, suggesting that white juries and appellate judges were primarily concerned with establishing the power of racial common sense: without overwhelming evidence to the contrary, white men must be considered capable of recognizing a black woman when they saw her—or else what did the ideal of white racial purity mean? Accordingly, in a case involving "Shreveport Sarah," who had lived for several years with a married white man, Charles Medicus, numerous witnesses sought to prove that Sarah was "negro" by her associations with black people. Medicus's wife, Ivy, who had apparently instigated Sarah's prosecution for felonious adultery, testified that Sarah "lived in a negro house with negro people," and that "you can tell by her looks she is a negro." Several other witnesses for the state testified about Sarah's "negro associates," including testimony that she "kissed Ruby goodbye [and] Ruby was a negro mighty near black." No white woman, obviously, would do such a thing.[58]

Sarah's defense attorney sought to avoid the question of what Charles

had and had not known by emphasizing ancestry: Did any of the witnesses personally know Sarah's ancestry? Ancestry was irrelevant, the witnesses repeated: appearance, associations, and performance were enough
to mark Shreveport Sarah as "negro." As Ivy Medicus put it when the trial
judge asked whether she had personal knowledge of Sarah's background,
"No,—but don't she live with Negroes,—she could not surely be white."[59]

The jury found for Ivy, continuing the pattern of juries weighing associations more heavily than documentary evidence (or the lack thereof). Sarah argued on appeal that the state had not met its burden of proof that
she was "negro," but the court rejected this argument, invoking racial
common sense and the jury's role as fact-finder: "In this jurisdiction certainly every person possessed of any degree of intelligence knows a negro." As the *Wilson* court had asserted, race was a matter of common
sense, and blood would make itself known through performance. Thus,
despite the narrowing of blood rules, courts continued to let witnesses testify about all aspects of individuals' lives and histories—just not to draw a
conclusion about "degree of blood."[60]

Indeed, reputation evidence continued to be crucial not only in cases
involving marriage but in other types of civic matters as well. A North
Carolina school admission trial raised the question of how much hearsay
testimony to allow about an individual's racial identity. In this case the racial identity of the children's mother, Nan Powers, was at issue. Although
she had been raised as Lucy Jane Powers's sister, rumors suggested that
Nan was in fact Lucy Jane's illegitimate daughter by a "negro" man, making her "of mixed blood," and so disqualifying her children from attending the "white" school. Rumor and community rivalries were central to
the proceedings. One witness testified that it was "generally reputed that
two or three men started the rumor that [Nan's] children were mixed
blooded." The plaintiff, J. R. Medlin, Nan Powers's husband, acknowledged that his children had been excluded from school after he had spoken up against the new law segregating local schools, but he insisted that
he had opposed it in general terms, not because his own children were of
mixed blood. "I had a conversation with Hardy Bagwell at Berry O'Kelly's
store about the new school law, I said I thought it was a mean law to let
people marry and not let the children go to free school. I was not referring
to anybody in particular."[61]

Certainly, despite his apparent opposition to segregated schools, Medlin was eager to establish his own wife's whiteness, and he had plenty of

white neighbors who were willing to help. Numerous white witnesses for the Medlins testified that they had been to church and socials with the Medlins, until "the stir in that community four or five years ago." No one directly explained in court what the "stir" was about—whether it originated with the school issue or with some earlier altercation.[62]

Some local residents, though, had come to see Medlin's wife as black. Thad Ivey, for example, claimed that Medlin had said to him: "Well, Ivey, what are we going to do about the school matter[?] . . . [T]hey won't let us send to school, and he said to me I married a negro, and it so shocked me there was very little else said, if anything at all." Hardy Bagwell also insisted that in his conversation with Medlin at Berry O'Kelly's store, Medlin had said, "This infernal Democratic legislature has changed the law and his children had no where to go to school." Surprised, Bagwell "asked him if he meant to say that he was colored and he said in my presence that he knew that his wife was one-fourth nigger. He said that he knew that he had married one-fourth negro. I hated mighty bad to hear him say that." As in other cases, the court was willing to allow witnesses to offer reputation evidence with regard to race—but not to draw their own (nonexpert) conclusions about it. The court instructed the jury that Ivey's and Bagwell's statements were to be understood only as impeaching Medlin's credibility, and not as "evidence that goes to the jury as to the color of the children."[63]

The court tried to distinguish between reputation evidence and simple rumor, asking numerous witnesses if they could tell the difference between a "general reputation" of mixed blood and simply a "report in the neighborhood." One witness remarked, "I notice the witnesses get mixed up on general reputation. Does it mean two-thirds, seven-eights [sic] or how many?" The lawyer answered: "The majority . . . The rule is this. Do you think you know what the people generally say in that community about this woman as to whether or not she is mixed blooded, and it is a matter for you to determine what is the general statement of the people." Yet even a neighborhood report could rise to the level of fact. Thus, the court amplified, "When a report becomes fixed in a neighborhood so it becomes like a fixed fact in the neighborhood, then it can be testified to like a fact when it becomes so general."[64]

At the end of the testimony, the judge addressed the jury. First, he promised to speed things along because it was "very hot, oppressively warm to you and all of us," and the issue of racial identity was "largely a question of fact . . . and not very much law in it." He then advised the jury

that it could rely on its own racial common sense, informed by performance and reputation evidence: "You can take into consideration your
own observation of this woman. You can consider the arguments about
that and consider the question. It is argued on the one side that her appearance shows upon its face that she is not a white woman, but it is argued on the other side that appearances—that appearances are not reliable in cases of that kind, that people are higher colored, tanned, or
something like that." Whether the jury believed that race was self-evident
or feared that they could be fooled by hidden essences, they were convinced that the Medlin children should be allowed to attend white schools,
and the Supreme Court upheld their verdict.[65]

Ultimately, despite the increasing rigor of "degree of blood" rules, juries both north and south of the Mason-Dixon line allowed numerous individuals whose whiteness was challenged to avoid a determination of "negro blood." Courts continued to permit juries to hear and see evidence of
individuals' and their ancestors' associations, performances, and appearance, and to use that evidence to decide whether an ancestor was in fact a
"negro." Many individuals benefited from the fact that such evidence
could not actually prove, however, that a distant ancestor was a "pure"
African—allowing them to escape prosecution for miscegenation, for example. While the law on the books was moving toward a "one-drop" rule
in many states, the law in action did not always work that way. Perhaps Jim
Crow–era juries, sympathetic to the horrors of being consigned to the
black race in an era of white supremacy, felt moved to give the benefit of
the doubt to the potentially white litigants who, after all, resembled them.
To do otherwise might have been to cast doubt on their own whiteness—
an increasingly important source of political, social, and economic capital
in a Jim Crow world.

As the United States moved toward more and more extreme versions of
racial separation, often through violence, African Americans reacted with
ambivalence. On the one hand, testifying in court, some ex-slaves reinforced ideals of racial separation by speaking up against people who may
have been trying to "pass" for white; on the other hand, their testimony often called attention to the high level of antebellum racial mixing, making it
harder for whites to suggest that there had always been segregation.

Black public figures and writers were equally ambivalent. Tuskegee Institute leader Booker T. Washington publicly reassured whites in his famous 1895 speech at the Atlanta Exposition that "in all things that are purely social [whites and blacks] can be as separate as the fingers, yet one as the hand in all things essential to mutual progress." Yet other prominent African Americans, especially those who were themselves of mixed ancestry, began in the late nineteenth century to write quite explicitly about the phenomena of "race mixing" and "passing," warning white Americans that race mixing was taking place all around them, that many people they believed were white were of "mixed blood," and that almost no one who was called a "negro" was wholly African in ancestry. Their writings called into question the meaning of racial difference. How important could it be, their work implied, if blacks could fool whites to such an extent?[66]

At the very time when whites were struggling to solidify the new legal edifice of Jim Crow and to make white associations synonymous with whiteness, writers like Charles W. Chesnutt and Frances E. W. Harper gave the lie to their efforts—even quoting from racial identity trials to demonstrate the absurdity of the notion of "racial purity" and exploring in fiction real-life trials such as the Rhinelander case. At the turn of the twentieth century, African American writers insisted, in the face of anti-miscegenation hysteria and legislation, that race mixing was inevitable and that what made it tragic was not its "unnatural" blurring of God-given distinctions but rather the legal and social proscriptions against it. W. E. B. Du Bois, the great black leader and author, wrote in 1921: "Amalgamation is still going on. It is not then caste or race prejudice that stops it—they rather encourage it on its more dangerous side. The Southern laws against race marriage are in effect laws which make the seduction of coloured girls easy and without shame or penalty." According to Du Bois, the only thing that would end race mixing was "the spreading and strengthening determination of the rising educated classes of blacks to accept no amalgamation except through open legal marriage." Likewise, in 1919 Joel Augustus Rogers, a Jamaican-born, Harlem-based popular historian and journalist, sought to show that race mixing was already under way and that it would not harm the white race: "We find this mixing is taking place between the males of the more developed race, and the females of the less developed . . . [T]he higher development of the male flows toward the less developed race and nothing from the lower race toward the higher. The Negro race is elevated without lowering the standard of the Caucasian."[67]

Charles Waddell Chesnutt, a lawyer and prolific author, had surveyed the inconsistent and arbitrary statutes and cases regarding the determination of racial identity in order to demonstrate the absurdity of racial line-drawing in his 1889 essay "What Is a White Man?" Chesnutt wrote the essay as an answer to the "wise men of the South" who believed that the "Anglo-Saxon race" must always rule the United States, warning them that there was no such thing as a pure white race. Reminding his readers that not all people of color were slaves before the Civil War, Chesnutt told the history of the "free colored people of North Carolina," including the "Croatan Indians," whose status was "anomalous but tenable."[68]

Two of Chesnutt's later novels, one published and one unpublished, dealt with the issue of "passing." In the well-known *House Behind the Cedars* (1900), the lovely, light-skinned Rena Walden decides to stay with her family and her people rather than marry a white man and pass for white, whereas her brother crosses over to the other side. The more interesting *Paul Marchand, FMC* (Free Man of Color), written in the 1920s, involves an incident of baby-switching in which Paul Marchand, a proud and well-educated "free man of colour," turns out to be the illegitimate white son of an old aristocrat. When he is restored to his inheritance and birthright, he insists on defending his honor against the cousins who had dishonored him when he was black. He refuses to abandon his "colored" wife, instead moving with his family to France, where they can (supposedly) live free of prejudice. The story contrasts sharply with Mark Twain's contemporaneous *Pudd'nhead Wilson* (1894), in which a white and a black baby are switched, but as they grow to adulthood, the white man (who is really black) is a vicious cheat, and the black man (who is really white) cannot succeed in a white world because he has been schooled in black ways. Twain's novel suggests the fixed nature of race even as he mocks society's willingness to be fooled by clever masqueraders. In Chesnutt's novel, by contrast, Paul Marchand is honorable both when he is black and when he is white, and the switching serves to reveal not the unfairness of a white world that denies its members the opportunities they need but rather the constructed and arbitrary nature of race.

Frances E. W. Harper also questioned the significance of racial categories in her turn-of-the-century writing. A poet, abolitionist, and Underground Railroad conductor who wrote and lectured before and after the Civil War on behalf of racial equality, Harper produced one remarkable novel, *Iola Leroy*. Published in 1892, the book depicts a young woman born into a white family and raised as white who discovers her "negro blood" only after her white father dies and she is sold into slavery. Quickly freed by the beneficence of a white family friend, Iola goes to work as a nurse in the Civil War. When a white doctor falls in love with her, rather than pass as white to marry him, she goes north, marries a light-skinned black man, and works for racial uplift.

Ostensibly Harper's work would seem to support the racial categories of the era: Iola refuses to enter into the white race, choosing instead to maintain the integrity of the black-white divide. Yet the fact that Iola's distinguished white lover never suspects her "negro blood" subversively suggested that educated people of color were indistinguishable from the white elite—certainly as far as the white elite was concerned—and that such racial confusion cast doubts on the entire basis of both segregation and the white supremacy that segregation was intended to uphold. As the white doctor asks himself: "Could it be possible that this young and beautiful girl had been a chattel, with no power to protect herself from the highest insults that lawless brutality could inflict upon innocent and defenseless womanhood? Could he ever again glory in his American citizenship, when any white man, no matter how coarse, cruel, or brutal, could buy or sell her for the basest purposes?" Harper also suggested that education would eventually enable all people of color to "pass" in the sense of becoming indistinguishable from white elites in every way that mattered—a radical notion indeed in the Jim Crow era.[69]

By the 1920s the theme of passing had become a major preoccupation of the black novelists of the Harlem Renaissance. These authors, too, emphasized the absurdity of whites' "common sense" of race, their belief that they could discern racial identity with confidence, and they too used passing stories to demonstrate the arbitrariness of racial distinction. As the heroine of Nella Larsen's *Passing* comments to herself: "White people were so stupid about such things for all that they usually asserted that they were able to tell; and by the most ridiculous means, fingernails, palms of hands, shapes of ears, teeth, and other equally silly rot. They always took her for an Italian, a Spaniard, a Mexican, or a gipsy." But these later authors were also concerned with the impossible dilemma of the educated black elite. Unlike Charles Chesnutt, who wrote sneeringly of the light-skinned members of the "Blue Vein Society," who looked down on "negroes" and gave themselves airs, writers like Nella Larsen portrayed with compassion the dilemmas of the women caught between two worlds. Blackness and whiteness are performances, Larsen reveals—and unlike either the black underclass or the white elite, the black educated elite might perform both, but could never be fully at home in either.

While black leaders and writers confronted the absurdity of racial identity, the rise of Jim Crow brought new forms of racial subjugation across the United States marked by separation rather than intimate domination. Racially ambiguous people challenged this separation, as did all historical artifacts of prewar intimacy and marriage. Courtroom battles over racial identity often became struggles to reimagine racial relations in the past as more separate than they had been, by rewriting individuals as purely black or white. Even the new "degree of blood" rules, and the limitations on lay testimony about "degree of blood," did not alter courtroom practices of testifying about racial associations and performances in cases involving intimate relations. These practices allowed some individuals to succeed in "passing" to the white side of the line, while others chose to identify as "negro."

Today most white youngsters attend predominantly white schools, and most black children attend schools predominantly populated by people of color. While many of us have co-workers of other races, relatively few have intimate relationships: friendships, marriages, family. It still seems possible to know someone's racial identity by his or her intimate associations. This assurance, and the need to tell stories about race by association even about circumstances in which people of different races in fact mixed a great deal, is an artifact of the post–Civil War world. In the aftermath of slavery, Americans re-created race by retelling the past as a history of separation. In doing so, they helped to shape the future.

CHAPTER FOUR

Citizenship of the "Little Races"

SOLOMON BOLTON was a "malungeon" whose family had migrated away from an isolated community of families like his to a large city, where his daughter married a man recognized as white. Yet other people identified as Melungeon continued to live in the Appalachian community of Hancock County, Tennessee, as a recognizable "racial island" long after the Civil War and well into the twentieth century. Up and down the Eastern seaboard, clusters of people who shared Indian, African, and European ancestry continued to live as distinct communities that were not readily racially identifiable to their neighbors. Not only individuals but also entire groups of people straddled the line between black and white that Americans were trying to demarcate more sharply after the Civil War. Indians, of course, had always posed a dilemma for those who would imagine the United States as a biracial society, but Indians who mixed with people of African descent raised even more challenges. These conflicts over black Indian identity came to a head in the Jim Crow era. The "little races," as they were sometimes known, followed different paths, some individuals retaining or struggling to retain Indian identities, others becoming known as "free people of color," and still others claiming whiteness. In each case they tried to stake a claim to citizenship, whether as citizens of Indian nations or tribes or as citizens of the United States.

As members of racially ambiguous communities came before courts and legislatures, challenged as "people of color" and claiming white or Indian identities, they and the witnesses in their cases gave evidence equating whiteness with full social and political citizenship and blackness with its denial. In the broad sense of participation in political and social life, only white people could become—and were seen as *capable* of becoming—citizens. Indian identity seemed to hold out the promise of an alternative—being part of a separate nation rather than a degraded race—yet that "national" alternative was always radically curtailed in the American legal system. Repeatedly Indians were offered full civic rights in the U.S. polity only to the extent that they abandoned their self-governance and distanced themselves from people of African descent.

Indian identity was understood differently from "negro" race in the courtroom. Indians occupied a unique constitutional category: "Indians not taxed" were the only group the Constitution formally put outside of "We, the People." All Indians did not gain formal U.S. citizenship until the Indian Citizenship Act of 1924, although under the Dawes Act of 1887 and the Curtis Act of 1898, Indians who accepted land allotments and disbanded their tribal governments gained U.S. citizenship, as did those who were "de-tribalized." Membership in an Indian tribe or nation was understood as a political identity, subject to determination by the nation itself. Yet from an early stage, Indians outside of recognized tribes had a hybrid legal identity as both race and nation. For example, in a South Carolina case in 1848 the court decreed that even an individual Indian who was not a member of a tribe counted as a "free Indian in amity with this Government" (a national identity) rather than a "free person of color." Yet the court based this distinction on the *racial* status of Indians, "the race of Shem," as higher than Africans, "the [race of] Ham and his offspring." Indians occupied both an "intermediate or third [racial] class," between whites and blacks, and an anomalous status as members of "domestic, dependent nations." In other words, Indians retained the legal presumption of a *national* identity, based on their status as an intermediate *race*. Furthermore, the borders of Indian nations were determined by race in a way that those of other nations were not; Indians could not absorb people of other races, the court decreed in *U.S. v. Rogers*. A white man who became a Cherokee citizen was still a white man, not an Indian.[1]

The recognition of Indian national identity was something of a double-edged sword. It allowed some Indians to escape the second-class citizenship of "free people of color" but also supplied the logic for denying Indians U.S. citizenship, even as it enabled Indian nations to be removed from and cheated of their land. As one missionary in Oklahoma exclaimed in 1846, "As tribes and nations the Indians must perish and live only as men!"[2] Thus at the same time that whites, especially in the South, sought to draw the line between black and white to be more congruent with the line between slave and free, Indian identity was increasingly racialized.[3]

Of course, Indians had been disappearing as nations and reappearing as individuals, often as "free people of color," for longer than the American nation had existed. The "vanishing Indian" has been as enduring an image as the "noble savage." Native populations did dwindle as a result of the encounter with Europeans, and with their diseases, guns, and alcohol, but whites also saw Indians as disappearing whenever they mixed with other populations, especially Africans and African Americans. Gideon Hawley, a white missionary to the Mashpee tribe on Cape Cod, first noted in a letter in 1776 that the district of Mashpee had "three hundred and twenty seven black inhabitants, 14 of whom are Negroes, the most of whom have married squaws." By "black" Hawley seems to have meant both Native American and the African-descended "Negroes," but clearly, the offspring of these dozen or so marriages between "Negroes" and "squaws" would produce "mixed-race" members of the Indian community. Hawley commented in another letter that Mashpee had become "an Asylum for the Indians and their Connections which have now become various & mixed almost beyond conception."[4]

In early America, Hawley and other observers noted the black-Indian connection dispassionately, or even approvingly, without necessarily casting doubt on the political sovereignty or cultural integrity of the Indian nations. Hawley did not appear to think that "mixture" was a bad thing: he wrote to the governor of Massachusetts in 1791 that Mashpee children had grown healthier "since their blood hath been commixed with English, Germans and Negroes" and that most children were now "mongrels." He also found that "mulattoes" had "generally made better husbands than the aboriginals." Despite Hawley's generally positive view of racial mixing, however, he did distinguish between "mulattoes" and "aboriginals," and he did refer to Indians as "black," revealing the process by which Indians were made to disappear, particularly as they mixed with people of African descent.[5]

Those Indians who mixed with Africans and African Americans throughout the seventeenth, eighteenth, and nineteenth centuries vanished through reclassification as "free people of color." Rhode Island officials changed individuals' racial designations, first from "Indians" to "mustee" or "mulatto," and then again to "Negro" or "black." The category "mustee" or "mestee" was often a way station en route to disappearance for native tribes, which may explain some of the antagonism certain native groups expressed toward African Americans. Thus Benjamin Austin was counted as an "Indian" in East Greenwich, Rhode Island, in 1767, but as a "Malatoo Fellow" in 1768. Numerous other individuals appeared as "Indian or Mustee Woman" one year, only to be redescribed as "Negro" several years later. Others were identified in the alternative as "Molatto or Indian," "Mustee or Mulatto," "Negro, Indian or Molatto."[6]

In colonial Virginia as well, Indians were both reclassified as "black" and lumped in with Africans and African Americans as "people of color" or even "mulattoes." The first law to define "mulatto" was a 1705 Virginia statute that deemed a mulatto "the child of an Indian" as well as "the child, grandchild, or great grandchild of a negro." This statute was not modified until 1785, when a "colored person" was defined as anyone with "one-fourth or more negro blood," whereas those who had "one-fourth or more Indian blood" and no "negro blood" were Indians. We can see this process taking place in the tax rolls of Charles City County, Virginia, where Indians underwent a variety of classifications. From 1783 to the early 1800s no race was marked for free persons; all were classified as "white-tithable." Then, from 1809 to 1812, "free negro" was placed after some names, but Indians and people of mixed blood were apparently treated as white. In 1813 the term "mulatto" appeared, apparently used to designate mixed-race offspring of various combinations, but also to indicate Chickahominy Indians—even, presumably, "full blood" Chickahominy—exemplifying the way that Indians were so often viewed not in their own terms but in relation to the categories of black and white.[7]

In other Virginia counties, relatives of reservation Indians who had taxable property were classified as "mulatto" or "free colored," and sometimes even "free negro," again revealing the extent to which Virginia lawmakers insisted on viewing Indians in terms of black and white. As late as 1818, "mulatto" was applied to those of white-Indian mixed blood by Virginia jurists in *Mercer v. Commonwealth,* in which the judge noted that "the free man sold, was not proved to be either a negro or mulatto, but by one witness, who said he had heard that he was the offspring of a white woman by an Indian."[8]

Many of these Virginia "free people of color" migrated to North and South Carolina in the eighteenth century, including the Goins, Chavis, Bass, and Bunch families. During the seventeenth century, these families were counted on tax rolls sometimes as "white" and sometimes as "mulatto." In South Carolina, early-eighteenth-century legislation distinguished between "negroes, Indians, mulattoes & mestizoes" who were slaves and "free Indians in amity with this government, and negroes, mulattoes, or mestizoes who are now free." As they settled in the Carolinas, or continued to migrate along the Appalachians into eastern Tennessee, these people formed entire communities of racially ambiguous people who became known in the twentieth century to anthropologists as "little races," "racial islands," or "tri-racial isolates." Their neighbors, as we have seen, gave them colorful and mysterious names such as "Melungeons," "Brass Ankles," and "Red Bones," sometimes meant as racial epithets and other times as affectionate monikers.[9]

Some of these groups always identified as Indian tribes, such as the Pamunkey of Virginia and the Croatan (now Lumbee) of North Carolina. Those who continued to identify as "Indian" made strenuous efforts to avoid being classed as "free people of color." Virginia Indians tried to take advantage of the Jeffersonian resurgence of interest in Indian-white marriage and the romantic myth of "Pocahontas" to gain favorable legal treatment. Pamunkey Indians in the early nineteenth century obtained "certificates of Indian descent" from local authorities, and wore their hair long despite adopting other aspects of European clothing, in order to demonstrate that they were racially distinct from African Americans.[10]

It is likely that both the Melungeons and the Croatan/Lumbee migrated along a path from Virginia through North Carolina along the Appalachian Range to eastern Tennessee in the late eighteenth century, according to present-day genealogical researchers. The earliest identified Melungeons who acquired land in Hawkins County in the first decade of the nineteenth century—Millington Collins, the Gibson, Goins, Bowlin or Bolton, and Bunch families, and the Denhan or Denman families—can be traced back to Virginia. It is possible that some of these individuals also intermarried with slaves imported from Portuguese trading posts or with Portuguese sailors, some of whom were also of African ancestry. Probably, then, these communities were indeed "tri-racial" amalgamations of Africans, Portuguese (including Portuguese-Africans), Indians, English, and others, who came into the hill country of the Carolinas and Tennessee in the eighteenth century.[11]

In Robeson County, North Carolina, there are records of "Indian" or "mulatto" residents as early as the eighteenth century already speaking

English when the first white settlers arrived. A colonial proclamation in 1773 listed the names of people who took part in a "Mob Railously Assembled together," apparently defying the efforts of colonial officials to collect taxes. The proclamation declared that "the Above list of Rogus," which included many characteristically Lumbee names, "is all Free Negors and Mullatus living upon the Kings Land." A colonial military survey described "50 families a mixt crew a lawless People possess the Lands without Patent or paying quit Rents." It is likely that the Croatan/Lumbee community grew out of an amalgam of different native peoples, including Siouan, Cherokee, and Tuscarora Indians, who mixed with ex-slaves, free people of color, and whites. Before the Civil War they were known to their neighbors as a distinct community of free people of color, within which some individuals were designated white, some black, and some mulatto, while some moved between identities from one census to the next. But it was only after the Civil War that they began to claim a specifically Indian identity and to transform themselves "from mulattoes to Indians."[12]

Many different people lived on the borderlands between black, white, and Indian in the East for years before the Civil War. From the 1840s on, they found themselves increasingly squeezed as whites put pressure into policing a single line between black and white. This pressure intensified in the aftermath of the war and Reconstruction—even as racially ambiguous groups all reacted differently to this pressure. While the Melungeons sought to fall on the white side of the line, the Croatan/Lumbee and the Narragansett insisted on Indian identity, the Croatan/Lumbee by denying any African American connection, and the Narragansett by embracing it. Each group struggled with the question of what citizenship meant under Jim Crow and how people who had once been known as "free people of color" could attain the full rights of citizens.

Melungeons: Portuguese as Passing for White?

After the "celebrated Melungeon case," there were no more official encounters between Melungeons and the state. Yet Melungeon identity has continued to be the focus of conflict outside of the courtroom. The mythology of European origins has repeatedly clashed with the efforts of state officials to police "blood" rules strictly against all "tri-racial" or racially ambiguous communities. When Melungeons began to garner attention from journalists, officials, and anthropologists, most of it was negative.

Romantic stories, like Lewis Shepherd's tale of the "celebrated Melungeon case" and the "Carthagenian" origins of the Melungeons, have been repeated and elaborated as a source of pride because Melungeon identity has continued to be the subject of struggle.

For example, on August 5, 1942, Dr. W. A. Plecker, the state registrar of the Commonwealth of Virginia and a leader in the Anglo-Saxon Club movement, wrote to the secretary of state of Tennessee in Nashville about the classification of Melungeons. Plecker had spent the 1920s and 1930s on a mission to prove that there were no true Indians in Virginia because "no Virginia Indians were free from black blood," and to deprive the Pamunkey, Mattaponi, and Chickahominy of Indian status. Writing to Tennessee officials in 1942, he explained that there were Melungeons in Virginia who had come from Hancock County, Tennessee, and who "are classified by us as of negro origin though they make various claims, such as Portuguese, Indians, etc." Not surprisingly, Plecker was investigating these claims carefully.[13]

Tennessee state librarian and archivist Mrs. John Trotwood Moore wrote back to Plecker that "the origin of the Melungeons has been a disputed question in Tennessee ever since we can remember." Moore quoted Captain L. M. Jarvis, who identified the Melungeons as "friendly Indians" who had come to Newman's Ridge in the late eighteenth century, and also quoted Lewis Shepherd regarding their "Carthagenian" origins. She concluded, however: "I imagine if the United States Census listed them as mulattoes [in 1830] their listing will remain. But it is a terrible claim to place on people if they do not have negro blood." Plecker wrote back to tell Moore that she and other Tennesseeans, including the judge in Lewis Shepherd's "celebrated Melungeon case," had been fooled. "All of these groups have the same desire, which Captain L. M. Jarvis says the melungeons have, to become friends of Indians and to be classed as Indians . . . [T]hey have always endeavored to tie themselves up as closely as possible either with the whites or Indians and are striving to break away from the true negro type." Plecker noted that many Melungeons were listed in Carter G. Woodson's "Free Negro Heads of Families in the United States" in 1830. He dismissed the claims of "Portuguese" or "Phoenician" origin, and concluded that Melungeons were no different from other people "who are now causing trouble in Virginia by their claims of Indian descent . . . We have found after very laborious and painstaking study of records of various sorts that none of our Virginia people now claiming to be Indian are free from negro admixture, and they are, therefore, according to our law classified as colored. In that class we include the melungeons of Tennessee."[14]

The Melungeons' legal battles faded as they assimilated into the surrounding population, yet the battle over Melungeon identity has taken on new life in recent years as family history and genealogy have become an increasingly important aspect of popular culture, especially in the South. Many Melungeons vigorously endorse theories of European origin against any suggestion of West African descent. Personal narratives by Melungeons who claim to be part black have stirred great controversy in popular forums. The best-known narrative of Melungeon origins is a history by Brent Kennedy titled *The Melungeons: The Resurrection of a Proud People; An Untold Story of Ethnic Cleansing in America.* While Kennedy does not deny the possibility of African American or Indian origins for the Melungeons, he insists on a Mediterranean connection: Melungeons descended from Moors and Turks, he writes, perhaps in connection with Juan Pardo's expedition to the New World, or perhaps brought by Sir Francis Drake in the 1580s. It is striking that today, even as "Melungeon" has become a term of pride and self-ascription rather than an epithet of opprobrium, its association with multiracial identity is still perceived by many as a taint, or at the very least a source of controversy.

Creating an Indian Identity: The Croatan/Lumbee

The Croatan—today known as the Lumbee—chose another response to the pressure of Jim Crow: they engaged in an elaborate process of self-definition as Native American. Although they probably shared a common "mixed" heritage with Melungeons, and though they were equally concerned to erase all traces of their African heritage, they began to identify not as white but as Indian. As Jim Crow emerged in North Carolina, the Indians of Robeson County sought a third way in a binary system.

In the immediate aftermath of the Civil War, the "free colored" community of Robeson County increasingly came into confrontation with whites in conflicts over land and labor. Indeed, the Croatan/Lumbee today are best known for the famed "outlaw band" led by Henry Berry Lowery, which during this period robbed white plantations, murdered members of the white upper class, and continually escaped arrest. As whites in the county struggled to regain control of their communities, they tried to come to terms with the identity of their attackers. Impressed by the bravery and defiance of Lowery's band, whites began to imagine them less as "mulattoes" and more as "Indians," acknowledging their mixed blood but emphasizing their supposedly Indian "savage" and "warlike" qualities. Several local whites wrote memoirs of the Lowery band, and others testified about the outlaws and their community before congressional hearings in 1872; their words reveal their confusion about Croatan/Lumbee racial identity.

For example, some contemporary whites attributed "superhuman qualities" to Lowery's "mixed blood." Mary Norment, whose husband was killed by Lowery's band, wrote a history of Lowery in which she tried to parse his heritage and his personal attributes, ascribing Lowery's "love for rude music" to the "negro trace," his affinity for "war and plunder" to his Indian character, and his "scrupulousness" and honor to his "cavalier blood." The lawyer Giles Leitch Jr., who had successfully defended the militia members who killed Lowery's father and brother, went to Washington to testify before a congressional committee investigating Ku Klux Klan activities in the region. Leitch attempted to identify Lowery's community in racial terms but eventually gave up: first, he testified that they were "a mixture of Spanish, Portuguese, and Indian" without "much negro blood at all . . . They are called 'mulattoes.'" But then, when asked, "The word 'mulatto' means a cross between the white and negro? . . . You do not mean that word to be understood in that sense when applied to these people?" Leitch answered, "I really do not know exactly how to describe these people." Whites in Robeson County could not decide whether the Croatan/Lumbee were tri-racial or whether they were some other thing entirely, something heretofore unknown and mysterious.[15]

The Croatan/Lumbee themselves began efforts in the late nineteenth century to establish their Indian identity, enlisting the help of state legislator and the amateur folklorist Hamilton McMillan. In 1885 McMillan was able to win state legislation changing the Robeson County Indians' legal status from "mulatto" to "Croatan Indian," based on the "lost colony" theory of their origins. Several years later McMillan published a pamphlet titled *Sir Walter Raleigh's Lost Colony*, in which he noted that "formerly these Indians called themselves 'Melungeans,' and some of their old people still adhere to that name," and traced both the Melungeons of Tennessee and the Croatans of North Carolina to the same roots on Roanoke Island. According to this theory, the Croatans were descendants of Sir

Walter Raleigh's second group of settlers, who disappeared from Roanoke Island in 1587 leaving only the word "CROATOAN" carved into a tree, and then intermarried with local Indians.[16]

Because of this change in legal status, the newly named Croatans were able in 1885 to establish their own school committee and a system of separate schools in Robeson County, including a segregated normal school in the town of Pembroke a few years later. Croatans also won separate schools in neighboring Richmond County, and briefly in Sampson County, although the Sampson County school law was repealed as a result of a fracas over allegedly mixed-race children attending the school. To the Croatans, this was an enormous victory: if they could not be educated alongside whites in the Jim Crow South, at least they did not have to be relegated to the manifestly inferior and stigmatized "negro schools." The establishment of these separate schools, however, provoked anger among some of the African-descended residents of Robeson County, leading to the first legal challenges of Lumbee/Croatan identity to reach the North Carolina Supreme Court.[17]

In 1888 Nathan McMillan of Robeson County (relation to Hamilton McMillan unknown) sued the school committee of the "Croatan Indian" public school district, seeking his own children's admission to the schools it operated. McMillan sought to establish the color line where white people in the Jim Crow South were increasingly prone to draw it: between white people and everyone else. McMillan claimed that "all children not white" in the district were entitled to the benefits of the Croatan school, and moreover, that his wife and the mother of his children was the sister of Preston Locklear, a member of the defendant school committee, proving that his children were as Croatan as anyone else and should be allowed to go to school. Preston Locklear, Hector Locklear, and William Sanderson, who constituted the school committee, did not think so, and wrote to McMillan that they would not admit his children to the school "until the law compels us to do so."[18]

McMillan did not claim to be a Croatan; he had been a slave, and his master, a white man, was his father. But he did not think Croatan identity was such a clear-cut affair: as one defense witness admitted on cross-examination, "The people now designated as croatans were called mulattoes up to the passage of the Croatan Act, but were always a separate race to themselves." The North Carolina Supreme Court affirmed the jury verdict that McMillan's children were "negro" and not "Croatan"; at best, according to the judge's instructions, they were "half-bloods," but they had not proved that they had no "negro blood" to the "fourth degree," that is, in four generations. The court decided not to "consider the testimony tending to show that those persons (the Croatans) were, in fact, of negro descent, or were formerly called mulattoes." In North Carolina, then, white lawmakers at all levels were still committed to distinguishing between people of African descent and everyone else. Even if the Croatans were not white, they were not black, and thus they had the right to exclude McMillan's children, just as the white schools had the right to exclude the Croatans.[19]

The North Carolina Croatans clearly considered their own separate school system to be a significant prize, and for the next several decades they continued to petition Congress for increased appropriations for their school system and for federal recognition as an Indian tribe. In January 1889 the U.S. Indian commissioner, John H. Oberly, wrote to J. W. Powell, director of the Bureau of Ethnology at the Smithsonian Institution, asking about the Croatan Indians, saying that he had no record of such a tribe. Powell advised Oberly to contact Hamilton McMillan for more information. In 1890 McMillan wrote to the Indian Office describing the Croatans as a branch of the "Melungeans," and recommending support for their petition. But nothing came of this brief show of federal interest.[20]

The Croatans became increasingly unhappy with the designation "Croatan," because local usage shortened the word to "Cro"—which, with its verbal associations with "Jim Crow," became a pejorative synonym for "colored." In 1911 they succeeded in changing their official designation in the state legislature from "Croatan" to "Indians of Robeson County," and then in 1913 to "Cherokee Indians of Robeson County." The legislature emphasized that this name gave them none of the benefits that belonged to the "Eastern Cherokee" tribe, but only the benefits that had belonged to the Croatans, namely, the right to run their own schools.[21]

In that same year, at the urging of Angus W. McLean, the state legislator to whom the Croatans had turned for support when Hamilton McMillan retired, the U.S. House of Representatives held hearings to discuss the Croatans. For the hearings, the secretary of the interior submitted a report to Congress on the Indians of Robeson County. These congressional investigations focused on the race consciousness of the Croatans, and on their desire to distance themselves from "negroes." At the House hearings, Representative Burke and McLean had an exchange about the tripartite separation of races in North Carolina. Burke asked, "The Indians are not prohibited from intermarrying with the whites?" McLean answered: "Yes sir. In other words, the Southern States have paid more attention to race distinction than any other States in the Union." Burke then suggested that Croatans should be allowed into white institutions. McLean answered that it would violate the "great feeling on the part of the southern people that there should not be any admixture of races. For instance, the Japanese and Chinese have never been permitted to intermix with the whites down there and, in that way, the segregation of races is complete." Burke agreed that the Croatans should not be allowed to enter Indian schools "because they are not full-blood Indians" and professed his "great sympathy with people in the South in dealing with the negro."[22]

Croatan Indians themselves had very little voice in the hearings. There was only one brief exchange, when the Croatan representatives were presented to the committee for questions. One representative asked a Locklear if he was an Indian; he replied, "Yes sir; not a full blood, I don't suppose." The congressman then asked Preston Lowry if he was a full blood, and Lowry answered, "No sir," adding, "I attended school at Lynchburg, Va." Another congressman asked if there had been any "objection to [him] at Lynchburg"? He answered, "I did not tell them I was Indian."[23]

While the testimony before Congress focused on the resemblance between Croatans and other non-black people of color (such as the Japanese and Chinese) and stressed the importance of segregating them from whites, the interior secretary's "Report on the Indians of North Carolina" suggested that the boundaries between white and Indian were rather blurred: "It is in no way surprising that enumerators should return so few Indians [in the U.S. Census of 1890], as many of them are not distinguishable from whites except on special investigation as to their racial relations . . . A body of people residing chiefly in Robeson County, N.C., known as the Croatan Indians, are generally white, showing the Indian mostly in actions and habits. They were enumerated by the regular census enumerator in part as whites."[24]

The report also offered evidence that the Croatans were indeed Indians, reprinting an August 1914 letter from Hamilton McMillan which observed, "Tradition is the Indian's history . . . These Indians call themselves Cherokees. During [the] past 30 years I have interviewed hundreds of them, and the inquiry as to their origin was, without an exception, in favor of their being Cherokees . . . Since their recognition as a separate race they have made wonderful progress. Their hatred of the Negro is stronger than that entertained by Caucasians." Clearly, Congress could not settle the question of who the Croatans were—but everyone agreed that they were not "negro," which was proved by their "hatred of the Negro."[25]

Having achieved a separate normal school, the Croatans, now known as "Cherokee Indians of Robeson County," in 1915 sought to exclude other students from the school who had "negro blood," including members of the subgroup of Croatan/Lumbee known as "Smilings," who had come from South Carolina. Three "Smilings" brothers with the surname Goins sought to have their children admitted to the normal school. In a long trial Willie Goins testified that he had brought his family from Sumter County, South Carolina, and that they "belong to the Indian race of people if any to my knowledge." He testified that their general reputation was "Indian" and that "we were not associated with that class of people [the "negroes"] and we pulled out from among them and built us a new church by the name of Hopewell and we tried to get them to see as we saw and do as we did and we couldn't do so and finally there was such a few of us we couldn't do anything ourselves and we came from there . . . up here."[26]

The Goins, like so many other members of tri-racial groups who had moved to white areas, experienced racial investigations. Willie's brother, Walter, or W.W., testified that the "Indian Baptist Association of Robeson County made an investigation before they admitted us." Three ministers were sent to Sumter to investigate the Goins' racial identity. "In South Carolina," W.W. explained, "we are sometimes called 'Red-bones'; some call us 'Croatans.'" A. S. Locklear, one of the investigators of the Goins, gave his opinion that "on the mother's side plaintiffs are Indians and on the father's side malungeans." Locklear was impressed that "these families had made every endeavor to keep themselves aloof from the negro. Did not want to associate with them in churches and in schools." Other plaintiffs' witnesses testified that the Goins were members of a race apart, perhaps white mixed with Indian, but not "negro," and especially emphasized their efforts to keep clear of black people socially. Lizzie Brown, the plaintiffs' sister, explained, "We are Indians in the North, but they give us the name of 'Red Bones' down there [in South Carolina]." A white witness who testified by deposition argued that the Goins "belong to a mixed race, indian predominant . . . They are commonly known as 'Red Bones' and that is a synonymous term for indian." The witness recounted approvingly that the Goins had withdrawn from their original church when it "got a negro for their pastor," and that he had helped them organize a new church, until they moved to North Carolina. Yet although he claimed that "they were not considered a mixture of the negro," on cross-examination he allowed that "as a matter of fact they are not pure blooded Indians. They have got some mixture in them. Mixture of some dark strain of blood I presume." A handwritten addition to his testimony reads, "Some of these red bones intermarried with negroes." No one appeared to think the Goins were "pure white"; all witnesses described some kind of "mixing"; but they respected the Goins' efforts to distance themselves from "negroes."[27]

The school board tried to introduce the testimony of Hamilton McMillan, now seventy-eight years old, about his recollections of the bill he introduced in the state legislature designating the "Croatan" Indians and establishing the normal school. McMillan asserted that he had intended the school for Indians residing in Robeson County and no others. He explained his theory that the Croatans were "descendants of John White's lost colony." The court asked McMillan, "Do these people here call themselves croatans?" He answered: "No sir. They call themselves malungeans." Other witnesses for the defendants, including the investigators sent by the school board to Sumter, South Carolina, testified to the plaintiffs' reputation as "colored people." One testified that Willie and Walter Goins "went with the darkies" and that Willie had lived with a black woman.[28]

The judge then reminded the jury that it was state policy to "give every child an opportunity to get at least a limited education," and also state policy "to separate the races," though occasionally "a mixture of blood . . . creates a discussion and trouble." He explained that if the mixture went back "a few generations and if it is then passed out so that it is hard to trace back," state policy was "to put the matter to sleep in a few generations and in that way provides so that every child shall go to school somewhere and to separate races as well as can be done." He went on to charge the jury that the law regarding the normal school should apply to all "croatans," not only those in Robeson County at a given moment, and should exclude only those with "negro blood" in the fourth generation, not any "trace of negro blood." He refused to submit to the jury special questions about the "negro blood" of the plaintiffs and instead submitted only the question "Are the plaintiffs entitled to be admitted into the Indian normal training school at Pembroke?" to which the jury answered "yes." Clearly the jury was less concerned with policing the black-Indian color line or with maintaining the racial purity (i.e., the lack of African heritage) of the Croatans than it was with simply establishing a tripartite system of racial identity: white, black, and Indian. In a Jim Crow world where whiteness was the political prize, white jurors were not prepared to bother too much about whether Indians had some "trace" of blackness.[29]

Croatans, by contrast, remained highly concerned with demonstrating that their community contained no "taint" of black blood and was instead purely Indian, and they were supported in their efforts by the North Carolina General Assembly, which in 1921 established a racial screening committee for the Robeson County schools, staffed only by Indians of Robeson County. The group also policed the boundaries of Indian identity in the pages of local newspapers as well as in the courts, so that in 1914 the *Robesonian* was forced to print a retraction for having referred to Amos Bell of Ten Mile Swamp as a "darky." "That was a mistake and if the reporter had not been too busy to observe when 'Uncle' Amos called he would have known better. 'Uncle' Amos is a highly respected Indian." As for the Smilings, although they won their case before the North Carolina Supreme Court, the county built them a separate school, and from then on they were regarded as a separate community.[30]

The Croatan/Lumbee took advantage of every opening to establish their Indian heritage and to win all the political rights that Indian identity implied. Thus in the 1930s, when John Collier took over the new Bureau of Indian Affairs and Congress passed the Indian Reorganization Act, allowing and even encouraging tribes to reestablish federally recognized tribal governments, the Croatans also pressed Congress for a bill to recognize "the Robeson Indians" as "Siouian Indians of the Lumber River." The bill was blocked by Secretary of the Interior Harold Ickes, who worried about extending federal recognition to tribes which had not received any federal benefits in the past. In 1953, however, the Croatans won a measure of state recognition when North Carolina officially changed their designation to "Lumbee Indians." Three years later Congress finally followed suit, though their new designation as Lumbee Indians did not bring with it any federal benefits. Still, in the Jim Crow South, any move toward Indian identity, and by extension away from "negro" identity, must have seemed to the Lumbee like a step forward.

The Croatan/Lumbee took a very different path from that of the Melungeons in the era of Reconstruction and "Redemption." Rather than passing to the white side of the color line with the establishment of Jim Crow, they sought a "third way." Demanding recognition as Indian allowed the Croatan/Lumbee to create an existence somewhat separate from whites and blacks—yet very differently from when they had "free people of color" status before the Civil War. Adamant that their intermediate status would *not* lead to any fluidity in racial identity, the Croatan/Lumbee rigorously policed the line between Croatans and other people of color, whether they were individuals suspected of "negro blood" or other racially ambiguous communities like the Smilings.

Even when Jim Crow ended, however, the Croatan preoccupation with racial identity did not cease. Since the 1960s the Pembroke School has been open to whites and blacks, and the school for Smilings closed—but the Lumbee did not cease resisting integration. One elderly Lumbee man, speaking in the late 1970s about a recent meeting attended by Indians, whites, and blacks, told an ethnographer: "An Indian stood up, right in front of Negroes, and said [to the whites], 'You've forced the Negro down our throats and now they're forcing him down yours. Don't you go pushing them off on us. If you take him, we'll take him.' And not before will we take them." This sentiment, combining Indian nationalism with anti-black racism, echoes conflicts in other nations which have struggled with racial identity issues.[31]

Meanwhile, in the twentieth and twenty-first centuries, the Lumbee and other groups who consider themselves to be Indians but who were deemed "mulatto" by Southern whites have continued to seek federal recognition as "Indian." Their claims, like the land claims of Northeastern tribes such as the Mashpee, have suffered because they have been able to demonstrate neither racial purity nor continuous tribal identity. For these Indian tribes that mixed with blacks and whites, "race" and "nation" have proven to be swords that cut both ways.

A Multiracial Indian Society: The Narragansett of Rhode Island

Unlike either the Melungeons or the Lumbee, the Narragansett of Rhode Island staked a claim to Indian identity without denying their African roots. Indeed, in repeated confrontations with state and federal efforts to strip them of tribal status, individual Narragansetts spoke eloquently of their refusal to accept U.S. racial hierarchies and designations. At the same time, they sought to maintain their tribal sovereignty and control over their territory.

For most of the nineteenth century, the Narragansett tribe of Rhode Island had fought the Rhode Island legislature in its attempts to gain access to tribal lands and repeal tribal rights. The "mongrel" characterization of the Narragansett figured prominently in the state's efforts to portray the them as unworthy of tribal status. In 1830 the General Assembly appointed a committee to "examine the present condition of the Narragansett tribe." The committee report depicted the Narragansett as "verging towards [a] state of complete extinction": while the tribe claimed two hundred members, "of this number however only five or six are genuine untainted Narragansetts all the rest are either clear negroes or a mixture of Indian, African and European blood." The committee concluded, "Forty years ago this was a nation of indians now it is a medly of mongrels in which the African blood predominates." The committee recommended the appointment of a white overseer for the tribe; the adoption of rules of membership to "prevent a transmigration of this tribe from an indian to a negro race"; the elimination of the tribal exemption from lawsuits for debt; and the opening of Narragansett lands for "publick uses" at such time as the tribe was found to be extinct. The Narragansett responded with strong objections to all of the committee's recommendations, noting that "the white citizens have got away all the best of our Lands. And we pray that we may be permitted to enjoy what we have left, and that no more of our Lands may be sold . . . And as to the mixture of African and European Blood with that of the native Indians; It has been done, and cannot be undone by any Legislative Act." Again, in 1852, another committee reported to the assembly about the Narragansett: "While there are no Indians of whole blood remaining, and nearly all have very little of the Indian blood, they still retain all the privileges which belonged to the Tribe in ancient times." This committee too recommended revoking their tribal status. Six years later the commissioner of the Narragansett Indians reported that "the Narraganset of the present day can boast of little else than the name, without exhibiting any of the traits of character that distinguished his ancestors."[32]

Yet before the Civil War, the Narragansett managed to turn away each of these committees, preserving its tribal status for several more decades. In the immediate aftermath of the war, however, the state of Rhode Island acted more forcefully to repeal the Narragansett's tribal status and make their individual members into citizens of the United States. The Narragansett reacted equally forcefully. In December 1866 they turned back the first investigative committee with the following words: "We have not sent for this committee, and we know of no particular occasion for its visiting us at this time."[33]

The Narragansett expressed their skepticism about citizenship, for they feared it would be the same second-class citizenship to which blacks were relegated:

> We have traveled much over the country; Have visited many States and have seen many men, both white and black. We have heard much said about the rights of the negro; of negro citizenship, and negro equality; but we have not found the place where this equality and these rights exist, or the negroes who enjoy them. Negro citizenship as we have seen it, means the right to have the negro vote for somebody, but not to be voted for; no white man votes for a negro.

After describing the status quo of Jim Crow, the Narragansett spokesperson explained why they did not want to submit to it themselves—not because they did not want to associate with "negroes" but because they saw the injustice of the "negroes'" place in society:

> We do not want this negro citizenship, and if we are to have some other citizenship, we prefer to see it enjoyed by some one else before we accept it . . . We are not negroes, we are the heirs of Ninagrit, and of the great chiefs and warriors of the Narragansetts. Because, when your ancestors stole the negro from Africa and brought him amongst us and made a slave of him, we extended him the hand of friendship, and permitted his blood to be mingled with ours, are we to be called negroes? And to be told that we may be made negro citizens? We claim that while one drop of Indian blood remains in our veins, we are entitled to the rights and privileges guaranteed by your ancestors to ours by solemn treaty, which without a breach of faith you cannot violate.[34]

This was a very different notion of Indian identity from that of the dominant society—a vision of Indians as a nation rather than a race, and a multiracial nation at that. Furthermore, it turned the emerging "one-drop rule" of "negro" identity on its head; the Narragansett claimed that even one drop of Indian blood entitled them to Indian national status and the rights and privileges guaranteed their nation by treaty.[35]

In 1880, at the outset of the allotment era, the Narrangansett of Rhode Island were finally "de-tribalized" and their tribal lands made available for public sale. The Rhode Island General Assembly concluded, after decades of committee investigations showing the "decline" and "mongrelization" of the tribe, that it had become extinct and should be terminated. Also in 1880 a new committee reported that "there is not a person of pure Indian blood in the tribe, and that characteristic features, varying through all the shades of color, from the Caucasian to the Black race, were made manifest at the several meetings of the Committee. Their extinction as a tribe has been accomplished as effectually by nature as an Act of the General Assembly will put an end to the name."[36]

The Narragansett had vigorously resisted this de-tribalization—not just in defense of tradition, and in order to hold onto their land, but in conscious rejection of American racial practices. In a series of public meetings in Charlestown in 1879, Narragansett Council members articulated the difference between their understanding of Indian identity, encompassing people of "mixed race," and the larger community's two-tiered hierarchy of whites and people of color. Joshua Noka explained why he did not want to be a U.S. citizen: "Now, for me as an individual to ask to be a citizen, under the present existing circumstances, I don't see anything that would be interesting to me. For a colored man to be a citizen, he will remain about the same as at the present time." In practical terms, citizenship would mean only being "brought out" to vote, but the "colored citizen" could not "expect ever to be President of the United States, or an Attorney-General. It makes no difference how well he is qualified, he can't be put into a jury box; to be drawn as a common juror, or anything of the kind; but if you have got a cesspool to dig out, put him in there." Under these circumstances, "what would be the object in throwing off the tribal authority and come out and be called a citizen, with nothing to do as a colored man? . . . Why should the Narragansett tribe be willing, just for the sake of being a citizen, to throw away the rights and privileges that they now have?"[37]

Another council member, Daniel Sekater, agreed: "I can't see for my life wherein we shall be benefited any more than we are at the present time by coming out as citizens under the present circumstances . . . Some argue that they ought to come out as citizens because they are mixed up with others. There are niggers, it is true—perhaps more niggers than anything else. But other classes are mixed up with other nations just as well. There is hardly one that can say, 'I am a clear-blooded Yankee.' So I can't see whereby I should be benefited." Tribal member Brister C. Michael, too, preferred to "remain as I am, and to hold the lands as we do at the present time. To be a citizen I don't think would be any use to me. I shouldn't be permitted, or any of my sons, to be a juryman. Might do, as some one said a little while ago, to dig out a cesspool, or some other job."[38]

When several congressmen protested that as citizens they would have the right to vote and sit on juries, Michael replied: "That may be, but in Rhode Island there is no such thing. I never knew one on a jury." One congressman tried to suggest that were it not for the land issue, Narragansetts would accept citizenship. But tribal council member Ammons insisted: "You can't bring us out as citizens . . . I don't think that many of these white gentlemen here would like to have any of our nigger tribe hang around your daughters and court them. If we come out citizens, it would be a name without any gain to it. It would sound rather large, it is true, but there wouldn't be much to it."[39]

Only one tribal member, Samuel Congdon, spoke in favor of detribalization, and he admitted that he was the only one in favor. And even Congdon compared tribal government favorably to the harsh rule of Jim Crow in the South: "We are not under restraint like the four and a half million colored people of the South; we are not led to the whipping-post; but I had just as leave be in that condition as under this tribal institution. I have always been in favor of coming out citizens, and having the rights and privileges that other men have."[40]

At the second and third public meetings, tribal members were examined in order to determine tribal enrollment for the purpose of distributing cash payments to the members upon dissolution of the tribe. One individual, Edward Cone, challenged the right to membership of several others, including Joshua Noka. Brister Michael spoke in Noka's defense: "Deacon Cone has made objections to the Noka family as not belonging to the tribe, and he is just as lame as they are. When you come to the point of the law, they have got to be begotten by an Indian man, and any other woman but a negro woman. Now, Cone's mother was a nigger woman, and I know it." Yet Michael raised the objection only to counter Cone's effort to exclude Noka; he did not try to exclude Cone, who he noted had voted and been a member of the tribal council without challenge. When Cone took the stand, council member Ammons expressed some skepticism about his claims to tribal membership: "If we can judge anything from color, we should judge that you was an African." Cone retorted: "Then I should judge that you were. There is not much difference in our color." There was also considerable testimony on tribal practices regarding intermarriage between Indians and Africans, in which several witnesses testified that the child of an Indian and a negro, whether free or slave, was an Indian.[41]

The record of these late-nineteenth-century hearings is striking in its account of such profound solidarity between people who identified as Narragansett and those of African ancestry, as well as in its evidence of the Narragansett's acceptance of racial mixture. There is some evidence that this may have changed by the mid-twentieth century. In 1934, in the aftermath of the Wheeler Howard Indian Reorganization Act, the Narragansett tribe incorporated and began to hold annual reunions and powwows and other cultural events, and to publish a newspaper, the *Narragansett Dawn*. The Indian Office investigated the Narragansett in 1935, finding that despite their history of "intermixture," many were now "strongly anti-negro." The investigators considered that the Narragansett "have suffered many injustices and they deserve a great deal of credit for having made a move to check intermarriage with true negroes." Perhaps by the mid-twentieth century, having grown up in a Jim Crow world, the children and grandchildren of those who had once fought to retain their tribal government had now lost their more inclusive and "national" sense of Narragansett identity. In the twentieth century, for many Indian tribes seeking recognition, like the Lumbee and the Narragansett, nationalism became associated with anti-black feeling. But for the Narragansett, unlike the Lumbee, this was something new.[42]

Other "Racial Islands" in the Jim Crow Era

The Melungeons, the Croatan/Lumbee, and the Narragansett all faced ongoing challenges to their racial identity, and in those conflicts had to adopt more or less conscious strategies to navigate the terrain of Jim Crow America. Yet there were other, smaller racially ambiguous communities that survived well into the twentieth century, particularly in the hollows of Appalachia, with little challenge to their status. Often it was only when members of these communities migrated elsewhere that they ran into challenge, as did the Smilings in Robeson County, and it is only through the records of their cases that we catch a glimpse of the insular "racial islands" from which they came.

Members of these racial islands confounded courtroom fact-finding because they associated with neither whites nor blacks, and lived neither as white nor black. For example, in 1922 Percy Reed faced prosecution for living with a white woman in Alabama. The prosecutor claimed that Reed's grandmother was black; Reed claimed she was mixed Indian and white; and much of the neighbors' testimony suggested that the woman had associated with neither blacks nor whites but was part of a racially ambiguous community like the "creoles." Although the jury found that Reed was a "negro," the verdict was overturned on appeal. Eleven years later the Alabama Supreme Court expressed frustration about the identity of another family, the Farmer children. The court wrote: "It appears the good people of the community are divided on the question . . . It seems from the weight of the evidence this family is of a group known locally in Toulminville as 'creoles.'" While the term was sometimes used to refer to whites, "locally it is applied to a mixed race in which negro blood is present." The court found, however, that "there is and has been, it seems, a division; some recognizing them as white people, others not. Evidence tends to show that in much these creoles, so-called, form a social group of their own. There is no evidence, we believe, that [Farmer] and his family have ever classed themselves as negroes, or socially so identified themselves." Without reaching a decision on their racial identity, the court upheld a jury verdict denying the Farmer children admission to white schools. Whatever the Farmers were, the court seemed to be saying, they certainly weren't "pure white" and so were not entitled to attend whites-only schools.[43]

Neighbors appear to have held different views of these "racial islands": some saw them as people of color, while others viewed them as an intermediate or separate group. This lack of consensus sometimes survived until one of the group moved to a new community, or until some event or person upset the status quo. Thus a Jim Crow–era slander case in Buchanan County, Virginia, reveals the willingness of several small Southern communities to allow racially ambiguous individuals to settle on the white side of the color line, or even to avoid classification altogether. At the same time, the 1914 case *Spencer v. Looney* bears a striking similarity to antebellum cases in which a self-appointed "racial investigator" could turn a family's life upside down by publicly challenging their whiteness and having their children expelled from school.[44]

The Spencers had been members of a racially ambiguous "colony" in Kentucky, probably related to the Melungeons; the other family names in the community included Collins and Ratliff, common Melungeon names.

But when the Spencer family moved to Buchanan County, Virginia, they became close to the Looneys, who were known in their own community as white. The Spencer and Looney families were linked by marriage, work, and social relationships—until Jack Spencer was accused of killing Henderson Looney. The accusation launched a family feud, and George Looney, Henderson's brother, began to accuse the Spencers of being "God damned negroes," going so far as to travel to Kentucky to collect testimony about the "mixed blood" of the Spencer family. Looney even had a Buchanan County school official travel with him so that he could certify that the Spencer children were unqualified to attend white schools. He was successful in having Spencer's children expelled—and Spencer sued Looney for slander some months later.[45]

Buchanan County was known for taking pride in its all-white status: five years before the lawsuit, Klan mobs had ridden through town. In fact this small Appalachian community was known as "the whitest county in Virginia," a rugged, rocky, and steep area with coarse and sandy soil whose main business was strip-mining coal. In the mid-1950s one denizen of the county remembered a lynching that had taken place there earlier in the century: "They rounded the negroes up—some people say that they captured one or two who were innocent—took them to a spreading tree near the brickyard and hanged them, riddling their dangling bodies with bullets . . . It may seem cruel, but it may be the best that the colored people avoid Buchanan County. As long as our County remains all white, we can have no segregation trouble." White supremacy was an unquestioned way of life in Buchanan County.[46]

Yet at the trial of *Spencer v. Looney,* one of the older citizens chuckled about a "right smart sprinkle of African and Indian blood" in the county. Numerous witnesses acknowledged that they had heard rumors about the Spencers yet still accepted them into white society. These witnesses portrayed the rumors of mixed blood as something that surfaced only when there were "difficulties" or when "people were mad," just as had been the case some six decades earlier for the Perkins family in Tennessee. Defense witnesses, by contrast, claimed that it was the "common report" that the Spencers had some negro blood, and that they had been treated as "darkeys." Yet many of the Spencers' white neighbors appeared to believe that the Spencers were white, even with a few drops of "negro blood," because of the way they performed whiteness.[47]

Most of the witnesses who betrayed reluctance to comment on the

Spencers' "blood" acknowledged a lack of familiarity with "negroes" on the grounds that they lived in a nearly all-white community. The witnesses who sent depositions from Kentucky, who did think the Spencers had some mixed blood, were not certain that it was "African blood"; the Spencers appear to have been part of a "colony" of people who lived apart, neither black nor white, even as they claimed to have Indian ancestry. In other words, in Kentucky the Spencers, along with the Collins and Ratliff families, were apparently part of a racially ambiguous family that had not lived as white; when they moved to Buchanan County, they successfully "passed and repassed as white" until they made people "mad." At this point the rumors surfaced. The Looneys, by contrast, were longtime Buchanan County residents: as one chronicler of county history put it, "Looneys, Looneys everwhere!"[48]

On behalf of the plaintiff, witnesses from Johnson County, Kentucky, mostly old men who remembered Spencer's grandfather, gave depositions indicating that the Spencers had attended churches and schools with white people, and had even eaten and slept with them, although they also reported old rumors of "mixed blood" and black hair painted red, rumors that, again, spread whenever "some man would get mad" at them.[49]

Looney introduced other witnesses from Kentucky who painted a somewhat different picture. In their view the Spencers were neither black nor white but "mixed," although the witnesses were not certain what the mixture was or how much "negro blood" the Spencers had. Yet even a witness for Looney confirmed that the "report" about Spencer's race "kindly depended on whether a man would call him a negro or not, when they would get into a difficulty."[50] On cross-examination, when Spencer's attorney tried to get this witness to say that the Spencers had lived among whites, he instead described the racial island the Spencers inhabited: "They had a church in a mile or two miles of where he lived, and about one-half of the congregation had as much color as the Spencers did, but they claim, and their ancestors claimed it was Indian, and some of them were as dark as Jordan Spencer or darker, that is the Collins and Ratliffs." On redirect examination Looney's lawyer asked "how the people in the county regarded that little colony of Spencers, Ratliffs, Collins, &c., I mean what did they think of them as to nationality?" The witness answered: "I don't know only what I heard, that they claimed the Collins, Ratliffs, and Jordan were part Indian . . . We took from his looks, general appearance, and demeanor that he was mixed blooded, and we did not associate a great deal with that class of people, and when he ate at our house he ate at the last table, he has eaten there several times. He never seemed to want to press himself at all; he recognized the fact, and of course, we explained to him, he was a good man, a good worker, and he did good work." He assented when asked, "So you and your family treated him as you would any other darkey?" and went on, "I was always in sympathy with the man, because he tried to be a good man, and tried to avoid looking like a darkey, and because he wanted to raise himself up instead of lowering himself." But the witness made clear that he sympathized with Spencer as a "darkey," not as a white man, at one point correcting the lawyer, "I never said they associated as white people, but with white people." He "had a very high regard for them, and especially the old man, because he wanted to be a white man," but he nevertheless treated him as a "darkey."[51]

Another witness, Wallace LeMasters, also gave evidence suggesting that the "colony" of Spencers and other families might have been a tri-racial community when he testified on the question of Spencer's "negro blood," saying, "I could not judge him; he might have been black Dutch, I don't know." "Black Dutch" was a name used for tri-racial communities like the Melungeons in the mid-Atlantic and Appalachian states, similar to the appellation "Portuguese."[52]

At the end of all the testimony, the jury gave a verdict for Looney, absolving him of the charge of slander. Presumably this amounted to a conclusion that the Spencer children had at least "one-sixteenth negro blood in them," for that is the way the judge instructed the jury. The Virginia Supreme Court overturned this verdict on a variety of grounds: that the trial judge had improperly excluded photographs from the evidence, and that the testimony of various defense witnesses should have been excluded because they were not competent to reach conclusions about the Spencers' racial identity.[53]

Despite the Supreme Court's verdict on technical grounds, the jury in *Spencer v. Looney* acknowledged what everyone in Buchanan County probably knew: the Spencers had some African ancestry, even as they and other families had lived in the racial borderlands of the Appalachian hollows for years. Unlike the Croatan/Lumbee, the Spencers retained no memory of their Indian identity. Unlike the Melungeons, they developed no elaborate origin myths to explain their dark skin. So long as their members did not upset anyone, these racial islands continued to survive, even into the twentieth century—and as the jury verdict made clear, local communities were agreeable to, even actively supportive of, families' claims that they had no "colored blood," despite everyone's implicit knowledge to the contrary. Perhaps neighbors resisted the idea of racial investigators' scrutiny being turned on themselves, and so they rejected the one-drop rule. Perhaps they defined racial identity for themselves more by performance—whether someone "passed and repassed as a white man," whether he "tried to be a good man, and . . . wanted to raise himself up instead of lowering himself"—than by fractions of blood. Perhaps they recognized the "Black Dutch" or "Portuguese" as something other than white but other than "negro" as well.

Another racially ambiguous community that lasted well into the twentieth century were the "white negroes" of Jones County, Mississippi. In fact the county was notorious for its resistance to the Confederacy, a time when it had actually been known as "the Free State of Jones." The Knight clan, leaders of the rebellion, found themselves in court periodically over the course of the century, but the last time was in 1949, when Davis Knight was put on trial for miscegenation for marrying a white woman, Junie Lee Spradley.

The deputy circuit clerk, Nell Graves, had issued the marriage license. She testified that "we can't very well ask them [their race]." She knew that Davis Knight and Junie Lee Spradley were white because Davis had walked into court "with a crowd of white ladies," and "the girl's mother was a white woman, and she was white." Despite Graves's testimony, the trial turned on the racial identity of Davis Knight's great-grandmother Rachel. If there were no other black ancestors, then Rachel had to be a "full-blooded African" for Davis to be more than one-eighth "negro." But the trial revealed complete disagreement within the community about whether Rachel was "negro" or of mixed Indian and European ancestry. In order to prove that the Knights had no black ancestry, the defense attorney, Quitman Ross, pressed witnesses on cross-examination to admit that most Mississippians followed a one-drop rule, asking one, "It is generally true that any person who is known or thought to have Negro blood in them, whether it is little or much, is considered a Negro by White people in the South, isn't it?" The witness avoided this conclusion, answering, "No, no, not necessarily, but you can tell—you can look at a man and tell if he has—if any remarks are made about him, you can look at a man and tell if it is true or not." The witness chose to focus instead on "blood" and racial science, saying at one point, "I think they can tell them by blood, can't they, Quitman?" and later, "If he's got Negro blood in him, he's a negro, isn't he?" The case also turned on associations. The Knights, who belonged to a racially ambiguous community of "white negroes," testified that their associations were neither with whites nor with blacks. Ella Knight, Davis's grandmother, explained, "I went to our private school, with my kind of people." The prosecutor clarified, "In other words, you don't associate with colored people nor white people, just among yourselves?" She answered, "Yes, our own selves."[54]

Although Davis Knight was convicted of miscegenation in December 1948, the Mississippi Supreme Court reversed the verdict, finding that the state had failed to prove beyond a reasonable doubt that Davis had one-eighth or more of "Negro (or Mongolian) blood." As in the racial identity trials of the previous century, courts had to choose between two untenable alternatives: to allow a "black" man to pass as white, or to deny the privileges of whiteness to a man who "deserved" them. Whatever the decision in an individual case, the preoccupation with defining the privileges of citizenship differently according to race continued.

Fifteen years later, in 1963, Davis Knight's sister Louvenia sought to send her children to the white school in Jasper County, Mississippi. The Mississippi State Sovereignty Commission, a state agency set up to protect Jim Crow and subvert the civil rights movement, kept files on the Louvenia Knight case and tried to discourage her from pressing her claim to whiteness. Quitman Ross, Davis Knight's lawyer in the 1948 miscegenation trial, wrote to the commission that he had no intention of helping Louvenia in her suit. Indeed, "in [his] opinion, the forced enrollment of these children in the school in question would bring about needless trouble which might well mount to serious proportions." Ross explained that he had taken Davis Knight's case because he thought it would have been "morally wrong" to let Knight fight in the war as a white man "only to return home and be sent to the penitentiary for, in effect, being a Negro." But he was not willing to help children he considered black attend a white school.[55]

The Sovereignty Commission report concluded that Louvenia Knight's children were white by Mississippi law as they were either one-sixteenth or one-thirty-second Negro. Nevertheless, they faced a problem: "The official attitude in [the town of] Stringer bars the children from the white school; yet, if they enrolled in a Negro school, because they are legally white, Jasper County would have an integrated, public school—the first integration of a public school in Mississippi history." Ironically, the state's most strenuous efforts to support segregation by keeping up a dual school system would result in integrating the "white negroes" into the white school.[56]

The "white negroes" of Jones County, Mississippi, like the Spencers, Ratliffs, and Collinses of Buchanan County, Virginia, all lived for years as distinct communities without a clear racial identification. When families moved out of the area where they had lived for generations, or when the community itself came into closer contact with surrounding neighbors, these ambiguous "mixed" groups were forced to claim a single racial identity. The pressures of Jim Crow, and especially segregated schools, encouraged the disavowal of "negro blood," which reduced a family to second-class citizenship and the dangers of racial violence.

The persistence of racially ambiguous communities challenges the notion of the United States as a binary racial system, but it also calls into question the naïve belief that the mixing of races will eliminate racial hierarchy or injustice. Indeed the histories of these in-between peoples suggest that intermediate and hybrid statuses were precarious, bred the tendency to subordinate the next group down the line, and increased the pressure on all individuals to perform whiteness in order to maintain one's place in a community. Racially ambiguous groups of Indian and African ancestry took radically different paths in the face of Jim Crow: the Melungeons claiming whiteness, the Lumbee asserting Indian identity and rejecting association with blacks, and the Narragansett asserting Indian identity without rejecting their African origins. Other small "islands" simply remained in the racial borderlands, trying to avoid state regulation.

Indian communities which had welcomed African Americans at one point in their history, as well as racially ambiguous communities with varied ancestry, faced enormous pressure during this era to comply with the new rules of Jim Crow. While some of these communities had survived quite successfully as "racial islands," despite all of these pressures in the years leading up to the Civil War—and a few even survived well into the twentieth century—Indian communities fought hard to maintain their place in the racial hierarchy. Those who thought of themselves as Indian and wanted to retain an Indian identity faced difficult choices. The Croatan/Lumbee were relatively successful in maintaining Indian status by distancing themselves from blacks and policing the Indian/black line themselves; the Narragansett, who refused to accept white notions of Jim Crow citizenship, were far less successful. Yet today the Lumbee still have not won federal recognition, despite massive and extremely expensive efforts over several decades. And the national identity of the Narragansett was reinstated only after the Bureau of Indian Affairs approvingly noted the extent of their rejection of blacks in the mid-twentieth century.

In every case, when racially ambiguous groups came before courts or legislatures, the state demanded that they exercise their claims to citizenship through the rejection of blackness. Whether proving Indian or white identity, the community or individual who could show the strongest hatred for "the negro" had the best claim. The only group that refused white imperatives to reject blackness, the Narragansett, suffered de-tribalization and near extinction as an Indian nation until they finally won a land claim settlement from the state of Rhode Island in 1978 and federal recognition as a tribe in 1983. Ultimately the lesson of Jim Crow America was that citizenship meant whiteness, measured in distance from blackness.

CHAPTER FIVE

Black Indian Identity in the
Allotment Era

JUST AS THE NARRAGANSETT lost their tribal sovereignty in the late nineteenth century and were reborn as "colored" U.S. citizens, tribes across the Western United States faced the demise of their tribes as sovereign nations and their rebirth as individuals defined by race. The transformation from nations to races was most dramatic among the "Five Civilized Tribes" of Indian Territory (what is now Oklahoma), all of which included African American members. These black Indian "freedmen," as they became known after the Civil War (whether they had been free or enslaved in the Indian nations, and whether or not they had mixed ancestry), found their possibilities for citizenship radically curtailed by the growing impossibility of a black Indian identity.

In the early twenty-first century the status of the "freedmen" of the Cherokee and Seminole nations is the subject of fierce court battles. In 2003 Seminole chief Kenneth Chambers expressed the official position of the Seminole Nation: "There is no black Seminole." Sylvia Davis, representing a band of Black Seminoles seeking redress from the federal government, said: "When they were on that Trail of Tears there weren't no Freedmen. When we were in Florida, there weren't no Freedmen. Who are these people to say I don't have enough Indian in my blood?" The litigation, which was concluded in favor of the Seminole Nation, turned on the status of Black Seminoles in 1823, the year when Seminole Indians were first removed within Florida by the Treaty of Moultrie Creek. Yet the real turning point for black Indians in what is now Oklahoma came with the era of land allotment and enrollment. The advent of Jim Crow in post–

Civil War Indian Territory drew new boundaries within Indian nations, redefining some people out of Indian identity.[1]

The turn of the twentieth century marked the high point of U.S. imperialism, as well as the country's most aggressive colonial policy toward its own native peoples. At the same time that the United States invaded the Philippines and overthrew the Hawai'ian monarchy, it was implementing an aggressive policy to "pulveriz[e] . . . the tribal mass" on its own shores. The Dawes Allotment Act of 1887, and the legislation that extended the Dawes policy to Indian Territory in 1898, sought to put an end to Indian tribes by breaking up Indian reservations, extinguishing tribal government, and allotting land to individual Indians. Reformers like Henry Dawes believed that individual ownership of land would transform Indians into proper U.S. citizens. All "surplus" lands remaining after Indians received their allotments were sold to white settlers, and most Indians lost their allotted lands within a brief span of years to sales, fraud, and graft.[2]

Before allotment could begin, the government had to decide who should receive allotments, which it did by compiling rolls of names. Land allotment set in motion a process of segregated tribal enrollment that made indigenous peoples into U.S. citizens by incorporating them into a Jim Crow racial order. Until that point, Indian identity under U.S. law had been a hybrid of "race" and "nation"; after that time, Indian nations were shattered and individual Indians were forced to take their places in the U.S. racial hierarchy. Enrollment extended the concept of blood quantum to Indian tribes for the first time, and soon afterwards, new laws tied the ability to sell and control land to a person's blood quantum. Perhaps even more important and far-reaching was the fact that enrollment took all of the familiar ways of knowing someone's racial identity—common sense, appearance, associations, performance—and fixed them forever. One administrative moment of racial knowledge was inscribed and transformed into a fraction or "quantum" carried by every descendant. Segregating the Indian rolls by blood guaranteed that "black Indian" would become an impossible identity.

Africans, Seminoles, and Cherokees

The Seminole Nation did not exist before contact with Europeans; it is rather the result of the political, social, and sexual mingling of Indians and Africans in colonial Florida, beginning in the late seventeenth century. Disparate groups of Creeks migrating from Georgia and Alabama in the wake of war and disease mingled with the remnants of Native Floridians to form the new tribe known as the Seminole Nation. "Seminole" meant "wild" or "runaway" in the Creek language, vividly encapsulating the tribe's identity as a conglomeration of people who had abandoned their former homes and come together in Florida. At the same time, Spain granted asylum to runaway African American slaves from the Carolinas, who created "maroon communities" in Florida, where they struck up alliances with Indians to ward off slave catchers. By the late eighteenth century, some African Americans were already known as "Black Seminoles" or "estelusti." Some whites in the 1830s even used the name "Seminole" to refer to runaway slaves.[3]

Although the Seminoles adopted African slavery toward the end of the eighteenth century, it was very different from slavery as it existed among whites, or even Cherokees and Creeks. Seminole "slaves" lived in separate towns, planted and cultivated fields in common, owned large herds of livestock, and paid their owners only an annual tribute, partly as "protection" from slave catchers. Historians disagree about the cultural integration of the estelusti into the Seminole Nation. Those who view the estelusti as maroon communities argue that they remained culturally separate, intermarrying very little, speaking related but distinct languages, and following different naming practices and religious rituals—two national peoples who maintained close and mutually beneficial military and economic alliances. Others have emphasized the role of those who did intermarry, and those who became valuable members and even leaders of the Seminole Nation, as interpreters and warriors, as well as their overlapping and syncretic cultural practices, including religious rituals, food, and language, which, while not identical, shared much in common. Although we do not know how the Black Seminoles referred to themselves in the early nineteenth century, by the time of the Civil War they were calling themselves "Seminole" or "estelusti," and even those who moved to the Texas-Mexico border in the decades preceding the war called themselves "Indios Mascogos" (Muskogee Indians) and their language "Seminole."[4]

During the 1820s and 1830s the estelusti and the Seminoles were allies in a series of wars against the Americans, although their alliance came under increasing strain. In 1823 six Seminole leaders, including one of some African ancestry known as "Mulatto King," signed the Treaty of Moultrie

Creek, removing the tribe from their fertile lands in northern Florida to swampland south of Tampa. The signers accepted bribes and ultimately unfulfilled promises that they would be allowed to stay on their lands. Another provision of the treaty required the Seminoles to return runaway slaves and turn away any future runaways. Because they rarely did so, other nations of the "Five Civilized Tribes" often considered the Seminoles bad neighbors who threatened the institution of slavery. During the 1830s Black Seminoles were some of the staunchest opponents of "removal" and played a major role in the Second Seminole War, fighting against removal from 1835 to 1842. General Thomas W. Jesup, the leader of the U.S. Army, claimed, "This, you may be assured is a negro and not an Indian war." The army saw its opportunity to divide and conquer by offering freedom to those Black Seminoles who separated from the Indians and surrendered; some did gain their freedom in this way.[5]

By contrast to the relative freedom and incorporation of African members into the Seminole Nation, the other nations of the "Five Civilized Tribes," and particularly the Cherokee, experienced far more stratified race relations. While in 1809 only 583 black slaves resided in the Cherokee Nation, this number had nearly tripled by the time of Indian "removal" to Oklahoma. The Upper Creek and Cherokee nations developed a version of plantation agriculture by the early nineteenth century, with some planters owning upwards of forty slaves. These nations placed increasing restrictions on slaves' autonomy, including attempts to regulate "interracial" marriages of "negroes" with Indians. The Chickasaw and Choctaw of Mississippi and Tennessee practiced particularly harsh forms of slavery, killing slaves for minor offenses by whipping or burning them. The Cherokee, Choctaw, and Creek nations all adopted regulations regarding intermarriage with whites and with "negroes." For example, white spouses and the children of Indian-white marriages became citizens of the Cherokee Nation, whereas marriages between Indians or whites and "negro slaves" was banned in 1824, and the 1827 Cherokee Constitution provided that "descendents of Cherokee men by all free women, except the African race," and "the posterity of Cherokee women by all free men" would become citizens. The child of a free black father and a Cherokee mother, while a citizen, could not hold "any office of profit, honor, or trust under this Government." The Creeks adopted a law making it impossible for children of Creeks and "negroes" to inherit property from their Creek parents, declaring that "the property shall be taken from them and divide among the rest of the children as it is a disgrace to our ~~people~~ Nation for our people to marry a Negro."[6]

By the early 1840s all of the Five Civilized Tribes had been "removed" to Indian Territory, in what is now eastern Oklahoma, and all of them brought African American members with them, some slaves and some free. Those of African ancestry made up 15 to 20 percent of both the Cherokee and Seminole nations, although the Seminoles refused to take a segregated census. Many of the Black Seminoles had won their freedom as a result of the Second Seminole War. Estelusti acted as warriors and interpreters, and held positions of power and leadership within the nation. By contrast, the Cherokees reestablished plantation slavery in Indian Territory. By 1860, although only 10 percent of Cherokee families owned slaves, some 3,500 to 4,000 slaves lived among 21,000 Cherokees. The 1860 Cherokee census also listed a small number of free black heads of household and slaves of mixed Cherokee and African ancestry.[7]

On the eve of the Civil War, the Black Seminole and the Black Cherokee experience stood in sharp contrast: at one pole, a relatively harmonious multiracial nation in which Black Seminoles maintained a strong identity as both African and Indian; at the other a slave society in which racial identity was closely linked to slave status. As a result of the enrollment and allotment process, however, Black Seminoles and Black Cherokees would find themselves in a very similar predicament by the early decades of the twentieth century.

As slaveholders, all five nations officially sided with the Confederacy to defend slavery, although there were also Unionists and even abolitionists among the Five Civilized Tribes. The U.S. government was able to take advantage of Indians' military defeat to further erode Indian sovereignty: when Confederate Indian forces surrendered to Union troops in 1865, the federal government declared all previous treaties nullified by their rebel status and required them to sign new treaties in 1866. Under these new agreements the Five Civilized Tribes ceded the lands that would become the Oklahoma Territory. And because the treaties assumed both that ex-slaves had not previously been citizens of the nations and that the nations would try to drive them away, the treaties provided that in order to be re-admitted to the Union, each nation had to "adopt" its "freedmen" as citizens. Before the Civil War, although the Five Nations did not have very clear-cut conceptions of "citizenship," they did have a concept of "adopting" or incorporating outsiders into the tribe—usually into one's clan or kin group, the most important unit of society. Individual Europeans, Shaw-nee and Delaware Indians, and African Americans had all been "adopted" into the Cherokee Nation back in Georgia. The treaties of 1866 now suggested that all ex-slaves would likewise have to be "adopted" as citizens. One Black Cherokee commented on the irony of the treaty provision: "You talk about adoption," he wrote to the *Vinita Indian Chieftain* newspaper. "It would be a hard matter for the Cherokees to adopt one of their own family." Whatever their status had been before the war—whether free or enslaved or even members of the family—all African Americans in Indian Territory became known as "freedmen."[8]

Like other African Americans during Reconstruction, freedmen spent the immediate postwar years reuniting their families and, in some cases, exercising newfound freedoms. Many returned to the Territory from great distances, especially ex-slaves whose Indian masters had taken them farther south.

Given the close and egalitarian ties between blacks and Indians in the Seminole Nation, the Seminole—and to some extent the Creek—were known as the Indians most "crossed with negro," as one white traveler put it in his diary. The traveler quoted a popular story to illustrate his point: "A Creek said to a Cherokee (Wm P Ross) 'You Cherokees are so mixed with whites we cannot tell you from whites.' The Cherokee Ross replied: 'You Creeks are so mixed with Negroes we cannot tell you from Negroes.'" As this traveler described Wewoka, the Seminole capital, "Shem, Ham & Japhet [representing red, black, and white men] dwelt together in unity & found it sweet & pleasant." Accordingly, Black Seminoles participated equally with other Seminoles in financial payments and land distributions, and even acted as interpreters in the 1866 treaty negotiations. Because the Seminoles of "both races" appeared to get along so well, an agent for the Freedmen's Bureau concluded that "the national laws and customs are sufficient for [the Seminole Freedmen's] protection." In 1869 the U.S. superintendent of Indian affairs could write, "The Seminoles are living in a state of more perfect peace than any other tribe within the superintendency."[9]

At the other extreme, although the Choctaw and Chickasaw reluctantly abolished slavery in the shadow of the Confederacy's defeat, both nations refused to grant citizenship to the freedmen despite long negotiations with the federal government. White travelers who reported back from Choctaw and Chickasaw country painted a dire picture in the immediate aftermath of the Civil War: one government agent wrote that several "colored men" had told him that "these tribes have the bitterest feeling toward the blacks" and had murdered "colored people attempting to travel through their territories"; the agent concluded that "the blacks are suffering a reign of terror." This corresponded with the reputation of Choctaw and Chickasaw slavery as the harshest Indian slave regime. In 1874 the commissioner of Indian affairs observed that the Choctaw and Chickasaw freedpeople were "in an anomalous condition": free but "without equal rights and privileges" since the two nations refused to accept African Americans as citizens. The Choctaw and Chickasaw treaty created a $300,000 fund to pay for Indian lands leased to the United States, but the U.S. government held the fund in trust until the tribes either gave freedmen full citizenship or used the money to buy separate lands for the freedmen. In the event, freedmen were neither accepted into the Choctaw and Chickasaw nations nor granted separate territories. They simply remained in the Choctaw and Chickasaw nations, where, as the Choctaw Colored Citizens' Association complained to the Dawes Commission several decades later, they were the victims of "unjust and ruinous discrimination." Choctaw Freedmen demanded the right to vote, a share in per capita annuity and "leased district" payments, equal allotments in land, and suitable schools. The Choctaw eventually adopted their freedmen in 1883, but the Chickasaw never did. The Chickasaw Freedmen sued for citizenship, but in 1904 the U.S. Supreme Court found that they were neither adopted citizens of the Chickasaw Nation nor entitled to the $300,000 set aside for their removal—because they had not been removed. Black Chickasaws were truly "people without a country."[10]

The struggles of Cherokee Freedmen for citizenship and land rights also began immediately after the Civil War. The "Southern faction" of the Cherokee, led by Elias Cornelius Boudinot and Stand Watie, advocated U.S. government removal of Black Cherokees to another territory at government expense. The Northern Cherokee under the leadership of Lewis Downing wanted the ex-slaves adopted and given an area of land for their exclusive use. In general, they opposed the postwar treaty with the United States and feared the loss of their sovereignty. Downing led a delegation to the Senate to ask: "Senators: Shall we stand dumb before you like a sheep before its shearer? Shall we lie down supinely and see our national governments destroyed and ourselves despoiled of our lands?" The result was a compromise in which the Cherokee Nation limited citizenship for "freedmen" to those who returned to the nation within six months, which excluded many of those whom Cherokees had enslaved.[11]

The debate over citizenship for those "too-lates" presaged the view that more and more Indians would take during the era of enrollment and allotment: that black Indians were not full citizens of Indian nations but rather intruders bent on taking land rightfully belonging to Indians. The editor of the *Cherokee Advocate* expressed "sympathy" for the "unfortunate colored persons" who had arrived too late to enroll, but added, "As much as we feel for the former slaves of Cherokee masters, we confess to feeling more for those Cherokees who did not own any slaves at all—by far the majority of the Nation—whose inheritance it was proposed to divide with the freedman."[12]

The freedmen themselves objected to what they saw as a disinheritance. Like many enslaved people under U.S. rule, they understood that their labor had built the wealth of the Cherokee Nation which was now proposing to exclude them. As one Cherokee Freedman complained in a letter to President Ulysses S. Grant: "Most of the Cherykees is down on the darkys. The Cherykees says they aint in favour of the black man havin any claim, that they had rather any body else have a rite than us poor blacks . . . [Lewis] downing is for us, Chelater [Oochalata], and mr. Six killer, them tree [sic] is in our favour, and what can they doo with so many [on the other side]: . . . [We] all don't think it rite to[o], after we have made them rich and built their land, doo you[?]" This freedman echoed sentiments expressed by many ex-slaves about their ownership in the land they had worked as slaves, and marked a growing rift within the Cherokee Nation along racial lines.[13]

The land known as "Indian Territory" had been established in 1830 to serve as the home for Indian tribes removed from the Eastern United States. At first it had spanned most of what is now Kansas, Nebraska, and Oklahoma, but in 1854 the Kansas-Nebraska Act carved two states out of it, leaving only the remainder as "Indian Territory." Many Indians had lived in that region before the Territory was established—Osage and others resided in the east, while the Wichita and Arapaho occupied the west—but Indian removal in the 1830s brought a major influx of Indian population from the Southeast, in particular the Cherokee, Creek, Choctaw, Chickasaw, and Seminole nations. Accordingly, the Osage were relocated within the Territory to make room for the Five Nations in the 1830s, and after 1866 the western Oklahoma tribes were conquered and relocated as well. After the Civil War, as punishment for siding with the Confederacy the federal government forced the Five Nations to sell a large part of their territory to the United States, some of which was used to create reservations for some of the previous occupants of "Indian Territory"—the Iowa, Kickapoo, Pottawotamie and Shawnee, Sac and Fox, Cheyenne and Arapaho nations—and some of which became known as the "Unassigned Lands." Thus, in the late 1860s, Indian Territory comprised three types of land: reservations for its former occupants, lands owned collectively by the "Five Civilized Nations," and "Unassigned Lands" owned by the U.S. government.

Indians were not the only ones moving to Indian Territory, however. In the aftermath of the Civil War, African Americans from the South saw Kansas and Oklahoma as a potential promised land of freedom. Moved by the exhortations of black leaders such as Booker T. Washington, who preached a doctrine of racial separation and black self-sufficiency, and drawn to the hope of frontier-style equal opportunity, some five thousand African Americans moved to Indian Territory in the first quarter century after the Civil War and established their own communities there. By 1900 they had built twenty-three all-black towns, mostly on sites that originated as freedmen's allotments in the Creek Nation—the allotments granted to the Creek Freedmen when the Dawes and Curtis acts carved up Indian lands into individual parcels. For example, the well-known black town of Boley, Oklahoma, was formed on the site of a Creek Freedwoman's allotment.

The black immigrants' purchase of freedmen's land for their communities gave rise to considerable tension and resentment among "native" freedmen, who resisted the arrival of those they called "state negroes" or "watchina." ("Watchina" was the Muskogee word for "white man," as in "white man's negro.") When interviewed by the Works Progress Administration (WPA) in the 1930s, many black Oklahomans recalled that Indian freedmen "broke up church services and other public gatherings with gunfire and periodically amused themselves by riding through Boley . . . late at night shooting out windows." Perhaps ironically, the two initially separate black communities—freedmen and immigrants—eventually united under the pressure of white and Indian hostility to all African Americans during the first decades of the twentieth century.[14]

While a source of friction, these all-black towns were dwarfed in significance by the massive white immigration to the Territory. After the Civil War ended, white settlers began streaming into Indian Territory. In the late 1870s and early 1880s they put pressure on Washington to open up the land they deemed "surplus"—land not assigned to reservations or being used for agriculture or ranching by Indians. In 1889 the Unassigned Lands were the first part of the Territory opened to white settlers in a massive "land run." "Boomers" gathered on the Kansas border to make a run to claim their homesteads; those who jumped the gun were known as "Sooners." Land runs were also used in the early 1890s to settle the Cherokee Outlet (a strip of the northern part of the Territory taken from the Cherokee), the Cheyenne and Arapaho reservation, and the Iowa and Kickapoo lands. In 1890 the Unassigned Lands and other parts of eastern Oklahoma were merged to form the new Oklahoma Territory, leaving still less land for Indians. While the Oklahoma Territory was opened to settlement in races and lotteries, white settlers came to Indian Territory not in rushes but in a slow stream over several decades. Cherokee leader Elias Boudinot, an advocate of the allotment policy, sent a letter to the *Chicago Times* in 1879, widely copied in other newspapers, advertising "unoccupied" public land in Indian Territory, and tens of thousands of white settlers poured in as a result. With no legal claim to Indian lands, they established themselves as squatters. White settlement was further spurred by the arrival of the railroad, with the first tracks laid between 1870 and 1872; throughout the 1880s rail mileage increased rapidly.

Thus, when Indian Territory was merged with the Oklahoma Territory to form the state of Oklahoma in 1907, whites constituted the vast majority of inhabitants, with Indians and blacks a small minority. Whereas in 1870 whites had made up only 3 percent of the population of Indian Territory, by 1890 they were 61 percent of its people; although the black population tripled during those years, blacks remained just 10 to 11 percent of the total population, and Indians dwindled from 87 to 28 percent of the total. Charles Meserve, the president of Shaw University in North Carolina, traveled to the Indian Territory in 1896 at the behest of the Indian Rights Organization to investigate the land allotment issue. He observed mordantly in his report: "Come with me to the Indian Territory, and remember when you enter it that all this vast domain with its tremendous natural resources belong to the *Indian* and that this property is all held (theoretically) in common. But whom do you see? *White* men, *white* men everywhere! The scarcest object is an Indian, and this is the *Indian* Territory set apart by solemn treaty obligation for the *Indian.*" Meserve noted that a white man in the Seminole Nation had defined an Indian to him as "a trustee of the title to the land in the interest of the white man."[15]

The white people flooding Oklahoma were predominantly Southerners and Midwesterners who had moved farther west in the hope of escaping sharecropping by buying their own farms, and most of them probably had not held slaves themselves. Yet their worldviews had been shaped by the doctrines of white supremacy, and many who came from the former states of the Confederacy were still seething with resentment at the Northern victory, for which they blamed Lincoln, the Republican Party, and the former slaves. These settlers did not necessarily discover in Indian Territory the economic opportunities of which they had dreamed. The Territory's new white residents soon found themselves once again tenants or sharecroppers, because immigrant aliens were not allowed to own land. The dusty desert that nobody had wanted—land so worthless that it could safely be reserved for Indians—shot up in value when oil and gas were discovered there at the turn of the century. The first oil well was drilled in 1897, and the big oil boom began in 1900. Over the next thirty-five years, 9 billion barrels of crude oil were pumped in Oklahoma, making the state the biggest oil producer in the country for twenty-two of those thirty-five years. During that time Oklahoma's agricultural economy became transformed into an economy dominated by oil and coal extraction; this enormous change led to increasing conflict between tenant farmers and laborers on the one hand and landlords and employers on the other.

What united the elite landowner and landless tenant was the Democratic Party, which came into power in Oklahoma—and throughout the United States—on a wave of white supremacy, encouraging rural farmers to blame African Americans and their "rich Republican allies" for the economic disenfranchisement resulting nationwide from the spread of corporate power and ever larger businesses. Throughout the United States the Democrats were heavily pro-segregation, and they rose to power in Oklahoma at a time when Jim Crow had already been established across the South and ratified by the U.S. Supreme Court in *Plessy v. Ferguson.* The Oklahoma state constitution, promulgated in 1907, was the result of popular agitation among virulently Jim Crow ex-Southerners, and of 112 delegates to the state convention, 99 were Democrats. Statewide, Republicans dominated the Territory until statehood; after statehood, not only did the Democratic Party triumph, but "lily-white Republicanism" drowned out memories of the "Party of Lincoln" as both parties united against the threat of "negro domination."[16]

The Oklahoma constitution set in stone an extreme level of segregation in public accommodations. Black people could not attend public schools, ride in railroad coaches, or drink from the same water fountains as white people or Indians. The constitution reflected the new understanding of race that had become current in America by the early twentieth century, so that, ironically, Oklahoma's constitution was more extreme and explicit on the subject of race than most of those in the former Confederacy. South Carolina and Mississippi, for example, adopted new constitutions in the late nineteenth century, mostly for the purpose of disfranchising African Americans through poll taxes and literacy tests for voting, but unlike the Oklahoma constitution, they did so in race-neutral language. The state constitution did not simply segregate black from white, however. It also specified that only those of African descent—not Indians—were subject to Jim Crow. This extreme separation—both the mindset that produced it and the specific racial designations on which it depended—was the result of the segregated tribal rolls created by the Dawes Commission for the purpose of land allotment. In separating Indians from blacks, the commission opened the door to Jim Crow, racialized Indians once and for all, removed the last vestiges of Indian nationhood, and guaranteed the separation of Indians from blacks in the new Oklahoma. The state constitution reinforced and extended the process begun in allotment. As Jim Crow progressed in Oklahoma, Indians hurried to associate themselves with whites and to separate themselves from "negroes."

Even the most integrated of the tribes, the Seminole, became segregated like the rest. Black Seminoles interviewed from the 1930s through the 1960s portrayed a pre-statehood society in which African Americans and Native Americans had mingled closely, including intermarriage and the cultural integration that resulted. Carrie Marshall Pitman was the daughter of a Seminole Freedman, born in Texas; in 1878 she moved back to the Nation and married a Seminole Indian. Fannie Rentie Chapman, a Creek Freedwoman, married a Seminole first and then a "colored non-citizen." Primus Dean, a Black Seminole, was born in 1896 of parents who had migrated with the tribe from Florida. Asked by a WPA interviewer in the 1930s whether the Black Seminoles had adopted Seminole customs and were "just almost identical in the way they lived," Dean agreed:

"That's right almost identical—we could make that obusky, sofky, echo dry that beef on the house, beat that up, call that—what did they call that, I forgot. The name we call that—but anyhow, we'd beat that beef up and it'd be kinda fine and stringy like, you know. And boy, you put that thing in your pot, little salt, little water . . ." Dean also recounted his parents' stories about slavery days: "No, these Seminoles they didn't consider them slaves. They just considered them one of the family." Dean remembered his parents' descriptions of cooking, eating, working, and going to sleep together with the Indians.[17]

Schools were also integrated in Seminole Nation before the state constitution established segregation. Dave McIntosh, a Black Seminole born in 1879, remembered going to school with mostly "colored" pupils but with two Indians as well. McIntosh's father had been a Seminole lighthorseman, or warrior. McIntosh remembered that there was "not a bit of difference" between Seminoles and Black Seminoles when he was young: "What you had, I had; what I had, you had." When the interviewer prompted, "An[d] if an Indian came to you, you shared with him, and—," McIntosh finished the sentence, "Just like I would anybody else, yes suh, yes suh." A number of other Black Seminoles also remembered integrated schools, telling interviewers about their attendance at the Mekuskey Mission School. As an anthropologist summed it up in 1951, "in the memories of most older Freedmen, the coming of statehood to Oklahoma is a very prominent event," for he was repeatedly told that before statehood Indians and blacks were "all as one."[18]

After statehood in 1907, however, blacks and Indians grew increasingly separate, not only in school but in the wider culture as well. Primus Dean remembered that "they Jim Crowed us, but we didn't quit school until 1910." According to Charlie Johnson, a "blood" Seminole born in 1901, a "lot of our Indian children those days couldn't speak a word of English. And we went to school in just one big building." As he recalled in 1969: "We must [have] had about four classrooms, I suppose. And we went to school with the colored children. I imagine those colored children were Freedman's children. And a lot of them spoke Indian. And then when we couldn't talk English, well we tried to talk in Indian. We'd get caught. Why we'd get demerits for it. But it was good for us. That was encouraging us to learn how to talk English." The interviewer asked Johnson if he remembered when the "Negroes" were "Jim Crowed" out of the school. Johnson answered: "That, I don't really remember. But I do remember them quitting school. I didn't know for what reason."[19]

As the Seminole narratives described, statehood in Oklahoma meant the separation of freedmen and Indians in numerous schools that had been mixed, accompanied by a vigorous effort in some areas to integrate Indians into white schools. Their memories are supported by contemporary evidence: in 1911 the federal supervisor of Indian schools, John B. Brown, reported that "county officials were urged to put the Indian on a level with the white neighbor" in schools, and that "in very few localities has there been found any race prejudice against the coeducation of the white and Indian." The Oklahoma constitution, defining Indians as legally "white," was found to "accentuate . . . the natural friendship and the ties of blood which in many cases unite the red and the white race in eastern Oklahoma. By contrast, [w]here an Indian shows any degree of negro blood, there is immediate and violent objection to his admission to the public school of the whites, and the State law forbids it." While the 1907 state constitution was the formal document that established segregation, that constitution would never have been possible without the allotment process that established the racial categories at its foundation.[20]

Enrollment and Allotment

The first stage in land allotment was enrollment. The Dawes Commission had to decide what criteria to use for enrolling tribal citizens and how to divide the rolls. In doing so, the commission for the first time instantiated "blood quantum" as a meaningful juridical category, first by separating the rolls for "Indians by blood" and "freedmen," and then by noting fractions of blood by individuals' names. The first step in this process was the 1898 legislation itself, which authorized the commission to make separate rolls for "Cherokees by blood," "Cherokee Freedmen," "adopted Shawnees and Delawares," "intermarried whites," and similarly segregated lists for each of the other nations except for the Seminole. There was to be only one Seminole roll: Congress had determined that in every other nation the freedmen required special protection of their rights, but that in the Seminole Nation their rights were secure. Furthermore, Congress considered the Seminole so mixed that separate rolls would not make sense. Yet the commission made separate lists for the Seminole Freedmen as well, explaining that "while the law does not specifically require a separate roll of [Seminole Freedmen], the commission's data will enable it to so separate them." The implication seemed to be that separation was so desirable as to require no explanation; if it was possible, it should be done.[21]

Despite its obsession with racial classification, however, the commission showed what to modern eyes seems a surprising lack of regard for accurate classification. The Curtis Act had specifically instructed the commission not to rely on earlier tribal rolls, which had been drawn up by the tribes on an ad hoc basis. Yet the commissioners made heavy use of the earlier rolls, especially to exclude individuals who had not appeared on one of them. Indeed, a 1909 Report on Enrollment by the secretary of the interior found this to be a major defect in the enrollment process and went on to detail the many inadequacies of these earlier rolls. For example, the Choctaw Census Roll of 1896 included many penciled notations such as "don't enroll," "dead," and "doubtful," and all of those names were left off the Dawes Commission rolls. Yet the Choctaw Census was hardly a rigorously prepared document: on one of the Choctaw rolls, the interior secretary noted disapprovingly, could be found "directions in regard to painting and paint brushes. On page 236 are cooking recipes for making buns and French rolls, for preparing brine to preserve butter, pickling tomatoes, and preparing chopped pickle, Chile sauce, and tomato catsup." Some other, much better preserved census rolls were found later, but these were never used by the Dawes Commission. Yet while the commission was willing to leave off people whose names were on the rolls, it almost never enrolled anyone whose name was *not* on a previous roll.[22]

The Dawes Commission was at pains to dispel the idea that "the work of making rolls of 'Indians' is a comparatively simple matter." Because the rolls had to include "full-blood Indians, negroes, and white men, with every intervening degree of blood," Indian "blood" was not "the sole qualification for citizenship in Indian Territory" and sometimes "was not even an element." The commissioners also lamented that an 1895 court decree, resulting from the Cherokee Freedmen's efforts to share in per capita payments to the tribe, required them to follow special instructions for enrolling the freedmen. The court decree prohibited the nation from discriminating between "Cherokee citizens of Cherokee blood or parentage" and "Cherokee citizens who are or were freedmen . . . as well as all free colored persons."[23]

In order to make payments to Cherokees for lands sold to the United States, Congress had already authorized several Cherokee Freedmen rolls, all of which the Cherokee Nation claimed were corrupt and "contain[ed] many names not properly belonging there." Finally, in 1901 the Dawes Commission began its own enrollment, starting from the earlier rolls, but enrolling less than half the number. In the end, the Dawes Rolls included fewer than half of the freedmen who applied, and even then, citizens of the Cherokee Nation sued the commission for enrolling too many freedmen. Although Cherokee citizens would all receive 160 acres regardless of how many people applied (with the remainder sold as "surplus"), Cherokees were convinced by the per capita payments of the late nineteenth century that the pie was finite, and that more freedmen citizens meant less to go around.[24]

Both officials and applicants painted a picture of considerable chaos at the enrollment sites. The Dawes Commission traveled with a caravan, pitching a small tent city of three commissioners, a stenographer, a translator, and several secretaries. In every town they tried to employ a member of the tribe to translate in each enrollment tent, though when this was not possible, they did without. There were two tents: one known as the "Indian tent" and one known as the "nigger tent" or "darky tent." Commissioner Archibald McKennon, who had been a Confederate army captain, was in charge of the tent for persons applying as freedmen, and Melvin Cornish, who later became the lawyer representing the commission, served as his stenographer. Cornish later claimed that no notes were taken in his tent beyond the information entered by clerks on "field or census cards," which included the names of family members, age, and sex. These cards were divided into "Straight" cards, for individuals who appeared on earlier tribal rolls, and "Doubtful" or "D" cards for those who did not; only a relatively small number of "Doubtful" applicants were ever later admitted to citizenship.[25]

Once an individual ended up in one tent or the other, it was assumed that his or her identity was already fixed; the true determination happened outside the tents. The tribal member standing at the door, along with any officials who may have been outside, directed individuals to one tent or the other on the basis of personal knowledge of an applicant's family or status in the community, or according to the applicant's appearance or performance. Applicants who later sought to be transferred from the freedman rolls to the Indian by blood rolls described these directions as arbitrary and unfair. Lula Seitz, who claimed to have a Choctaw citizen father and freedman mother, testified before the commission that she was enrolled by "Mr. Linton Tell [one of the commissioners] and a fellow by the name of Cohee [Charles Cohee, a "mixed" Black Choctaw leader] and a colored man. There were a lot of tents there, but Mr. Tell says 'That is where you go.'" Her lawyers questioned her, "Did you ask to be enrolled as a freedman?" and she answered, "I knew I didn't have anything, any right, of course." Rebecca Williams testified in the same case about the way she had enrolled, and, like Seitz, she too seemed to feel she didn't "have . . . any right." She first described her conversation with an agent sent to the Indian Territory town of South McAlester to publicize enrollment. He "said they were going to close the rolls and they said they were enrolling everything from one to a thousand." Rebecca recalled asking, "Are they giving the mixed bloods a right?" and was told, "Come down and see for yourself." She described going to Tishomingo, one of the local enrollment centers, to appear before the commission, intending to enroll as a Choctaw by blood: "I went there and I didn't want to go in with the negroes and then one of them [the officials] almost forced me to go." Rebecca described her conversation with "those leading men" about which tent she should go into:

> I asked Linton Tell what was going on in that tent. He says "Enrolling."
> And I says "What is going on in that tent?" And he says "Enrolling." I ask
> him about several tents and then I says "What about that tent" and he says
> "The niggers," and then I asked him about another tent and he said "Indi-
> ans." I started to go there but Mr. Linton Tell stopped me. We got into a
> little fuss. He spoke very insulting to me, told me that was the place for me,
> among the negroes. I told him that wasn't. He disposed of me so: he says to
> me "You are nothing but a negro." I says "you are blacker and you look
> more like a negro than I do" . . . Me and him had quite a little quarrel out
> there.

Rebecca explained that after this quarrel she was crying loudly, having "a big bellowing spell," and finally Julius Folsom, a local judge, took charge of her enrollment himself, taking her before Captain McKennon in the "freedman tent" and giving McKennon the information that she was a former slave, even though she contradicted him. As she said: "I spoke to Captain McKennon. I told him I wanted to file with the Indians. Judge Folsom told who I was . . . and I was so swelled up I didn't say anything." Nevertheless, she asserted that she was "never a slave. It is no disgrace to say it if it was so." Judge Folsom claimed to know Rebecca's former owners, and to speak from personal knowledge. Later, before the commission, Rebecca denied that he knew her owners, indeed denied having been a slave, but she had shrunk from pressing her case before the commissioners at the time of enrollment.[26]

In many cases, "freedman" applicants showed reluctance to describe themselves as slaves, or else revealed understandings different from the commissioners' of what it meant to be enslaved. For example, Ellen Perry, who was about eighty when she went before the commission to ask to be transferred to the "Choctaw by blood rolls," was asked, "You were a slave of a Chickasaw Indian?" She answered: "Yes sir. My mother was a Choctaw but they held me as a slave." After discussing her enslavement to the family of Frank Colbert, she was reminded of her earlier testimony in Bill Colbert's case before the commission: "At that time this question was asked you . . . 'Were you a slave during the war?' Your answer was 'No sir.'" When asked to explain, Ellen answered: "In one sense I would consider I was not a slave. My mother was a Choctaw and I don't see how I could be a slave." Asked, "Did you know at that time that you were the slave of Frank Colbert during the war?" she replied, "I don't know whether I was or not but I know I was taken as a slave and used as a slave." Ellen distinguished between the *fact* of having been "held" or "taken" or "used" as a slave and her Choctaw status, which affected someone's *right* to hold her as a slave, suggesting that she had been a slave in fact, but not rightfully so. Later Ellen was asked about her mother's status, and she answered: "I can't say my mother was a slave—I can't say that . . . My mother was a Choctaw and I just can't see how it was that we were held slaves. My mother was called an Indian and we were called slaves." Nancy Fulsom, Ellen's half-sister, similarly explained how she knew that her father was a slave to Frank Colbert: "He had to stay there and work for Frank and Frank whipped him. I saw him myself tie him up and whip him until the blood run to his heels. That is the reason he must have belonged to Frank." Nancy did not think that her mother was a slave because "she always told us she was an Indian by blood," and "she had horses, hogs and cattle."[27]

Just as antebellum Southerners tried to prove whiteness by citing their civic participation, so did applicants from the Five Civilized Tribes try to prove Indian membership by testifying about ways that the tribe had recognized their Indian identity besides putting their names on the tribal rolls. For example, Kelo Brown testified that he "held the jury and voted and everything," and that he mustered in the Chickasaw militia. Brown sought Chickasaw citizenship not on the basis of Chickasaw blood but be-

cause his mother, a Creek Indian, had been stolen and adopted by Chickasaws back in Mississippi. They also relied on a version of racial common
sense. Joe Stanley, a "Choctaw freedman," testified at length about his
ability to distinguish Choctaw from Chickasaw Indians. The freedmen's
lawyer elicited testimony from Stanley that a certain person was a Choctaw: "Do you know he was a Choctaw?" the lawyer asked. "I know it."
Stanley repeatedly insisted on his knowledge but refused to state a basis
for knowing a man's identity. The questioning by the lawyer continued:

"Can you, by looking at an Indian tell whether he is a Choctaw?"

"Certainly I can tell."

"Can you tell the difference between a Choctaw and Chickasaw?"

Stanley shifted his ground slightly: "He always went as a Choctaw." This
answer was stricken. The second answer he gave was "Pretty Much; if I
can't do it that way I can by the language." Asked again if he could distinguish in general between Choctaws and Chickasaws, Stanley again insisted
that he could tell about the individual in question. The lawyer asked the
question again several times. Stanley answered: "The difference I don't
know—there is as much difference as there is between a white man and a
black man."

"There is as much?"

"Not so much; I can't tell these Creek Indians; I can hardly tell, but I
know it's the tribe."

After a while Stanley admitted that "by looks you couldn't tell," but nevertheless reiterated, "I come here swearing he is a Choctaw and I'll go
back swearing it and money can't make me say anything else."[28]

Susan Brashears described the moment when she was directed toward
enrollment as a freedman. She did not know the people who were enrolling at Goodland; "they were strangers to me." Later, when Susan applied
to transfer from the freedman rolls, she was asked:

"Who was off to one side? Indians at one table and colored people at
one table?"

"Yes sir."

"You went where the colored people were did you not?"

"Yes sir."

"If you were an Indian and claimed Indian rights why did you not go
where the Indians were?"

"Well, they would have pushed me away."

"You are quite positive that they would have pushed you away?"

"Yes sir."

Her own lawyer then questioned her:

"Why did you say that if you had have gone up to the table where they were enrolling Indians they would have pushed you away, what makes you think they would?"

"My old man wasn't there at the time, I couldn't go up by myself, if he had been living I might have walked up with him."

"Well, that would not be sufficient for making you think you couldn't go up there, wasn't other colored people going up there?"

"You see we just had to go in and come right out, they would not allow us in there."[29]

Individuals who testified about their enrollment as freedmen repeatedly expressed a sense of helplessness: despite their own belief in their claims to Indian identity, they were quite certain that they had no choice but to enroll as freedmen because white officials had already made the determination of their identity, whether on the basis of their appearance, reputation, or associations with other freedmen.

Meanwhile, inside the "Indian" tents, people were being classified with a blood quantum as either "full blood," "half blood," or "three-quarters blood." Records of the questioning that went into these designations suggest that the interviews may have been quite cursory and the determinations arbitrary. For example, Redbird Smith stated that his mother's father was a "Dutchman." Commissioner Clifton Breckinridge (who replaced McKennon in 1900) then asked him, "You are about three-quarter Cherokee then are you?" Smith replied, "About that." He was then listed as "three-quarters," although historians always refer to him as a "full blood." This may be a result of Redbird Smith's later testimony before a 1905–6 Senate committee investigating problems with enrollment and allotment. Smith and the committee had the following exchange:

The Committee: Are you a full-blood Indian?

Smith: I am Cherokee.

The Committee: Are you a full blood or part blood?

Interpreter: From my experience he must be a full blood.

Smith: I think I must be a full blood; I don't know, but I think I am.

The Committee: From your experience you must be a full-blood Cherokee Indian?

Smith: Yes, sir.

In this exchange Redbird Smith seems initially to reject the distinction between "full blood" and "part blood," and certainly to express uncertainty about what a "full blood" is; the interpreter bases his own determination on "experience," and the committee seems to accept this as a valid basis. Yet Smith had apparently stated in 1900 that he was three-quarters Cherokee. Clearly these distinctions meant far less to him—at least at the time—than they meant later to both whites and Indians, after enrollment had greatly expanded the significance of blood quantum.[30]

Before the allotment process began, designations of "full blood" and "mixed blood" had been politically salient terms. White officials used the terms "half blood" and "mixed blood" to stand for "politically progressive"—that is, assimilationist, in favor of U.S. citizenship and adoption of American land use practices—whereas "full blood" meant to them "conservative" or "traditionalist" as much as it referred to any actual designation of ancestry. But these distinctions first took on legal and economic significance only after enrollment and allotment, when federal legislation passed in 1904 and 1908 lifted restrictions on the right to sell or transfer one's land allotment according to blood quantum. Initially, according to the Curtis Act, all land allotments were inalienable—could not be sold or transferred—for twenty-five years. This paternalist provision was supposedly for the protection of ignorant and naïve Indians. Nevertheless, unscrupulous grafters were still able to secure ninety-nine-year leases on Indian allotments for rents as low as one dollar per 160 acres. The 1904 and 1908 laws created a new system marked by "blood": people of less than "one-half Indian blood," "intermarried whites," and "freedmen" could sell their land with no restrictions, while "full bloods" maintained the full twenty-five-year restriction, and those of one-half to three-fourths blood could sell all but their forty-acre homestead, which was restricted. Thus the distinction between "full" and "part blood" that seemed insignificant to Redbird Smith in 1900 came to have enormous import just a few years later.[31]

Appealing Enrollment

Because no records exist of how people ended up on "freedman" or "blood" rolls, the best extant evidence of these decisions comes from an unusual set of hearings the Dawes Commission held in cases in which individuals sought to transfer from "freedman" onto "blood" rolls. The commission had followed conflicting practices with regard to children who had one parent on a "freedman roll" and one on an "Indian roll," enrolling such children with one parent or the other, either allowing them to "elect" which parent to enroll with or simply enrolling the child as a freedman if the official believed that the child had any "negro blood." In 1905 the assistant attorney general of the Department of the Interior issued a decision in the "Joe and Dillard Perry Case" declaring that children should be able to elect to enroll with one parent or the other. This decision led to a series of cases in which individuals formerly enrolled as freedmen on the basis of their mother's affiliation sought to transfer to the "by blood" rolls because they had an Indian father.

The reach of the "Joe and Dillard Perry Case" extended only to the Choctaw and Chickasaw nations, for it was only among these peoples that officials believed the freedmen were being denied their rights. The 1909 Dawes Commission Report on Enrollment explained: "Persons of mixed Indian and negro blood who were enrolled as freedmen, in the Cherokee, Creek and Seminole nations did not suffer a property loss by reason thereof owing to the fact that such freedmen became citizens of the respective nations by adoption, acquiring thereby all the property rights of citizens by blood in respect to the final distribution of the land and money of said tribes." The words "did not suffer a property loss by reason thereof" were written in and the words "is not a matter of much importance at this time" were crossed out beneath them. Either way, except among the Choctaw and the Chickasaw, the commissioners claimed that the designation of "Indian" or "freedman" would make little difference to any citizen of Oklahoma—a belief that was sadly out of kilter with the 1907 Oklahoma state constitution, which brought strict Jim Crow regulations to schools and public places. Focusing narrowly on the question of how many acres each allotted citizen would receive, the commissioners ignored the larger issue of second-class citizenship for African Americans in the United States.[32]

For a brief window in 1906–7 the Dawes Commission considered hundreds of applications from people enrolled as Choctaw and Chickasaw Freedmen to transfer from the "freedman" to the "by blood" rolls. Most applicants for transfer claimed to be children of Choctaw or Chickasaw fathers and "freedman" mothers, although some claimed to have an Indian mother and a "negro" father. In their transfer hearings, virtually all of them described how they had been enrolled as freedmen despite having asserted an Indian identity or told about an Indian father.

Fannie Rodgers, who had enrolled her children as Chickasaw Freedmen, remembered that she had told the Dawes Commission that the children's father was Charles Eastman, an Indian enrolled on the Chickasaw Indian roll, but that they "just laughed a little and put the children down just the same; got their rights." Her lawyer asked, "Did you tell the Dawes Commission at that time that your children was of white blood or colored blood or what?" The lawyer for the Chickasaw Nation objected to the question as leading and suggestive, so her lawyer changed his question to ask simply, "Tell what you said about it?" Rodgers explained: "They asked who was their father; I told them Charles Eastman was their father; they asked me if I was married to him and I told them no; they just laughed; that is all that was said."[33]

In the midst of the Dawes Commission hearings on applications for transfer, the Senate Committee on Indian Affairs held hearings on the Choctaw and Chickasaw Indians to consider legislation specifically to authorize the transfer from "freedman" to "by blood" rolls "the name of any person who is of Indian blood or descent on either his or her mother's or father's side." Webster Ballinger and Albert J. Lee, the lawyers for many of the transfer applicants who had been "arbitrarily enrolled as freedmen," urged Congress to act because, despite the lengthy hearings, the commission had not actually approved any transfers: "Not one single name of a person on the freedman roll has been transferred to the roll of citizens by blood," asserted Ballinger and Lee. The commission and the Department of the Interior had "resorted to every technicality known to them" to keep from transferring freedmen to blood rolls. The main device they used was section 4 of the legislation, which prohibited transfer "unless application for enrollment as citizen by blood was made within the time prescribed by law." This catch-22 meant that unless the Dawes Commission had recorded the applicant's effort to be enrolled by blood, or the applicant could produce some documentation of an application to enroll on the blood rolls, the applicant was now denied transfer to those rolls. Yet it was precisely because the Dawes Commission had refused to allow applicants the opportunity to apply for "by blood" enrollment that they had been enrolled as freedmen.[34]

At the Senate hearings, attorneys Ballinger and Lee described typical cases in which families were divided between the two rolls. Ballinger reported that "nine of [Joe Jackson's] children are on the freedmen roll with their mother. The last-born child is on the Indian roll with its father." The senators questioned the freedmen's lawyers about "Indian customs." All of the senators apparently assumed that the Indians must have followed a "one-drop rule" regarding African ancestry. Ballinger explained that the commission had used such a rule—"that where any person had a strain of negro blood in them descending from an ancestor once held in involuntary servitude that the servile blood contaminated and polluted the Indian blood and render such person incapable of taking land under a treaty with the United States"—but the tribes had not followed any such rule. One senator pressed, "What had been the tribal law?" but later amended his question to concern "tribal *custom* then." Another senator asked "how they come [sic] to make up their rolls?" Ballinger explained to both senators that the tribes had "in many instances . . . enrolled [people of mixed blood] as citizens and their names appear on the tribal rolls." In other words, the Five Nations had considered people citizens for many different reasons—if they were members of their mother's clan, if they had been adopted by marriage or custom—none of which corresponded to a "blood" rule.[35]

Melvin Cornish, the attorney for the Choctaw and Chickasaw nations, appeared before the Senate to rebut the testimony of Ballinger and Lee. Cornish contended that both Commissioner Tams Bixby, who headed the Dawes Commission, and Captain McKennon, the commissioner who was in charge of freedman enrollment, "absolutely and positively" denied "that there were persons swarming around the Commission and forced to go to the freedmen's tent—that statement is absolutely untrue." Several senators asked Cornish about testimony that there were "representatives to direct their people" standing outside the two tents, and "the evidence was that [people of mixed blood] were misdirected." Cornish replied that he had been a stenographer with the commission before he went to law school and never saw such misdirection while he worked in the freedman tent. One senator, however, pointed out that if Cornish had been sitting in the freedman tent, he could not know whether someone who appeared before him had previously been put out of the "Indian by blood" tent. To this Cornish had no answer.[36]

The senators also considered an affidavit by Charles Cohee, the Chickasaw Freedman who had been the tribal member hired to sit with the Dawes Commission "for the purpose of identifying applicants for enrollment as freedmen." Several applicants for transfer had named Cohee as the person standing outside the tent who directed them to the freedman tent or the Indian tent. In his affidavit Cohee claimed that the committee had at first "made particular mention of those who claimed to have Indian blood," but that after only fifteen days the committee was told that "applicants who were born to slave mothers or to negro women who were descendants of slaves, were freedmen," and that they should therefore "discontinue hearing the statement of applicants as to their Indian blood, as in no case would they be enrolled as Indian citizens." From that time forward, even when the committee knew applicants were of mixed ancestry, it noted only their freedman family relations.[37]

Cornish insisted that the central issue for the commission's inquiry had been not Indian blood but whether a person appeared on the earlier tribal rolls, which included some people "possessed of negro blood." He went on to explain that the Choctaw and Chickasaw had given citizenship to some people of mixed blood, because children followed the status of the mother; the tribes, however, had made a distinction between children of legitimate marriages and illegitimate children, and that all "persons begotten by Indian men in an intercourse which had no relation to a marriage . . . are illegitimate just the same as the mulattoes who have grown up in the South."[38]

Indeed, the representative for the tribes echoed the frequent statements of the Dawes Commissioners themselves that determinations of identity were based *not* on blood, and certainly not on blood alone, but on documentation in tribal rolls. Thus the claims of the mixed-blood freedmen were portrayed as racially based, whereas the commission's decisions were seemingly based on the neutral category of citizenship.

In the end, the legislation failed to pass, and few Choctaw or Chickasaw Freedmen changed rolls. Joseph Howell, who was sent as a special commissioner to report on enrollment to the Department of the Interior in 1909, again made the case for moving many of the freedmen onto the "Indian rolls" of all five tribes. Although Howell wrote that "from my personal examination and observation of a considerable number of persons claiming to be of mixed Indian and negro blood, I found that, as a general rule, such person were not obviously and visibly Indians," he also concluded that "there were still others who, I am thoroughly persuaded, are related by blood to recognized Indian citizens" and in fact "instances . . . where part of the members of a family have been enrolled as freedmen while others of no greater natural right have been enrolled as Indians by blood." This lament—that families were arbitrarily divided between "freedmen" and "Indians"—became a central claim of "freedmen" who found themselves excluded from citizenship in the Five Nations. The theme of a family torn apart is one that arises again and again in their struggles to claim an Indian identity.[39]

The most important issue in the aftermath of land allotment was the alienability of land on the basis of blood quantum. There had been some discussion among government officials about whether it was right to remove restrictions on freedmen's right of alienation. A Dawes Commission memorandum argued that "[the freedmen] are a simple, uneducated people and need protection in most instances as much as the fullblood Indians . . . These people, if they are now required to shift for themselves with no restriction upon their right of alienation, will no doubt soon become in a large measure a dependent class of citizens." The commission decided, however, that only Indian blood should mark incompetency. Violet Crain, a Seminole Freedman, wrote to the secretary of the interior in 1908 "explaining as near as possible the condition of things here in the Seminole Nation among the Freedmans and Mixbloods." She warned that grafters and speculators would take advantage of freedmen: "It's a burning shame in the sight of God the way these people are being treated in this land buying business. This country is made up of a class of cold hearted Land Gobblers who've left all thoughts of fair dealing behind and are here for no other purpose than to rob and cheat these ignorant people out of their homes, for a few baubles barely enough to cover notary fees and the paper the so-called deeds are written upon." Crain insisted that the freedmen and mixed bloods were no better able to manage their own affairs than full-blood Indians: "They are all uneducated . . . They are no more capable of controlling their affairs than a child." Likewise, Seminole Freedman Witty Cudjo wrote to the secretary: "We are Indians yet so far as we are governed by their laws. Therefore we can not understand why we should be thrown on our own ignorance in the care of the property coming to us. I ask the question of you plainly. Does your Department recognize these sales good or bad so far as the Seminole freedmen are concerned." Cudjo's use of the word "ignorance" was meant not as a slur upon his people but as a means of calling attention to the fact that the Seminole had always dealt with land collectively and could not understand the consequences of being thrown suddenly into the nexus of buying and selling property.[40]

Some of the freedmen who had sold their land for a pittance turned to the courts to recover their allotments. In several cases people enrolled as freedmen argued that their sale of land should be revoked because they were in fact of "Indian blood" and so should not have been allowed to alienate their land. In effect they were claiming retroactive protection from the laws restricting Indians from land sales. Thus, Hattie Rowe sold 120 acres of her allotment in the summer of 1904, but in *Rowe v. Sartain* in the early 1920s sued to recover that same land, claiming that she should never have been allowed to make the sale. Rowe was enrolled as a Creek Freedman—which technically gave her the right to sell away her property—but in ruling on her case the Oklahoma Supreme Court noted that "the evidence indicat[ed] that she possesses seven-eights Indian and one-eight negro blood."[41]

Rowe acknowledged that she was enrolled as a freedman. Nevertheless, she argued, her right to alienate her allotment should have been restricted because she possessed "7/8" Indian blood, and Congress had not removed restrictions from people of more than one-half Indian blood but only from "half bloods," whites, and freedmen. The Oklahoma court rejected Rowe's argument, holding that "the adjudication by the commission to the Five Civilized Tribes fixed her status, and so far as her allotted lands are concerned, she is deemed to be not of Indian blood . . . The Commission . . . must of necessity have determined that she was a negro." Following the tradition that allotment had established, the court could not see any possibility of Hattie Rowe's being both a "freedman" or "negro" and an Indian.[42]

In this same trial Hattie's mother, Susie Harrison, testified at length about her own enrollment, notably claiming that she had not understood what the "freedman roll" was or how it was differentiated from the "by blood" roll. Susie testified that she was the daughter of a Creek father and a Cherokee mother; she had had two husbands, the second a "colored man," which was why her children had ended up on the freedman roll, although Hattie was her first husband's child. In an echo of the racial identity trials of the 1840s, Hattie's lawyer asked Susie to demonstrate her Indian features: "Take off your hat, Susie. I call the Court's attention to her straight black hair and Indian characteristics." The opposing lawyer objected to the demonstration, but the court overruled the objection.[43]

Beyond demonstrating Hattie Rowe's Indian heritage, her lawyer sought on numerous occasions to prove that the people whom the Dawes Commission enrolled had not realized what was happening. He frequently tried to elicit testimony from Creek Freedman witnesses that they had recognized no significance in the segregated rolls; that they had not understood what it meant to be enrolled as a freedman. Implicitly Rowe's lawyer was trying to explain why someone with a right to be enrolled as an "Indian by blood" might have ended up on the freedman rolls. Rowe's lawyer also sought to elicit testimony that living in a "colored" or "freedman" town, such as Arkansas Town, did not necessarily make one a "negro," because the populations even in these supposedly all-black towns were mixed.

Both issues—whether people understood at the time what the rolls meant, and whether Indians lived in "all-black" towns—played a part in the testimony of E. S. Jacob, a Creek warrior and former "king" of Arkansas Town. The lawyer first asked Jacob what was "the common understanding of the Indians with reference to what the Dawes Commission were doing?" Jacob answered, "The enrollment, I understand it was only to consider who were citizens and who had a right to be." The court then sustained an objection to a question about what Indians understood to be the difference between enrolling as "Freedmen" or "Indians," as well as to a question about when Jacob found out he was enrolled as a freedman. Finally the lawyer asked, "Did it make any difference to the Indians whether they were placed upon the Freedmen rolls or placed upon the Indian roll?" and Jacob answered, "No sir."[44]

Jacob was also recalled to the stand to talk about Arkansas Town, "whether it was all colored or Indians or negroes from the southern states or what?" He answered, "Some Indians and some colored." He was then asked to be more specific: What were "most of the citizens living in the town during the years 1890 and 1895?" Jacob answered, "They were citizens." The lawyer replied, "I know they were citizens," and Jacob gave him no more specific answer than "They were colored and mixed at that time."[45]

The lawyer's difficulty stemmed from the different meanings that Indians and whites assigned to different terms—"colored," "mixed," even "slave"—as well as the fluidity of the concept of "blood" among Indians. Billy Barnett, a Creek, testified that Hattie's father, Billy Harrison, was "Creek but belonged to Hickory Town," another so-called freedman town. The lawyer then asked—just as he had asked Jacob—"Now at the time of the Dawes Commission enrolling Indians, what was the common understanding of the Indians as to what the Dawes Commission was doing?"

A. When I filed for my land there was a fellow by the name of Billie Brown interpreted for all full bloods.

Q. What did the Dawes Commission do?

A. Had me three-fourths.

> Q. I am not asking about you, Billy, what did the Indians understand the Dawes Commission were doing?
>
> A. There was a fellow interpreted, gave a fellow land, fellow interpreted it for me, had me three-fourths blood.
> [Lawyer asks to use interpreter. The previous witness, Jacob, serves as interpreter.]
>
> Q. What was the common understanding among the Indians as to what the Dawes Commission was doing here? I am not asking you about yourself, what did the Indians generally understand what the Dawes Commission was doing?
>
> A. He said that he don't know exactly, but that his best understanding it was to find out who are citizens and who had a right to allotment.[46]

Despite the lawyer's difficulties eliciting testimony, it seems fairly clear that at the time of enrollment, Indians had little notion how significant the Dawes Commission's "blood" distinctions would turn out to be. Billy Barnett appears to have identified himself as a "full blood," yet he acknowledged that the Dawes Commission "had me three-fourths"; he was aware that the commission was determining citizenship and the right to land allotment but did not necessarily understand how those decisions were being made or that blood quantum figured in them so heavily.

Yet arbitrary as they clearly often were, the Dawes Commission's designations of blood quantum fixed families' racial identities for a century afterward. Any living enrolled Cherokee today can tell you a story about the randomness—or craftiness—behind her ancestor's blood quantum designation on the Dawes Roll. Whether because people did not realize the enormous significance those notations would come to have, like Redbird Smith; because they were not even allowed to acknowledge their Indian parents, like the many people who identified themselves as "Indian" or "mixed" but were directed to the freedman tents; or because they knew that a smaller fraction of Indian blood would allow them to sell their land, many Indians ended up with a blood quantum that did not even correspond to their own self-identification, and many were excluded from the rolls entirely. The Certificate of Degree of Indian Blood (CDIB) card Indians hold today, according to which they prove eligibility for a host of tribal and government programs, establish Indian identity according to fractions of "blood" calculated by reference to the Dawes Rolls.

Contemporary Litigation

From the moment that allotment was completed, each of the Five Nations became embroiled in litigation with its freedmen over efforts to exclude them from sharing in distributions of land or money. Once land allotment had set the stage for Jim Crow, creating the new juridical category of the "freedman"—who was therefore a "negro"—the growing rift between freedmen and Indians led to conflicts over resources that increasingly spilled into the federal courts. Segregated enrollment drove a wedge between people who had previously been united in various ways. Both the Black Seminoles and Black Cherokees spent a good part of the twentieth century embroiled in litigation with their tribes, going back to their first efforts after the Civil War to ensure that they would share in any disbursements of national funds or common property. Each time the Cherokee Nation took another census of freedmen, a group of Cherokees challenged the roll in an effort to exclude some freedmen from citizenship. The Cherokee Nation itself litigated for thirteen years a losing claim against the United States, trying to recover payments to the Cherokee Freedmen. Then, in 1933, the Cherokee Nation brought suit against the federal government to recover money for the lands that had been designated "surplus lands" after individual allotments were given out and then taken from the nation and sold to white settlers. The Cherokee Freedmen successfully sought to intervene in these lawsuits to secure their own share of these funds.[47]

By the mid-twentieth century, Indian efforts to sue the federal government had largely failed, whereas the freedmen had used the courts relatively successfully to prevent the Indian nations from excluding them. Then, after several decades of inactivity, the passage of the Indian Claims Commission Act in 1946 spurred a new round of legal activity. The Cherokee Freedmen's Association formed to advocate for the rights of Cherokee Freedmen, especially those who had been left off the Dawes Rolls. Finally, in 1960 the association gained a hearing before the Indian Claims Commission. Eighteen aging Black Cherokees testified to the dispossession of their land, despite the fact that their names had been listed on two of the original pre-Dawes freedmen's rolls.[48]

Fred Martin, a Cherokee Freedman, described waiting in line for the Dawes Commission at Tahlequah, but his line was "cut off" before he could be enrolled—a story similar to that of many Indian freedmen testifying at Claims Commission hearings or being interviewed in the mid-twentieth century. Now, in 1960, Martin was asked:

"Are you part Indian[?]"

"I'm supposed to be."

"That's not my question. Are you part Indian?"

"I'm supposed to be, I told you. My grandmother was."

"You couldn't prove that, though, before the Commission, could you?"

"No, naturally, they wouldn't know. I didn't try it, fellow. What's the matter with you? Did you ever try to prove—I never tried to. Go down and see if I did."[49]

Fred Martin and other Black Cherokees understood themselves as sharing an Indian identity without much caring whether it was based on Indian "blood" or shared culture: either way they viewed themselves as intrinsically Cherokee. How could the Cherokee Nation adopt "one of their own family"? The process made no sense to them. How could you "prove" your Indian identity? Fred Martin reacted as though the questioner were asking something indecent, as well as impossible. To the claims commissioners, however, the question "Are you part Indian?" was a question *only* about racial identity or "blood"; in their eyes Fred Martin could not be "Indian" by ascription, political membership, or shared culture.[50]

Compounding the cultural miscommunication, the Court of Claims dismissed the Black Cherokees' suit in 1963 because the court considered it "a series of individual claims over which the Commission lacked jurisdiction." This idea that the Black Cherokees' claims were individual rather than collective made sense in the context of individual inquiries into "blood"; but Fred Martin and his fellow Black Cherokees saw the issue as one of group political and cultural identity. Just as land had been held collectively, so was identity—not a matter of individual blood quantum that might vary from person to person, but a shared membership in a commonly held entity.[51]

Controversy over the freedmen's right to membership in the Cherokee Nation continued. When the Cherokee reorganized their government in 1975, their new constitution defined eligibility for tribal membership "by reference to the Dawes Commission Rolls." The membership provision explicitly mentioned adopted Delaware and Shawnee Indians as citizens but made no mention of the freedmen. Cherokee Nation officials interpreted this to mean that the 1975 constitution excluded freedmen from citizenship, and in 1983, for the first time, freedmen whose names appeared on the Dawes Rolls were turned away from a tribal election as ineligible to vote. The freedmen appealed their exclusion from voting in federal court, and in 1989 the Tenth Circuit rejected the Black Cherokees' appeal, holding that a finding of race discrimination would "in effect eviscerate the tribe's sovereign power to define itself, and thus would constitute an unacceptable interference 'with a tribe's ability to maintain itself as a culturally and politically distinct entity,'" an opinion based on the assumption that the freedmen could not have been culturally and politically part of the Cherokee Nation. A decade later the Cherokee Nation's highest court also ruled that freedmen could not be enrolled as citizens under the 1975 constitution.[52]

Both the federal and Cherokee Nation courts have begun to be more sympathetic to the freedmen's claims, yet at every turn the nation's elected leaders have sought to exclude the freedmen, now by constitutional amendment. After numerous skirmishes in federal court and in correspondence with the Bureau of Indian Affairs over the nation's repeated refusals to restore voting privileges to the freedmen, the freedmen won several big litigation victories in 2006–7. Freedman Marilyn Vann sued the Bureau of Indian Affairs in federal court, and freedman Lucy Allen sued the Cherokee Nation Tribal Council in the Cherokee Nation courts, for the right to vote in tribal elections as a citizen. Although by early 2008 there had been no final ruling in the federal court case, the D.C. district court did deny the Cherokee Nation's motion to dismiss, ruling that the freedmen had a legitimate Thirteenth Amendment claim, and therefore the nation could not invoke sovereign immunity to escape liability. In other words, because the nation's denial of voting rights to the freedmen could be considered a badge of servitude, the United States has a right to encroach on the nation's sovereignty in order to enforce the freedmen's right to be free from the badges and incidents of slavery. Even more significantly, in 2006 the Judicial Appeals Tribunal of the Cherokee Nation gave a victory to the Cherokee Freedmen in Lucy Allen's case, overturning its earlier decision and reinstating the freedmen to citizenship. That decision, however, relied on a reading of the 1975 constitution. The Cherokee Tribal Council responded to this decision by passing a resolution to amend the constitution to require Cherokee "blood" for citizenship, and that amendment was upheld in a vote on June 23, 2007. The freedmen lost a motion in federal court to enjoin that election. Some freedmen, who had enrolled in the year since Lucy Allen's victory, were allowed to vote in the 2007 election. It was then up to the federal court to decide whether the constitutional amendment violated the treaty of 1866 and the Thirteenth Amendment.[53]

Seminole Freedmen have fought a similar battle over the last century, but especially since the 1990s. Just as in the Cherokee Nation, freedmen's claims have been a part of the Seminole Nation's century-long efforts to gain compensation from the United States for lands taken in removal from Florida, as well as for "surplus" lands in Oklahoma sold to non-Indians when the Indians' land was allotted in 1906 and 1907. In 1933 the Seminole Nation also sued the United States in the Court of Claims to reclaim lands that had been issued to the freedmen. The nation argued in that case that the freedmen, though citizens, did not have any rights to property; the Court of Claims ruled in favor of the freedmen. Then, in 1950, the nation sought compensation for land taken by the United States in the 1823 Treaty of Moultrie Creek. The Seminole won their claim in 1976, and Congress awarded the nation over $70 million, including interest, which is now known as the "Seminole Judgment Fund." The fund finally began to be disbursed to individual Seminoles in 1991. In that year Congress decided to allocate 75 percent of the Judgment Fund to the Oklahoma Seminole Nation, 25 percent to Florida Seminoles, and nothing to the freedmen.[54]

Congress's action was based on a Bureau of Indian Affairs (BIA) memorandum written in 1976, titled "Results of Research Report on Seminole Judgment in Dockets 73 and 151 before the Indian Claims Commission." As background, the report detailed the early history of the Seminole—the incorporation of Lower Creeks, Indian remnants, and "Negroes." The report acknowledged that these African Americans were "escaped slaves of Americans who became essentially free under the Seminoles, or who became slaves of Seminoles, and who intermarried with them to some extent." The report chronicled the way that even Seminole slaves lived apart from their masters, farmed separately, and experienced "extremely amicable and tolerant" relationships with Seminoles. The memorandum also noted the important role of Black Seminoles as warriors, translators, and diplomats during the Seminole Wars, in the "Negro Fort," and as scouts for the U.S. Army. Nevertheless, it concluded that "despite the long and close relationship between the Seminole Negroes and the Seminoles, the Negroes, whether entirely free and residing with the Seminoles, or nominally slaves, did not acquire any interest in tribal lands or other property, and did not become members ('citizens') of the Seminole Nation in Indian

Territory until 1866." Therefore the BIA found "all Seminole Negroes and their descendants . . . to be ineligible to participate in the subject award."[55]

In September 1989 the Senate held hearings on the Judgment Fund Act, and there was a brief exchange between the chairman of the Select Committee on Indian Affairs and Walt Mills, deputy assistant secretary of the Department of the Interior, in which the chairman asked Mills about the status of the freedmen with regard to the Judgment Fund. Mills explained that "the Freedmen . . . were not members of the tribe until, I believe, it was 1866 . . . So we feel we have no [government-to-government] relation in this particular bill." Chief Jerry Haney of the Seminole Nation gave a slightly different response, however. When he was asked by the chairman if it was his "contention that the Freedmen will not share in this award," Haney replied: "At this time we haven't addressed that. It is something that we will have to take up with the tribal members."[56]

On the basis of this history, the U.S. Solicitor's Office approved the tribe's limitation of eligibility for programs *not* to Seminoles by blood but to a standard "based on descent from a member of the Tribe as it existed in 1823." Of course, if the tribe used the 1906 Dawes Rolls to make a determination about who had descended from a member of the tribe in 1823, then they would almost certainly be making the "blood"/"freedmen" distinction as it was made in 1906. But the U.S. regional solicitor, Tim Vollmann, concluded that "we should not assume that the Tribe will administer these programs in an arbitrary and discriminatory manner." He suggested in a footnote, "Perhaps a contemporary Freedman member will be able to trace some Indian blood in his or her lineage."[57]

Correspondence among government officials in the 1990s makes it clear that BIA officials and Seminole leaders concurred in their hope to avoid "the Freedmen issue." A September 1990 memo from the "Area Tribal Operations Officer" to the "Muskogee Area Director" recounted a Seminole Judgment Fund Committee meeting at which the "Freedmen issue" was "a very sensitive matter and the Committee does not want to include them [Freedmen] in the usage plan." A lawyer from the Solicitor's Office in Tulsa suggested to the tribal members that there was a "possibility of [the] plan slipping through if Congress is busy with the Middle East crises on their mind," or of legislators going along with the interpretation limiting the award to "members by blood," even though Congress had used the more inclusive language "members by blood or members of the Seminole Tribe."[58]

In 1996 Sylvia Davis, along with two bands of Seminole Freedmen, brought suit against the U.S. government to protest the refusal to issue CDIB cards and to disburse Judgment Fund benefits to Black Seminoles. Most of the payments are small individual grants for education, housing, and basic needs; Sylvia Davis's son Donnell had been denied $125 in clothing assistance from the Judgment Fund. In January 2000 the U.S. government warned the Seminole Nation Council that the entire fund would be frozen pending the outcome of the Davis case. Immediately the council decided to hold a referendum election on the issue of voting the Black Seminoles out of the Seminole Nation. On June 28, 2000, the BIA informed Chief Haney that the bureau had to approve referendum issues before the election could be valid. Nevertheless, on July 1 the Seminoles held the election and voted to amend their constitution to add a one-eighth "blood" requirement for membership, thereby excluding the Seminole Freedmen from citizenship. The BIA responded by designating the Seminole Nation an illegal government. The Seminole sued in D.C. District Court for an injunction and held a new election for chief.[59]

From 2001 to 2003 there were two rival governments: the newly elected government of Kenneth Chambers, and Jerry Haney's government, recognized by the BIA but not by the Seminole Nation. Haney and the freedmen both intervened in the Seminole Nation's litigation in the D.C. District Court over the question of whether the nation had the right to exclude the freedmen. Haney, who had made the original decision, began to argue on the freedmen's side. The D.C. court denied the Black Seminoles' motion to intervene and berated them for their "attempt to broaden the scope of the lawsuit currently before the Court" to include the Judgment Fund questions being litigated in the Western District of Oklahoma. In September 2002 the D.C. court granted summary judgment to the BIA, upholding its right to refuse to recognize Haney as chief of the Seminole Nation until new elections were held in which the freedmen were permitted to vote. The court found, however, that the BIA had "acted contrary to law by refusing to recognize the nation's General Council members" who had been elected after the unconstitutional one-quarter Seminole blood requirement, "absent evidence that there were candidates that would have run for those positions but for" the new requirement. On March 5, 2003, the BIA recognized Chambers's government, and seven months later announced to the freedmen that "the regulation that defined an Indian has been changed" so that freedmen would now be eligible for some benefits, including health, school, clothing, and burial funds, although not CDIB cards. In 2005 the freedmen were preparing to bring suit again, this time naming individual Seminole Nation representatives.[60]

Throughout the course of litigation with the freedmen, some representatives of the Seminole Nation have insisted on a racial definition of Indian identity rather than one of political or cultural affiliation. Charles Grounds, lawyer for the nation for several decades, kept in his papers a definition of "Indians" gleaned from various dictionaries: "'Indians' is the name given by the European discoverers of America to its aboriginal inhabitants. (1) The term 'Indian,' when used in a statute without any other limitation, should be held to include members of the aboriginal race, whether now sustaining tribal relations or otherwise." Grounds used this definition in his correspondence with U.S. government officials and others to bolster his contention that the Black Seminoles could never be the intended recipients of benefits meant for "Indians."[61]

At a 1983 Seminole Tribal Council meeting several representatives of Seminole bands articulated five reasons for opposing Black Seminoles' participation in the Judgment Fund: "(1) The ancestors of the Freedmen owned no lands in Florida but were the Seminoles' slaves . . . (2) The Freedmen were not made citizens of the Seminole Nation until 1866 . . . (3) Others of the Five Tribes were able to have their Freedmen excluded . . . (4) the Freedmen [should not have] taken their case to Washington . . . and (5) the Freedmen [should not have] used the influence of the [Congressional] Black Caucus" to put pressure on the Bureau of Indian Affairs. Many Seminoles voiced "the opinion that the blacks had to decide whether they were blacks or Seminole tribal members—they could not be both."[62]

Despite their disagreement on other matters, the two chiefs agreed on one thing: the freedmen are not Seminoles. Ken Chambers put it most bluntly: "There is no black Seminole." Jerry Haney described the status of the freedmen: "They were always looked at as non-Indian. They were always a separate people. I remember seeing black people speaking Indian, but now they go their own way. It is kind of like military service. You fight with each other and you have things in common but once you get out you lose those things . . . We were both fighting the white man. Now that relationship is gone."[63]

Some people who identify as "Seminoles by blood" and supported the newly elected Chief Chambers argued that the dispute with the U.S. government concerned sovereignty rather than race: the right of Indian nations to determine their own membership. As Chambers explained: "We're a sovereign nation. Our government was here before the U.S. government." Yet some of his supporters told a different story. Yogi Harjo, standing sentry in front of Chambers's offices, told a reporter: "We're not black—we're Indians. We're trying to keep the black people out." And others demonstrated how race and sovereignty merge in the desire for self-determination of racial boundaries. Jerry Bread, Native American Studies professor at the University of Oklahoma, claimed that the dispute "is really not a matter of race; it's a matter of politics and the right of the people to define their own blood . . . How far do we go in allowing the U.S. government to dictate the rights that we have?"[64]

In the Seminole Nation, with its relatively peaceful multiracial origins, the freedmen are now completely shut out. By contrast, the Cherokee Nation has recently made a complete about-face, legally if not in the attitudes of its people. Ironically, many Seminoles would claim that they have always defined their nation in this way, separating African from Indian, despite their long history of alliances, intermarriage, language exchange, and unity against the U.S. government and the white slaveholders of the South. African Americans had become part of the Cherokee, Seminole, Creek, Choctaw, and Chickasaw nations in a wide variety of ways. Indian nations had held slaves, freed slaves, and offered havens to runaway slaves as well as free black people. African Americans had married Indians and become part of Indian families. In the Jim Crow era they all became "freedmen" rather than "Indians" and legally separated from the communities of which they had long been part. Indians were no longer nations but races, whose integrity was measured by blood quantum. Defining Indian identity through blood quantum has made a black Indian identity virtually impossible to imagine, and has set Indians and blacks against each other politically. Today many Seminole Indians believe that what undermined their sovereignty was the 1866 treaty provision forcing them to make the freedmen citizens—not unlike the Lumbee in the 1970s who told whites, "We'll take the Negro when you take him, and not before." This is a profound revision of a history in which blacks had always been part of Indian nations. Likewise, the separate freedmen rolls may not have appeared terribly consequential at the outset because, at least among the Seminole and Cherokee, freedmen received land allotments. But within only a few years the Jim Crow rolls made an enormous difference, because everyone on the freedmen rolls was deemed a "negro," and "negroes" were excluded from public accommodations, schools, and political institutions in the new state of Oklahoma.[65]

From the mid-twentieth century through the present, blood quantum has taken on still greater significance for both Indian nations and individual Indians. From the moment the Dawes Rolls were created, people who wished to identify as Indian had to trace their lineage back to those rolls to prove citizenship in the Cherokee, Choctaw, Chickasaw, Creek, or Seminole nations. The determination made in a dusty tent by ill-informed white officials supervising the enrollment and allotment process during a few hectic months in the early twentieth century determines whether today an Indian's Certificate of Degree of Indian Blood card reads "1/32" or "3/64" or "5/128" Indian blood—numbers that might determine whether the cardholder can vote in Indian elections or qualify for government aid. The CDIB cards determine as well how large an Indian nation is considered to be—too small a degree of blood quantum and tribal identity is lost—and so the cards further reinforce the idea of the vanishing Indian. These consequences certainly were not clear to those Indians who took part in the enrollment and allotment process one hundred years ago.

CHAPTER SIX

From Nation to Race in Hawai'i

JUST AS THE QUESTION of whether the Seminole and Cherokee are races or nations animates the litigation over freedman citizenship today, native peoples' identity as race or nation is the subject of struggle in courtrooms, legislatures, and tribal councils across the United States. These struggles have taken on great urgency in recent years in the wake of a U.S. Supreme Court decision concerning voting for the Hawai'i state agency that administers programs for native Hawai'ians. In 2001 the Supreme Court held that limiting voting for the Office of Hawaiian Affairs to "Hawaiians" violated the Fifteenth Amendment because that was a racial classification, not, as previously understood, a political and national identity.[1]

The roots of the current dilemma surrounding Hawai'ian identity may be found in the same era as the drama that unfolded in Oklahoma. Just as native identity in Indian Territory became racially fixed during the era of allotment and enrollment in the first decades of the twentieth century, native peoples from the United States' imperial adventures abroad were also incorporated into citizenship and racially marked through the process of land allotment. The policies of individual land allotment and the breakup of tribal governments served as models for the treatment of the native peoples conquered beyond U.S. borders. In 1898 the United States made a bid to join the European powers in acquiring an empire, reaching beyond its shores to Hawai'i, the Philippines, Cuba, and Puerto Rico—and its treatment of conquered peoples would reflect its new imperial identity.

By 1898 the "Five Civilized Tribes," already conquered and removed to Indian Territory, were treated not as citizens of a rival government but rather as subject peoples to be integrated into American society via the

Curtis Act. U.S. notions of race—including the centrality of "blackness" and African heritage in American racial theories—were a major factor in this transformation of the Five Nations from nations to conquered people. Certainly the imperial nations of Europe also invoked race in their appropriation of territory in Africa, Asia, Latin America, and the South Pacific. Only in America, however, did the rise of empire take place both internally and externally at the same time—with Indians in North America and with Hawai'ians, Filipinos, Cubans, and Puerto Ricans abroad—organized around an explicitly racial means of identifying who had a right to their own government and who might be incorporated as a subject race within the United States.

Just as the allotment process and the dynamics of Jim Crow helped to create each other in Indian Territory and Oklahoma, so did America's imperial adventures abroad interact with the final conquest of Indian nations at home. In establishing its dominance over a subject people, the U.S. government introduced the notion of blood quantum to divide those who were considered too incompetent to sell or transfer their land from those who would not receive legal protection; that notion of "blood" then took on a life of its own to separate once united peoples along the lines of white and black, pure and mixed.

These notions of racial purity were born out of the centuries-long need both to incorporate enslaved African Americans into U.S. society and to keep them at a distance. Now, in the Age of Empire, the ideas of "blood" and "blood quantum" would be applied even to situations in which there were no people of African descent: the allotment of land to native Hawai'ians in the conquered land of Hawai'i. No longer subjects of Queen Lili'uokalani but racial types, they too were given their individual parcels of land—and in their case, racial impurity became the pretext for depriving most Hawai'ians of even that. Hawai'ians of 50 percent or greater blood quantum had a right to forty acres of the farmland that was formerly theirs, but mixed bloods or Japanese—even those who had been living in Hawai'i for generations—had no such rights, which freed huge acreages for the sugar companies and cattle ranches. In Hawai'i as in Oklahoma, race became the substitute for nationhood.

The Conquest of Hawai'i

As with that of the North American Indian nations, the native Hawai'ian conception of identity was based on lineage or genealogy, as set forth in the Hawai'ian origin narrative, the Kumulipo. Anyone who could trace her ancestry through either the maternal or paternal line of descent to a particular *'ohana,* or extended family, was a member of that family. Unlike blood quantum, Hawai'ian genealogies were about connectedness to land and people, with no racial or genetic connotations. Although Europeans and Americans, missionaries as well as merchants, began arriving on the islands after Captain James Cook's "discovery" in 1778, they continued to be called "foreigners" rather than "Hawai'ians." As most nations do, the Hawai'ian kingdom made numerous legal distinctions between "natives" and "foreigners," including a head tax on foreigners, a prohibition on the sale of liquor to natives, and a law against enlisting sailors on foreign vessels. "Foreigners" were classified as such even after naturalization. Nonetheless, Hawai'ian law contained no definitions of "Hawai'ian" and "foreigner." A Hawai'ian was someone related to or descended from Hawai'ians.[2]

The first 125 years of European, American, and Japanese residence in Hawai'i saw an enormous shift of land away from "Hawai'ians" to "foreigners," as well as a movement from traditional forms of landholding to "a system of exclusive, transferable private property rights." Before European contact, Hawai'i's agricultural economy was organized in a more or less feudal system, in which chiefs *(ali'i)* owned the land but commoners *(maka'ainana)* had rights of use and occupancy and paid taxes to the chiefs. A number of factors combined to put pressure on this system. While Westerners in the Hawai'ian government strongly promoted private property rights, demographic and economic forces were important as well. The severe population decline following contact greatly reduced the tax moneys available to chiefs and the king; private property rights were a way to raise public revenue, both through government sale of lands and through increased leasing to the new sugar plantations that were beginning to spring up.[3]

In 1845 the minister of the interior, Dr. Gerrit Judd, proposed the conversion of customary rights in land into private property rights. This conversion took place in a series of steps over the next few years. What became known as the Great Mahele (Land Division) of 1848 created three categories of land: "crown lands," reserved for the king and his descendants; "chiefs' lands"; and "government lands" or "public lands," which were to be used for individual allotment. While many Europeans and Americans were already living in Hawai'i, and some, like Gerrit Judd, occupied positions of power in the government of King Kamehameha III, Hawai'i was not yet a colony. Hawai'ian elites, however, recognized the writing on the wall as European presence on the island increased, and they sought to protect their lands from foreign settlement by undertaking a form of allotment ahead of colonization. Thus, foreign influence may be part of the explanation for the Mahele, but it was also a self-conscious effort by the king and the *ali'i* to generate revenue and to protect their lands from conquest. While the rights of commoners as tenants were supposed to be protected through the Mahele, in point of fact they received very little of the land allotted. The Mahele was thus a rehearsal for the land allotment undertaken by the U.S. government in the twentieth century.[4]

The division of Hawa'ian land took place in several steps. In 1845 Kamehameha III created a Board of Commissioners to Quiet Land Titles; all people had to file their claims to land by February 1848. The first division was between the king's lands and the chiefs' lands, and the second divided the king's lands into crown lands and government lands. Finally, the Kuleana Act "granted fee simple titles to commoners 'who occupy and improve any portion' of land belonging to the government, to the King, or to a chief, 'for the land they so occupy and improve.'" In other words, acreage was set aside out of each category of land for commoners to claim individual allotments, provided they used the land for individual farms. The last step in the Mahele came in 1850, when the legislature allowed foreigners to acquire land in fee simple.[5]

Throughout this process, few Hawai'ian commoners actually gained title to land, while foreigners took an ever greater share of it. By 1855 there were 1 million acres of crown lands, 1.5 million acres of government lands, and 1.6 million acres of chiefs' lands, with less than 1 percent of the total acreage of Hawai'i—only 28,600 acres—allotted to individual commoners. But the system of property in land had changed fundamentally, and the main transformation involved alienability: land could now "be sold by anyone to anyone, whether foreigner, commoner, chief, or the king."[6]

And it was: the royal family, government officials, and chiefs all sold land to foreigners. By 1896, on the eve of Hawai'ian annexation, 57 percent of taxable land belonged to foreigners, while Hawai'ian commoners owned only 14 percent. To some extent, Hawai'ian elites had succeeded in their objective of protecting their own landed estates; the U.S. government recognized title in chiefs' lands and other Hawai'ian land titles after annexation. But while the Mahele had distinguished crown lands, the

king's own private holdings, from government lands, the United States refused the distinction. Upon conquest, Queen Lili'uokalani was forced to
"cede" the crown lands to the United States. It was a portion of these
"ceded lands" that was deemed to be held in trust for the native Hawai'ian
people.[7]

When Hawai'i was conquered with the toppling of Queen Lili'uokalani's
government in 1893, it hardly registered as a military event. Faced with a
force of only 150 U.S. Marines, the queen surrendered in a mere three
days. By the time of official annexation in 1898, the Hawai'ians were already viewed as a subject population, and the extinction of their national
government happened far more quickly and thoroughly than the conquest
of many Indian peoples—including the Five Civilized Tribes. Significantly,
when allotment took place among mainland Indians, the United States
had tribal governments to deal with, and these helped to shape the terms
on which enrollment took place. In Hawai'i, by contrast, conquest and annexation eliminated all vestiges of Hawai'ian political identity, so that by
the time land was allotted in the 1920s, there was no longer any national
entity to extinguish. No Hawai'ian government existed to advocate for the
rights of its people, so the allotment process—again, in a racialized form—
could proceed pretty much unopposed. After annexation, Hawai'i became
a territory of the United States, just like the Oklahoma Territory before
statehood, with a territorial legislature and a governor, but ultimately governed by the U.S. Congress. And just as native identity in Indian Territory became racially fixed during the era of allotment and enrollment in
the first decades of the twentieth century, so were native peoples in the
United States' imperial acquisitions abroad also incorporated into citizenship and racially marked through the process of land allotment. In
the simplest possible terms, when Hawai'i was conquered as a nation,
Hawai'ians were remade as a race; and, as in the case of the Seminole and
Cherokee, it was in battles over land allotment that native identity was
precisely adjudicated and legislated.

Land Allotment and Racial Rehabilitation

The annexation of Hawai'i made it even easier for foreigners—especially
Americans—to gain control of Hawai'ian lands. In 1900 Congress passed
the Organic Act, in which all Hawai'ian public lands—some 1.8 million
acres of crown and government land—were officially "ceded" to the United

States. It was a portion of these lands that would be allotted in response to
what native Hawai'ians and their advocates began to call "rehabilitation," a
term developed to express the fear that the "race" of native Hawai'ians
was dying out and needed to be rehabilitated—not only restored to their
former numbers but also returned to their former purity and nobility.
While some Hawai'ian activists framed their people's claims to land in
terms of entitlement or justice for commoners, deferred since the Mahele,
many Hawai'ian leaders and virtually all U.S. politicians, businessmen,
newspaper editors, and others residing in Hawai'i spoke about land ownership for natives as the only way to prevent the ever-growing possibility of racial extinction for the native Hawai'ians. Unlike Indians, who
were supposedly vanishing as a result of warfare, disease, and assimilation,
Hawai'ians were seen as dying out because they had left the land for the
tenements of the cities, where they were degenerating as a race and dwindling in numbers. Returning the natives to the land, reformers believed,
would "rehabilitate" the race.

The language of racial "rehabilitation" is a striking departure from the
way mainland Indians discussed land claims. To some extent the writings
of native Hawai'ian leaders about the "Hawai'ian race" during this period
appear to use the term synonymously with the "Hawai'ian people," to con-
note the indigenous people of the Hawai'ian islands. But the rhetoric of
"rehabilitation" also suggests the extent to which native Hawai'ian leaders
adopted the European missionaries' romantic racialism, paternalistically
referring to the needs of a childlike race in danger of dying out without
charity. The Ahahui Pu'uhonua, the advocacy organization begun by native Hawai'ians, articulated its mission as a kind of middle-class "uplift"
project for the Hawai'ian people: to improve conditions for Hawai'ians but
also to teach them to be better citizens. Reading their words today, we find
it difficult to know to what degree native Hawai'ian leaders used this language instrumentally, because it was the best language available to appeal
to U.S. decision makers, or whether the middle-class members of these
organizations had actually come to share the romantic racialism of Christian reform.

The U.S. Senate seemed to support native Hawai'ians' control of their
own lands through a 1910 amendment of the Organic Act that provided
for the homesteading of any ceded lands when demanded by a petition of
twenty-five or more eligible citizens, while limiting non-homesteading
leases to one thousand acres each. This "general homesteading" how-

ever, was open to anyone who applied, European, Japanese, or Hawai'ian. Many Hawai'ians applied for these homesteads, seeking to regain some of the land that the sugar companies had been taking for decades. The sugar planters opposed homesteading because it limited their access to large acreages of agricultural lands, and they mobilized great pressure to amend the Organic Act yet again in order to expand the lands available for long-term leasing and limit the reach of homesteading.[8]

Support for homesteading also came in 1911 from the last vestiges of Hawai'ian resistance as Jonah Kuhio Kalanianaole lodged his "complaint against the administration of Hon. Walter F. Frear, governor of Hawaii," that "homesteading and small holdings remain an exotic in the industrial life of Hawaii." Prince Kuhio, as he was known, had been next in line for the Hawai'ian monarchy at the time of its overthrow. Educated in Honolulu, California, and England, and imprisoned for his resistance to U.S. annexation, Kuhio was eventually elected as the nonvoting Hawaiian delegate to the U.S. Congress from the Territory of Hawaii for decades until his death in 1922. He spent his life advocating the claims of Hawai'ian commoners; accordingly, in the 1910s, Kuhio and other native Hawai'ian leaders began to press for the expansion of homesteading. They accelerated these efforts in 1918, after the United States entered World War I, which disrupted shipping to and from Hawai'i and doubled prices on food staples, creating yet more pressure from native Hawai'ians for additional homestead lands.[9]

Kuhio and others formed two political advocacy organizations, the Hawaiian Protective Association (Ahahui Pu'uhonua O Na Hawai'i) and the Hawaiian Civic Club, which generated homesteading plans as a way to promote Hawai'ian welfare and culture. The Ahahui Pu'uhonua published its own newspaper and recruited politicians to support "rehabilitation." The circular launching the organization began by using racial language to express national claims: "Aloha Oe: We all know it to be a fact that the Hawaiian race is about to be a race of the past . . . To labor or help in the rebuilding of a dying race whose only fault is its big-heartedness, its kindliness, is a work emphasized by our Master." Its first political effort was to petition for Prohibition, which was also put forth in racial language: "Explanations are unnecessary, for all of us know that liquor has reduced the race from 400,000 in 1749 to the present-day 'extinct' number of 28,000." According to Ahahui Pu'uhonua, the native Hawai'ian "must wake up and must fully realize that he is 'nobody' and that he has 'nothing' . . . That it is only by bettering his condition, pulling himself up to the standard of the other more enlightened and earlier civilized races that he can ever expect to be their equal." Although native Hawai'ian leaders used the term "race" as a synonym for "people," the notion of "blood" did not enter into the discussion.[10]

The first time a "native Hawai'ian" was defined in law was in the 1920s, to facilitate the land allotment process. As World War I ended, Hawai'ian "rehabilitation" came to the forefront of legislative debate in the United States when the sugar companies and large ranchers took up once again their claims to increasing shares of Hawai'ian territory. By this point the native population had been decimated by smallpox and other foreign diseases, falling from more than 400,000 to between 20,000 and 40,000 people, depending on who was counting—and on who counted as "native." By any measure, native Hawai'ians had been dispossessed of their land and livelihood, while their culture and their language were suppressed by law. The schools were established as English-only beginning in 1896 (under the brief Republic of Hawai'i between conquest and annexation), and children were punished for speaking Hawai'ian in school. This process was not unlike what happened to Indians in North America after the breakup of tribal governments. Under the imperial model, native peoples, whether at home or abroad, were to be educated in American ways and Christianized before they could be ready for citizenship. Squeezed economically even as they were silenced culturally, more than half of all native Hawai'ians had moved to Honolulu in the 1910s. As they sought work and crowded into city tenements, the farm workers on Hawai'ian sugar plantations and ranches were increasingly drawn from the ranks of Japanese, Chinese, and Filipinos imported to take low-wage jobs. By 1920, out of a total population in Hawai'i of 255,192, there were 109,274 Japanese, 23,507 Chinese, and 21,031 Filipino residents—leaving only 20,000 to 40,000 native Hawai'ians, or somewhere between 10 and 20 percent of the total. Hawai'ian politicians began to talk about "returning native Hawai'ians to the land" as the way to "rehabilitate" a "dying race."

Meanwhile, between 1917 and 1921 many of the leases on Hawai'i's highly cultivated sugar cane lands—as well as an even larger area of public lands leased to the sugar companies and subleased to cattle ranchers— were about to run out, raising the question in the U.S. Congress whether to extend the leases, and whether to open more public lands to leasing. The sugar companies known as the "Big Five"—Castle & Cooke, Alexan-

der & Baldwin, C. Brewer & Co., Amfac, and Theo. H. Davies & Co.—
dominated the Hawai'ian economy and politics during the territorial period, and they had a keen interest in extending their leases on public lands
and opening more lands for leasing.

The allotment of land to native Hawai'ians thus mirrored allotment on
the mainland, in that it resulted in small numbers of native people gaining
small parcels of less desirable land, while large swaths of land were made
available for, in the Hawai'ian case, the "Big Five" sugar companies and, to
a lesser extent, the cattle ranches. Unlike in the case of Indian allotment,
however, in which each Indian and freedman received his or her allotment initially regardless of blood quantum (with the exception of the
Choctaw and Chickasaw freedmen), in Hawai'i the law that eventually was
passed limited land allotments to only those with more than one-half native Hawai'ian blood. This blood quantum limitation directly determined
how much land would be available as "surplus" for the sugar companies
and ranches.

The politics of racial identity became central to land distribution in
Hawai'i. Claims that Hawai'ians rightfully owned the lands of their former
nation as a matter of justice were quickly subsumed to arguments based
on the need to rehabilitate a "noble race of people." Congressional advocates conjured images of the vanishing Hawai'ian, a happy and childlike
native imbued with the spirit of "aloha," who needed government assistance to compete with aggressive, hardworking "Caucasians" and Japanese
("Far Eastern Yankees"). Racial comparisons and the "science" of racial
mixing were the currency of the debate. On the one hand, Hawai'ian rehabilitation was presented as a way of staving off the dominance of a "bad"
racial group, the Japanese; on the other hand, some commentators presented the romance of race mixing in the Hawai'ian islands, in which the
"crossing" of Hawai'ians with other races had produced not only racial
harmony but better workers as well. Opponents of rehabilitation used the
science of "race mixing" to argue that "part-Hawai'ians" were sturdy and
prolific, and needed no help. All of these arguments converged in the debates over blood quantum: a low blood quantum requirement meant rehabilitation for more "part-Hawai'ians"—and less land available to the sugar
companies. The connection between blood quantum and available land
was thus evident and explicit.

The overt comparison of Hawai'ians to American Indians was prominent in the debate. Opponents of the Hawaiian Homes Commission

Act (the land allotment legislation) argued that the act would reduce Hawai'ians "to the status of blanket Indians," making them dependent on the federal government; some proponents spoke paternalistically of Hawai'ians as "our wards," and considered the reservation solution. But proponents also drew the comparison more positively when talking about sovereignty and land claims: both mainland Native Americans and native Hawai'ians had rights to land that had been taken from them, and both deserved recognition as nations from the federal government.

In 1919 the territorial legislature put forward two resolutions urging congressional action to amend the Organic Act. The first was a "Hawaiian rehabilitation" bill, written by John Wise, a part-Hawai'ian delegate known as something of a radical. Wise's bill would have allotted approximately 200,000 acres of the "ceded lands" (formerly crown and government lands) for settlement by "individuals of Hawaiian blood in whole or in part." The resolution proposed that "members of the Hawaiian race or blood should be encouraged to return to the status of independent and contented tillers of the soil, preserving to posterity the valuable and sturdy traits of the race." Here Wise drew on the reformers' language of racial rehabilitation, but in other settings, he and Prince Kuhio, who introduced the bill in Congress, also put the idea of land allotment in terms of claims for justice. A second resolution, put forward by the pro-sugar interests, asked Congress to amend the Organic Act to empower Hawai'i's territorial governor to exempt one-fifth of cultivated sugar lands under general leasing from homestead laws, and to continue existing leases for the highest bidder. This bill aimed to protect from homesteading as much land as possible for leasing by sugar plantations and ranches.[11]

The territorial legislature appointed a legislative commission to bring both resolutions to the U.S. Congress. The commission was composed of Wise, the advocate of "native Hawai'ians"; territorial senator Robert Shingle, one of the leading Republicans in Hawai'i, who advocated for the sugar and ranch interests; territorial representative William T. Rawlins, a lawyer and chairman of the Public Lands and Internal Improvements Committee, also sympathetic to the sugar lobby; territorial representative Norman Lyman, a part-Hawai'ian homesteader from Hilo; and Charles McCarthy, a Woodrow Wilson appointee who served as Democratic governor of the territory, who generally opposed the Big Five sugar companies and sympathized with the cause of Hawai'ian rehabilitation—in part because of his virulent anti-Asian sentiment.

John Wise wrote the legislative commission report on his own resolution, in which he explained that the Mahele had "brought about a regrettable result for the Hawaiian people." Because "the Hawaiian people are not naturally an acquisitive people . . . the natural acquisitiveness of the 'haole' [white people] has brought about the unfortunate result [that] . . . this fine race of people will soon be entirely exterminated." Wise justified the proposal for Hawai'ian homesteading by both the need for "the rehabilitation of the race" and the argument that "the Hawaiian people as a matter of common justice, are entitled, even at this late date, to a more liberal treatment in the matter of the disposition of the public lands of the Territory." Thus the original rationale for the bill included claims of justice as well as racial arguments about the rehabilitation of a naïve and dying race.[12]

In February 1920 Wise and the rest of the commission appeared before the U.S. House Committee on the Territories in hearings on the rehabilitation bill as well as the proposed amendments to the Organic Act. In the hearings the chairman of the House committee advised the commission to consolidate the two bills into an "omnibus bill" before introducing it in Congress. The first draft of this bill contained several prizes for the sugar companies. It exempted from homesteading not one-fifth but *all* of the first- and second-class "highly cultivated" agricultural lands. These would be leased to the plantations and ranches for periods of up to fifteen years. Third- and fourth-class lands were set aside for homesteading by native Hawai'ians. The new bill linked rehabilitation and land policy by using 30 percent of the revenues from the leasing of the highly cultivated sugar cane lands to finance a $1 million Hawai'ian home loans fund, which would provide every native Hawai'ian homesteader with a $3,000 start-up loan. These substantial concessions to the sugar companies were designed to garner their support for "rehabilitation," but they did not necessarily do the trick. Territorial senator Shingle, who supported the Big Five, remarked at the time of consolidation, "There is no question in my mind but that these bills conflict." Yet supporters of rehabilitation saw no way to win their program without linking the fortunes of rehabilitation to the political goals of the powerful Big Five companies.[13]

Prince Kuhio introduced the bill into Congress as H.R. 12683. In a speech back in Hawai'i he declared that he had "introduced this bill to set aside for the Hawaiian people lands that originally belonged to the Hawaiians." In the House hearings on the rehabilitation bill, Wise likewise made arguments based on the native Hawai'ians' rightful claim to the land. He

described the Great Mahele, and lamented the fact that Hawai'ian commoners had received only 28,000 acres of land. But the claims of justice
for the people fell on deaf ears compared to the familiar concerns about
the Hawai'ians as a dying race.[14]

Wise: We contend that the crown lands belong to the common people.

Rep. Dowell: How would you discriminate between the citizens there?

Rep. Strong: He [a Hawai'ian citizen] would have to have an admixture of
Hawaiian blood.

Prince Kuhio Kalanianaole: Were these crown lands under the monarch
open to settlement by citizens?

Wise: No.

Prince Kuhio: Then these lands were held by the crown in trust for the common people?

Wise: Yes; of the Hawaiian race.

Chairman [of the House Committee]: There is an equity and justice in saying
that these crown lands belonged to the Hawaiian people.

Rep. Dowell: I want to get the information.

Wise: I believe the Hawaiians should have the first choice. There is only a
little of this land left.

Chairman: And there are only about 40,000 Hawaiians and part-Hawaiians.

Rep. Dowell: Suppose he discriminates between Hawaiians?

Wise: The reason why this Senate resolution 2 was introduced was to overcome that difficulty. The Hawaiian people, those of Hawaiian blood, have
rights to these crown lands, for the Government of the United States and
the Territory have given them these rights. We feel that we have not got
all that is coming to us . . . The United States Government has seen fit to
set aside lands for the Indians. Why do they do that? Was it not because
you recognized that they had some rights?[15]

During this discussion Wise several times brought up the question of
Hawai'ians' "equitable" rights to the land; by "equity" Wise meant "justice." This was different from the legal sense of "equity," a right to the land
that would be upheld in a court of equity. In addition to his claims that giving land to native Hawai'ians was the "equitable" thing to do, Wise also
made the "dying race" argument. He asked the U.S. government to "pause
for one moment and instead of giving all your help to Europe, give some
help to the Hawaiians and see if you can not rehabilitate this noble peo-

ple." As always, the discussion of rehabilitating the race quickly led to the
issue of blood quantum:

> *Rep. Dowell:* One other matter. I notice in the resolution that you provide
> for those of Hawaiian blood.
>
> *Wise:* Yes.
>
> *Rep. Dowell:* How far do you go with that?
>
> *Wise:* Anybody with Hawaiian blood . . . I contend that anybody, even to the
> thirty-second degree should be included . . .
>
> *Rep. Humphreys:* I do not think that would be a big problem.
>
> *Rep. Dowell:* How many mixed blood people are there?
>
> *Wise:* Sixty thousand six hundred and sixty estimated in 1918.
>
> *Rep. Dowell:* What are there?
>
> *Wise:* Mostly white.
>
> *Rep. Dowell:* Mostly Americans?
>
> *Wise:* Americans, English, Germans, Europeans, and Chinese.
>
> *Rep. Strong:* Are there very few Japanese?
>
> *Wise:* Very few.
>
> *Gov. McCarthy:* There are quite a number of Chinese.
>
> *Dowell:* About how many?
>
> *Gov. McCarthy:* The Chinese and Hawaiian mixture makes a fine people.[16]

As would be true throughout all discussions of Hawai'ian land allotment, the experience of Indians in North America was widely viewed as
the template. While some thought that Hawai'ians had fewer rights than
Indians because they lacked any tribal government or acknowledged land
base, others thought the analogy was stronger. Thus, several congressmen
sought to differentiate Hawai'ians' rights from those of Indians, for whom
land was held in trust by the federal government. The committee chairman, by contrast, tried to argue that native Hawai'ians did have something
like a trust, suggesting that "from [the native Hawai'ians'] standpoint these
crown lands never really vested in the Federal Government except in trust
for the common people . . . That they were placed in trust for the common
people when in possession of the king, and just as we have provided lands
for the Indians, we may use these lands to provide for the Hawaiian race."
He sought to argue that the crown lands were analogous to lands that had
been taken from Indians and were now recognized as land held in trust for
their benefit.[17]

In the House hearings, the congressmen drew numerous connections between native Hawai'ians and Indians. One representative asked John Wise about the feasibility of turning part of Hawai'i into a big reservation, and Secretary of the Interior Franklin K. Lane warned that "the natives of the Islands, who are our wards, . . . and for whom in a sense we are trustees, are falling off rapidly in numbers and many of them are in poverty." When some congressmen argued that there was no parallel to the Indians because there was "no government or tribe or organization to deal with here," others pointed out that land had been taken from both groups and that "we have the law of the land of Hawaii from ancient times right down to the present where the preferences were given to certain classes of people." By drawing the analogy to Indians, these reform-minded sympathizers with the plight of the native Hawai'ians hoped to strengthen the case for passing a law that singled out native Hawai'ians for land allotment. Arguments about the constitutionality of legislating on behalf of the native Hawai'ians, which could be characterized as "class legislation," were answered by the analogy to Indians and other "wards of the government," including veterans. Yet the Indian analogy took on a life of its own in the debate as well, because the image of the Indian had so many meanings; Indian tribes may have once been proud nations, but by this time "blanket Indians" were dependent and even destitute "wards" of the government.[18]

Hawai'ian rehabilitation was also discussed in the context of strong anti-Asian sentiment, mostly directed at the Japanese in Hawai'i, rather than the Chinese, because of their greater numbers. Accordingly, congressmen referred to the decline in the Hawai'ian population by way of making ominous remarks about the rising number of Japanese. Wise played into white U.S. congressmen's fears of Japanese influence in Hawai'i, and of Japanese competition for land and jobs, by alluding to the Chinese and Japanese as "Far Eastern Yankees." How could the easygoing Hawai'ians, with their spirit of "aloha," prevail against them? As Wise testified: "A good many of our young people to-day are forced to take other trades than carpentry or mechanics simply because there is no opening for them. They could not compete with the Asiatics."[19]

The rehabilitation bill faced heavy opposition in the U.S. Congress, particularly from the Big Five companies, which found the bill in its existing form to lean too heavily toward homesteading, without enough protection for the sugar lands. They too framed their opposition in racial language, focusing on the definition of "native Hawai'ian." Because the land allot-

ment had been justified as the "rehabilitation" of a dying race—on the basis of an incompetent population's need rather than the entitlement of
people with rights to the land—it was possible to portray part-Hawai'ians
as self-sufficient, prolific, and competent, with no need of being "rehabilitated," and hence no need for (or claim on) Hawai'ian land.

The analogy to American Indians continued to be on everybody's mind,
both supporters and opponents of homesteading. Newspapers in the islands used the image of American Indians negatively, with the *Pacific
Commercial Advertiser*'s editorial page on March 28, 1920, calling the rehabilitation bill "An Act to Reduce the Hawaiians to the Status of Blanket
Indians." The "blanket Indians" epithet raised the specter of Hawai'ians
becoming dependent wards of the government rather than the self-
sufficient "yeoman farmers" conjured up by rehabilitation advocates. In
the same issue of the newspaper, Dr. J. H. Raymond of the Raymond
ranch wrote: "The proposed statute plays directly into the hands of the
powerful corporations doing business here—in many cases founded by
those who came to Hawaii bearing the banner of the cross upon their
shoulders and the message of 'peace on earth, good will toward men' in
their hearts—and reduced the Hawaiian people to the state of the lowliest
blanket Indian, living on the sufferance and bounty of those corporations
and of the federal government." Here even a representative of one of
the great ranches tried to portray his position as opposed to corporate interests, although the ranchers' main concern was to limit the scope of
homesteading to a small number of "pure" native Hawai'ians. The language of romantic racialism was thus used to mask the fact that it was the
foreign interests that were taking ever larger portions of native Hawai'ians'
national heritage—their land—and reducing the Hawai'ians to "blanket
Indians," that is, to native peoples dispossessed of their nation.[20]

The *Honolulu Star-Bulletin*—which tended to support the Republican
Party, and hence the sugar and ranching industries—likewise opposed the
need for "rehabilitation," and continued to invoke both the language of
race and the specter of impoverished and disenfranchised North American Indians. An editorial published on July 22, 1920, made light of the
claim that native Hawai'ians deserved rehabilitation on the grounds of
having unjustly lost lands in the Mahele of 1848: "As a matter of fact this
alleged wrong is unadulterated political bunk and no one realizes it better
than those first using it as a means of misrepresentation. The proposed law
is supposedly framed for a dying race, and includes among its beneficiaries

fractional blood Hawaiians who, according to the census, are steadily increasing. In its present form the law will not help, as intended, the pure Hawaiian."[21]

Yet the *Star-Bulletin* also argued against the claim that rehabilitation would end homesteading, as well as "the specious plea that the Rehabilitation Act will relegate the natives to the status of reservation Indians"; it came down in support of the bill, provided the blood quantum requirement were amended. The newspaper, like the representatives of the ranches and the sugar companies, actually wanted land reform to pass in order to open more lands for sugar cultivation and ranching. The aim of these interests in opposing the rehabilitation bill was simply to limit its beneficiaries to as few native Hawai'ians as possible so that *even more* land would be available for the big companies. Racial arguments supported this effort to limit land allotment to a smaller class of beneficiaries. And "blood quantum" was the mechanism by which it took place.[22]

The argument that Hawai'ians were a "dying race" was key to the movement for rehabilitation—and so this notion was debated fiercely, with anthropological studies of Hawai'ians and "race mixing" proliferating on either side of the debate. Proponents of rehabilitation cited studies claiming that the Hawai'ian race was indeed dying out and so needed to be protected. Opponents emphasized anthropological studies showing that while "full-blood" Hawai'ians might be "dying out," "part-Hawai'ians" were thriving. From this they concluded that "rehabilitation" was not necessary. In March 1921 the *Pacific Commercial Advertiser,* which frequently advocated for the sugar industry and opposed rehabilitation, published an article by Professor Louis R. Sullivan of the American Museum of Natural History, who proclaimed that according to his research, "the Japanese are not the most prolific race in the islands, as generally supposed . . . [T]he part-Hawaiians [are] the most fruitful racial unit in the territory." This research suggested that perhaps Hawai'ians were not after all a "dying race" in need of rehabilitation—and so, presumably, land did not have to be set aside for them. In Sullivan's arguments we can see how racial science played into the rehabilitation debate. On the one hand, Sullivan's research represented modern cultural anthropology's efforts to suggest that racial mixing was inevitable, normal, and not necessarily a bad thing; on the other hand, his inspections of "Hawaiian teeth" suggest the persistence of early-nineteenth-century forms of racial knowledge and "common sense." Both cultural and physical anthropology tended toward the same end, however; whether the argument was "nurture" or "nature," the final result was to erase from the debate all notions of political justice—the idea that the native Hawai'ians had a *political* claim to their own land. Instead the argument turned into one about the viability of their "race," replacing the concept of political justice with that of racial survival.[23]

A number of times during the congressional hearings, the superiority of the "cross" between Hawai'ians and Chinese was mentioned. This opinion echoed the anthropological studies of Hawai'ian "race mixing," which attributed traits to each racial group and then sought to determine which mixture was best. Some of the impetus behind this research was quite explicitly to counter eugenics arguments that race mixing created mongrels and led inevitably to the degeneracy of society. Thus the anthropologist Stanley Gulick found the "Chinese-White-Hawaiian" cross "superior"; he sought to prove that "contrary to popular opinion it is not true that the crossing of races begets offspring that inherit the 'bad qualities of both the parental races and the good qualities of neither.'" Two other U.S. anthropologists characterized Hawai'ians as easygoing and good-natured, bad at business, and sometimes possessing a childlike criminality. Whites had intellect and strength of character, these anthropologists believed, and, because of their strong-willed individualism, they resented regulation, discipline, and routine. Chinese were characterized by their "persistence in the face of difficulties, their docility and obedience to regulation," while the Chinese-Hawai'ian had the best "capacity and willingness for manual labor." Some anthropologists held Hawai'i out as a new kind of racial and cultural melting pot, a laboratory that would prove to the world how much could be learned from "other" races and their cultures. At the same time, the emphasis on the capacity of Chinese-Hawai'ians for labor suggested that anthropologists, like missionaries and other reformers, still thought of native Hawai'ians not so much as potential citizen freeholders but as workers for American companies.[24]

"Making Hawai'ians work" became itself a justification for rehabilitation. From the earliest stages of the legislative wrangling, the sugar industry had succeeded in exempting the "highly cultivated sugar lands" from homesteading. This meant that the land available for allotment would be poor-quality agricultural land fit mostly for pasture. Proponents of "rehabilitation" insisted that they were not asking for government handouts; indeed, they supported the policy of giving third- and fourth-class lands (as opposed to the highly cultivated sugar lands) to native Hawai'ians for homesteading by arguing that a lower grade of land would benefit Hawai'ians by requiring them to work harder.

The need to make Hawai'ians work harder seemed to be an idea on which all participants in the debate agreed, even native Hawai'ian organizations. For example, a flyer mailed by the Hawaiian Protective Association in February 1918 in support of rehabilitation declared that the Hawai'ian

> must wake up and must fully realize that he is "nobody" and that he has
> "nothing"; that he must start a new life, by going back to the soil and by
> fishing, as his ancestors did . . . That he must work, and work hard every
> day . . . That his best friends are the Athertons, Baldwins, Castles, Cookes,
> Dillinghams, Joneses and Rices [the "old American families" who owned
> the sugar companies and ranches]; that said "old families" and their chil-
> dren will always help him when he proves himself deserving, and that it is
> to his advantage to "look up" to them . . . That it is only by bettering his
> condition, pulling himself up to the standard of the other more enlight-
> ened and earlier civilized races that he can ever expect to be their equal.[25]

Likewise, the Reverend Akaiko Akana, a founder of the Hawaiian Protective Association, published a pamphlet titled "Sinews for Racial Development" in 1918, calling for "race consciousness," by which he meant "pride for, and faith in the race," and exhorting Hawai'ians: "Back to the soil and work! Work! Work! Will be their future salvation in health and general welfare." Akana, a middle-class part-Hawai'ian educated by missionaries, found it easy to draw upon the romantic racialism of rehabilitation to reassure Republicans and the companies they represented that native Hawai'ians would not step out of their place once they owned land.[26]

If native Hawai'ians believed that their own people had to work harder, the U.S. officials who ran the annexed island could not but agree. Governor McCarthy wrote to Interior Secretary Lane: "Those who contend that if there is to be any distribution of public lands exclusively in favor of Hawaiians, they ought to have first choice of the highly cultivated lands, completely misunderstood the purpose of rehabilitation. We don't want to make the Hawaiians rich, we want to make them work."[27]

The rhetoric of "making them work" made quite explicit the gulf between the discourse of "rehabilitation" and any idea of claims to land as a matter of justice; the Hawai'ians were understood not as a nation who deserved to have their land returned to them but as a labor force who should be allotted homesteads to turn them into good laborer-subjects of the United States.

When hearings on rehabilitation moved from the House to the Senate Committee on the Territories, senators were already familiar enough with the issue to zero in on the aspect of it they understood from the U.S. experience with Indian land allotments: blood quantum. This became the focal point in the Senate hearings in December 1920, with opponents of the bill focusing sustained criticism on the "one-thirty-second" requirement, which had been written into the bill on the basis of John Wise's somewhat offhand comment in the previous hearings. Supporters, meanwhile, were in retreat, facing the opposition of the Big Five, the ranches, and the Republican Party.

The turning point in the hearings was the testimony of Alexander G. M. Robertson, a former U.S. district judge and chief justice for the Hawai'ian Territory, an organizer of the Hawai'ian Republican Party, and a delegate to the Republican national convention. Robertson appeared on behalf of the Parker Ranch, a 500,000-acre landholding owned by a single minor child on the island of Hawai'i (the "Big Island"). Robertson argued against the policy of reserving homesteads for native Hawai'ians, not because such a policy would reduce the amount of land available for people like his client but rather on humanitarian grounds, saying that "[the] bill cleaves the Hawaiian community in two" by distinguishing one Hawai'ian from another "according to the color of his skin and the kind of blood that God has put in his veins." Robertson's language of blood drew on the ideology of racial distinctions, even though he claimed to be against using these distinctions as the basis for social policy.[28]

In particular, Robertson claimed that the Hawai'ians were not a dying race. For while "aboriginal Hawaiians of the pure blood are dying out," the bill applied to part-Hawai'ians as well, and they were thriving and successful. He personalized his opposition by pointing to another witness before the committee: "Here is the Rev. Akaiko Akana—part Hawaiian and part Chinese, why should I be taxed for his rehabilitation? . . . [The part-Hawai'ians] do not belong in the same class here with these unenterprising, apathetic, thriftless natives of the pure blood." Senator Chamberlain asked, "Why do you draw the line of those having one thirty-second of the pure blood in them?" Robertson replied, "I think that Senator Wise got that from the grandfather's law." (Robertson was probably referring to "grandfather clauses" in Southern laws that set up educational restrictions on voting but created a loophole for people whose grandfathers had been eligible to vote—thereby giving uneducated whites the right to vote but excluding even the most educated blacks. It is not clear what these laws had to do with the one-thirty-second fraction, except for the racial thinking they had in common.) Chamberlain, evidently meaning to be supportive, commented, "You take a man that has one thirty-second of native blood as compared with one who has [one] thirty-third, and you could not distinguish between them to save your life." Robertson agreed: "The Hawaiian blood is so readily absorbed that a person of one-eighth Hawaiian blood can not be distinguished from a white person, in ninety-nine cases out of one hundred." By assimilating "part-Hawai'ians" to whites, Robertson sought to limit the reach of the law.[29]

Robertson also brought up evidence of individual wealthy part-Hawai'ian families—"mixed" with either Chinese or whites—in order to argue for a "full blood" definition of native Hawai'ian; in other words, although there may not have been many wealthy "pure" Hawai'ians in Hawai'i, the Hawai'ians had mixed to advantage with more enterprising "races." He also asserted that in Hawai'i, "nobody is indigent out there by reason of the lack of opportunity to work," suggesting that poverty could only be the result of incompetence or laziness, which he related again to "pure Hawai'ian" identity. As with the North American Indians, racializing the Hawai'ians was a way to erase their *political* claim to Hawai'ian lands, replacing the notion of sovereignty with the notion of blood quantum.[30]

Yet Robertson sought to refute the comparison of Hawai'ians to Indians, on both political and racial grounds:

> The Hawaiians are not Indians. The status of the Hawaiians is diametrically opposed to that of the Indians on the mainland. The Indians have been regarded as aliens. They get their rights, such as they have, by treaties between them and the Federal Government. They have no right to vote, unless under subsequent circumstances they become naturalized. As I understand it, they are aliens and not citizens, and their inherent character is by no means that of the Hawaiians. The Indians were a roving, nomadic race of people. They did not take to civilization the way the Hawaiians did. The Hawaiians took to civilized customs there like a trout to a fly. They were right in line for it.[31]

Supporters of rehabilitation had used the Indian analogy to bolster the case for giving Hawai'ians land, just as Indians had been allotted land.

Ironically, though, much of the opposition to the rehabilitation bill, in the newspapers and in legislative debate, had *also* been grounded in the Hawai'ian-Indian comparison: "Let us not reduce the Hawai'ian to the status of a blanket Indian," suggesting that Indian policy had been a failure and Hawai'ians should not be treated the same way. Robertson was doing something different: he argued *against* land allotment for Hawai'ians by denying the comparison. Indians were "aliens," foreign nationals, whose relationship to the U.S. government was by treaty, whereas Hawai'ians could become citizens and assimilate to American society. They took to civilization "like a trout to a fly." Robertson's backhanded compliment captured the irony of citizenship as a subject status.

Prince Kuhio Kalanianaole, in rebuttal, declared that Robertson was "trying to lead you [senators] to believe that he is representing the white people. In Hawaii we do not know of such a thing as the white people. All we know is, we are all Americans. My belief is that the majority of the so-called white people are back of this bill." Whereas Robertson had compared the "one-thirty-second" Hawai'ian to a white person, parsing racial differences according to fractions of blood, Prince Kuhio sought to change the field of debate, denying that categories such as "white" were meaningful in Hawai'i. Instead he tried to deploy the rhetoric of interracial unity in support of rehabilitation.[32]

W. B. Pittman, brother of U.S. senator Key Pittman, appeared on behalf of the Raymond Ranch on Maui. Pittman claimed that he had "talked to many intelligent Hawaiians in Hawaii who bitterly oppose being placed in the category of Indians, who say, 'We are capable of taking care of ourselves. We do not need any rehabilitation.'" The ranching interests contended that the bill was all for the benefit of the sugar companies.[33]

The Reverend Akaiko Akana appeared on behalf of the Ahahui Pu'uhonua, arguing that rehabilitation was preferable to "charity" because it would "enable Hawaiians to make a start" and would effectively destroy "whatever feeling of bitterness was left in the heart of many Hawaiians not only by reason of the greedy and selfish exploitation of their ignorance by land speculators, but largely by the passing away of what they, as a nation, possessed by reason of conquest and annexation of the islands to the United States." He claimed that the Hawai'ian race could best be rehabilitated by helping them to help themselves.[34]

Senator Pittman responded by questioning Akana about the "highly cultivated cane lands." Why not give those lands to the native Hawai'ians?

Akana echoed Wise and Prince Kuhio in affirming that "Hawaiians don't want the sugar lands," and that it was necessary to continue leasing them to raise revenue for the Hawaiian Homes Commission Fund. In other words, advocates of rehabilitation would not risk alienating the sugar companies by decoupling their legislation from the goals of the Big Five; they would settle for lower-quality lands and leave the sugar lands to the Big Five.[35]

George McClellan, appearing on behalf of the Hawaii Chamber of Commerce in opposition to rehabilitation, called the bill "frankly class and race legislation." These buzzwords meant that the bill discriminated unconstitutionally on behalf of a single class or race of people, the native Hawai'ians, in violation of the Fourteenth Amendment. Again this led to the Indian comparison, because Indian tribes, as national peoples, did have a special status under the law, different from merely a class or a race. McClellan, however, saw the Hawai'ians as a race, not a nation. He argued that this was the first proposed legislation to give "rights to a dark race above and against the rights of the white race." Senator Reed Smoot answered, "Oh, the Indians have such legislation, right along." Prince Kuhio pressed McClellan on his use of the term "race," asking whether McClellan thought "color" was the basis of the bill, and McClellan said, "You may call it racial blood, if you prefer, Mr. Delegate . . . It is avowedly drawn on race lines." Kuhio noted that some Hawai'ians had opposed the bill because they feared that "it would put them in the category of wards," like Indians, but that he had explained to the Hawai'ians "that it was not so, but it was for their salvation."[36]

Once again, the nation/race question—so tied up with the comparison to Indians—cut in several directions. To whites who saw Hawai'ians as a race, any "special legislation" on their behalf was impermissible. To Hawai'ians who saw themselves as a people, the comparison to Indians could either make Hawai'ians appear more like nations, which could be singled out for different treatment under the law, or like wards of the government—domestic, dependent nations—a status not worth having.

The Hawaiian Homes Commission Act, as the rehabilitation act was now known, passed both the House and Senate committees on the territories and then inspired a flurry of letters among the principal opponents and proponents in early 1921. On January 10, 1921, Judge Robertson wrote to Senator Smoot that he was "opposed upon principle to all that part of the bill which relates to the disposition of the public lands of Hawaii." If, however, the bill were to go forward, he wrote, it should be amended "along the lines suggested by Mr. W. B. Pittman and Mr. Geo. M. McClellan. The privileges conferred by the bill, clearly, should be limited to Hawaiians *of the pure blood* who alone arquire [sic], deserve, or are entitled in the slightest degree to rehabilitation at the expense of the taxpayers of the Territory."[37] In this round of negotiation the question of blood quantum became the explicit ground of contention. Opponents of rehabilitation, like Robertson Ranch representative W. B. Pittman, sought to limit its reach by limiting land allotment to "pure" or "full blood" Hawai'ians. Supporters had opened the door for this tactic, however, by invoking "rehabilitation" of a race, rather than political justice for a people or a nation, as the basis for ordinary Hawai'ians' land claims. Opponents also argued that the bill was class legislation, benefiting only a special class.[38] Prince Kuhio lobbied Senator Smoot from the opposite perspective, arguing that the bill was necessary both from the perspective of rehabilitation (otherwise "the Race will become extinct in a very short period of time") and in the general interest, because the new homesteading would raise revenues through taxation.[39]

Despite this spate of lobbying, though, the bill stalled in the Senate. The prince's report to the Senate expressed his frustration that the senators were quarreling over the "blood-fraction giving the right to share the privileges of the act," with some believing the criterion should be one-half, one-fourth, or one-eighth Hawai'ian blood. The prince asserted that he had done his best to reflect everyone's wishes, and that had the bill gone to the Senate floor, it would have passed. To Prince Kuhio, the blood quantum still appeared to be a tangential issue, a technicality, when in fact to many of the players it was the central concern. Had the prince been more aware of the history of Indians in Oklahoma, he might have been more wary.[40]

Later that month Prince Kuhio wrote to Governor McCarthy, expressing his belief that Dr. Horner, the sugar expert, was responsible for the failure of the bill in the Senate. Frustrated, he wrote: "The rehabilitation feature is only a portion of the bill. It is not the most important feature. You know, and I know and Dr. Horner is aware of the fact, that the rehabilitation portion is clearly an experiment. It is a step toward placing the Hawaiians back on the soil and away from the tenements. It injures no one, and may be beneficial to many of Hawaiian blood, should the scheme prove successful." Kuhio was convinced that a cable signed by Horner and others sent to the Senate in the final hours of debate had been the last straw. The *Honolulu Star Bulletin* of January 31, 1921, reported that the signers opposed rehabilitation with the following arguments: "(1) For the first time in Hawaii it brings up the question of race distinction, (2) It is an unjust discrimination against other loyal American citizens, (3) It will not rehabilitate the Hawaiian people[,] (4) The part Hawaiians do not need rehabilitation."[41]

Governor McCarthy then held two meetings at his residence in Hawai'i to amend the bill to make it more palatable to the Big Five companies. At this point John Wise distanced himself from the idea of entitlement and from the "one-thirty-second" definition of native Hawai'ian, asserting that he would support no less than "one eighth or one fourth or even one half" blood quantum. The 1921 draft contained two major changes: the one-thirty-second definition had been revised to one-half blood quantum, and the one thousand–acre limitation on leaseholdings by corporations had been deleted from the Organic Act. In the *Star-Bulletin* of April 18, 1921, Senator Russell objected to the "railroading" of the measure, commenting ironically on the amendment eliminating the thousand-acre limitation for sugar lands. This new draft provided for two things the sugar companies and ranches dearly wanted: a much smaller class of people eligible for land allotments through a new racial definition, and a much greater area of land available for the Big Five. U.S. business interests in Hawai'i were slowly but surely gaining ground.[42]

The House Committee on Territories again held hearings in June 1921. When Wise and Prince Kuhio Kalanianaole were asked about whether Hawaiians supported one-thirty-second or one-half blood quantum, Wise gave inconsistent answers: Hawai'ians would "bless" the chairman, Wise said, if he put the one-thirty-second figure back in the bill, but he also said that Hawai'ians generally supported a one-half or even full blood limitation. "We came over here as beggars, and so we took what we could get," he told the senators. Wise spoke emotionally about the reasons for rehabilitating the part-Hawai'ian, claiming that the future for the "pure" Hawai'ian depended on intermarriage with the part-Hawai'ian. He told the committee that he himself was part-Hawai'ian and had ten children, and "that is not anything to be laughed at."[43]

As a result of this debate, native Hawai'ians did in fact "take what they could get." The bill that made its way into law as the Hawaiian Homes Commission Act (HHCA) in 1921 enshrined a definition of native

Hawai'ian as having "one-half of the blood of the races inhabiting the Islands in 1778." For the first time, the law defined Hawai'ian identity, and it did so explicitly in racial terms, after a debate specifically about entitlement to land. Native Hawai'ians were defined by one-half blood quantum because that definition gave the sugar companies access to the lands they wanted. Just as the blood quantum laws in North America had eventually resulted in railroads, oil and gas companies, and big farmers and ranchers taking over Indian lands, so did the same process—and the same tactic—take hold in Hawai'i.

The practical result of the Hawaiian Homes Commission Act thus mirrored the results of Indian allotments in North America. First-class and second-class lands were leased to plantations and ranches, while the lands chosen for homesteading were third- and fourth-class lands, "rough, rocky, and dry," including 55,000 acres covered with barren lava and another 7,800 acres on steep mountain slopes. Moreover, in the seventy years following the passage of the HHCA, fewer than 6,000 native Hawai'ians received land leases, 30,000 died while on the waiting list, and 22,000 were still waiting. In addition, nearly 14,000 acres of home lands "were transferred to other government agencies through 29 Executive Orders although the Governors had no authority to do so," and other lands were leased, licensed, or otherwise unavailable to homesteading, leaving only 20 percent of the ceded lands that were to have been allotted actually to be homesteaded by native Hawai'ians. Unlike the situation in Indian Territory, in which individual Indians and freedmen in fact received their allotments but lost them to sales and fraud, most native Hawai'ians never received a homestead at all under the Homes Commission Act. When Hawai'i became a state in 1959, the Admission Act transferred about half of the original ceded lands to the state to manage as a trust; the federal government withheld the remainder, primarily for military use. The Admission Act required the ceded lands to be used for five purposes, one of which was the betterment of native Hawai'ians, as defined in the HHCA. Few of the funds, however, went toward programs for native Hawai'ians before 1978.[44]

Hawai'ian Identity Today

In the aftermath of the Hawaiian Homes Commission Act, numerous programs have been adopted to benefit native Hawai'ians, although they have done little to redress the enormous harms of conquest. In 1978 Hawai'i adopted a new constitution, which wrought two important changes in the status of native Hawai'ians. First, it provided that they would be entitled to 20 percent of the revenues from the Ceded Lands Trust and created the Office of Hawaiian Affairs to manage the revenues. Second, it established a major expansion of the definition of "native Hawai'ian." According to the proceedings of the constitutional convention, "The time has come to include all native Hawaiians, regardless of blood quantum." While the new constitution kept the HHCA's definition of native Hawai'ian as an individual with 50 percent blood quantum, it added a new category of "Hawai'ian" defined as anyone who could trace her lineage to the aboriginal people inhabiting the Hawai'ian islands in 1778, with no reference to blood quantum. Although native Hawai'ians who fall within the 50 percent blood quantum have brought several lawsuits challenging the extension of benefits to people of lower blood quantum, the new lineal definition has been consistently upheld by both state courts and the federal Ninth Circuit. Hawai'ians, as descendants of the people whose land was "ceded" to the United States by Queen Lili'uokalani, and therefore the beneficiaries of the Ceded Lands Trust, are the only people eligible to vote for trustees of the Office of Hawaiian Affairs, which administers that trust.[45]

State legislation has created other definitions of native Hawai'ian that are more expansive, allowing classification by reputation, and including adopted or *hanai* persons. In a 1995 case the Hawaiian Supreme Court left open the question of whether "non-Hawaiian members of an 'ohana'— meaning 'family, relative, kin group; . . . extended family, clan' . . . may legitimately claim rights." Native Hawai'ians have also been included in major federal legislation aimed at Native Americans, including the Indian Education Act, the Indian Self-Determination and Education Assistance Act, and the Indian Financing Act, using the broader definition of native identity.[46]

Hawai'ians achieved a major milestone toward recognition of native Hawai'ian sovereignty in the Apology Resolution passed by Congress and signed into law by President Bill Clinton in 1993. Under the Apology Resolution, the United States government apologized to native Hawai'ians "for the overthrow of the Kingdom of Hawaii on January 17, 1893 . . . and the deprivation of the rights of Native Hawaiians to self-determination" and "expresse[d] its commitment to acknowledge the ramifications of the overthrow of the Kingdom of Hawaii, in order to provide a proper foundation for reconciliation between the United States and the Native Hawaiian people." The movement for federal recognition for native Hawai'ians has taken place under the auspices of this "reconciliation" process, which has involved a series of hearings about the best way to redress the problems of native Hawai'ians, and an advisory committee to the U.S. Commission on Civil Rights.[47]

Native Hawai'ians today are divided about whether they should be defined by "blood" or only by descent from an aboriginal ancestor. In Hawai'i there is a complicated relationship among the national independence movement fighting for political sovereignty for native Hawai'ians, the Hawai'ian language movement emphasizing culturally based definitions of Hawai'ian identity, and those who emphasize blood as the basis for native identity. As part of the "reconciliation" process begun after the 1993 Apology Resolution, the Department of the Interior and the Department of Justice held "reconciliation meetings" in Hawai'i in 1999, and the Hawaii Advisory Committee to the U.S. Commission on Civil Rights held hearings there in 2000, both of which recorded a great deal of testimony regarding native Hawai'ian identity and sovereignty. Some who spoke before the committee advocated a "more inclusive approach" to native Hawai'ian identity; Dr. Lilikala Kame'eleihiwa, director of the Center for Hawaiian Studies, University of Hawai'i at Manoa, argued that "the American government's requirement that Native Hawaiians be 50 percent blood quantum" usurps native Hawai'ian sovereignty and the right of native Hawai'ians to determine their own membership. Others defended the 50 percent blood quantum measure, arguing that any dilution of this identity requirement would designate so many people as native Hawai'ians that those meeting the "50-percent-plus blood quantum" would suffer a loss of benefits.[48]

In the midst of this conflict among native Hawai'ians about the best way to define themselves and to begin to redress the forcible conquest of their nation, the Supreme Court dropped a bombshell in 2001. For the first time the Court suggested that native identity was a racial category rather than a national one, throwing into jeopardy the special status not only of native Hawai'ians but of all Indians as well. Despite two centuries of assault on Native American and Hawai'ian sovereignty, the Court had established that "Indian" was a political status in the mid-1970s, saving federal and state programs for Indians from Fourteenth Amendment racial discrimination challenges. The Supreme Court's 2001 decision in *Rice v.*

Cayetano upset this consensus. *Rice* struck down the law that limited voting for trustees of the Office of Hawaiian Affairs to "Hawaiians," defined as "descendants of the aboriginal peoples who lived in Hawaii before 1778." The *Rice* majority opinion for the first time held that a native identity—even one defined without blood quantum, based purely on descent from an aboriginal ancestor—was a proxy for race. While the opinion avoided the plaintiffs' Fourteenth Amendment claim, deciding only on Fifteenth Amendment grounds, *Rice* threw into question any understanding of indigenous people's unique relationship to the U.S. government.[49]

Rice v. Cayetano brought to center stage in the political conflict the relationship of native Hawai'ians to "Indians," and of "race" and "blood" to "sovereignty" and "nationhood." The majority opinion avoided the issue of whether native Hawai'ians were analogous to Indian tribes, although the concurring opinion addressed it directly. Justices Stephen Breyer and David Souter, while observing that native Hawai'ians might be analogous to Indian tribes, joined the majority because they considered the category of "Hawaiian" too large, indicating that had the definition been limited by the 50 percent blood quantum, it might have survived their analysis. The dissent, by contrast, found that ancestry was not a proxy for race in the native Hawai'ian case and should not be prohibited as the basis for a voting qualification.

Native Hawai'ians, Indians, and their advocates have seen the case as a dangerous attack on sovereignty. Critics of *Rice* fear that because of the case's emphasis on the distinction between tribal Indians and other native peoples, tribal enrollment will become the sine qua non of Native American identity, cleaving a dichotomy between a "national" identity for tribal Indians and a "racial" identity for all other Native Americans. Indeed, in Hawai'i, *Rice* has had a cataclysmic effect. White plaintiffs have brought lawsuits challenging nearly every public and private program benefiting native Hawai'ians. On the mainland, in the aftermath of *Rice,* many Indian tribes are debating whether to drop blood quantum requirements and conceptualize Indian identity in terms of race, culture, language, or political affiliation. In the fall of 2000, 15 percent of the Confederate Flathead tribe's members signed a petition to eliminate the one-fourth "blood quantum" requirement for tribal membership; most of the "full bloods" in the tribe vehemently opposed the move.[50]

Fears of the impact of *Rice* have led directly to a move for federal recognition of the native Hawai'ian people. Senator Daniel Akaka of Hawai'i
introduced in 2005 a bill in the Senate to designate native Hawai'ians
as the equivalent of Indian tribes in response to the reasoning in *Rice*.
While some native Hawai'ian groups supported Senate Bill 147, informally
known as the Akaka Bill, others feared that it would amount to an acceptance of less than sovereign status, making them "wards" of the federal
government.

Since *Rice,* the organizations that backed Freddy Rice and the lawyer
who represented him, John Goemans, have brought lawsuits attacking
other programs and institutions for native Hawai'ians on the grounds
that they constitute illicit racial discrimination. In 2006 the Kamehameha
Schools, private schools established by the last surviving member of the
Hawai'ian monarchy, Princess Bernice Pauahi Bishop, for the education of
native Hawai'ian children, defended against a race discrimination lawsuit brought under the civil rights statute used to desegregate Southern
schools. The Ninth Circuit Court of Appeals, in an en banc decision of all
twenty-three judges, found in favor of the school system, in part on the
ground that the schools are wholly private, receiving no federal funds, but
also noting that the schools are racially diverse, with no blood quantum requirement, the only criterion being descent from one aboriginal ancestor.
The schools, however, reached an out-of-court settlement with the plaintiffs in 2007 to avoid having their case heard by the U.S. Supreme Court,
fearing that the Ninth Circuit decision would be overturned.[51]

In order to protect native Hawai'ians from these challenges, the Akaka
Federal Recognition Bill provided for the establishment of a United States
Office for Native Hawaiian Relations and a "Native Hawaiian governing
entity" that would be recognized by the United States. Under the bill, a
"Native Hawaiian" is defined as:

> (i) an individual who is 1 of the indigenous, native people of Hawaii and
> who is a direct lineal descendant of the aboriginal, indigenous, native peo-
> ple who (I) resided in the islands that now comprise the State of Hawaii on
> or before January 1, 1893, and (II) occupied and exercised sovereignty in
> the Hawaiian archipelago, including the area that now constitutes the State
> of Hawaii; or (ii) an individual who is one of the indigenous, native people
> of Hawaii and who was eligible in 1921 for the programs authorized by the
> Hawaiian Homes Commission Act or a direct lineal descendant of that in-
> dividual.

The bill provided for a nine-member Commission of Native Hawaiians with "expertise in the determination of Native Hawaiian ancestry and lineal descendancy" to prepare a roll of native Hawai'ians. Individual applicants for enrollment would then submit documentation to the commission, which could consult with the Office of Hawaiian Affairs and other government agencies in determining whom to enroll.[52]

Proponents of the Akaka Bill argued that it would protect existing federal and state programs for native Hawai'ians, "reaffirm the rights of Native Hawaiians as indigenous people," facilitate the establishment of a native Hawai'ian governing entity, and make it possible for native Hawai'ians to pursue claims for "the lands and resources that were taken from them." The Hawaii Advisory Committee cited the "benefits of formal political status" for native Hawai'ians: "the ability to seek federal funding for housing assistance; the ability to sue the government for breaches of trust; the right to place native children in a culturally appropriate environment; the ability to promote their economic opportunities through favorable tax treatment of ventures within their jurisdiction." In part, the Akaka Bill was a direct reaction to *Rice v. Cayetano,* an attempt to insulate programs for native Hawai'ians from constitutional attack. Mahealani Kamau'u, executive director of the Native Hawaiian Legal Corporation, contended that the Akaka Bill would "possibly recast . . . our status from a racial classification in such a manner as to escape the pernicious application of constitutional law devoid of contextual conscience." Proponents insisted that the Akaka Bill would not foreclose future native Hawai'ian claims, including claims before international tribunals.[53]

Opponents of the bill argued that native Hawai'ians should not give up claims of independence to become wards of the federal government, and that rather than seek federal recognition, Hawai'ians should pursue reparations claims under international law. Opponents also asserted that the Akaka Bill unacceptably narrows the definition of "Hawai'ian" and "native Hawai'ian" by requiring Hawai'ians to prove their lineage through nineteenth-century Hawai'ian kingdom records and 1920 homestead eligibility. On the opposition Web site stopakaka.com, opponents argued: "The bill installs a racial definition of 'Hawaiian' where no such definition ever existed in Hawaii outside of U.S. law. In other words, foreigners will 'help' you decide who is Hawaiian and who isn't. Would you want a stranger to have the power to decide who is a member of your 'ohana' and who isn't?"[54]

As J. Kehaulani Kauanui has written, "Besides defining Hawaiians on a blood-quantum basis, the proposals for federal recognition now before us refuse to acknowledge our inherent sovereignty as a people over our national lands." Kauanui, a historian of Hawai'i, argues that "in evaluating the dangers of federal recognition, Hawaiians should look to cases from Indian Country, Native Alaska, and the U.S. Territories of the Pacific, which all shed light on the problems and pitfalls of domestic dependent nationhood." In testimony before the Senate Committee on Indian Affairs in 2003, Kauanui argued that "there is no guarantee whatsoever that federal recognition for Hawaiians would guarantee . . . protection [against lawsuits like that of Freddy Rice]." Kauanui also pointed out that

> while the 1893 marker provides a timeline tied to Hawaiian sovereignty, it complicates any definition that is exclusively aboriginal . . . [T]he specific requirement that one also be the lineal descendant of a Hawaiian also works to limit broader sovereignty claims that could be made not only by Hawaiians but also by any lineal descendent of a Kingdom citizen. This containment of the sovereignty claim staves off demands for Hawai'i's independence and decolonization from the United States, based on international law, for both Hawaiian people and others.[55]

Many opponents tied federal recognition to the notion of defining Hawai'ians "as just a race." Alani Apio writes, "When the queen's soldiers were disarmed after the overthrow of a viable nation, America was enabled to recognize Hawaiians solely by race." Apio identifies the HHCA as a "major act of racism . . . By setting a blood quantum instead of a 'nationality' quantum, America employed 'race' . . . to pit us against ourselves over land. Equally important, it gave all non-Kanaka the grounds on which to call the program racist." These opponents saw federal recognition as an extension of the Hawaiian Homes Commission Act further racializing native Hawai'ians.[56]

Of course, federal recognition was also opposed by those seeking an end to all recognition of native Hawai'ians, whether as an independent nation or as a quasi-sovereign body similar to an Indian tribe. These included the same groups that were funding the onslaught of litigation against the Office of Hawaiian Affairs (OHA) and the Kamehameha Schools, including the *Rice* and *Arakaki* lawsuits. These opponents speak the language of unity, equal protection, and color-blindness. For example, H. William Burgess, attorney for the *Arakaki* plaintiffs, argued, "The bill would erase aloha and impose apartheid." In his version of the history of overthrow and annexation, "Hawaiians, unlike the American Indians, decided not to remain separate and apart. Hawaiians welcomed the new immigrants and their ways and chose the path of assimilation because both the ali'i and the commoners decided it was in their own interests to do so." Burgess asserted that he had "never seen or heard of any Japanese tribe or Irish tribe or Hawaiian tribe or quasi-sovereign entity or separate enclave of any kind" in Hawai'i. Just as talking about all people white or black or green or blue, when in fact no green or blue people exist, makes the notion of racial hierarchy appear ridiculous, so the invocation of a "Japanese tribe" or an "Irish tribe" makes the idea of a quasi-sovereign native Hawai'ian nation appear absurd.[57]

The comparison between native Hawai'ians and American Indians or Alaskans remained a contentious issue, as opponents of the Akaka Bill emphasized that they did not want to become "wards" of the federal government like mainland Native Americans, echoing similar arguments eighty years earlier about "blanket Indians." At the same time, Indian tribes today have better-established rights to sovereignty than do native Hawai'ians. As the Hawaiian Advisory Committee notes, "on the one hand, Hawaiians reject the comparison to American Indians, stating that they are not a tribe; on the other hand, they compare themselves to American Indians to justify their right to self-determination."[58]

Extensive hearings were held in Washington, D.C., and Honolulu on an early version of the federal recognition bill in August–September 2000. Most of the native Hawai'ians who testified opposed the bill. Some supported it with reservations about the blood quantum limitation. For example, Mililani Trask, a former trustee of OHA, testified that "we do not favor the 1921 definition of blood quantum, because most of our people were not born in hospitals at that time. My grandfather was not born in a hospital. He does not have a birth certificate, saying that he is a Native Hawaiian . . . That is why, in the bill, we are asking to bring in our own genealogical records." Others who supported it emphasized that it was only a first step. As Robin J. Puanani Danner argued, "this bill does not represent the end all, be all of Hawaiian self-determination." She also commented: "Much has been said over the many months, and even in this hearing today, about whether this bill attempts to turn me, a Hawaiian, into an Indian, or an Eskimo. Neither this bill, nor any bill can accomplish this."[59]

Native Hawai'ians who spoke at the hearings in opposition to federal recognition emphasized sovereignty, self-determination, and resistance to allowing the United States to define their identity. Repeatedly they rejected the names "Hawaiians" or "Native Hawaiians" and insisted on the name "Kanaka Maoli." Many used the term "genocide" to describe what would result if the bill were passed. In the case of Hawai'i, as among tribes on the mainland, sovereignty and self-determination have become inexorably tied to the determination of racial identity.[60]

As with the Seminole and Cherokee nations, issues of sovereignty and intervention by the federal government remain potent in the struggles of the native Hawai'ian people to define themselves. In both cases racial identity, and in particular "blood quantum," became meaningful at the historic moment of land allotment, and adjudications of identity from the first decades of the twentieth century continue to cast a long shadow on current debates. Perhaps most unfortunate is the fact that so many members of these nations have come to equate sovereignty with the right to exclude on the basis of blood quantum, despite the relatively recent history of "blood" as a factor in the determination of citizenship, and its association with policies that destroyed indigenous peoples' land base.

CHAPTER SEVEN

Racial Science, Immigration, and the "White Races"

WHILE STATE COURTS frequently litigated individuals' racial identity, the U.S. Supreme Court rarely did. Between the 1816 case of "negro John Davis v. Wood" until 1923 there were no U.S. Supreme Court cases directly addressing the subject of whether one person or a group of people were white, "negro," or something else. But in 1923 the Supreme Court decided two cases within three months that did directly take up the question of racial identity. One of these cases concerned the identity of Bhagat Singh Thind, a highly educated immigrant from the Punjab region of India. As a "Hindu," was Thind white for the purposes of naturalization to U.S. citizenship?

In an unusual move, Thind submitted his own personal "Statement Regarding His Race" to the Court. In this statement, Thind tried to bring to bear the weight of a new racial science, cultural anthropology. He asked: "What is the 'white' race and of what peoples is it composed? A very slight study of anthropology will convince even the most skeptical person *that there is no clearly defined 'white' race.*" He then argued that courts should abandon the absurd effort to classify people racially. Needless to say, the Supreme Court did not heed Thind's call to abandon racial determination. But he was able to have this unusual argument recorded for the first time in an American courtroom, because such questions were now beginning to be raised within racial science itself.[1]

The early twentieth century was the heyday of a new racial science to which courts turned for answers about racial identity. Two scientific movements vied for authority, both within the courtroom and beyond: eugenics and the new science of cultural anthropology. Racial scientists gave conflicting answers to questions of who counted as white, whether there were five or fourteen "races," and whether "race" itself was a meaningful category of human differentiation. Yet litigants, lawyers, and judges turned to these new scientific experts—professors rather than local doctors—in order to resolve claims of whiteness, this time in cases involving the right to formal U.S. citizenship as "free white persons."

In trials involving questions of black and native identity, law had equated whiteness with full social and political citizenship. An individual was white if he proved himself capable of acts of civic participation. And only if proven white would he be allowed to vote, to marry a white person, to live where he wanted, and to participate fully in society. Some Indians carved out a space for independent schools and institutions, but only to the extent that they distanced themselves from black identity. Yet even if they enjoyed only second-class citizenship, most of these people were formally U.S. citizens, with the right to remain on American soil: African Americans, whether formerly enslaved or free; Indians who had accepted individual land allotments and forsaken their tribal allegiance; and racially ambiguous people who had successfully won status as white, like the Melungeons.

At the turn of the twentieth century, for the first time, who could become a *formal* citizen of the United States became a burning question on the national agenda. This was not only an era of massive immigration of new groups to the United States but also a time of legislative and political efforts to restrict that immigration. In the courtroom the question was, how would the United States recognize citizenship among the thousands of new immigrants from Europe, Asia, and Mexico once they were here? Could any immigrant to the United States become an American citizen, or would some people be barred even from formal citizenship? Federal courts wrestled with these questions in trials over the racial identity of national groups—Armenians, Syrians, Japanese, Mexicans, and South Asian Indians. The Federal Immigration and Naturalization Act made formal citizenship an issue of racial identity by limiting naturalization to "free white persons" (since 1790) and people of "African nativity" (since 1866).

The largest influx of immigrants that had yet been seen in America occurred in the late nineteenth and early twentieth centuries, as hundreds of thousands of eastern and southern Europeans entered U.S. ports. These southern Italians, Poles, and Germans, as well as Jews from all over eastern Europe, faced hostility because of their Catholic or Jewish religious identity and their real or imagined radical politics, as well as their swarthy resemblance to people of color. They faced overt discrimination in employment, housing, and public accommodations, and some nativist ideologues and political demagogues even spoke of them as separate and inferior races. Yet despite the discrimination and racialization they faced, these Europeans were never deprived of U.S. citizenship: they became naturalized as citizens, voted, attended white schools, joined the armed forces and served in white units, and married white people without restriction. In all of these important respects, these Europeans were "white on arrival." Indeed their whiteness was established by means of their contrast to people whom America understood as "black."[2]

By contrast, immigrants from Asia and Mexico faced a very different legal, political, and ideological regime in California and the Southwestern borderlands. The first Asians to arrive—Chinese, then Japanese—worked on the railroads, in the gold mines, and in agriculture. Likewise, most Mexican immigrants worked in agriculture. In the nineteenth century, these Asian and Mexican immigrants were nearer to peons than free wage workers, degraded in status in order to provide cheap plantation-style labor, not unlike the freed African American slaves in the post–Civil War Southeast.

We may be tempted to attribute this difference in status between European immigrants on the one hand and Mexicans and Asians on the other to the idea that the latter truly *were* less white than the Europeans, and so were subject to color biases that centuries of African slavery and battles with Indians had already established in American minds. But in fact, among the Greeks, Mexicans, Punjab Indians, Spanish, Japanese, Italians, Irish, and Chinese, it would not have been a simple and obvious matter to sort people according to color, appearance, or cultural assimilation, nor even according to performance of "whiteness." Who would seem "whiter" or a better candidate for U.S. citizenship: the British-accented Punjabi doctor or the olive-skinned Greek bricklayer who spoke not a word of English? The Japanese farm worker or his Italian counterpart? The carpenter from Spain or the one from Mexico? Only in retrospect is it obvious who "was" and who "wasn't" white—precisely because of the legal and social processes set in motion by the trials of racial identity. These trials, unlike trials of earlier cases involving individuals, turned less on personal appearance or performance of whiteness and more on the attributes of an entire people. Racial science held out the hope of definitive answers to these questions, but scientific battles of the experts, as in the nineteenth century, often gave way to racial common sense.

Though nonwhite immigrants, enslaved Africans, and conquered native peoples were all denied citizenship at one point or another, and though in all cases, racial identity trials were significant legal and social mechanisms that helped determine who might be entitled to citizenship, the processes were different for each group, and so was the spirit in which the trials were conducted. In nineteenth-century trials there was a kind of spontaneous quality to courtroom behavior, with the trials providing a window onto the wider culture's anxieties and assumptions about race, albeit mediated through legal language and practice. In these twentieth-century trials, however, the discussions and uses of racial identity were more conscious and strategic on both sides. The difference was made by the Fourteenth Amendment. Now that the U.S. Constitution explicitly insisted that every citizen had the right to equal protection under the law, regardless of race, color, or creed, efforts to discriminate on the basis of race would have to be carried out in a different spirit than in the America in which Justice Roger Taney famously declared that blacks at the time of the founding were "so far inferior, that they had no rights which the white man was bound to respect." Racial discrimination continued, to be sure, and the state was often its agent—but now that activity had to be carried out *as though* the Fourteenth Amendment's promise was still being kept. As a result, trials reflected the elaborate processes which judges, lawyers, juries, and participants employed to fit their own views of race into a legal framework that declared race to be irrelevant, rather than into a body of law that validated racial discrimination at its heart.[3]

"A Race So Different from Our Own"

The annexation of California in 1848 led not only to American expansion toward Asia but also to the migration of Asians to America. The first Asians who arrived on U.S. shores were Chinese immigrants who came during the 1850s for sanctuary from the Opium Wars, peasant rebellions, and harsh economic conditions; most came voluntarily and paid their own way. By 1852, 20,000 Chinese were immigrating per year, and by 1870, some 63,000 Chinese were living in the United States. During the 1860s, two-thirds of these Chinese immigrants were working in California gold mines,

but as mining profits decreased and heavy "foreign miners taxes" were levied, more and more went to work for the Central Pacific Railroad, run by
Leland Stanford, so that at its peak, the railroad employed 12,000 Chinese
laborers, 90 percent of its workforce. The harsh conditions in the mines
and railroads killed hundreds and perhaps thousands of Chinese workers,
whose contribution to the development of the U.S. economy endures in
the railroads that by 1900 spanned more than 200,000 miles and crossed
the continent. When the railroad was finished, Chinese workers moved
to cities, particularly San Francisco, where employment discrimination
pushed most Chinese into self-employment, especially the laundry business and restaurants. Most men had come to the United States alone; of
the small number of women, the majority came over as prostitutes, usually
held in debt peonage for the price of their passage. By the late nineteenth
century, the Chinese had become an urban population, disproportionately
male.

Chinese immigrants arrived with some economic resources and were
extremely well organized. Most of them were recruited by the Chinese
"Six Companies," or Chinese Community Benevolent Associations, clan
organizations in such major cities as San Francisco which helped immigrants and served as a bridge to the wider society, especially to American
employers. Once in the United States, Chinese immigrants pooled their
resources in these benevolent associations and other organizations, not
only for economic advancement but also to fight discrimination through
litigation.

Throughout the nineteenth century, the Chinese were subject to harsh
discrimination. For example, ordinances in San Francisco prohibited men
from wearing their hair in a long "queue" in the back, a law clearly aimed
at humiliating Chinese men; other laws prohibited carrying laundry in bas-
kets on a stick, in the customary manner of Chinese laundrymen. At the
same time, small numbers of Chinese immigrants were able to naturalize
to citizenship before the 1882 Exclusion Law, and they proved to be remarkably adept litigants, fighting discriminatory laws and the application
of the 1882 law with more lawsuits per capita than any other ethnic group
in the United States.

More often than not they lost, as most courts assumed that Chinese,
members of the so-called "Mongolian race," were not white. They harked
back to an 1854 precedent, *People v. Hall,* in which a California court determined that a Chinese person could not offer testimony against a white

criminal defendant, deciding that the statutory disqualification of "Black or Mulatto . . . or Indian" witnesses should extend to the Chinese as well. The court based its opinion on three things: first, a scientific claim that American Indians were related to the "Mongolian race"; second, a historical claim that the drafters of the statute understood "Black person" to mean nonwhite, so that the term "necessarily excludes all races other than the Caucasian"; and third, a stark statement of white supremacy. The court did not want to extend "equal rights of citizenship" to "a race of people whom nature has marked as inferior, and who are incapable of progress or intellectual development beyond a certain point, as their history has shown; differing in language, opinions, color, and physical conformation; between whom and ourselves nature has placed an impassable difference." Accordingly, "Mongolians"—a term that presumably extended to Japanese and Koreans—were marked as racially inferior and culturally inassimilable. After the Civil War, this opinion helped bolster the view of an impassable gulf between white and nonwhite: anyone who was not white must be black, or something like black.[4]

This view of the Chinese as essentially "African" in their inability to rise to the elementary requirements of citizenship continued basically unchallenged, so that four decades later, in 1896, the "Great Dissenter," Justice John Marshall Harlan, while dissenting from the U.S. Supreme Court's imposition of "separate but equal" to justify Jim Crow segregation in *Plessy v. Ferguson,* nevertheless partook of the same logic to relegate Asians to a nonwhite status. Harlan was willing to imagine full citizenship for the freed slaves, whom he saw as truly American, but he could not envision extending such citizenship to Asians. Consequently, in a little-noted paragraph of his *Plessy* dissent, he compared African Americans, who were finally citizens of the United States (albeit citizens whom some wished to separate entirely from the polity), to Asians: "There is a race so different from our own that we do not permit those belonging to it to become citizens of the United States. Persons belonging to it are, with few exceptions, absolutely excluded from our country." This view was so uncontroversial that Harlan's words have received almost no attention. His dissent is generally seen as a prescient judgment on the injustice of Jim Crow, and a moving paean to the possibility of full citizenship for African Americans. Yet even while Harlan argued for African American inclusion in the polity, Asian American citizenship remained unimaginable to many.[5]

In the antebellum and Jim Crow eras it seemed that the Chinese could be seamlessly assimilated to the position of African Americans—in law, politics, and social practice. Just as discrimination against black people was the organizing principle of the new state of Oklahoma, with the Democratic Party rallying poor, formerly Southern whites to loyalty on the basis of Jim Crow, so did anti-Chinese agitation become the rallying cry for California unions and the nascent Democratic Party after the Civil War. The state party also appealed to migrants from the South, drawing explicit analogies between blacks and Chinese, even as the unions expressed their members' economic anxieties in racial rather than class terms. They successfully fed on workers' fears of competition, effectively building a movement to exclude the Chinese completely. After Chinese exclusion, the process was repeated with other Asian immigrants. Big farmers and ranchers recruited first Japanese and then Mexican and Filipino workers. Each time the farmers found a new source of cheap immigrant labor, immigration restrictionists responded by lobbying for the exclusion of that group.

Nativism cannot be wholly explained in economic terms, however. Some of the leading lights of the national movement to limit immigration were old-line Anglo-Saxon Protestants from the East Coast establishment who had no personal economic stake in restricting immigration. Indeed, big business interests by and large resisted efforts to keep out laborers, as they correctly saw immigration as driving down the price of labor. People like Henry Cabot Lodge, Prescott Hall, Charles Warren, and Robert DeCourcy Ward, however, founders of the national Immigration Restriction League in 1893, and Madison Grant, the author of *The Passing of the Great Race,* were Boston Brahmins distressed by the power of Irish and Irish American political machines. They hoped to preserve Anglo-Saxon America by restricting immigration. These men, fighting to recapture the world they had dominated at mid-century, feared both the laboring masses and the new, dynamic, upwardly mobile capitalists—self-made men such as Andrew Carnegie and J. P. Morgan—and they voiced their fears in increasingly racial terms.[6]

Such concerns found their logical expression in the eugenics movement, whose aim was to purify the white race by selective breeding and the elimination of "race mixing." The eugenics movement provided the language for these men to portray entire nations as different races. Not only the Chinese and Japanese but also southern Italians, "Mediterraneans," Jews, and other southern Europeans were viewed as dark and inassimilable peoples who could destroy "the Aryan race." These eugenicist arguments were picked up more broadly—by business and political leaders, and even unions—as a way to play on fears of economic competition. The Democratic Party in California adopted the racial vocabulary of eugenics to appeal to southern migrants, who were more than ready to substitute "Chinese" for "black."

Nativist activity by California union leaders and politicians, as well as some Eastern advocates of immigration restriction, culminated in the 1882 Exclusion Act, which made it unlawful for Chinese laborers to enter the United States for the next ten years and denied naturalized citizenship to the Chinese already here. Six years later the prohibition was broadened from laboring Chinese to include "all persons of Chinese race."[7]

Immigration restrictionists then turned their attention to the Japanese, who had been in the United States since the 1870s, mainly in Western states, working first on railroads and then in agriculture. The first generation of Japanese immigrants, despite having arrived in the United States with high rates of literacy and education compared to the Chinese, nevertheless found themselves relegated to the lowest positions as farm laborers. When new to an area, Japanese workers initially accepted low wages, but once established, they began fighting for better conditions and higher wages. This threat contributed to employers' hostility, especially as some Japanese immigrants began to earn enough money to buy their own land and become small farmers. Even more threatening was the formation of the Japanese-Mexican Labor Association, established in 1903 by some eight hundred Japanese and Mexican farm workers in Oxnard, California. Nativists and union leaders viewed the Japanese, like the Chinese, with suspicion and prejudice, as inassimilable and dangerous foreigners. But because Japanese women—many of them "picture brides" who had never met their future husbands—did immigrate in increasing numbers between 1900 and 1920, the fears of the "Chinaman" as sexual threat were not extended to the Japanese.[8]

Still, white workers were anxious about the possibility that the Japanese would take their jobs, if not their women. In 1900 the first mass meeting aimed at excluding the Japanese was held in San Francisco; that year both the national Populist Party and the American Federation of Labor (AFL) came out in favor of restricting Japanese immigration. Delegates from a number of trade unions in San Francisco founded the Japanese and Korean Exclusion League in 1905 to combat Japanese immigration, which had reached ten thousand people per year, mostly to the farms of California's Central Valley, but also to such West Coast cities as Los Angeles, San Francisco, and Portland. Three years later, under pressure from union leaders and politicians in California, President Theodore Roosevelt negotiated with Japan a "Gentleman's Agreement" in which Japan agreed to stop issuing emigrant visas to its own laborers—but to little effect. Japanese workers continued to immigrate, but faced increasing discrimination from a population who continued to view them as a race apart.

In California, for example, school segregation laws and "alien land laws" restricting land ownership to citizens were passed, aimed at "Mongolians," a term that, since the 1854 *Hall* decision, was understood to encompass Chinese, Japanese, and Koreans. The 1913 land law particularly harmed Japanese immigrants, who worked in agriculture, were more likely to own land than the Chinese, and remained a largely rural population. Clearly, both competing workers and the owners of agribusiness saw the industrious and assertive Japanese as an economic threat. As a result, some Japanese moved to urban areas, where they primarily went into domestic service and founded small businesses, in large part because they were denied access to higher-paying industrial jobs by employers who refused to hire them.

Land and employment were not the only issues: numerous states revised their miscegenation statutes in the twentieth century to include a marriage prohibition between whites and "Mongolians," though some specified just Chinese, just Japanese, or just those two nationalities. While some of these states had significant Asian populations—in particular California, Nevada, and Oregon—others were home to relatively few Asians, such as Georgia, Idaho, Maryland, Missouri, Nebraska, and Virginia. Many of the latter states, however, had large black or Indian populations, and long histories of dealing with the question of social and/or political citizenship on a racial basis. These state legislatures adopted broad statutes prohibiting marriage between whites and a growing list of other races. Clearly, Western unions and politicians had been successful in placing anti-Asian hysteria on the national agenda, leading not only to the passage of the national Exclusion Act but also to anti-miscegenation laws in states that had no Asian immigrants but feared them nonetheless. Eastern eugenicists had successfully allied with Western Democrats to create fears of a sexual threat to white womanhood and of the "mongrelization" of the white race—even in places where there were no actual Asian bodies onto which to project those fears.

Old-line New Englanders provided the crucial political support for restricting immigration not only from Asia but from Europe as well. Once they had succeeded in curtailing Chinese and Japanese immigration, they lobbied for the imposition of a literacy test on all immigrants, which was passed in 1917, and finally, in 1924, the National Immigration Act. The 1924 act, known as the "Quota Act," cut off almost all Asian immigration. By pegging immigration quotas for each nation to its percentage of the U.S. population in the 1890 census—before the great influx of immigrants from southern and eastern Europe—it effectively cut off immigration from those regions as well. This law, combined with the Great Depression of the 1930s, did curtail the flood of immigrants—from nearly 6 million in the 1910s to about a half-million in the 1930s—until well after World War II.

Within the overall restriction on Asian immigration, a single loophole prevailed: because the Philippines was a "ward" state of the United States, Filipinos had the ambiguous status of American "nationals." While it was clear that they were not U.S. citizens, they were allowed to immigrate freely in the 1920s, especially after the exclusion of the Chinese and Japanese led to labor shortages on commercial farms. Accordingly, by 1930, out of a total of 65,000 Filipinos in the United States, 34,000 were living in California, the great majority working as migrant laborers together with Mexicans.

California saw several anti-Filipino "race riots" in 1929 and 1930 in Exeter (Tulare County) and Watsonville (Monterey County). Angry white mobs attacked dozens of Filipinos and murdered one man; no one was indicted for these crimes. The *New York Times* editorial page portrayed the Exeter "affair" as the product of "economic jealousy": Filipinos were "willing to work for less—and to work harder—than white laborers. This is their 'crime.'" What really drove the conflict, however, was not simply that Filipinos worked for lower wages but that they fought for higher wages. As Carey McWilliams explained in the pages of *The Nation* at the time, Filipinos were "militantly race-conscious" and "protest[ed] against [their] exploitation."[9]

Yet despite the militancy of Filipino workers, most contemporary journalists and sociologists attributed anti-Filipino sentiment to sexual rather than economic competition. Even more so than the Chinese, Filipino immigrants were exclusively young and male, so that their only option for female companionship was non-Filipino women—mostly Mexican and white "dancehall girls." Thus, in addition to expressing fears of Filipino "cheap labor," California newspaper editorialists and politicians began calling attention to the dangers of Filipino male sexuality. Just as in the South under Reconstruction the politically and economically threatening black man became the target of hysterical fears of rape, now Filipino men were portrayed as a threat to white womanhood. According to one contemporary author, Filipinos "raised a much greater question than was the case with the previous Chinese and Japanese immigration" because they posed a sexual as well as an economic threat. Unlike the Chinese and Japanese workers who had immigrated earlier, workers of a lower social class, the recent Filipino immigrants were "of a much higher intellection level . . . gifted along artistic and social lines," educated and "ambitious." In the evenings "they are to be seen dressed in their best parading down the main streets." The Filipino was a "lounge lizard." The president of the Immigration Study Commission, C. M. Goethe, wrote in a popular journal in 1931 of the "peril" of Filipino immigration. He attributed the recent anti-Filipino riots in California to the "primitive moral code" of this "jungle folk" more than to economic competition. Goethe argued that Filipino men tended "to interbreed with near-moron white girls. The resulting hybrid is almost invariably undesirable. The ever increasing brood of children of Filipino coolie fathers and low-grade white mothers may in time constitute a serious social burden." Unlike the supposedly inassimilable Chinese and Japanese, many Filipinos spoke English, wore American clothes, and had already assimilated to American culture in the Philippines before arriving in the United States. Thus the prevailing stereotypes of Filipino men were more like those of the oversexed African American—fully American, perhaps, but especially dangerous.[10]

Even contemporary supporters of Filipino immigrants' rights saw conflict over miscegenation looming larger than economic competition. In his exhaustive study of race riots, the sociologist Emory Bogardus found that most were triggered by interaction between Filipino men and white dancehall girls. The social worker and reformer Bruno Lasker pointed out the irony that some employers preferred Filipinos to Mexicans because "the latter bring their families with them and are apt to create problems of dependency," yet at the same time, "one of the strongest objections to the Filipinos . . . is that they *do not* have families and wish to mix socially with the white community, and especially the fair sex." As in the post-Emancipation South, economic and sexual fears merged into racist hysteria aimed at Filipino exclusion. Anti-immigrant sentiment made for some strange bedfellows: the AFL, the American Legion, and the same upper-class New England nativist groups which had fought for the 1924 Quota Act all called for Filipino exclusion in the late 1920s.[11]

At the same time, political leaders in the Philippines began making more insistent demands for immediate and complete independence from the United States. Surprisingly, advocates for Filipino exclusion joined forces with supporters of Philippine decolonization, despite the gap between their goals. By tying independence for the Philippines to tariffs on Philippine imports, the right to retain military bases in the Philippines, and the right to exclude all Philippine citizens from the United States as "aliens," the proposed independence legislation met all of the nativists' goals. Although the United States would lose one of its foreign colonies, it would retain the benefits of unrestricted access to the Philippine market and to its strategic military assets, while curtailing emigration to America.

Finally, in 1934 the Philippines Independence Act, known as the Tydings-McDuffie Act, granted the Philippines the status of a commonwealth, with a ten-year transition period to independence. It also cut off immigration to the U.S. mainland almost completely, labeling all Filipinos residing in the United States "aliens." The Immigration and Naturalization Service began a campaign of repatriating Filipino "aliens," both voluntarily and involuntarily. Although over two thousand Filipinos returned to the Philippines, tens of thousands remained. The depression era gave rise to a movement to deport Mexican nationals (and some Mexican Americans) to Mexico when there was no work for them in the fields; this was the same tactic that would be used against Filipinos a few years later, making the 1930s the peak of anti-Filipino agitation in California.

Not surprisingly, given the sexualized fears of Filipino men, the first efforts to reckon with the racial identity of Filipinos arose in the context of marriage between Filipino men and white women, which came before California courts in growing numbers in the 1930s. Because the marriage law in California banned only marriages between whites and "Mongolians, negroes, and Indians," when prosecutors tried to enforce the law against Filipino-white marriages, courts had to decide whether Filipinos were "Mongolian." When several courts decided that Filipinos did not fall into that category, the anti-Filipino lobby secured new legislation to add "Malay" to the marriage ban.

Despite the efforts at exclusion and restriction, by the first decades of the twentieth century, a substantial number of people of Asian origin were living on the West Coast, including Filipinos, Japanese, Chinese, and Indians. They faced violence, segregation, restrictions on their rights to marry and own property, and even deportation if their naturalization to citizenship was invalidated. While some Americans viewed these new immigrants from the start as "a race so different from our own," others joined together with them as striking workers and as husbands and wives. But in order for these Asian Americans to remain in the United States as citizens, and especially to attain the full rights of social and political citizenship, they had to prove that, though Asian, they were also "free white persons" eligible for naturalization to citizenship, and thus had a right to own land and marry other white people.

Asian Americans' battles to prove that they were not "a race apart" ran headlong into the burgeoning debates over the "science" of race. The kind of racial expertise that had developed out of nineteenth-century racial identity trials—in which medical doctors and laypeople discussed the characteristics of the African and Caucasian races—was now being claimed by a new generation of racial scientists, the eugenicists, and their challengers, the new culturalists.

Eugenics and Anthropology

The first science of race developed in the mid-nineteenth century on both sides of the Atlantic, concerned with classifying human beings according to a great "Chain of Being." These natural scientists, from Johann Friedrich Blumenbach at the end of the seventeenth century, to the natural historians Buffon and Linnaeus, sought to classify human beings as they classified other species of plants and animals, according to their physical, mental, and moral features. These were not neutral classifications, however; they were hierarchical.

By the turn of the twentieth century, a new academic discipline had been born in American universities: anthropology. This discipline constituted itself around classifying "the peoples of the world" into races, building on the work of the natural historians. For example, A. H. Keane, one of the first professors of "ethnology," began participating in the meetings of the Anthropological Institute in 1879 and eventually became a leader in the organization. He published the first edition of his treatise on ethnology in 1890 and, in 1908, his best-known work, *The World's Peoples:*

A Popular Account of Their Bodily and Mental Characters, Beliefs, Traditions, Political and Social Institutions. Today the descriptions of each "people" contained in the work would not sound very scientific to us. For example, of the "Mongolic or Yellow Division" he wrote: "Mental Characters: Generally somewhat reserved, sullen, and apathetic (Mongols proper); very thrifty, frugal and industrious (Chinese and Japanese); indolent (Malays, Siamese, Koreans); nearly all reckless gamblers; science slightly, arts and letters moderately developed; porcelain, bronze work, ivory carving, and decorative painting scarcely surpassed (China, Japan, Korea formerly); but all plastic and pictorial art defective, lacking perspective, and the human figure mostly caricatured." But courts and legislatures relied heavily on Keane's work and that of other early anthropologists when they sought to define race.[12]

Over two years from 1910 to 1911, the Dillingham Commission issued a series of reports to Congress on immigration, including an exhaustive "Dictionary of Races or Peoples" hundreds of pages long, listing different "races" or "peoples," including, for example, "Mongolian": "That grand division of mankind which is typically, as to color, yellowish, and as to origin, culture, and present habitat, Asiatic. An important subject in immigration." The Dillingham Commission's recommendations eventually led to the adoption of stringent immigration restriction legislation in 1921 and 1924, establishing immigration quotas based on national origins that were designed to keep the racial composition of the United States as it had been in the census year 1890.[13]

Nativists who sought to exclude Asian immigrants from American shores drew upon even more avant-garde scientific theories, however, to make their case that Asians constituted a "peril" to white America: theories of eugenics. The eugenics movement aimed to improve humanity—especially the "Aryan races"—through selective breeding and race-specific policies of immigration restriction. The popularizers of eugenics in the United States preached that racial purity could be achieved only by keeping the races strictly separate and keeping America a white nation. They advocated not just immigration restriction but also the passage of stringent segregation and sterilization laws aimed at blacks, Indians, and Mexicans. Eugenicists also warned that "race mixing" would lead to the "mongrelization" of the white race, which went beyond a strictly "racial purity" issue to fears about the survival of humans in general: eugenicists feared that the products of racial mixture would be weaker, less intelligent, and less able to reproduce than their parents.

In addition to their primary theoretical and political focus on selective breeding—conscious efforts to "improve the race"—the eugenicists were also preoccupied with restricting immigration, which they justified by the fear that America would become a "mongrel" nation. Eugenicist leader Alfred P. Schultz wrote in his book *Race or Mongrel*, "The intermarriage of people of one colour with people of another colour always leads to deterioration." Proof of this danger could be found in Brazil's "mongrel nondescript type, deficient in physical and mental energy," or in Mexico, where the vice president of the Immigration Restriction League, Madison Grant, argued, "the absorption of the blood of the original Spanish conquerors by the native Indian population has produced the racial mixture which we call Mexican, and which is now engaged in demonstrating its incapacity for self-government." Accordingly, the eugenicists scoffed at the idea of "foreign races" improving while in the United States and rejected even the possibility of their being assimilated. Schultz wrote: "The opinion is advanced that the public schools change the children of all races into Americans. Put a Scandinavian, a German, and a Magyar boy in at one end, and they will come out Americans at the other end. Which is like saying, let a pointer, a setter, and a pug enter one end of a tunnel and they will come out three greyhounds at the other end."[14]

The eugenicists were certain that "race mixing" always resulted in reversion to the lowest common denominator. They insisted that "mulattoes" were like mules, which could not reproduce, and were weaker and less intelligent than others of pure blood. Madison Grant explained: "Whether we like to admit it or not, the result of the mixture of two races, in the long run, gives us a race reverting to the more ancient, generalized and lower type. The cross between a white man and an Indian is an Indian; the cross between a white man and a negro is a negro; the cross between a white man and a Hindu is a Hindu; and the cross between any of the three European races and a Jew is a Jew." Consequently Grant recommended segregation and sterilization of the "lower races" and restriction of immigration to avoid "sweeping the nation toward a racial abyss."[15]

In response to the eugenicists, advocates for Asian and Mexican immigrants argued for better "race relations"—a new term in the 1920s—and an end to racial discrimination. During the 1920s and 1930s liberal sociologists inaugurated a massive "Survey of Race Relations in California," chronicling a great deal of anti-"Oriental" prejudice. Eliot Grinnell Mears, the executive secretary of the survey, sought to downplay racial difference and emphasize economic competition as the cause of problems between natives and immigrants. Mears argued: "Entirely overemphasized in the popular California stand is an alleged racial inferiority factor. In fact, even the rabid talkers admit in private, if not in public, that there is no basis for assuming that the Oriental civilization is inferior to our own; it may be superior. The important point is its marks of difference which appear to make assimilation biologically and culturally exceedingly difficult." With such statements as these, liberal culturalists of the early twentieth century hoped to convince fellow Americans that differences among nationality groups should not be seen in racial terms, and that they should give up race prejudices.[16]

Mears and liberals like him drew upon racial science, and in particular the new cultural anthropology, as did the Asian immigrants who challenged their second-class status in court in naturalization and miscegenation cases. They had a great deal of new science to help them, for in the early twentieth century, the anthropologist Franz Boas and his students released an outpouring of studies aimed at refuting eugenic understandings of race. Boas and his students called on Americans to see human difference in terms of history, culture, and environment rather than immutable biology. Many, including Boas himself, testified in court cases litigating the racial identity of various immigrant groups.[17]

Yet for the most part, the new culturalism was of little benefit to Asians in court. Its arguments most directly benefited members of "the white races"—that is, Europeans—rather than people from one of the other great "divisions of mankind," for while the cultural anthropologists considered race much less important than culture in explaining human difference, they did believe that race existed. Although they repudiated the eugenicist belief in several dozen races (Aryan, Celtic, and Nordic, among others), the cultural anthropologists did maintain the "grand divisions of mankind"—white, red, yellow, brown, and black. They were also inconsistent, invoking two contradictory arguments: first, that race was a fiction, not a meaningful biological category; and second, that race was *only* biology, with no cultural implications.[18]

At the time, these two arguments did not seem contradictory, for they were generally made in different contexts. The first—that race was a biological fiction—was raised in response to the eugenicists' claim that dozens of different races existed. Late-nineteenth-century and early-twentieth-century Americans used the term "races" to indicate "large groups like Nordics and Mediterraneans, medium-sized ones like the Celts and Hebrews, or smaller ones like the North or South Italians," in a manner that corresponds more closely to what would today be called "nationality" or "ethnicity." Cultural anthropologists were at pains to show that this notion of "race" had no biological basis: it was not possible to distinguish biologically between, say, Swedes and Italians.[19]

Turn-of-the-century uses of "race" could also refer to the "grand divisions," or what the historian Thomas Guglielmo has called "the "color-races," of black, brown, white, red, and yellow. Here the cultural anthropologists accepted the divisions—the biological distinctions among African, Latin American, European, Indian, and Asian—but argued that these biological categories had no bearing on culture, intelligence, or qualification for citizenship.[20]

In keeping with the political decision to admit Europeans to citizenship while excluding Asians and Mexicans, courts picked up on new culturalist arguments about the absurdity of competing lists of races, especially subdivisions of the European races. But they also insisted on the primacy— and the manifest common sense—of "color race."[21]

Much of the early work of Franz Boas and his students was directed toward demonstrating that there was no such thing as a "pure race" or a "mongrel," and that race mixing was inevitable. Moreover, the new culturalists sought to reassure white Americans that, contrary to the eugenicists' fears, race mixing would neither degrade nor extinguish "the white race." In his early study *The Half-Blood Indian*, Boas argued that Indian-white "mixtures" were actually stronger, taller, and more fertile than their parents of either race. Perhaps white people would become slightly darker, but they would not weaken or die off. Boas extended this argument to the European "races," combining it with his emphasis on culture over race as determinative of most human difference. In "Changes in Immigrant Body Form," he found that a group's average head size and stature increased after immigration to the United States. He argued that in America, "mental traits as well as physical traits will be modified by the effect of environment." This countered the eugenicist claim that inferior European races such as southern Italians and Slavs would cause the American "racial stock" to degenerate; Boas argued, instead, that they would be improved by the healthy American environment, and by mixing with Americans.[22]

Boas and his students tentatively applied this belief in environmentalism and race mixing to "the negro." In opposition to the prevailing view that blacks were immutably racially inferior, Boas wrote that "the traits of the American negro are adequately explained on the basis of history and social status." In other words, if "negroes" seemed inferior—a proposition with which Boas evidently agreed—it was because of the history they had endured and the social status to which they had been relegated. Unlike the eugenicists, who saw "race mixture" as unnatural and therefore as something that one ought to be able to prevent, Boas considered "race mixture" of whites and "negroes" to be inevitable, writing, "That there is no racial sexual antipathy is made sufficiently clear by the size of our mulatto population." He even suggested that the answer to the "Negro problem" *was* racial mixture. Boas wrote in a letter to a fellow member of the U.S. Immigration Commission in 1910 that perhaps "we should fare better by encouraging the gradual process of lightening up this large body of [black] people by the influx of white blood." Again, in 1921, he wrote, "The Negro problem will not disappear in America until the negro blood has been so diluted that it will no longer be recognized, just as anti-Semitism will not disappear until the last vestige of the Jew as Jew has disappeared." Although to modern ears the notion of "lightening up" the Negro race or eradicating "the last vestige of the Jew as Jew" carries disturbing overtones, Boas was a steadfast opponent of Nazism and racism; he truly believed that racial distinctions would and should become irrelevant, thus eliminating the basis for the terrible crimes of the twentieth century. Like others of his generation (and many in ours), Boas saw "white" as a natural, common sense category, whereas he was generally comfortable with the notion that race mixing would enable the stigmatized categories of "black" and "Jew" to disappear. Though a liberal in his time, Boas was still committed to a flawed racial science.[23]

Yet Boas played an important role in undermining the basis of biological racism. He summed up the view that race referred *only* to biology, and hence was unimportant in explaining human differences in comparison to culture and environment. In his entry on "Race" for the new *Encyclopedia of Social Sciences,* he explained that he used the term "race" solely to apply to "the biological grouping of human types," not for "groups of men differing in appearance, language or culture." Furthermore, he wrote, "all racial differences which have been established thus far are so much subject to outer circumstances that no proof can be given of innate racial differences"; what small differences may arise "are altogether irrelevant as compared with the powerful influence of the cultural environment." Thus

Boas's work pointed in the direction of an extreme separation between "race" and "culture."[24]

Like Boas, his students had faith that better racial science would improve "race relations" by giving the lie to the idea of a "Chain of Being" or hierarchy of races. They assumed—correctly—that the notion of racial hierarchy was used by white people to justify their ongoing discrimination against those deemed "not white," and they hoped, with perhaps too much optimism, that by showing the biological equality of all races, they could establish their political equality as well. Accordingly, Claude Lévi-Strauss, in his groundbreaking book *Race and History,* inveighed against the assumptions of white supremacy in writings about race, arguing that better science would allow investigators to find every race's bell curve. Lévi-Strauss was confident that objective scientists would find little variation among races, both physically and mentally, writing in *The Significance of Racial Differences* that most differences between races could be attributed to culture and historical circumstance, not biology.

Some of Boas's students also took up his exhortation to investigate the "mulatto," finding the results of black-white mixing to be positive and arguing in favor of "race mixture." The sociologist Robert Ezra Park extolled the benefits of race mixture for "acculturation," as evidenced by intermarriage in Hawai'i. Park also wrote that "in the United States, the mulattoes are on the whole . . . the cultural advanced guard and the leaders of the Negro people," desirable traits they exhibited as "the product of a double inheritance, biological and cultural." Likewise, Edward Byron Reuter attributed intellectual differences between whites and mulattoes to access to education and social status "rather than to innate and unalterable traits." Melville Herskovits, in an encyclopedia entry on "Race Mixture," argued that "the undesirability of [racial] crossing cannot be substantiated by objective proof. There is no reason to suppose that such deficiencies as are seen in some hybrid populations cannot be referred to the social situation in which these people are found." These social scientists reached the conclusion Boas was not confident enough to make, that even black-white racial mixture led only to racial improvement on both sides rather than to the degradation that the eugenicists—and much of contemporary racial common sense—assumed.[25]

As opposed to the prevailing view that race mixture would degrade the white race, the new cultural anthropology sought to show the inevitability and even salutary nature of race mixing, undermining the bases for miscegenation laws as well as racially or ethnically based restrictions on immigration. The new culturalists applied these arguments equally to the white races and to all other races, even to blacks. Boas and his students were liberals opposed to racism and Nazism, and they truly hoped that their research would help prove that race should play a much smaller role in determining people's life chances than it did at the time. Nevertheless, they rarely argued that "race" itself was not a meaningful category—and in this they inadvertently contributed to a kind of cultural racism that would become increasingly important in discrimination against both Asians and Latinos.

"Free White Persons" in the Courtroom

What happened when the new racial science entered the courtroom in immigrants' battles to naturalize to citizenship? New culturalist criticism of "white" racial distinctions was helpful to some immigrants from the Near East seeking citizenship, since these were people with a plausible claim to European identity who had nevertheless been excluded from citizenship on the ground that they were not white. Racial science worked against most Asian groups, placing them firmly in the nonwhite category, and it went in contradictory directions for people from India, who could claim to be "Caucasian." Yet despite the eugenicist description of Italians as a separate race, no federal court or government official ever seriously suggested that any immigrant from northern, central, or southern Europe, no matter how swarthy, should be excluded from citizenship. There is no evidence that any member of the "white races" appeared racially ambiguous enough for his or her identity to become the subject of litigation.

In the 1922 case of *Rollins v. Alabama*, a Sicilian immigrant, Edith Labue, was implicated in a miscegenation suit against Jim Rollins, her black husband. If Labue were white, Rollins would be guilty of miscegenation, so he defended himself by pointing out that the state had never actually proved Labue's whiteness. At trial there was no discussion of whether Labue's Sicilian identity made her white or not. Rollins simply argued that calling his wife "Sicilian" did not *prove* she was white rather than "negro," any more than calling her "Swedish" or "German" would have proven her racial status; she might be any nationality and still be either white or not white. Indeed the state lost its miscegenation prosecution solely on the grounds of that technicality, with no formal finding on what Labue's race actually was. While *Rollins v. Alabama* has been put forward as an example of a case litigating whether Italians were really white, all the case really demonstrates about Italian identity is that at least some Italians intermingled with blacks in early-twentieth-century Alabama.[26]

Nevertheless, it is certainly true that Italians in the South as well as in Northern cities were seen in racial as well as cultural terms. In 1899 the U.S. Bureau of Immigration began distinguishing between "Keltic" northern Italians and "Iberic" southern Italians. There was prejudice against southern Italians, and occasional threats to their status as "white"—for example, a 1903 attempt in Louisiana to exclude Italians from voting in "white primaries." (Democratic primaries were limited to white voters, which despite the Fourteenth Amendment was considered constitutional at the time because political parties were interpreted to be purely private institutions that, unlike branches of government, could legally discriminate on the basis of race.) And in 1911 the House Committee on Immigration and Naturalization debated whether to regard "the south Italian as a full-blooded Caucasian." Yet "if U.S. congressmen openly debated whether southern Italians were 'full-blooded Caucasians,' writes Guglielmo, they never went so far as to deny *meridionali* [southern Italians] naturalization rights based on their doubts; if magazines like *World's Work* called for the exclusion of Italian immigration, Congress never seriously considered the matter; and if some Louisianans tried to disenfranchise Italians, their efforts, in direct contrast to those regarding African Americans, failed miserably." Italians may have been a race apart, but they shared the *color race* status of whites. Certainly in court and in immigration rulings, Italians and other southern Europeans were white.[27]

There were two groups of immigrants from the geographic borderlands between Europe and Asia, however, whose whiteness *was* litigated: Syrians and Armenians. Near Eastern immigrants presented courts with a difficult conundrum. In color they could be very dark or quite light; they came from ancient civilizations of the highest culture; and many were highly educated—all of which would seem to make them "white." Yet often enough, because of their dark skin, they did not resemble "Anglo-Saxon" whites. As one court described a Syrian claimant, he was "in color, about that of a walnut." Nevertheless, both Syrians and Armenians eventually won their claims to whiteness before state courts, drawing on both common sense and racial science. Cultural anthropologists argued on their behalf that they belonged to the "white" or "Caucasian" races, and their theories provided an effective tool for arguing that subdivisions of the "white races" into Iberic, Nordic, and Mediterranean, or further micro-categories, were absurd and arbitrary. Courts also turned to the legislative intent of the framers of the 1790 Naturalization Act, arguing that the relevant question was what "white" meant in 1790. While U.S. officials argued that "white" meant "European," an argument that a few courts accepted, most found that the common sense understanding of "white" to "the average man on the street" was "not negro" and, more recently, "not Mongolian."[28]

In several cases involving Syrian applicants for citizenship, the state argued that Syrians were outside the boundaries of whiteness because they fell outside common understandings of Europe, geographically and culturally. Tom Ellis was described by a federal district court in Oregon in a variety of terms: he was a Turkish subject; he was Syrian; he was a native of Palestine; he was Maronite; he was from Beirut; he was ethnologically "Semitic"; his color was white. Ellis spoke English well, practiced the Catholic religion, and seemed in all other ways fit for U.S. citizenship. The U.S. attorney conceded that Ellis was a "member of what is known as the white or Caucasian race," but argued that the term "free white persons" in the 1790 statute was "intended to include only those peoples of the white race, who, at the time of the formation of the government, lived in Europe and were inured to European governmental institutions, or upon the American continent, and comprehended such only of the white races who, from tradition, teaching, and environment, would be predisposed toward our form of government, and thus readily assimilate with the people of the United States."[29]

This argument equated whiteness with European culture and fitness for citizenship—just as in the antebellum trials, whites (particularly white men) were people who were capable of performing citizenship. In this view, as in earlier racial identity trials, race, culture, and character were all aspects of the same fundamental identity. A person who was technically "Caucasian" according to current scientific definition, but who fell outside the common sense understanding of a white person capable of performing citizenship, could not be white. Yet the Oregon District Court rejected this argument, insisting that the plain meaning of "white" was "white," as used in "common parlance." According to the court, in common usage both then and in 1790, "white" referred to everyone who was not "negro" or "Mongolian," which manifestly included Syrians. In other words, since

Syrians were clearly neither "negro" nor "Mongolian," they simply had to be white, regardless of how dark-skinned they appeared or how "foreign" they seemed.[30]

Around the same time, the United States made a similar argument—that "white" meant "European"—in order to exclude several Armenians from citizenship in the Massachusetts case of *In re Halladjian* in federal district court. Yet that court, too, found the equation of "white" with "European" problematic, since one of the petitioners had been born and resided not in "Asiatic Turkey" but in a suburb of Constantinople, then considered part of Europe. In trying to exclude Halladjian, an Armenian man, the government argued that "European, or its analogous term, white man, . . . is intended, not merely to describe the local habitat of the person to whom applied, but as a brief and convenient designation descriptive of the prevailing ideals, standards, and aspirations of the people of Europe."[31]

But if the court was unwilling to let the government rule that Armenians were "not white," it also disapproved of the plaintiffs' suggestion that "the education and intelligence of the petitioner furnish part of the test of his statutory color." The questions in nineteenth-century racial identity trials concerned an individual's ability to perform whiteness, thus demonstrating his or her distance from blackness. In the twentieth century, individual performance was not the issue—but cultural performance was. What interested the court was not whether a single Armenian man "acted white" but whether an entire group of people could live up to the standards of performing whiteness.[32]

Accordingly the government also tried to make a common sense argument that ordinary people saw certain nationalities as "not white"—implicitly, as not capable of performing the duties of whiteness: "Without being able to define a white person, the average man in the street understands distinctly what it means, and would find no difficulty in assigning to the yellow race a Turk or Syrian with as much ease as he would bestow that designation on a Chinaman or a Korean." In other words, the U.S. attorney argued, both common sense and common usage divided the world into a white European race and a yellow Asiatic race, and that common sense put Armenians squarely into the latter category. The court, by contrast, disputed both points: first, that "white" did in fact mean "European" (some non-Europeans might be "white") and that "Asiatic" automatically meant "yellow" (some Asians might be of other colors); and second, that

Armenians were either Asiatic or yellow. Maintaining its skepticism that the world could even be accurately divided along racial lines, the court concluded, "If we are compelled by statute to classify for the purposes of American naturalization every man living on the earth as a member of some one race, we shall find that the Armenians have always been classified in the white or Caucasian race, and not in the yellow or Mongolian."[33]

Finally, the court drew on other arguments common to cases involving Near Eastern immigrants: first, that the Near East was the cradle of Western civilization; and second, that in 1790, when Congress passed the Naturalization Act, "white" meant everything but "negro," and later also everything but Chinese or Japanese. As the court explained, "white" was a "catch-all word" for people who were not "negro" or "Mongolian." A few years later a Massachusetts court applied the same logic to a Syrian applicant in *In re Mudarri*.[34]

By contrast, the court in two South Carolina cases rejected the "cradle of civilization" argument, and applied common sense and legislative intent tests to find that "white" in 1790 did in fact mean European, even as it bemoaned the inconsistency of relying on racial science and judicial discretion to draw distinctions among individuals for naturalization: "One Syrian may be of pure or almost pure Jewish, Turkish, or Greek blood, and another the pure-blooded descendant of an Egyptian, an Abyssinian, or a Sudanese. How is the court to decide? It would be most unfortunate if the matter were to be left to the conclusions of a judge based on ocular inspection." In the nineteenth century, "ocular inspection" had been perfectly acceptable as a basis for determining racial identity—but again, that was when "African" was the only race at issue, and the ocular inspection concerned whether an individual *was* in fact African. In this case there was no argument about the individual's specific identity; rather the question was about the racial identity of the group to which everyone agreed he belonged.[35]

The court concluded that although the easiest criterion would be "European habitancy," the correct rule regarded European *descent:* Europeans or European-African "mixtures" could become citizens even if they had lived in Asia; everyone else from Asia was to be excluded. Consistent with its previous dismissal of "ocular inspection" as too individual a way of determining racial identity when group determinations were wanted, the court also insisted that such traditional markers of racial performance as high culture or the capacity for citizenship should not play a role in contemporary citizenship decisions: "If the matter were placed, as some decisions would indicate, on intellectual status and achievement, then the Japanese and certain of the Chinese would be clearly entitled to stand with many of the so-called white nations and with the Parsee, the Brahmin, and the Persian, and far above the negro races." Instead, the court ruled, eligibility for naturalization should stand or fall on race alone, and whiteness should be defined, as the U.S. attorneys had been urging in other cases, by "Europeanness."[36]

Yet when one of the South Carolina cases, involving a Syrian named George Dow, reached a higher federal court, the decision was overturned, following the well-established line of cases that used both racial science and common sense to find Syrians white. The *Dow* court argued that while Blumenbach's classification of Syrians as white may not have been known in 1790, that classification and other ethnological works in the eighteenth and nineteenth centuries would have been known to the legislators who adopted amendments to the Naturalization Act. Yet these legislators did not change the definition of distinctions for explaining human difference; rather they confirmed the existence of "the white race" and persisted in the practice of classifying people in racial systems. As we can see, this type of racial classification was extremely persistent, and very difficult to overcome once it had been established over several centuries, in part because it was a convenient way to support the prevailing racial bases for dividing society even when its practitioners were aware of its shortcomings.

Thus in order to demonstrate that Armenians could assimilate with Europeans, Franz Boas cited evidence that Armenians intermarried with non-Armenians at a "similar to average rate" compared to other European immigrant groups. In other words, by showing that Armenians "amalgamate readily with the white races, including the white people of the United States," he sought to demonstrate their own white identity.[37]

Despite the arguments of some modern historians that Jews, Italians, and Armenians were "not white"—arguments well supported if we look only at the writings of the eugenicists at the turn of the century—it is clear that courts determining citizenship and miscegenation issues did indeed accept those "races" as "white." Even immigrants from the Near East, despite the questions raised about their "Europeanness," were able to harness both ethnological claims to Caucasian identity and common sense claims to be part of the white "color race," by contrast to African "negroes" and Chinese or Japanese "Mongolians."[38]

All of the arguments that surfaced in federal courtrooms when Syrians and Armenians sued for citizenship collided in disputes involving immigrants from Japan and India. According to ethnological classification, "Hindus" and "Parsees" may have been "Caucasian" or "Indo-European," while according to individual performance of civic character, actual color, and cultural capacity for citizenship, many Japanese Americans looked and acted white. Yet courts decisively rejected these grounds for finding Asian applicants white, embracing a simpler version of racial common sense, in which the "color races" of black, white, yellow, red (and possibly brown) were upheld even while courts affirmed the unity of the "white races." At the very time when eugenicists were elaborating long lists of "races," courts were reiterating the common sense understanding of "color race" and rejecting any subdivisions. They did so in part by reference to the way they imagined Americans had understood "whiteness" in 1790, but more generally by reference to the average man on the street, who would not recognize someone from East Asia or India to be white no matter what scientists said.

In the course of these court battles, petitioners for naturalization from India had racial science on their side, as most anthropologists considered "high caste Hindus" to be part of the "Indo-Aryan race" or a branch of the "Caucasian race." Their argument for inclusion in the class of "free white persons" rested on this scientific claim, and indeed federal courts did allow a significant number of immigrants to be naturalized in the first two decades of the twentieth century on these grounds. Yet, interestingly, even the courts that did find "Hindus" to be "white" resisted making science the basis of their decision, citing arguments by now familiar to us contrasting expertise with the democratic knowledge of the common man. Accordingly, both the "white" and "not white" decisions relied more heavily on arguments from racial common sense.

For example, in the 1910 case of *U.S. v. Balsara*, the government argued, as it had in the cases involving Armenians and Syrians, that "free white persons" should include only Europeans. Balsara, a "Parsee" from Bombay, argued that "free white persons" should include all members of the "white or Caucasian race," clearly referring to scientific classifications of "Parsees," originally from Persia, as Caucasian. The Second Circuit Court opinion found for Balsara, allowing him to be naturalized. Yet it was not willing to do so on scientific grounds, noting that most Americans in 1790 had probably never heard the term "Caucasian race" and suggesting thereby that it placed great store in racial common sense as a democratic principle: whatever "most Americans" chose to codify into law ought to trump the expertise of scientists, who spoke in technical language that "most Americans" would not understand.[39]

The court made this argument even as it rejected the notion that naturalization should be limited only to those groups that commonly immigrated in 1790: "We think that the words refer to race and include all persons of the white race, as distinguished from the black, red, yellow, or brown race." While the court did not want to concern itself with the "nice discriminations" involved in drawing lines among races, it did not think these five color races presented such close distinctions. "For practical purposes," noted the court, "there is no difficulty in saying that the Chinese, Japanese, and Malays and the American Indians do not belong to the white race" and that Parsees did belong. The court seemed to be acknowledging that notions of "racial common sense" had evolved since 1790—now, in 1910, the five color races were commonly acknowledged in a way that perhaps earlier they might not have been—but that it was still common sense rather than scientific expertise that determined racial classification for purposes of making new citizens.[40]

In a similar case, Mohan Singh, a twenty-nine-year old Indian butler in Los Angeles, petitioned in district court for naturalization in 1918. His petition was denied that March, "it appearing that petitioner is not a white man—being a hindo." The following year, however, a federal judge overturned this denial. He began by quoting *Balsara* regarding the "nice discriminations" that racial line-drawing might require, and went on to summarize the "preponderance of respectable opinion" that classified Hindus "as members of the Aryan branch of stock of the so called Caucasian or white race." The phrase "preponderance of respectable opinion" might have referred either to scientific opinion or to racial common sense. But the court's ultimate conclusion in favor of Singh rested on class and culture—that is, racial performance—as much as on science. Indeed the court's opinion explicitly noted that science could not adequately resolve the question of Singh's race: "In the absence of an authoritative declaration or requirement to that effect, it would seem a travesty on justice that a refined and enlightened high caste Hindu should be denied admission on the ground that his skin is dark and therefore he is not a 'white person,' and at the same time a Hottentot should be admitted merely because he is 'of African nativity.'" In other words, racial common sense found a "refined and enlightened high caste Hindu" to be a far more acceptable citizen—or, more specifically, far more "white"—than an African "Hottentot." If the amended Naturalization Act admitted Africans, it *must* admit Hindus, or at least Hindus who could clearly (in the court's eyes) perform whiteness more adequately than the "Hottentot." Once again, people of African heritage were cast as the absolute pole of "blackness" or "nonwhiteness," and the whiteness of other ethnic groups and nationalities was measured in terms of their distance from Africa. Skin color, the courts acknowledged, was not necessarily the only or the most important determinant of whiteness; a man whose skin was "dark" might still be "whiter" than an African, particularly if he was "refined" and "high caste."[41]

In 1917 a district court in Pennsylvania used a similar common sense logic to the *Balsara* court but reached an opposite conclusion. The Pennsylvania court considered several possible tests of whiteness. Unlike antebellum and Jim Crow–era courts considering whiteness, this district court explicitly rejected "the complexion or color test" because of its "utter impracticability" and "possible consequences." Once "nonwhite" included groups other than "African," color ceased to be a useful common sense measure: in this respect it was "impracticable" and might have dangerous "consequences." The court went on to consider the basis for the 1790 Naturalization Act and the reasons for limiting citizenship to "free white persons," stating, "Assuming the intention to have been to limit the privilege to those who were like unto themselves in blood, previous social and political environment, laws, usages, customs, and traditions, what has been called the geographical test (for which the representatives of the Bureau of Naturalization contend) might have been inserted in the law." In other words, in the vocabulary of the act, "white" could have been meant to signify "European." The court, however, rejected the idea that Congress had intended to specify "European," since in 1790 no one could have anticipated that the United States would become a "melting pot of almost all the nations of the earth."[42]

If neither color nor nationality could determine whiteness, what could? "The only remaining test," the court found, was a kind of a common sense test: "Our people, when the first naturalization act was passed, had a really definite idea of those to whom the privilege of citizenship was to be extended. The difficulty was, not in getting into accord upon the thought, but the difficulty was in finding a word or phrase which would express it. Resort was had, as the only recourse, to the common speech of the people, which provided a phrase ready at hand, which expressed the thought meant to be conveyed. The phrase was 'white person.'" In other words, we know whiteness when we see it. And by this common sense test, the court found, "white" must obviously exclude people from India.[43]

Although common sense clearly had a larger meaning than appearance in these cases, appearance certainly played a role in determining whiteness. Both a declaration of intent to naturalize and a petition for naturalization required the applicant to record "color" and "complexion" as part of establishing that he or she was white. While "complexion" might acceptably be noted as "dark" or "dark white," the only correct answer for "color" was "white." *Balsara* followed this logic: although the refined and high-caste Hindu might be "dark," he was also "white." Not surprisingly, these terms were often confusing to immigrants seeking U.S. citizenship, and many, like "Hindu" Deir Chand, made mistakes in their applications. Chand, who filed his declaration of intention to naturalize in 1913, discovered his error after his petition was denied, presumably on the grounds that he had not appropriately declared his whiteness. He pled later "that while his color is therein stated as 'copper color' he is, as a matter of fact, a white man," and added further evidence of his worthiness to become a citizen, pointing out that he had filed his declaration "after serving said United States in the recent world war." Likewise, Indian national Akhay Mozumdar noted that while in his "certificate of naturalisation, the blank after 'color' is filled in by the word ' brown' . . . [t]hat is merely a clerical error for which the defendant cannot be held responsible."[44]

Similarly, Japanese petitioners for citizenship lost on the basis of common sense even when racial scientists left open the possibility that they too might be white. In a 1912 case involving the son of a German father and a Japanese mother, a district court in Washington held that "the term 'white person' must be given its common or popular meaning. As commonly understood, the expression includes all European races and those Caucasians belonging to the races around the Mediterranean Sea, whether they are considered as 'fair whites' or 'dark whites,' as classified by Huxley, and notwithstanding that certain of the southern and eastern

European races are technically classified as of Mongolian or Tartar origin."
Thus, reasoned the court, "it is just as certain that, whether we consider
the Japanese as of the Mongolian race, or the Malay race, they are not included in what are commonly understood as 'white persons.'"[45]

This "common sense" logic was used frequently in the naturalization
cases, in which courts routinely seemed to agree: whatever the scientists
say, however they classify racial distinctions, we know who is not white. Indeed, having seen the trajectory of "race as common sense" from the antebellum period through the Jim Crow era into the twentieth century, we
can hardly be surprised by the courts' insistence that race is something
"any white man" should know when he saw it. For at least a century, whiteness had been an inextricable element of U.S. citizenship—both formally
and socially. At times it almost seemed that the whole notion of democracy
rested on the premise that whiteness could be determined not by scientific experts but by the ordinary white citizen—the man who, no matter
how poor, was entitled to vote, sit on a jury, and serve in the armed forces.

The U.S. Supreme Court addressed the question of whiteness and naturalization in two 1923 cases: *U.S. v. Ozawa,* in which the petitioner was
Japanese, and *In re Thind,* discussed at the beginning of this chapter, involving a "high caste Hindu" from the Punjab region of India. Takao
Ozawa had been in the United States for twenty years when he first applied for naturalization in 1914. He had attended the University of California at Berkeley, then settled in Hawai'i. He spoke English and insisted
that his children speak only English at home. In a brief he wrote himself,
he earnestly explained his desire to "do something good to the United
States before I bid a farewell to this world." He claimed that his own skin
was white, and also cited anthropologists' studies of Japan observing that
"in Japan the uncovered parts of the body are also white," and that Japanese "are whiter than the average Italian, Spaniard, or Portuguese."[46]

Yet in his Supreme Court opinion, Justice George Sutherland held that
Ozawa, despite his white complexion, was of the "Mongolian" race. Un-
usually for racial identity cases of the period, the Court relied on racial science as well as common sense, drawing on ethnological taxonomies to
show that "Mongolians" were one of the grand divisions of mankind, separate from whites or "Caucasians."

The case of Bhagat Singh Thind—a highly educated immigrant from
Punjab—came before the Supreme Court just three months later. In this

case, however, racial science suggested that Hindus were Caucasian, a decision that, as we have seen, seemed to run counter to common sense notions of race in early-twentieth-century America. Accordingly, the Supreme Court asserted the now familiar "common man" test of whiteness that whiteness was whatever the "common man" believed it was. On those grounds, regardless of what the scientists said, the Court found Thind wanting.

In both cases, however, the briefs and what little survives of the testimony make particularly clear the connection between racial common sense and the performance of whiteness. Ozawa sought to show that he had lived his life as a white man and was perfectly fit for American citizenship; yet the Court considered his evident nonwhiteness to render him automatically unfit for citizenship. In Thind's case, the prosecutor argued that whiteness and "civilization" were synonymous.

Ozawa, a "Mongolian," knew that racial science—with its faith in the "color races"—would place him squarely in the "yellow" camp. Consequently, his central argument was that "free white persons" meant in 1790 "free whites as distinct from blacks, whether slave or free." Ozawa expanded on this argument by asserting that whiteness was a status, referring to those "fit for citizenship . . . a superior class as against a lower class." Ozawa felt that if he could prove he was simply "not black," he would have established that he was white—a space that American Indians had occupied in the antebellum and Jim Crow eras and that, ironically, Asians may often occupy in U.S. society today. In 1923, however, the Japanese, though decidedly not black, were not white, either, in the "common man" view of race. Ozawa's brief sought to demonstrate that ethnologists could not agree on the number of races and whether the Japanese fit into the Mongolian race or another. In addition to questioning whether science was the proper basis for interpreting the racial definition of "free white men," he also cast doubt on the ability of science itself to establish clear notions of race—not unlike the way litigants in antebellum courtrooms cast doubt on the medical experts testifying for the other side.[47]

Ozawa's opponents had two arguments available to them. The amicus brief of the California attorney general relied solely on "the great weight of scientific opinion" that "either the Malay or Mongolian or both of these stocks predominate in the Japanese race," and that both legislatures and courts intended "white persons" to "exclude the Mongolian-Malay type." The state's brief quoted extensively from the testimony of Ales Hrdlicka, a physical anthropologist from the Smithsonian Institution, to the effect that the Japanese were "a part of the yellow-brown people or race" and that no "reliable scientific men" had classed the Japanese as "a white race."[48] The brief for the United States relied less on science and more on common sense. It began by equating "white persons" with "what is ordinarily and in common speech known as the white or Caucasian race." Because the drafters of the statute had not anticipated immigration from China or Japan, "white persons" should not be read as a "'catchall' for all people not black or red." And while science was not completely reliable—"the views of ethnologists have changed in details from time to time"—the bottom line was easily agreed on by experts as well as laypeople: "It is safe to say that the classification of the Japanese as members of the yellow race is practically the unanimous view."[49]

When Justice Sutherland delivered the opinion for the Supreme Court in *Ozawa,* he acknowledged that Takao Ozawa had appropriately performed whiteness; indeed his opinion began by noting all of Ozawa's achievements of education and assimilation, from going to college at Berkeley to speaking English at home: "That he was well qualified by character and education for citizenship is conceded." But Sutherland rejected the notion that Ozawa's civic performances and character were evidence of whiteness—by contrast to nineteenth-century trials in which an individual's performance and character could prove his whiteness. For Ozawa was white only if *all* Japanese Americans were white.[50]

Nor did Sutherland feel it necessary to "follow counsel in their extensive researches in [the science of ethnology]." Again this departed from the earlier practice of consulting racial science; all that was necessary, Sutherland wrote, was to conclude that the "words 'white person' are synonymous with the words 'a person of the Caucasian race'"—perhaps the ultimate statement of racial common sense. Sutherland admitted that this tautological formulation did not absolutely settle all questions; there would be "border line cases." But to Sutherland, consulting common sense, a Japanese man did not present a borderline case.[51]

Three months later the case of Bhagat Singh Thind, a "high caste Hindu, of full Indian blood, born at Amrit Sar, Punjab," was argued before the Court. Both sides in *Thind* agreed that this *was* one of the borderline cases. The United States in *Thind* made very similar arguments to the ones Ozawa had made on the opposite side:

The words "free white persons" meant to [the drafters of the naturalization statute] men representative of a composite type, a combination of color, race, and social institutions, with which they were familiar, men who collectively had developed and were maintaining a civilization of which they themselves were a part, the civilization of white men . . . The word "free" cannot be wholly ignored. It was not merely the opposite of African slavery. It referred to a type of civilization. All peoples whom they knew in this sense were of they type commonly and popularly called "free white" men, and it is undoubtedly true that the word "white" was by them indicative of type rather than color.[52]

It was this idea of racial status as a "type of civilization," a status of freedom and fitness for citizenship, that led to the "common sense" or "common man" test of whiteness: "The test must be a more open and obvious one [than that of science] . . . It is to be found not by the researches of scholarship but by the practical application of the good sense and common understanding of ordinary men in the light of history and experience . . . Neither in popular speech nor in literature has the term 'white man' ever been used as appropriate to describe the Hindu." By contrast, Thind's lawyer relied exclusively on racial science, arguing that experts recognized Indians as white.[53]

Justice Sutherland again delivered the majority opinion in *U.S. v. Thind*. His problem was to distinguish Thind's case from Ozawa's, for Thind could point to the holding in *Ozawa* equating "white" with "Caucasian" and argue that Hindus from Punjab were part of the "Caucasian race" according to leading scientific opinions. Nevertheless, Sutherland explained, "'Caucasian' is a conventional word of much flexibility . . . and while it and the words 'white persons' are treated as synonymous for the purposes of that case, they are not of identical meaning." The statute used the phrase "white persons," which were "words of common speech" rather than scientific terms. Likewise, the "racial test" was not a scientific test but—again—one of common sense. While Sutherland, like Thind himself, evinced a strong skepticism about racial science, he did not abandon the project of defining "free white persons."[54]

The claimants to citizenship in the cases discussed in this chapter fervently wanted to be Americans. Ironically, each and every one could have become so by claiming to be of African descent. Yet instead they all chose to make the case that they were white. It is impossible to know what they actually felt about their own identities, but it is certain that they understood that full citizenship in the United States was reserved for white people. Unlike the Jews, Italians, and Poles who immigrated to American cities, suffered employment and housing discrimination, but always exercised the rights of citizens, Asians remained resident aliens for generations. And even those who had slipped through the bureaucracy in the first decades of the twentieth century, when state officials and courts were undecided and conflicted about their racial identity, found themselves stripped of citizenship after the Supreme Court came down in favor of racial common sense.

After *Thind,* the Bureau of Immigration began to revoke Indians' citizenship retroactively; sixty-five people were "denaturalized" in 1923 and 1924, and one committed suicide. One of the most poignant—and revealing—of these cases involved Sakharam Ganjit Pandit, who had immigrated to the United States from India in 1906, became a citizen in 1913, promptly attended law school, and represented numerous Indian petitioners in their efforts to obtain citizenship. Pandit mounted vigorous efforts to turn back the denaturalization of a number of immigrants, including Mohan Singh, Akhay Mozumdar, and, in the end, himself. He was successful only in his own case—not on the grounds that he was a "free white person" but only on the grounds of "equitable estoppel," a legal term indicating that this particular case only was decided so as to avoid injustice to this litigant. Although the California court insisted in 1925 that Pandit was not white—in light of the *Thind* decision, it could hardly do otherwise—it considered the denaturalization of such an accomplished and successful lawyer and landowner too great an injustice.

The court also noted that the legality of Pandit's marriage to Lillian Stringer, a "White American woman citizen, born in the state of Michigan," would have been thrown into question were it found that Pandit was not a "free white person," because in California "it was required, in order that he procure such [marriage] license, that he should be a White person." Furthermore, his wife would lose her citizenship for having married a non-citizen, and would then lose 320 acres of property under California's alien land laws. The district court was unwilling to inflict such punishments on Pandit and his wife, particularly given Pandit's exemplary performance of whiteness, regardless of his actual (retroactively determined) racial status.[55]

Pandit also argued—persuasively in the court's opinion—that by moving to the United States and marrying a U.S. citizen, he had "lost his said high social station in India, and if he should return to his native land he would be an outcast; and if such certificate is now canceled the defendant will be a man without a country." Reluctant to make Pandit an outcast, the court was willing to grant him citizenship—albeit not to reconsider the larger issue of whether "Hindus" were white.[56]

Despite the U.S. Supreme Court's ruling only that year that Hindus were not white, Pandit nevertheless tried to reopen the issue. He introduced numerous expert witnesses to make his case that Hindus were in fact white. Grafton Elliott Smith, professor of anatomy and ethnology from the University of London, gave a deposition expounding on the question "What is the meaning of the word 'race'?" According to Grafton: "We interpret race in the sense of groups of men who present similar, physical characters and whom we believe to have been separated up into groups at a very remote period of time; that is, we divide existing men into six races . . . the Australian Aborigine; the Negro; the Mongol; and then the three races which are often grouped together as Caucasian, and which we regard as strict races: the Mediterranean, the Nordic, and the Alpine." As in other new culturalist testimony, Smith was not challenging the existence of color races but merely arguing that people from India belonged in the "white" category. Smith also testified that color was not a definitive marker of race, and that Hindus "belong to the same race as the Mediterraneans and, if the Mediterraneans are white people, the majority or chief element in India is white also." On cross-examination the lawyer for the government made the point that Smith used the term "white person" as a scientist, not as a judge would—that legal whiteness and scientific whiteness were *not* the same thing. And indeed, despite the fact that the court's decision ultimately favored Pandit, it too refused to allow racial science to trump racial common sense.[57]

Pandit also sought to introduce testimony by a philosopher, a sociologist, and a historian, to show that

Hindus were always regarded as Caucasians and of the white race by the general concensus [sic] of scientific opinion, and are so regarded today; that in popular opinion in this country they were also similarly regarded in 1875, and are so regarded at the present time; . . . That the term, "White person," has been used historically in this country and also in popular parlance mainly as a convenient designation for any and every person except one of the Negro or American Indian races; . . . [and] that the dark complexion of a large number of people in India is due to the effect for several generations of the tropical sun on white skins, as in the case of the English planter who returns from a long sojourn in India with his skin charged with a dark pigment which no amount of Pears' soap can remove during the rest of his life.[58]

Pandit's efforts to prove whiteness thus drew on racial common sense in a number of ways, referring to "popular opinion," "popular parlance," and arguments about appearance: even the whitest Englishman turned dark under the Indian sun. Besides those versions of racial common sense, Pandit also tried to introduce evidence of race by association, asserting that all of his "associates" were "white people." The government might have drawn on its own version of racial common sense, but that did not prevent it from objecting to Pandit's efforts to establish race as association and performance. Pandit's associations were irrelevant, the government argued, and his "personal qualifications" were likewise not at issue—only the status of his racial group.[59]

Although racial science included "Hindus" among the "Caucasian or white race," courts preferred to apply common sense. This accorded with judges' sense of legislative intent as well: the drafters of the naturalization statute had known what they meant by "white," just as the judge himself knew what he meant; they just could not put it into words. While these cases, like nineteenth-century trials of individual racial identity, appear to represent a triumph of common sense over science, the discourse of "common sense" worked somewhat differently than in those trials. Here we do not find local juries of "ordinary men" applying their own understandings of racial identity. Instead we have judges imposing what they imagine to be the understandings of a generic "common man."

This line of reasoning outraged Sakharam Pandit, who had spent two decades defending his countrymen against deportation and then found himself on trial. For both his countrymen and himself, Pandit argued that both science and culture made Indians white. In the end, he lost every case but his own.

The last group of Asian immigrants to remain racially undefined in the law was Filipinos, who continued to immigrate because of their anomalous status as American "nationals." In 1930 the sociologist Emory Bogardus published an article titled "What Race Are Filipinos?" He noted that courts and scientists called Filipinos either Mongolians or Malay, but, Bogardus argued, "there is no Filipino race, but a Filipino race in the making. They are in a similar boat to ours, for there is no American race, but only an American race in process—out of Nordics, South and East Europeans, Jews, Negroes, Mongolians." Bogardus sought to use the Filipinos to challenge the old racial science. "The Filipinos are daily becoming culturally more like Caucasians. They are a people *on the move racially*, from Mongoloid toward Caucasoid, but still colored by an ancient tinge of Negroid. They are approaching an average of the whole human race."[60]

Just as Franz Boas had suggested that the "new" European immigrants would be racially transformed in the United States, losing their distinctive racial and/or cultural traits, Bogardus extended the argument to Filipinos, who could actually become white, even "Caucasoid." Likewise, Filipino writer Alfonso Santos, in "A Filipino Race in the Making," wrote, "Today, notwithstanding the uncertainties that yet hover around the prospects of Philippine independence, there are already authentic proofs and evidences that a distinct and real Filipino race is in the making, in spite of the opinions of prominent authorities that the Filipinos belong to the Mongolian race." Liberal advocates of Filipino rights sought to distinguish the Filipinos from other groups who were the targets of prejudice and discrimination—"Mongolians" in particular—but also to assert that both racial and cultural identities could change with assimilation, and that Filipinos, like Europeans and Americans themselves, were undergoing a transformation and could even become white.[61]

In a series of cases in Los Angeles, courts reached conflicting conclusions about whether Filipinos counted as "Mongolians" for the purposes of California's anti-miscegenation laws. The disputes very much resembled naturalization cases from the same period, with heavy resort to racial science and common sense. Although a California appellate court resolved the issue in favor of Filipinos in 1933, the legislature quickly nullified the decision by adding the category "Malay" to the anti-miscegenation statute. Filipinos did not fit into the template of "Mongolian," either according to scientific classification or everyday practice, yet panic about Filipino male sexuality led the legislature to create this new category for them.

The first case, *People v. Yatko,* involved a Filipino man, Timothy Yatko, who married a white "dancehall girl" and then, after she left him, followed her and her white lover home one night and stabbed the lover to death. If Yatko was her rightful husband, then he could invoke the "jealous husband" exception, reducing the charge to second-degree murder, or even manslaughter, rather than first-degree murder. The issue of Filipinos' racial classification arose when the state contended that the marriage had been "null and void from the beginning on the ground that the defendant, Yatko, was a Filipino."[62]

Unlike in the case of Japanese people, whom racial scientists placed squarely in the "Mongolian" race, or "Hindus," who could use racial science to argue for whiteness, Filipinos' racial classification was much less clear, leaving the field open for argument on either side. Accordingly, lawyers for both sides brought in voluminous evidence from scientific "authorities," including eighteenth- and nineteenth-century natural scientists such as Blumenbach, Linnaeus, Buffon, and Cuvier, and the Dillingham Commission's "Dictionary of Peoples" entry for "Mongolian, Mongol, Mongolic, Mongoloid, Asiatic or Yellow Race."[63]

Furthermore, the state sought to introduce evidence of Filipinos' racial tendencies toward criminality. According to a contemporary sociologist who followed the litigation: "Counsel for the state called attention to the 'homicidal mania' of Malays, called 'running amuck,' which he stated was a neuropathic tendency imbuing them without any reason or motive to kill persons of other races. He discussed the evil effects of miscegenation generally and cited Mexico as a specific example of the effects of race mixture." Thus the state attorney sought to tap into public fears of miscegenation and "mongrelization" so that the jury would look at the defendant and make the "obvious" leap from Filipino male sexuality to murder.[64]

Yatko, for his part, made a slippery slope argument, warning that voiding Filipino-white marriages would mean that "marriages of Indians and white persons would also be void since the same authorities declaring the Filipino a Mongolian also include Indians as a branch of the Mongolian race."[65]

In finding for the state, the judge alluded to his "long residence and experience in the South" to demonstrate his expertise in matters of race and the necessity of white racial purity. He opined,

from my reading of history, that the Negro race will become highly civilized and become one of the great races only if it proceeds within its own lines marked out by Nature and keeps its blood pure. And I have the same

feeling with respect to other races . . . I am quite satisfied in my own mind
. . . that the Filipino is a Malay and that the Malay is a Mongolian, just as
much as the white American is of the Teutonic race, the Teutonic family, or
of the Nordic family, carrying it back to the Aryan family.

Clearly, for this judge, racial science—the division of humankind into Teutonic, Nordic, Malay, and Mongolian races—only reinforced beliefs that
were by now common sense, that the races should remain separate, given
the experience of Jim Crow in the South.[66]

The California attorney general, U. S. Webb, then issued an advisory
opinion on June 8, 1926, to the effect that Filipinos, being Malays, were
properly classed as Mongolians, and therefore Filipino-white marriages
were illegal. Edward T. Bishop, however, the assistant county counsel for
Los Angeles, gave L. E. Lampton, the Los Angeles county clerk, the opposite advice. Bishop's research showed that "scientists are not agreed upon
the divisions of mankind into races," but that "ordinarily when speaking of
'Mongolians' reference is had to the yellow and not to the brown people
and we believe that the legislature in Section 69 did not intend to prohibit
the marriage of people of the Malay race with white persons."[67]

In successive cases, different judges gave Lampton conflicting orders
about whether or not to issue marriage licenses to Filipino men, indicating
the unsettled nature of Filipino racial identity. State officials could not
agree whether Filipinos were "Mongolian" or not. In 1930 Judge J. A.
Smith prohibited the issuing of a license to Tony Moreno and Stella Robinson on the ground that Moreno was Filipino and a "Mongolian." But the
following year Judge Walter Guerin granted a license for Gavino Visco,
the Filipino grandson of Spaniards, to marry Ruth M. Salas, a "Mexican
Indian," born in Sonora (although her mother was born in Los Angeles).
Sociologist Nellie Foster reported that "the judge stated he would have
decided in favor of Mr. Visco [even] had Miss Salas been a white person"—that is, he would have allowed a Filipino-white marriage as well as a
Filipino-"Indian" marriage.[68]

Marriages were even more likely to be found valid if one of the spouses
was seeking an annulment rather than the couple demanding a license in
the first place, just as in the Jim Crow South, courts were reluctant to let
men out of their obligations to their wives by claiming later that they were
not white. In *Laddaran v. Laddaran* the Filipino husband, Estanislao
Laddaran, sought but failed to win an annulment from Judge Myron

Westover. One month later Judge Thomas Gould refused to allow Ilona Murillo to annul her marriage to Tony Murillo on the ground that she "was in ignorance that the laws of the State of California prohibited the marriage of white persons and those of the Mongolian race." Both of these judges were reluctant to end marriages on the basis of an unclear law, just as courts across the United States, in cases involving white husbands and black wives, were reluctant to grant divorces on the ground that these men had been fooled into an interracial marriage. Whether because of their belief in the sanctity of marriage, or because it was easier to pretend that racial mixing was not occurring than to confront it head-on, twentieth-century courts rarely allowed annulments on the basis of miscegenation.[69]

Just as other courts had been reluctant to invoke racial science to prove the whiteness of people from India, so was Judge Gould unwilling to rely on science rather than racial common sense. Hence he made clear his belief that California legislators had not intended "Mongolian" to include "Malay," and he expressed skepticism about scientific classifications of race in general:

> To hold this marriage void, it is necessary to hold that, ethnologically, Filipinos are Mongolians, and that the Legislature . . . had in mind the prohibition of marriages between Filipinos and whites. The older classification of races divided the human family into five branches, generally and popularly designated as the white, black, red, brown and yellow races . . . It is true that modern ethnologists . . . have limited the number of race groups to the white, the black and the yellow. But these writers warn us that there is no fixed line of demarcation . . . It cannot be said that the legislators of that day anticipated the scientific classification of this.[70]

In other words, at the time the law was passed, it could well have been that Filipinos were "brown" and Mongolians were "yellow"; therefore it could not be assumed that Filipinos were intended to be the targets of the law. More generally, the fluctuation in racial classification made racial science an unreliable basis for legal determinations of racial identity.

The final case began in 1932, when Lampton denied Salvador Roldan and Marjorie Rogers a marriage license and appealed Judge Walter S. Gates's decision in their favor. At trial Roldan described applying for the license: "They asked me also whether I was white, or yellow, or brown, or red. They asked me also whether she was an American, and I told them that she was an English girl. I did not tell them anything further about her.

They did ask me if she was white and I said 'yes.' Then they told me that I could not have a license. They did not tell me why and I didn't ask them." On cross-examination Roldan was asked about his ancestry, and apparently was asked what "tribe" he belonged to. He answered: "I was born in the northern part of Luzon Island. There is no tribe but they call them provinces or Ilicanos, that is a group. It is not a tribe." The official, assuming Roldan was from a "primitive" group, imagined he must be part of a "tribe," like American Indians.[71]

At the end of the trial the judge stipulated, and the attorneys agreed, "that I may refer to texts, sociologists, ethnologists for the purposes of forming my decision." This stipulation allowed the judge to consult racial science although it had not been invoked by the litigants. Clearly, despite the general preference of the courts for common sense over racial science, at least some judges felt the need to lean on scientific expertise in their decisions.[72]

The judge ruled against Roldan, apparently concluding that Filipinos were Mongolian. Roldan appealed, again drawing on racial science ("authorities agree Filipinos are Malay"), citing Blumenbach and T. H. Huxley, and arguing that the effort to apply miscegenation laws to Filipinos was a political one: "those who want the courts to engage in judicial legislation" were "influenced by labor, social and immigration agitation" against Filipinos.[73]

Significantly, the state's brief also relied on racial science, but insisted that the "most recent and best" science eliminated two of the five races. It quoted the anthropologist Hrdlicka's testimony before the Congressional Committee on Territories. Asked, if "the term 'Mongolian' was applied to all of the yellow-brown people?" Hrdlicka replied: "To all of the yellow-brown people, yes; except that originally the Malays and the American Indians were kept separate, until they were sufficiently studied." In other words, the newest racial science did include "Malays" among "Mongolians."[74]

The attorney general of California's amicus brief likewise invoked racial science, elaborating on its timelessness despite the changes in classification schemes: "We think the only question that need be considered is the question whether the Filipino people are Mongolians. If they are Mongolians now they were Mongolians in 1905, in 1880, and always theretofore . . . 'Once a Roman always a Roman.'"[75]

Nevertheless, there was a great deal of back-and-forth in reply briefs and "additional memoranda" about which "common school geographies" were being read in the 1880s in order to prove which racial classification schemes would likely have been familiar to the legislators who drafted the miscegenation statute. On this basis this district court judge found that the legislature did not intend to include "Malays" in "Mongolian," because during the 1880s all of the "agitation" about "Mongolians" was aimed at the Chinese. Thus, whatever racial science may have been around in the 1880s, the ordinary person understood "Mongolian" to mean Chinese. Salvador Roldan's Filipino-white marriage could stand because the statute did not prohibit Filipinos from marrying whites.[76]

The California legislature rendered the *Roldan* decision irrelevant the following year by amending its miscegenation statute to include "Malays." Numerous other legislatures followed suit in expanding their marriage prohibitions to Indians, Asian Americans, and "Malays," some in states that had substantial populations of Asians and others in states that did not.[77]

On February 19, 1942, President Franklin D. Roosevelt signed Executive Order 9066, authorizing the secretary of war to exclude Japanese Americans from designated military areas. One month later Manzanar, the first American concentration camp, opened. For the next three years, 120,000 people of Japanese ancestry, a majority of them U.S. citizens, were evacuated from California, Oregon, and Washington to harsh desert camps. Before internment, Japanese Americans had owned more than twelve thousand acres of land in California. Nearly all of it was lost during their time in the camps. Only the American Civil Liberties Union and the Society of Friends opposed internment; the U.S. Supreme Court upheld its constitutionality on the grounds of executive war powers. It was not until 1988 that the U.S. government admitted wrongdoing and paid reparations to living victims of the internment and their descendants.

How could this have happened while the United States was fighting a war against fascism and racism, a war for freedom? What made internment possible was an understanding of the United States as a white nation, of nationhood in racial terms, and of Asians as an alien race. This understanding developed over one hundred years of Asian immigration to the United States and several decades of litigation about the contours of American citizenship.

CHAPTER EIGHT

Mexican Americans and the
"Caucasian Cloak"

IN 1954, TWO WEEKS BEFORE the U.S. Supreme Court handed down its famous decision in *Brown v. Board of Education*, it decided the case of *Hernandez v. Texas*, striking down Pete Hernandez's murder conviction because Mexican Americans had been systematically excluded from the Texas jury that tried him. The Court held that Mexican Americans, whether or not they were legally white, had been treated as a "separate class . . . distinct from 'whites.'" For the first time in several decades, the state of Texas lost its claim that a Mexican American defendant suffered from no discrimination because he was white and the jurors in his case were white too. As Hernandez's lawyers argued, "about the only time that so-called Mexicans—many of them Texans for seven generations—are covered with the Caucasian cloak is when the use of that protective mantle serves the ends of those who would shamelessly deny to this large segment of the Texas population the fundamental right to serve as . . . jurors."[1]

As Asian immigrants to the United States learned in the early twentieth century, whiteness was a necessary qualification for becoming a U.S. citizen. Yet there was one group of immigrants to the United States who did not have to prove their whiteness to attain formal citizenship. When the United States annexed Texas and California at the end of the Mexican-American War, thousands of people already living there, in formerly Mexican territory, became U.S. citizens through the 1846 Treaty of Guadalupe Hidalgo, which established Mexicans' right to naturalize as formal citizens. Unlike the Japanese and South Asian Indians, who had argued before federal courts that they should be citizens because they were white, Mexican immigrants in the twentieth century were held by federal and state courts to be white because they were citizens—"white by treaty."

Formal citizenship did not mean full social and political citizenship. While a small elite of Mexican American landholders who identified as Spanish maintained white status, the majority of Mexican Americans were treated by Anglos as a separate, inferior race, a notion supported by their economic status as the poorest agricultural laborers. As Mexican immigrants flooded into the United States in the early twentieth century, they joined the ranks of sharecroppers and other impoverished farm workers isolated in segregated labor markets. Unlike European immigrants to Northern cities, who were able to move out of urban ghettoes through access to education and political patronage, Mexican Americans, like blacks, faced a more thoroughgoing exclusion from full social and political citizenship, and were the victims of violent, racist prejudice on both economic and social levels. Nevertheless, despite the institutional similarities between the forms of discrimination experienced by Mexican Americans and African Americans under Jim Crow, the two groups' legal status was significantly different. State segregation statutes did not specifically target Mexican Americans; their exclusion was de facto, in practice, rather than de jure, by law.

Mexican Americans' formal citizenship and nominal legal whiteness meant that race played a more complex role in their exclusion from full social and political citizenship. On the one hand, state officials in Texas and California—county attorneys, sheriffs, and school board presidents—viewed Mexican Americans as an inferior race, offering unself-conscious explanations of their unfitness for jury service or school attendance in terms of "Mexicans'" dirtiness, lack of innate ability, and inferior intelligence. On the other hand, over the course of the mid-twentieth century, they learned to explain their exclusion of Mexican Americans on the basis of language and culture rather than race. They could not exclude (white) "Mexicans" from juries and schools—but they could and did bar "Spanish speakers." Thus Cecil Walston, the sheriff of Menard County, Texas, explained to a court that Mexicans were inferior in intelligence and customs to whites, and yet at the same time maintained that his choice to exclude Mexican Americans from juries did not constitute discrimination on the basis of race—because Mexicans were "not a separate race but are white people of Spanish descent." As Gus Garcia, a leading civil rights litigator, commented, mimicking a Texas state court judge who had accepted a similar argument: "Caucasians were on the jury. Mexicans are Caucasian. So what's all the fussing about?" If Mexicans were white, they could not claim *racial* discrimination—even if their Mexican heritage or their Spanish language skills were the explicit grounds for their exclusion.[2]

The term "Mexican Americans" reflects the public usage of most mid-twentieth-century Mexican American civil rights advocates and litigators, distinguishing people who made claims on U.S. citizenship (Mexican Americans) from those who identified as Mexican nationals (Mexicans). Many "Mexican Americans," however, referred to themselves as "Mexicans" or "mexicano," and most Anglos lumped both citizens and non-citizens together as "Mexicans." To some extent the term "Mexican American" is itself an artifact of the era in which Mexican Americans expressed their claim to civil rights through their claims on U.S. citizenship (and eventually through their own concomitant claims to whiteness).

Unlike earlier trials, these twentieth-century trials were less the genuine efforts of a white society to determine what race was and how it should be treated than the strategic attempts of a self-consciously racist society to segregate a group perceived as nonwhite without admitting that the segregation was based on race per se. In the court records, unself-consciously racist statements sit side by side with elaborate efforts to deny racial prejudice, and the court actors seem less concerned with understanding race than with finding acceptable ways to enforce the racial views they already held—efforts that were to some extent prohibited by the Fourteenth Amendment. In the same vein, arguments by Mexican American civil rights advocates were made strategically to achieve entrance into white schools, places on white juries, and other markers of full citizenship. We cannot take their legal strategies as a direct reflection of their actual beliefs about their racial or national identity but must see them as an often circuitous if sometimes sincere attempt to win a legal victory.

But even if these were the ways early-twentieth-century Americans publicly expressed their racial views, they were struggling just as much as their nineteenth-century counterparts to figure out how race should determine citizenship. White citizens of the time were not at all certain of the relationship between Mexican heritage and full participation in American society, and it was partly during these twentieth-century trials that they worked out their contradictory feelings in this matter. Just as it had taken work to create the antebellum binary system of black and white, not at all obvious in a society that was in fact multiracial and diverse—and just

as it had taken work to create the Jim Crow system of absolute racial segregation, not at all obvious in a society that was in fact created of a wide
variety of interracial relationships—so did it take work to establish this
contemporary view of race, in which racial segregation is justified not on
the grounds of biology but rather on those of social science: the culture of
poverty, the negative effects of the ghetto, the "matriarchal family," and so
on. While these trials may not lay bare the psychology of the participants
in ways that earlier trials did, they do reveal state officials working out
their strategy of cultural racism, even as Mexican American civil rights litigators adjusted their own strategies in response.

Mexican American Whiteness before 1930

Mexican Americans' racial identity depended on class and geography in
Spanish Texas and California. In the 1840s debates over the annexation
of Texas, Anglo politicians often referred to the inferiority of the "Mexican race," using metaphors of dirt, including the epithet "greaser," which
probably derives from the work some Mexicans performed greasing the
axles of mule carts. As Representative Levi Woodbury of New Hampshire
argued, Texans were "men of the true Saxon race" who were "humiliated,
and enslaved to Moors, Indians, and mongrels" when governed by Mexico. The characterization of Mexicans as "mongrels" because of Spanish-
Indian mixture was effective in rallying support for the annexation of
Texas—as it was for eugenicists railing against immigrants—because it
conjured up fears of the white race becoming degraded and subsumed by
an inferior people through mixture. The combination of "slave" and "mongrel" was a deadly epithet.[3]

Because of pervasive prejudice against Mexicans, already framed in racial terms, Anglos who married Mexican women often "whitened" their
spouses by calling them Spanish. Meanwhile, many of the new immigrants
from Mexico in the years between 1890 and 1910 had "learned whiteness
and 'whitening' before coming to the United States." In Mexico, during
the years of Porfirio Díaz's dictatorship preceding the Mexican Revolution
of 1910, a racial hierarchy predominated in which people of a higher
class claimed "Spanish blood," regardless of their actual ancestry or color.
Thus, immigrants to the United States during this period would have
found familiar the close association there between landholding and white
or "Spanish" status.[4]

In those instances and many others, racial distinctions tracked class and landownership, at least to some extent, so that landholders were viewed as "Spanish" and white, while farm laborers and ranch hands were perceived as "Mexican." Patterns of Mexican-white segregation correspond to the divisions between the state's "ranch counties," where Mexicans continued to be landholders, and "farm counties," in which commercial farming took over in the first decades of the twentieth century and where Mexicans therefore became sharecroppers for Anglo landholders. Simply put, where Mexicans held land of their own, they were far less likely to be excluded from schools and other public accommodations, and "Mexican" was less likely to be a racialized identity as opposed to a nationality.[5]

Government versions of Mexicans' racial identity were ambiguous and contradictory. The 1848 Treaty of Guadalupe Hidalgo guaranteed U.S. citizenship to all Mexican citizens in the Mexican Cession without reference to racial identity. But in the antebellum and Jim Crow periods, before the federal courts ever considered the matter of Mexican whiteness, U.S border officials made their own racial determinations, placing some Mexicans in the category "Spanish race" and others—usually darker-skinned people—in the category "Mexican race." At the same time, the whiteness of "Spanish" landholders probably had more to do with their social status and class position than their ancestry or color; Spanish/white appears to have been the description for people with power and Indian/brown for people without. This kind of informal classification lasted for half a century through the antebellum and Jim Crow eras without public or legal challenges.[6]

Not until 1896 did a federal court consider the question of whether Mexicans could be eligible for naturalization to citizenship on the grounds of identification as "white" or some other basis. Although the Treaty of Guadalupe Hidalgo had guaranteed formal U.S. citizenship to all Mexicans then in the Southwest, what about new immigrants from Mexico? Did they have to be "free white persons," according to the 1790 Naturalization Act—and were any of them in fact free and white? In 1893 Mexican citizen Ricardo Rodriguez filed an application for naturalization papers in San Antonio, Texas, after having lived in the United States for ten years. Just as in the cases involving "Hindus," Japanese, Syrians, and Armenians, the federal district court had to address the question of whether Rodriguez was eligible for naturalization as a free white person. But unlike most Asian Americans, Rodriguez won his claim to citizenship.[7]

The district court's statement of Rodriguez's case began with a description of the plaintiff's coloring: "As to color he may be classed with the cop-per-colored or red men. He has dark eyes, straight black hair, and high cheek bones." Likewise, the lawyers at trial tried to elicit testimony from Rodriguez to place him in either a "Spanish" (white) or "Indian" racial cat-egory, although, like the Indians in the Dawes Commission hearings, Ro-driguez resisted this dichotomy. He was asked, "Do you not believe that you belong to the original Aztec race in Mexico?"

"No, sir."

"Do you belong to the aborigines or original races of Mexico?"

"No, sir."

"Where did your race come from? Spain?"

"No, sir."

"Where did your race come from?"

"I do not know where they came from."

Rodriguez's own expression of his identity was as a "pure-blooded Mexi-can," neither Indian nor Spanish. He resisted the idea that "Spanish" and "Indian" represented two distinct streams of blood in the Mexican's veins, claiming a national identity rather than a racial one—or perceiving "Mexi-can" to be itself a racial identity. It is also possible, of course, that he an-swered as he did strategically, coached by his lawyer to avoid giving an answer so that his racial identity could not be proved.[8]

Several San Antonio politicians submitted amicus briefs to the court ar-guing that Rodriguez's nonwhite racial identity made him ineligible for naturalization. Like the judge, local official Floyd McGown based his dis-cussion on Rodriguez's "appearance," which "indicates that he is a descen-dant of the original races of Mexico"—that is, an Indian, a category that, by 1896, had been sufficiently racialized for McGown to think its invoca-tion was sufficient to establish Rodriguez's lack of whiteness. McGown then cited anthropological "authorities" regarding the racial identity of the "original races of Mexico." This wording suggests the dual meaning of "races" to denote both "peoples" and "racial groups," reflecting the confu-sion in anthropology at the time. Thus he began with the *Encyclopaedia Britannica*'s division of humanity into the "white, yellow, brown, and black races," though he acknowledged that "for scientific purposes, greater ac-curacy is required." He then considered several other classification sys-tems, all of which, he claimed, placed the "aborigines of this continent" outside the white race. McGown concluded that Rodriguez was not white, whether "by the scientific classification" or "in the sense in which these words are commonly used and understood in the every-day life of our people," and therefore should be denied the right of citizenship.[9]

Another brief writer, A. J. Evans, also consulted scientific experts. Since he considered it an "admitted and proven fact" that Rodriguez was "of pure Aztec or Indian race," his only task was to establish that such Aztecs/Indians were common in Mexico. Accordingly, he quoted *Dana's American Encyclopedia:* "The population of Mexico comprises about six million Indians of unmixed blood, nearly one-half of whom are nomadic savage tribes of the mountain districts of the north; about five million whites or creoles, chiefly descended from the early Spanish colonists; perhaps twenty-five thousand Africans or hybrids, possessing some negro blood, whether mixed with the European or the Indian element; and the Mestizos, or half-breeds, derived from the union of the whites and Indians." From both the testimony and Rodriguez's appearance, Evans argued, it was "clear" that Rodriguez was one of the 6 million Indians, and therefore manifestly neither white nor eligible for citizenship.[10]

Yet despite the trial testimony and the briefs' focus on Rodriguez's racial identity, the Fifth Circuit Court decided the question on the basis of the Treaty of Guadalupe Hidalgo, or in other words, on Rodriguez's national identity. Although the court agreed that Rodriguez was probably not white according to ethnologists, nor perhaps even to laypeople, it concluded that the treaty required the United States to bestow citizenship on Mexicans regardless of their race. The court avoided reaching a conclusion about whether Mexicans *were* white but felt obliged to treat them legally *as though* they were white. Because naturalization to citizenship was reserved for free white persons and people of African descent, becoming naturalized in effect meant that Mexicans received a presumption of whiteness. Whether or not this is what the *Rodriguez* court intended, that is what the precedent came to stand for. *Rodriguez* provided the backdrop for all future litigation involving Mexican Americans in state courts. Later courts treated the bracketing of Rodriguez's racial identity as a presumption that Mexicans were Spanish—that is, white—unless proven otherwise; in court this led to an effort to tease out an individual's Spanish and Indian ancestry, an effort most Mexicans stubbornly resisted, whether because the distinction appeared irrelevant to them or because they refused it for strategic advantage.

In miscegenation cases after *Rodriguez,* when state courts enforced statutes that criminalized white-black marriage, they began with the presumption that Mexican Americans were white. The records of these trials reveal the clash between popular understandings of Mexican American racial identity and the legal binary of Spanish/Indian.

In 1910 Francisco Flores was convicted of "unlawfully marrying a negro within the third degree" and sentenced to two years in the penitentiary. According to the court, Flores was "a Mexican, or at least of Spanish extraction. There is no evidence in the record that he had any negro blood in his veins," whereas his wife, Ellen Dukes, was identified as having "negro blood in her veins," namely, a Mexican mother and a father with "some negro blood."[11]

It is hard to know exactly why local officials were intent on prosecuting black-Mexican marriages, particularly given the level of social interaction between blacks and Mexicans revealed by the trial testimony. Perhaps the governing elite wanted to keep blacks and Mexicans apart in an effort to prevent racial solidarity that could turn against upper-class whites. Or perhaps they considered Mexicans, if not actually white, at least above blacks in the racial hierarchy, and the Jim Crow–era preoccupation with "blood" and racial purity led to efforts to police even the mixing of two "inferior races."

At all events, Jim Derrick, the deputy constable at Nacogdoches, who testified that he had known Flores for two years, "peddling tamales and peanuts around the depot and town," had stopped Flores when he saw him going to the courthouse to marry Ellen Dukes and warned him that he could not marry a negro woman. When Flores expressed his belief that he should be able to marry her because he was Mexican, just like Ellen's mother, Derrick took the couple upstairs to see the county attorney, Angus Russell, who, as Derrick testified, "told him [Flores] it was against the law to marry a negro woman or a woman with any negro blood in her."[12]

When the lawyer for the state asked Derrick to testify about Dukes's race, Flores's lawyer objected that "unless he knows her antecedents, he can't say unless he qualifies himself." In other words, Flores's lawyer argued that the basis for testimony about racial identity had to be either personal knowledge of an individual's ancestry or scientific expertise. The court ruled that the witness could at least "describe [Dukes's] physical features," and so Derrick obliged, casting his "objective" description in decidedly racial terms: "She has the physical appearance of a negro, she is kinky headed and very dark, what we would call a dark yellow color." He was then asked, "Any other physical appearances of a negro?" He answered,

"Well just a plain old fat negro woman is all," which was stricken from the testimony at Flores's objection.[13]

On cross-examination Derrick elaborated, revealing once again the difficulties of using physical observation to determine race: "It is not a fact that she favors a Mexican greazer [sic] more so than she does a negro; her skin is a different color from that of a black negro; I suppose her skin is more of the color of a Mexican than it is a negro of that peculiar hue or type, it is a copper color, Mexicans most of them have a copper color . . . I would determine the quantity of negro blood in her by her kinky hair." Other witnesses seemed to feel that Ellen Dukes looked more black than Mexican. State witness W. B. O'Quinn judged Dukes "from her personal appearance . . . at least half negro" but could not say "what extent of negro blood she has in her, I am not a negro geologist."[14]

The sheriff of Angelina County offered a twentieth-century version of race by association: "During the years I have known [Ellen Dukes] I have never known her to associate with white people in a social way, she has always associated with negroes." Yet on cross-examination he admitted that association with "negroes" did not necessarily prove nonwhiteness (always assuming Mexicans were defined as white), because "Mexicans, such as this defendant here, that we commonly term as greasers generally associate with negroes. I would not undertake to say whether these greasers have any negro blood in them or not, I was not there at the beginning."[15]

Ellen Dukes Flores, in her testimony, evinced not only the fluidity of her own identity but also uncertainty about her husband's, revealing once again the shakiness of all three bases of racial identity that had been so far invoked—appearance, lineage, and association:

> My mother was a Mexican; my father had some negro blood in him; I do not know just how much . . . [M]y father's color was very bright, he was a great deal brighter color than I am; my father's hair was not kinky or nappy like the ordinary negro, his hair was not as bad as my hair, it was straighter . . . Flores always associated with negroes and not with white people . . . [W]hen I was at home I always associated with the Mexicans; since I have been in Angelina or Nacogdoches Counties I have not associated with the white people or white race.

Ellen Dukes appeared to consider Mexicans to be white, but she treated her own identity as somewhere in between since she associated at times with Mexicans and at times with "negroes"; likewise, her husband, who was Mexican, associated only with "negro" people. Evidently, like Indians, Mexicans occupied a shifty "third territory" between black and white: when contrasted with whites, they were "greazers" and colored; but when contrasted with blacks, they were white, to the point of not being allowed to marry black people without violating the miscegenation laws.[16]

Apparently relying on the determination in the *Rodriguez* case that Mexicans must be treated as though they were white, the trial judge reminded the jury that a Mexican "shall be deemed a 'white person' within the meaning of this law" while also explaining to the jury how "negro" and "white person" were defined under the state miscegenation statute: a "negro" was anyone of "negro blood within the third degree," and a white person was everyone else. Accordingly, the jury found Flores guilty. Although a representative of the law could call him a "greazer" in open court as though that were an acceptable racial designation, for the purpose of the miscegenation statute Flores was white and so could not marry a black woman, even one who was part Mexican. The jury convicted Flores, although he later won an appeal to the Court of Criminal Appeals.[17]

Flores v. State reveals a great deal about popular and legal understandings of Mexican and "negro" identity in Texas. On the one hand, it is fairly clear from the testimony that many Mexicans and blacks associated socially, and that some intermarried. On the other hand, the court interpreted the law to define Mexicans as "white," to the point of proscribing Mexican-black marriage as part of a larger attempt to keep whites and blacks from marrying. While the state attempted to demonstrate Dukes's "negro" identity by her associations, this proved difficult because of the evidence that Mexicans associated at times with both whites and blacks. And although the trial judge allowed, as in most racial identity cases, testimony about appearance, associations, and reputation, the Court of Criminal Appeals accepted the defendant's argument that the state had not met its burden of proof in showing the couple's ancestry. As in other miscegenation cases from the South, strict degree-of-blood rules could actually make it more difficult to prove someone a "negro."

Another miscegenation case from the same era also suggests the fluidity of popular understandings of Mexican racial identity, even as the state struggled to create and police a single, unambiguous racial boundary between black and white. In the 1921 Arizona case *Kirby v. Kirby,* Joe Kirby sued his wife, Mayellen, for an annulment rather than a divorce, on the ground that their marriage had violated the state's anti-miscegenation law because he was "a person of Caucasian blood" whereas she was "a person of negro blood." The trial immediately ran into complications regarding Joe Kirby's white status when his mother, Tula Kirby, took the witness stand, testifying in Spanish with an interpreter. Joe's lawyer asked, "To what race do you belong?" Tula answered, "Mexican." He pressed, "Are you white or have you Indian blood?" and she answered, "I have no Indian blood." On cross-examination, Mayellen's lawyer asked about Tula's father, "Was he a Spaniard?" She answered, "Yes, a Mexican." That was not what the lawyer meant; when he asked whether Tula's father was born in Spain, Tula told him he was born in Sonora—a city in Mexico. To the question "Who was your mother?" Tula answered, "Also in Sonora." Tula then explained that her mother was a Spaniard on her father's side and Mexican on her mother's side. Mayellen's lawyer asked, "What do you mean by Mexican, Indian, a native?" Tula answered, "I don't know what is meant by Mexican." The lawyer, still equating "Mexican" with "Indian," asked, "A native of Mexico?" But Tula, who understood "Mexican" as an identity in itself, answered, "Yes, [from] Sonora, all of us."[18]

So far Tula had been established as "Mexican," but did that mean she, and therefore her son, were not white? Mayellen's lawyer hoped to prove that Tula had Indian ancestry, thereby overcoming any presumption that Mexicans were "Spanish," or white. Yet Tula did not adopt what would have been the easiest strategy—to declare herself Spanish and thus white.

Mayellen's lawyer then asked Tula about each of her grandparents, all of whom Tula also described as "Mexican," save her father's father, whom she identified as a Spaniard named Ignacio Quevas. The lawyer then prodded her, "As a matter of fact, you don't know what your blood is at all?" Tula answered, "I do know that my mother is Mexican and my father is Mexican, half Spaniard." The lawyer then turned to the issue of her daughter-in-law's identity, asking Tula what she knew about "Mrs. Kirby's family." Tula replied that she "distinguish[ed] [Mayellen] by her color and the hair; that is all I do know." The cross-examination ended with one final exchange. Mayellen's lawyer asked her, "And you call yourself white, is that because you are colored too?" Tula replied, "We have no such description as white, we are called Mexicans."[19]

Tula Kirby's testimony is evidence of a popular counternarrative of Mexican identity that defies racial categorization. Tula apparently considered "Mexican" to be her racial identity, or at least identified strongly as Mexican and considered that to be her primary source of identification, with "race" perhaps less important than nationality and culture. Ultimately, Tula explained, "we have no such description as white." Indeed not: the category had meaning only in a world that had replaced nation with race—a substitution that had not yet occurred in the Mexican culture that Tula occupied. Revolutionary Mexico celebrated the mestizo Mexican—*la raza*, the Mexican race, combining all colors and ancestries. Accordingly, Tula may have understood herself as "Mexican" and therefore of one Mexican race, rather than describing herself in terms of "color races" such as white or brown. If she was acting strategically to help her son, she was not adopting the easiest strategy, which would have been simply to claim whiteness.[20]

When Joe Kirby took the stand, his lawyer asked him the same question he had asked Joe's mother: "What race do you belong to?" Mayellen's lawyer objected, "I think, if Your Honor please, that calls for a conclusion." But the judge disagreed: "Oh, no, that is a matter of pedigree." In other words, as in the nineteenth-century trials, racial identity—pedigree—was always a matter of fact to which witnesses could testify, as opposed to a matter of documentation that required hard evidence or a matter of conclusion that had to be left to the jury. Joe answered, less than emphatically, "I belong to the white race I suppose." On cross-examination Mayellen's lawyer asked, "Joe, haven't you repeatedly told Mrs. Kirby that you didn't claim to be a white man, that you were not a white man, that you were a Mexican?" Joe denied this, and also denied the notion that his father had been raised by Indians, insisting that his father was an Irishman. His goal was to prove that neither his father nor his mother could be connected with Indians or "negroes," thereby establishing himself as white.[21]

Not surprisingly, given the overlapping and conflicting stories about Joe's racial identity, Joe's lawyer claimed at the testimony's end to have established Joe's "Caucasian" identity, whereas Mayellen's lawyer claimed that Joe had "failed utterly to prove his case" and that Joe's mother "only claims a quarter Spanish blood; the rest of it is native blood." Drawing upon the precedent set by the *Rodriguez* case, the judge ruled for Joe. As his opinion explained: "Mexicans are classed as of the Caucasian Race. They are descendants, supposed to be, at least of the Spanish conquerors of that country, and unless it can be shown that they are mixed up with some other races, why the presumption is that they are descendants of the Caucasian race."[22]

Here was a case in which a popular narrative of Mexican racial identity (as not necessarily white, including the possibility of being "raised by Indians") clashed with the legal presumption of Mexican whiteness, in this case to the disadvantage of Joe Kirby's "negro" wife, whose racial identity was seen as facially self-evident. As in the *Flores* case, people who claimed "Mexican" identity were equivocal about what that meant in racial terms, even though "everybody" seemed to agree on what "black" identity was and on the illegality of its "mixing" with "white." In the *Flores* case the court concluded that whiteness had not been proven, whereas in *Kirby* the court ended its inquiry with the presumption of whiteness—but both cases revealed the gap between popular understandings (Mexicans as a distinct race) and legal ones (Mexicans as white).

Twenty years later the Supreme Court of Arizona again considered a marriage involving a defendant identified as part Mexican, but in this case both husband and wife had some Mexican ancestry. Frank Pass was found guilty of murder in 1941, over his invocation of the spousal privilege to exclude the testimony against him of Ruby Contreras Pass; the lower court overruled his objection on the ground that Frank and Ruby's marriage violated the state's miscegenation statute, because "a descendant of an Indian may not marry a member of the Caucasian race."[23]

Who was who in this case? Frank testified that his mother was half English and half Paiute Indian; his father was Mexican. The Arizona Supreme Court therefore concluded that Frank was "a descendant of three races, to-wit, Caucasian, Indian and Mexican." This seems to suggest that "Mexican" was a separate race in which none of the "color races" predominated—unlike, presumably, "negro" ancestry, which would have trumped all others. Ruby testified that her father was Spanish and her mother was half French and half Mexican. She was then asked, "Do you have any Indian blood in you?" and answered, "Not that I know of." That was enough for the lower court, as well as the Supreme Court of Arizona, to conclude that Ruby was "Caucasian," that is, "Spanish and French." Since Frank was "Indian and Mexican" while Ruby was "Caucasian," their marriage violated the miscegenation statute, and Ruby could therefore legally testify against her "husband."[24]

Frank's lawyer tried, without success, to argue that Mexicans were not white and thus could marry Indians: "It is, I believe, common knowledge that the Mexican people . . . are derived from some cross between Indian and other races or between an intermixture of people." The lower court judge, however, refused to "take judicial knowledge of that fact at all": so long as Ruby testified that she did not have "Indian blood" and no evidence was presented of "Indian blood," she was presumed white, just as in *Kirby* and *Flores*. The Supreme Court also found that "in [Ruby's] veins nothing but Caucasian blood flowed," although it urged the legislature to set a more precise blood quantum into the law so that people of mixed blood would be able to marry somebody without violating miscegenation laws in one direction or the other. The ironic result of the *Pass* case was that someone with Indian ancestry from the United States—a Paiute grandparent—could not marry someone with Indian ancestry from Mexico.[25]

Thus in cases involving interracial marriage, in which Southwestern courts were most concerned with drawing the line between black and white (rather than with establishing Mexican racial identity per se), courts placed "Mexicans" firmly on the white side of the line—even when trial testimony revealed a considerable amount of Mexican-black social interaction and distance from other "whites," as well as the refusal of both "Mexicans" and other "whites" to identify Mexican Americans as white socially. Indeed, by the 1930s and 1940s this social distance was exhibited in every aspect of life in the Southwestern United States. The clash between the varied social realities of Mexican Americans and their legal classification in court became even more problematic with the spread of Jim Crow practices.

Jim Crow and Mexican American Whiteness in the Southwest

In the 1930s and 1940s Mexican Americans in the Southwest began to organize in response to the increasing antagonism they were experiencing from their Anglo neighbors. During this period exclusionary practices— from deportation to segregation—spread. One of the strategies Mexican Americans employed in response was to claim the rights of white citizens. But this was never the only strategy, and it often coexisted alongside appeals to race pride and solidarity with other victims of racism.

From 1890 to 1930 between 1 and 1.5 million Mexicans immigrated to the United States, especially in the aftermath of the Mexican Revolution in 1910. In the 1920s alone the Mexican population of California doubled from 121,000 to 368,000. The Southwest was transformed by this massive influx of people, which fed an enormous expansion of agriculture and agribusiness. In 1880 there were only 7,436 miles of railroad track in the

Southwest; by 1920 that number had increased nearly fivefold to 36,000. In 1890 there were 1.5 million acres of irrigated land in California, Nevada, Utah, and Arizona combined; by 1909 there were 14 million irrigated acres in the Southwest. The expansion of railroads and irrigation enabled massive increases in agricultural production and marketing.[26]

Thanks to the dependence of Southwestern agriculture on Mexican workers, there had been little opposition to Mexican immigration before the 1920s. But with the passage of the 1924 Immigration Restriction Act, which set quotas limiting immigration from Europe, nativists' attention turned to Mexicans, especially the "wetbacks" who crossed the Rio Grande without documentation. As Congressman Albert H. Vestal of Indiana complained in April 1924, "What is the use of closing the front door to keep out undesirables from Europe when you permit Mexicans to come in here by the back door by the thousands and thousands?" Even politicians whose constituents were very unlikely to be in competition with Mexican workers were reluctant to abandon nativist rhetoric because of its power to unite whites of disparate economic situations against a common scapegoat. Until the Great Depression, little sustained effort was made to restrict Mexican immigration—but the rising anti-Mexican sentiment expressed itself in a tightening of Jim Crow. Beginning in the 1930s, nearly half a million Mexican Americans were pressured to repatriate to Mexico, some voluntarily, but the majority under great duress. Those who remained found themselves second-class citizens.[27]

In Texas in the 1930s and 1940s, as in much of the Southwest and California, most Mexican American children attended separate schools; indeed, by 1930, 90 percent of all south Texas schools were segregated. The situation was even more severe than in the Southeast, since in the agricultural areas dominated by big farms and ranches, many Mexican Americans lived in "company towns" like Taft Ranch with separate institutions—company stores, churches, schools, and so on—all run entirely by the rancher and attended exclusively by the migrant and/or resident workers. Mexican Americans were discriminated against in jury selection and in voting; and in many places they were shut out of public facilities such as swimming pools, theaters, and restaurants, or segregated into the "colored" section together with African Americans.[28] California maintained similar levels of discrimination, although extreme segregation existed primarily in agricultural areas and less so in the cities.[29]

Most segregation of Mexican Americans was de facto rather than de

jure, set in place by custom and local administration rather than state statute. Thus in Texas, school segregation was left to the discretion of local officials, who insisted that all separation was for educational purposes. In
California, Section 8003 of the state school code, promulgated in 1902,
provided that separate schools be established for "Indians under certain
conditions and children of Chinese, Japanese or Mongolian parentage." In
1931 a state legislator proposed a bill that would add the phrase "whether
born in the United States or not" immediately after the words "Indian
children" in that statute. As the *New York Times* noted, this addition
"could only apply to Mexican children, for there are in California no other
youngsters of Indian blood in sufficient numbers to be segregated, and
not born in this country." Although this effort to enshrine segregation of
Mexican Americans in state statute failed, most school districts simply interpreted the existing statute to include them already in the category "Indian."[30] As the journalist Carey McWilliams explained, the "common practice has been simply to assign all children with Spanish or Mexican names
to a separate school. Occasionally, the school authorities inspect the children so that the offspring of a Mexican mother whose name may be
O'Shaugnessy will not slip into the wrong school." When, in 1945, Mexican American groups helped introduce an anti-segregation bill to repeal
Section 8003 of the school law, it died in committee in the state senate.[31]

Although there was no specific legal basis for doing so, many government agencies explicitly counted Mexican Americans as a separate racial
category. The first efforts to include Mexicans in the U.S. Census, in 1930,
counted them among "people of other races," with "Mexican" being one of
the other races. Thus the census counted 686,260 "people of other races"
in Texas, but only 3,692 "white people born in Mexico." Because of the
vigorous opposition to this racialization of "Mexican" by the League of
United Latin American Citizens (LULAC) as well as by the Mexican government, the 1940 census categorized Mexicans as white unless "definitely
Indian or some race other than white" (although the census questionnaire
did ask about "language spoken at home in earliest childhood"). In subse-
quent decades the census used a variety of methods to count people of
Mexican origin in the five Southwestern states, including lists of Spanish
surnames and the categories "Spanish Mother Tongue," "Spanish Language," "Spanish Heritage," and "Spanish Origin." In 1980 the general
term "Hispanic" was introduced as a separate category following the "race"
question on the census form, making it possible to check the box for "Hispanic" and any of the racial categories as well.[32]

Yet state officials continued to classify "Mexicans" or "Latin Americans" as a nonwhite race well after 1940. For example, on July 10, 1941, José E. Martinez of San Angelo, Texas, complained to LULAC that "the Vital Statistics Department of said city is classifying births of the Latin Americans as of the Mexican race instead of the white race as has been recommended by the Federal Government." As late as 1954 the Texas Department of Health used forms with the categories "W," "M," and "C," for "white," "Mexican," and "colored," or "AA," "LA," and "C" for "Anglo American," "Latin American," and "colored." After LULAC complained, the state health officer instructed officials to change the forms, as he "agree[d] that Latin American citizens should be treated as white."[33]

Anglos in Texas who supported segregation of Texas Mexicans reported in a 1950 survey that they viewed Mexicans as a different race. According to the *American-Statesman*, an Austin newspaper: "Most of those who approve segregation make no attempt to cover up their prejudice against Latin-Americans. They say Latin-Americans are 'a different race,' 'socially inferior,' 'not clean,' 'we don't believe in mixing races.'" In 1950, according to that newspaper, one-third of all Texans favored separate schools, explicitly on the basis of their fear of race mixing. Nearly half cited other reasons relating to culture or social performance for preferring separation, including language differences and the Mexicans' not "act[ing] like whites." The Good Neighbor Commission, a government agency tasked with improving relations between the state of Texas and the nation of Mexico, also collected letters expressing virulent racism aimed at Texas Mexicans.[34]

Thus in Texas and California, Mexican Americans suffered many of the same Jim Crow practices endured by African Americans there and in the South. And, like blacks, they responded to racial injustice by organizing, petitioning, and litigating. In the 1930s and 1940s Mexican Americans formed several organizations to battle Jim Crow.[35]

The League of United Latin American Citizens, formed in 1929 to unite a number of Mexican American fraternal organizations in Texas, was the most important organization advocating on behalf of Mexican Americans. It consciously promoted both "race pride" and "100% Americanism."[36] Early LULAC leader Alonso Perales described the goals of the organization as developing "among the members of our race the better, more pure and perfect type of true and loyal citizens of the United States of America," as well as attacking all discrimination based on "race, religion, or social position," and emphasizing "the acquisition of the English language." LULAC made American citizenship a requirement for membership in its organization, orienting itself toward protecting the rights of citizens and distancing itself from Mexican nationals and "wetbacks."[37]

During this period LULAC officials talked about race pride, referred to "the Mexican Race, as a Race," and spoke of the need for an organization to promote understanding "where two races are brought together under one flag." At the same time, LULAC used claims of whiteness to push for Mexican American civil rights: in 1941, 1943, and again in 1945, the group pushed unsuccessfully for a bill in the Texas legislature guaranteeing "equal . . . privileges" to "all persons of the Caucasian race." Though the bill never passed, a toothless resolution declaring that "all persons of the Caucasian Race . . . are entitled to the full and equal accommodations, advantages, facilities, and privileges of all public places of business or amusement" did work its way through the Texas legislature in 1941 after lobbying by the Mexican government and LULAC leaders.[38] Local LULAC chapters also policed against the classification of Mexican Americans as anything other than "white."[39]

A few years after World War II, Hector Garcia founded another important Mexican American organization, the American G.I. Forum (AGIF). Despite the fact that the AGIF, like LULAC, worked to combat discrimination and segregation, in 1954 Garcia insisted that "we are not and have never been a civil rights organization," presumably to avoid any association with black groups. "Making any distinction between Latin Americans and whites," he wrote, "was a 'slur,' an insult to all Latin Americans of Spanish descent." In 1951 the AGIF passed resolutions urging restriction of the "wetback tide," although by 1954 Operation Wetback had led to such egregious violations of Mexicans' civil rights that even AGIF and LULAC protested.[40]

Many of the complaints by Mexican Americans to the Good Neighbor Commission of Texas, as well as to LULAC and other activist organizations, relied on a claim of whiteness, in essence diagnosing the problem of discrimination as one of misapprehension: we are being treated as though we were not white, but in fact we *are* white. One Mexican American activist wrote to the Good Neighbor Commission in 1945 to request an investigation of "the latest case of racial discrimination of which we have knowledge in our city, with a view to eradicate from the minds of ignorant Texans of Anglo-American descent the erroneous and pernicious idea that we, the Mexicans or descendants of Mexicans, do not belong to the Caucasian race." Another wrote to the coordinator of inter-American affairs to complain about a "No Mexicans Allowed" sign at the Toasty Tasty Café in San Angelo, asserting that "such discrimination is un-American and breeds a bad feeling between the people of Mexican blood and others," and at the same time noting that "the laws of Texas and the United States provide for no segregation of Mexicans and other white Americans." Such interchangeable discussion of "people of Mexican blood" and Mexicans as white was common.[41]

Some of the letter writers insisted that Mexicans should not be subject to Jim Crow because state law sanctioned only the segregation of "negroes" or "colored" people. And some took this even further, expressing outright hostility to African Americans: "Let us tell these Negroes," LULAC member Gregory Salinas urged in 1936, "that we are not going to permit our manhood and womanhood to mingle with them on an equal social basis."[42]

Even as late as the 1950s and 1960s, when the African American civil rights movement was in full swing, Mexican American activists and ordinary individuals continued to bring claims based on whiteness to state officials. In 1950 Hector Garcia of LULAC sent the acting director of the U.S. Census a copy of a Texas Department of Public Welfare form, complaining that it included a "race-nationality" category of "Latin." The director reassured Garcia that the Census Bureau planned "for persons of Mexican origin to be included under the race classification of white." In 1958 Rosa Deras Reyes complained to Lauro Izaguirre, the general consul of Mexico (who forwarded the complaint to the Good Neighbor Commission), that she had been refused service by a carhop at Tunie's Drive Inn number 2 in San Antonio. When told by the carhop "she was sorry but that the Tunie's Drive Inns did not cater to negroes or Mexicans," Reyes "showed the waitress her drivers license pointing out that the race of the bearer, hers, is 'white.'" Similarly, in 1963, when LULAC complained to the Good Neighbor Commission that a camp in rural Texas advertised "No Latin Americans or Colored People accepted," the GNC director wrote to the camp to explain that "the Latin race is a purely white race."[43]

While Mexican American advocates used whiteness claims to push for civil rights for Mexican Americans, state officials tried to turn such claims to their own advantage as they sought to widen the gap between Mexican Americans and blacks. Good Neighbor Commission officials responded to complaints about Jim Crow practices involving Mexican Americans, as did state prosecutors and judges, by drawing the distinctions between state discrimination against Mexicans and "Negro" or "colored" people, insisting that the two were extremely different. For example, when towns found themselves on the Mexican consulate "black list" for incidents of discrimination against Mexican nationals or Mexican Americans, they often wrote to the Good Neighbor Commission to protest. J. Conrad Dunagan, school superintendent of Monahans, Texas, wrote to the GNC in defense of state segregation practices that "our Mexican friends . . . misinterpret our motives in the arrangements which we make for the education of our Spanish-speaking citizens." Dunagan blamed this on the "furor over segregation of the Negro population," but warned that "it will do a serious injury to the Mexican-American to confuse his problem with that of the Negro. These are two distinct ethnic groups and their problems, with one or two exceptions, are about as different as they can be. It would be about as sensible to try to lump them together as it would to hitch up a Percheron and a Shetland pony to the same plow with the same harness."[44]

In spite of the prevalence of whiteness claims, many Mexican American scholars and activists consistently recognized the problems facing Mexican Americans as problems of racial discrimination, saw the connections between their plight and that of blacks, and drew the contrast between American ideals and racism, which they associated with Nazism. In this way they turned on its head the equation between Americanism and whiteness, instead claiming that Americanism equaled anti-racism. In 1937 LULAC supported Texas legislation to withhold government funds from "any school district which fails to provide equal educational facilities to all children of school age residing therein," including blacks as well as Mexicans. The Mexican-American National Association, founded in 1949, chronicled among its early activities "the first Mexican observance of Negro History Week" in the Maravilla Mexican community of Los Angeles. In its founding document, MANA declared, "We have pledged ourselves to eradicating the force and violence so repeatedly used against Mexican, Negro, and other minority peoples by local police and lynch-minded racists."[45]

This sentiment was not limited to leaders; the American G.I. Forum's *News Bulletin* reported in 1955 the results of a survey under the headline "Mexican-Americans Favor Negro School Integration." The article commented that the support of Mexican Americans for black civil rights could stem from two sources: "because they know what segregation of their own children means or because traditionally people of Mexican and Spanish descent do not share in the so-called doctrines of white supremacy and racial prejudice." This article, however, provoked an angry letter from Hector Garcia to Texas AGIF chairman Ed Idar complaining: "Anybody reading it can only come to the conclusion [that] we are ready to fight the Negroes' battles . . . for sooner or later we are going to have to say which side of the fence we're on, are we white or not. If we are white, why do we ally with the Negro?"[46]

Mexican American activists drew a sharp contrast between American ideals of equality and Nazi racism. Manuel Ruiz wrote to Jack Busch, mayor of Delano, California, that "when local officials condone community segregation of Latin Americans, our professed victory in Europe against the ideology of a super race, is looked upon with suspicion." Likewise, José de la Luz Sáenz, an early Progressive leader in Texas, a schoolteacher, and a co-author of LULAC's constitution, upheld an idealistic view of American multiracial solidarity. Fighting side by side with whites of many ethnicities during World War II had made him optimistic about the opportunities for Mexican Americans in the United States, leading him to emphasize that Americanism was opposed to racism. Luz consistently opposed all racial discrimination, denouncing the treatment of blacks in no uncertain terms: "The colored people has been subjected to accept, by brutal force, the mandates of the unfair Jim Crow Law promulgated by snobbish legislators."[47] Luz insisted that Mexican Americans suffered discrimination as a race, and he linked their struggle to the world struggle against racism and nativism. In an essay titled "I Am an American," he argued against "supporters of the skin deep theory of Americanism, that is, those who base Americanism on the color of the skin . . . I firmly believe that the Nordic element is not an essential factor in 'I am an American,' and that those who use the Nordic skin theory to foster racial discrimination are un-Americans in the first degree." He signed the essay "J. Luz Sáenz, Veteran of foreign wars." He also described himself as "an Aztec" in some of his early writings and referred to Texas Mexicans as "the Indians of Texas." To Luz, at least, vigorous advocacy on behalf of Mexican Americans, and claims to U.S. citizenship, did not preclude identification as a race or solidarity with African Americans against racism. Anti-racism was the true Americanism.[48]

Numerous historians have argued that working-class Mexicans, both immigrants and U.S. born, were far less likely to identify as white or Spanish than the middle-class people who joined organizations such as LULAC and AGIF. For example, Neil Foley comments: "For the masses of working-class Mexicanos . . . many of them first generation, the idea that they were members of the white race would have struck them as somewhat absurd. Anglos were white; mexicanos were, well, mexicanos—raza, and later, chicanos." Likewise, historian Ben Johnson notes that Progressive Mexican American leaders in Texas "displayed little interest in the whiteness strategy. They did not seem to think of themselves as white, or even to aspire to such a status." Thus the newspaper *La Crónica* noted that in the United States "the problem of race is a question of color" and referred to Mexicans as a "latin multicolor race."[49]

Yet it would also be a mistake to caricature all middle-class Mexican Americans as aspiring to be white and Mexican American workers as proponents of racial pride. Claiming whiteness was *one* of the strategies Mexican American individuals and organizations employed when making civil rights demands on state and national government officials. They also used other strategies, both compatible and contradictory: "100% Americanism," appeals to the Mexican government and "good neighbor policy," race pride, solidarity with other oppressed groups, and comparisons of racism to Nazism. Perhaps to modern ears, used to the militant claims of Black Power and La Raza or to the separatist notions of identity politics, such strategies sit uneasily side by side. To activists in the mid-twentieth century, however, there were no apparent contradictions in drawing on all of these approaches—sequentially or in various simultaneous combinations. Claims of whiteness might easily be used to supplement various notions of racial pride and cultural integrity, both in activism and in racial identity trials.

Litigating Mexican American Whiteness

Mexican Americans' status as white had been articulated in 1897 by the *Rodriguez* court in the context of naturalization to citizenship, and this status had been accepted in miscegenation cases in state courts. Yet before 1930, whiteness claims had never been raised directly in challenges to discrimination. Beginning in 1930, LULAC enlisted lawyers to bring suit in Texas state courts against segregation of Mexican American children in schools, as well as against the exclusion of Mexican Americans from juries, and throughout the decade these claims were framed in terms of racial discrimination. In the 1940s, however, state courts began to dismiss claims by covering Mexican Americans with the "Caucasian cloak" and to chastise civil rights litigators for presenting their "white" clients as victims of racial discrimination. In response, litigators turned to a more explicit whiteness strategy, arguing that Mexican Americans *were* white—but that because they were treated as nonwhite in Texas and California, they were entitled to Fourteenth Amendment protections against racial discrimination.

With the *Del Rio Independent School District v. Salvatierra* case in 1930, LULAC attorney M. C. Gonzales inaugurated efforts to integrate racially segregated school systems, arguing racial discrimination against Texas Mexicans. The court went along with this designation, explaining that the plaintiffs were "designated, for convenience of expression in the opinion, as the Mexican race, as distinguished from . . . all other white races," and beyond that, there was no discussion of "Mexican" racial identity. At least initially, Mexican Americans perceived the case to be a victory, because the court ruled that school districts could not segregate indiscriminately against "Mexican" children.[50]

Yet in fact the case was a setback. The court dissolved the temporary injunction against the school district and approved segregation on the basis of language and migrant worker status. This "cultural discrimination" became the template for future state-sanctioned racial inequities, making *Salvatierra* a harbinger of modern racial discrimination cases. From this point on, until a brief "affirmative action" period in the 1970s, courts would recognize only explicitly race-based classifications or intentional bias as true discrimination, whereas classifications based on supposed cultural, linguistic, or behavioral differences—even those highly correlated with race—would be considered acceptable. In *Salvatierra* the court accepted the testimony of the school superintendent that "people of Spanish or Mexican extraction" or "descent" had different talents from those of "Anglo Saxon parentage," including differing abilities in math, music, and handicrafts, even as the superintendent denied any "motive of segregation by reason of race or color." The ascription of different characteristics on the basis of Mexican ancestry did not count as "race"-based differentiation.[51]

On appeal the school district argued that "segregation" of children "of Spanish or Mexican descent" from "children of Anglo-Saxon parents . . . had been for educational purposes only." The Mexican American plaintiffs

insisted they had shown that their children belonged to and were part of
the white race, and "do not belong to nor are they Negroes or belong to
the colored race." In their motion for rehearing the plaintiffs explained:
"Segregation not being a discretionary matter, we are simply insisting
upon the plain application of CONSTITUTIONAL AND STATUTORY RIGHTS
as they now exist. Being white folks, we claim to be immune, and in fact
are immune, under their solemn pronouncements, just the same as if we
were arraigned before the Court for trial on a charge of Felony without a
Jury." The court's decision, allowing school officials discretionary authority
to segregate for educational purposes, they argued, "operates as a 'white
wash' for Appellants" and allowed them to discriminate racially "under the
guise or subterfuge" of "the best educational interest of such children so
segregated."[52]

It is instructive to compare *Salvatierra* to *Ramirez v. State,* the Texas
jury discrimination case of the following year. In *Ramirez,* the Mexican
American appellant (represented by an Anglo attorney) "charged that
there had been an unjust discrimination against the Mexican race" because the jury that had convicted him in 1930 of castrating his young
daughter's lover contained no one "of the Mexican race and Mexican descent known as Mexican." County officials argued that they were discriminating against Mexicans not on the grounds of race per se but rather because of Mexicans' presumed incapacity for jury service. County attorney
Joe Flack testified that Mexicans "in the County do not know the English
Language well enough and are otherwise ignorant"; he averred that there
was no "special discrimination against Mexicans as a race." Cecil Walston,
sheriff and tax collector, explained that he did not "think the Mexicans in
this County are intelligent enough and speak English well enough and
know enough about the law to make good jurors. Besides, their customs
and ways are different to ours and I do not consider them, for that reason,
to be well enough qualified as Jurors." While this might be true as well of
"some of the white jurors who we have upon our juries . . . I do not consider those white Jurors well qualified." In any event, Walston and other
county officials were adamant that there was "no discrimination on the basis of race or color" in jury selection.[53]

Ramirez's suit failed. Perhaps even more significantly, the court simply
reported county officials' testimony in its opinion and accepted it without
discussion, apparently finding it self-evidently sound.[54] Thus, efforts by
Texas Mexican plaintiffs in the 1930s to raise claims of race discrimination,

whether concerning juries or schools, fell victim to courts' willingness to accept almost any justification for exclusion or differentiation that did not explicitly refer to "race or color." For the purposes of anti-discrimination law, "race" meant "skin color," and only discrimination based explicitly and intentionally on color counted as racial discrimination. Mexican Americans could thus be effectively excluded from juries on the pretext of language or cultural difference.

Significantly, Ramirez's appellate lawyers considered that the jury commissioner's disparaging statements about Mexicans' intelligence proved that race discrimination had taken place. In their motion for rehearing they argued that "it is not the province of the Jury Commission to pass upon the Mexican race in Menard County as a whole as to their intelligence . . . [T]his Jury Commission also in passing, showed some of the race arrogance and haughtiness that is too common, especially in matters of court procedure that is characteristic probably of all races when dealing with different races, but especially with the white race." But their arguments found little welcome in the appellate courts. Whether or not white people were guilty of "race arrogance," the courts were comfortable allowing Mexicans to be disparaged as long as the terms were not *explicitly* racial.[55]

Throughout the 1930s and much of the 1940s, then, Mexican Americans brought civil rights lawsuits on the premise that they were a race that was being denied equal protection under the Fourteenth Amendment. Given the Supreme Court's response to African American civil rights suits, this was not a particularly promising strategy: the Court proved reluctant to find racial discrimination even when practices—all-white juries, all-white schools—clearly indicated that racially based criteria were being used to exclude African Americans (or Mexican Americans) from participation in civic life. As a result, neither the Mexican American plaintiffs nor their Anglo opponents discussed the racial identity of the Mexican people. The question whether or not Mexicans *were* a "race" was simply ignored, though trial transcripts and opinions suggest that both sides spoke loosely and interchangeably of Mexican Americans as a "race," a "people," and a national group. In *Carrasco v. Texas* (1936) the court found "nothing in the record to indicate that Mexicans were excluded or discriminated against solely because of race" in jury selection, even though the jury was all white in a largely Mexican American community. In this decision the court was not too particular about racial definitions, using "Mexican race" and "Mexican nationality" interchangeably in its opinion. Likewise, in *Lugo v. Texas* (1939) the court found that although jury commissioners had excluded members of the "Mexican race," they had done so on the basis of language qualifications, without intentional discrimination.[56]

But the 1936 Supreme Court case of *Norris v. Alabama* was to transform the legal climate entirely, though it took a while for its effects to percolate through the system. Clarence Norris was one of the Scottsboro Boys, nine young men wrongly convicted of rape by an all-white jury in Jackson County, Alabama. With the help of the American Communist Party and the NAACP, the case of *Norris v. Alabama* went all the way to the Supreme Court. Norris's suit charged that the jury which had convicted him of the rape of Victoria Price and Ruby Bates—a conviction that had led to a death sentence—had been all white in a largely black community. As an African American, he had been denied equal protection under the Fourteenth Amendment—not because any law had prevented the appointment of black jurors, but because the policy of excluding black jurors was, in effect, a denial of equal protection. In a landmark decision, the Court agreed. For the first time in U.S. history a racially biased practice (as opposed to a racially biased law) had been found unconstitutional. *Norris* offered Mexican Americans an extremely useful precedent. They, too, were being excluded from juries in their own communities, as well as from schools, elections, and other civic institutions. If Mexican Americans were a race, then under *Norris* their exclusion from juries was racial discrimination.

Ironically, Mexican American civil rights lawyers found it difficult to make use of the *Norris* precedent in part because of a victory by Mexican American activists on another front. In 1940, after lobbying by the Mexican government and Mexican American leaders, the U.S. Census reclassified Mexican Americans as white unless the census taker believed an individual was "clearly Indian or of another nonwhite race." But instead of winning for Mexican Americans the full range of social and civic citizenship rights they sought, this reclassification merely made available to state courts the argument that Mexicans were in fact white and therefore not victims of racial discrimination.[57]

One of the most dramatic legacies of the *Norris* case was *Sanchez v. State,* which reached the Texas Court of Criminal Appeals in 1944. Serapio Sanchez was convicted by an all-white jury of murdering his father's employer. Mariano Sanchez, Serapio's father, had been a farmhand for Bill

Hargrove. One day Mariano did not go to work, so Hargrove drove into town, found him, slapped him, and told him to get in the car and come back to work. In the ensuing fight Serapio killed a man who had come out to help Hargrove. Serapio, who had killed the man with a broken beer bottle, said that the action was self-defense; the district attorney called it murder. An all-white jury agreed, convicted Serapio Sanchez of murder, and sentenced him to death.

At trial the lawyers and litigants for the most part referred to Mexicans as "the Mexican race" and to whites as "Americans." When examining one witness, Sanchez's attorney, a man named Carlton, explained that "for the sake of the record. When I refer to the Mexican race I am referring to the Spanish and American descent." The judge then clarified, "People of the Mexican descent." Carlton asked a witness, "Do you have an opinion as to what the ratio is as between the so-called Spanish-American citizenship of the County and what they call American citizenship?" The witness replied that "the Spanish-American citizens number about 40 per cent." What went unremarked was the equation of "Americans" with whites.[58]

Sanchez's lawyer also elicited testimony about racial discrimination to demonstrate that Mexican Americans had been treated as a race apart in the county. When asked whether he thought Sanchez could get a fair trial in that county, the same witness answered that "there is a certain amount of prejudice against the Mexican race whether we like it or oppose it or not, the evidence of that is that we do not associate with them nor class them with ourselves." The state's attorney then cross-examined the witness. Despite the D.A.'s efforts to make him say otherwise, the witness suggested that Mexicans were treated significantly differently than white ethnic groups.[59]

The prosecutor attempted to portray relations among Anglos and Mexican Americans as amicable, with any segregation being self-imposed rather than evidence of discrimination, but the witness consistently answered that there were indeed "racial issues" involving the "Mexican race." And although the prosecutor at times tried to downplay race, he also referred at trial to Serapio and Mariano Sanchez as "these Mexicans," which Sanchez's attorney argued on appeal "was calculated to prejudice the minds of the jury against the Defendant" by reminding the jury that "the Defendant was a Mexican, a member of the Mexican race, a person of Mexican descent, and he was charged with and was being tried for the killing of one George A. Cox, a member of the American race."[60]

Sanchez appealed his conviction to the Texas Court of Criminal Appeals, arguing discrimination against the Mexican *race,* as the appellant had done in *Salvatierra* and *Ramirez.* But now the appeals court held that "Mexican" was a nationality, not a race; hence (white) Mexicans had *not* been discriminated against because the jury had consisted of their fellow white citizens. Since race was not the basis for excluding Mexicans, the court explained, *Norris* did not apply. Indeed, the judge explicitly identified Mexicans as a nationality rather than a race, writing that "[in] the absence of a holding by the Supreme Court of the United States that nationality and race bear the same relation, within the meaning of the [Fourteenth Amendment]," he would not apply the *Norris* rule to "members of different nationalities." The judge appeared to adopt the logic of the El Paso district attorneys in their brief for the state, which compared Mexicans to blacks in order to show that Mexicans were not in fact a race and so did not merit protection under the Fourteenth Amendment:

> The differences between the position of negro and the Mexican are multiple. The negro is of an entirely different race to that of the members of the jury commission, to wit: the black race, whereas, the Mexican is of the white race.
>
> Negroes were formerly in slavery under the white race, the Mexicans were not.
>
> Negroes are practically all citizens of the United States, whereas, the record will disclose that most of the Mexicans are not.
>
> The negroes speak English, whereas most of the Mexicans do not.
>
> There is a feeling in the South about the negro, which is evidenced by our Jim Crow Law, and their exclusion from our Democratic Primary Election, that does not exist toward the Mexican. If any prejudice exists against the Mexican, it is of a different kind.[61]

Ironically, the point of this elevation of "the Mexican" above "the negroes" was to sanction forms of discrimination against Mexican Americans that were now at least formally prohibited against African Americans.

The same thing happened in the next three challenges brought by civil rights litigators to jury exclusion in Texas: *Salazar v. State* in 1946, *Bustillos v. State* in 1948, and *Rogers v. State* in 1951. LULAC lawyer M. C. Gonzales was hopeful that *Salazar* might be different—that he might be able to convince the courts that Mexican Americans were treated as a separate race in jury selection. As he wrote in May 1946:

This is the case that I have selected as the best to use as a test to determine if it is lawful to deny the right to citizens of the United States of Mexican descent [to] sit on juries. Bee County is exceptionally good for this test because at no time during the past 100 years has a Mexican served on the jury on a criminal case and about one third of the population is Latin and we have about one thousand who have paid their poll taxes and about 500 who are able to read and write and speak the English language sufficiently well.[62]

But Gonzales's hopes to set a precedent against jury exclusion were dashed. Instead the lower court "held that Mexicans belong to the same race as that of the jury which tried [Salazar], although they are of different nationality." Gonzales had hoped to establish the racial status of Mexicans through the testimony of experts who could explain "that in theory and in practice the Mexicans belong to a different race to such an extent that they are being denied the federal constitutional right to serve on juries." Despite LULAC's earlier efforts to win "white" status for Mexican Americans in the 1940 census, by 1946 the organization's lawyer was trying to establish in court that whether or not they were "really" white, in *practice* Mexican Americans belonged to a different race.[63]

The 1951 jury selection case of *Sanchez v. State* turned on the same question—and foundered on the same contradiction. Aniceto Sanchez, a farm worker, was tried for the murder of a fellow laborer, convicted by an all-white jury in Fort Bend County, and sentenced to ten years in prison. Civil rights attorneys John Herrera and James DeAnda took Sanchez's appeal, and in their brief invoked racial language, complaining of "discrimination against Mexican-Americans as a race and people of Mexican extraction and ancestry as a class." They argued that "although a person of Mexican descent is a member of the White race, from a practical standpoint this segment of our population is not so considered in this State." Despite Texas courts' designation of Mexican Americans as white, the litigators insisted that *in practice,* Mexicans suffered racial discrimination and so were, *in practice,* a race. Moreover, they argued, "this court has, on numerous occasions, recognized this fact," citing *Carrasco* and other jury cases, and quoting the *Ramirez* judge, who had drawn a contrast between the "Mexican race" and the "white race."[64]

But fearing the consequences if *Norris*-style protections were extended to Mexican Americans as well as blacks, the courts were having none of it.

In its *Sanchez* ruling the Court of Criminal Appeals berated the two law-yers for their "exhaustive brief . . . citing cases which, either intentionally or loosely, refer to Mexican people as a different race. They are not a sepa-rate race, but are white people of Spanish descent."[65]

Local officials had obviously also learned the lesson about referring to Mexican Americans as a nationality rather than a race, for the Fort Bend grand jury commissioner testified: "We did not pick any American citizens of Mexican descent as Grand Jurors . . . A lot of these Mexicans are not cit-izens, and we just don't know them. I wouldn't say that I don't know of any Mexicans that were qualified for Grand Jury service. I will say we just didn't select them." On cross-examination he elaborated: "I don't think we put any man on the Grand Jury of French descent. I did not refrain from putting anybody on the Grand jury of French descent . . . I did not put anybody on the Grand Jury, that I know of, of English descent. Of the men that we put on the Grand Jury, we did not go back to their ancestors to see what country they originally came from." And when pressed again by DeAnda, he insisted that he had "never made any differentiation between people of Mexican descent in this County and all other white Americans." All of the jury commissioners answered the same way: there was no dis-crimination against any nationality in jury service, and Mexican Americans were just like any other nationality of the white race.[66]

Meanwhile, Mexican American leaders were still trying to make head-way against continuing school segregation.[67] In the *Delgado v. Bastrop Independent School District* case in 1948 in Texas state court, M. C. Gon-zales, the LULAC leader, tried to build the case that Mexican schools were inferior to white schools, and that Mexicans were arbitrarily sent to separate schools, regardless of language ability or any other qualifica-tion. LULAC officials inspected the Bastrop schools and filed detailed re-ports on the inequality of conditions between the "Latin" and the "Anglo" schools with regard to the building, transportation, lunchroom, plumbing, and the like. The plaintiffs used that evidence to argue both that they were being denied Fourteenth Amendment equal protection "solely because of their ancestry" and that they were being deprived of "benefits accorded . . . to other white children" for no pedagogical reason. The plaintiffs in *Delgado* cited the recent California case of *Mendez v. Westminster,* in which the state supreme court had overturned segregation of Mexican American children in separate schools. They sought further support from

Salazar to assert that Mexicans were "of the white race," so that, they conceded, "there is no question of race discrimination in this case."[68]

This strategy proved successful, for the plaintiffs won. The district court agreed that Mexican American children had been wrongfully excluded from white schools and confirmed its condemnation of discrimination that was supposedly based on Mexican children's language skills but did not involve actually testing the children to find out whether they could speak English or not. The Texas state superintendent of public instruction then issued "Instructions and Regulations to All School Officers of County, City, Town and School Districts" providing that segregation "applies only to persons of Negro ancestry" and not to members of any other race. "There has never been any requirement or authority for segregation of children of Latin American descent, and attempts at segregation of pupils of Mexican or other Latin American ancestry on account of race or descent have been held unconstitutional by the State courts of Texas and by the recent United States District Court decision in the case of Delgado v. Bastrop ISD." The Good Neighbor Commission's executive secretary, Thomas Sutherland, also sent letters to thirty segregated schools, requesting "that the schools reduce the number of grades in which children are segregated or eliminate segregation altogether." It appeared as though the whiteness strategy had given Texas Mexicans a true victory—although the state court decided not to publish the *Bastrop* opinion, preventing it from having precedential value in other cases.[69]

Yet despite this apparent victory for the activists, most school districts continued their traditional practices of segregation. Hector Garcia of the G.I. Forum inspected fourteen schools in the late 1940s and reported, "It is the consensus of opinion of the Latin leaders in their community that the school officials and especially the School Boards are not trying to abide by the spirit of the decree given by Judge Ben Rice." And when Mexican American parents met on January 10, 1949, with the Edcouch-Elsa school board to discuss desegregation of the high school, officials expressed reluctance to take action. When questioned by parents, board members said, "The anglos will have to think about that . . . The Americans are not going to like that."[70]

Despite the clear ruling in the 1930 case of *Del Rio ISB v. Salvatierra*, by 1948 the Del Rio school district still had not acted to desegregate the schools, so LULAC was forced to keep up the pressure for changes. In

1948 LULAC investigator C. P. Aldrete interviewed the Del Rio school board president, who seemed remarkably complacent about continuing segregation in the wake of litigation:

> *Aldrete:* Mr. Wallace, I come to see you on a question concerning our schools; specifically the segregation of "Mexican" children in West End and Garfield.
>
> *Wallace:* Nobody has ever complained before . . .—I would think they were satisfied. Is somebody complaining?
>
> *Aldrete:* Do you remember the Salvatierra case, or are you acquainted with it?
>
> *Wallace:* Not exactly, but I seem to recall something about it.
>
> *Aldrete:* Ever since the Salvatierra case the "Mexican" people have been complaining about segregation . . . I represent a significant number of those parents . . .
>
> *Wallace:* Who is behind you? Who is stirring up all this trouble?
>
> *Aldrete:* . . . Suppose that I, as a Latin American, bring a Latin American child to Central whom I wish to register there—would you refuse him admittance?
>
> *Wallace:* Yes, we would send him over to West End.
>
> *Aldrete:* Why?
>
> *Wallace:* Oh, custom; that's our policy—maybe because of language difficulties, I would say . . .
>
> *Aldrete:* Mr. Wallace, do you think there will be a change of policy any time in the near future?
>
> *Wallace:* As far as I'm concerned, no. That's the way it has been and that's the way it'll be unless we are ordered to change.[71]

By contrast, in California, Mexican Americans won a major victory with the Ninth Circuit case of *Mendez v. Westminster* in 1947. This class action on behalf of all students of Mexican descent in Orange County drew national attention to the segregation of Mexican American schoolchildren and attracted national civil rights organizations to join in the appeal as amicus curiae, including the NAACP and the American Jewish Congress. The case could have been as great a landmark as *Brown v. Board of Education* had it gone as far as some of the briefs urged and declared segregation to be a violation of the Fourteenth Amendment. Instead the court decided narrowly on the ground that the California school law approved only segregation of "negros, Indians, and Mongolians," not Mexican Americans.

The victory in the *Mendez* case was all the more significant because, before desegregation, Orange County had been a bastion of Jim Crow. Marge and J. D. Gobbel, Anglo residents of El Modena, remembered that Mondays used to be "Mexican day" at the local swimming pool. The pool would be drained and refilled on Tuesdays so that the "white kids" could swim in unpolluted waters Wednesday through Sunday. Likewise, Esther and Ralph Danker recalled "holding their noses" to avoid the "Mexican odor" when they went into the "Mexican school" or other places where Mexican Americans congregated.[72]

At the *Mendez* trial itself, despite the plaintiffs' official stipulations regarding Mexican whiteness, several witnesses referred to themselves as "Mexican" as opposed to "white." Each time the court reminded them that legally Mexicans were considered white. One young high school student, Carol Torres, was asked, "Do you have any neighbors in that same district, in the El Modena School District, who are children of your own age that are not of Mexican descent?" She replied, "Yes, there are plenty of white children, Americans, as they say there." When, asked to clarify her statement, she said, "Americans, as they say they are. They don't consider us—" the court interrupted: "You are pretty white yourself, Carol. You don't mean white people, do you?" Carol had been trying to point out that Anglo students claimed whiteness and Americanness for themselves, but the court insisted on the nominal whiteness of "people of Mexican descent." The plaintiffs' lawyer, however, continued to refer to students as either "American" or "of the Mexican race," more in line with the way the lay witnesses used the terms.[73]

As in the Del Rio case, school officials wanted to justify their segregationist policies on educational grounds, without admitting their racial basis. Thus the school superintendent testified that the district's policy of segregation was a matter of custom that had existed before he took his job and that it was in the best interests of Mexican children because of their language deficiencies. Since he admitted, however, that no tests were administered to determine language ability, he was in effect agreeing that once a child was identified—presumably by appearance and surname—as "Mexican," that child was segregated into a separate school regardless of his or her individual abilities. This kind of behavior had passed muster in previous cases, such as *Del Rio,* but it would not survive in the

California Supreme Court, by this time one of the most liberal state courts in the country, which in the same year struck down California's antimiscegenation statute. The superintendent also made clear his own racially based distaste for Mexican children, testifying that they had "lice, impetigo, dirty hands, face, neck, and ears; that they were generally inferior to the white children in personal hygiene." Eventually the lower court ruled in favor of the Mexican American schoolchildren and their parents, and the school districts appealed.[74]

In their reply to the appeal, the civil rights attorneys conceded that "this case does not involve any issue of race discrimination—for Mexicans are of the 'white' race." Indeed, given the mass of legal precedent finding Mexicans "white," they could hardly do otherwise. But in a sense the Mexican American activists were still trying to have it both ways, even though now the terms were reversed. Previously they had cited racial discrimination as evidence of their need for Fourteenth Amendment protection, even as they claimed whiteness as the basis for their entitlement to full citizenship. Now they reluctantly acknowledged their theoretical whiteness but nevertheless claimed that "appellants' acts have clearly fallen into 'the ugly abyss of racism.'"[75]

Mendez also revealed a new unity between African Americans and Mexican Americans, despite the use of a whiteness claim. After World War II, a war fought against racism, calling for integration could now be an American ideal. David C. Marcus, an African American civil rights lawyer from Los Angeles, argued the case for the plaintiffs in 1943, drawing heavily on rhetoric about the "four freedoms" and the "War for Freedom." Segregating Mexican American children on the basis of "color and ancestry," Marcus proclaimed, was "utterly inconsistent with our traditions and ideals . . . [and] at variance with the principles for which we are now waging war . . . To say that any group cannot be assimilated is to admit that the great American experiment has failed."[76]

The district court's response to the case managed to sidestep the question of Mexican American racial identity and never ruled on whether Mexicans were a race or not. Judge Paul J. McCormick's opinion emphasized that segregation "foster[ed] antagonisms in the children and suggest[ed] inferiority among them where none exists," and that any separation would have to be based "wholly upon indiscriminate foreign language impediments in the individual child, regardless of his ethnic traits or ancestry."[77]

When the school district appealed McCormick's decision, numerous civil rights groups weighed in on the appeal. The amicus briefs submitted by the NAACP, American Jewish Congress (AJC), and ACLU were some of the first to argue that separate could never be equal, anticipating *Brown v. Board of Education* by six years. The AJC's brief, written by the young African American attorney Pauli Murray, was particularly forceful in arguing that "when a 'dominant' group segregates an 'inferior' group it can never be equal," and that "any racial distinction is immediately suspect." Despite her eloquence, however, the Ninth Circuit declared that "we are not tempted by the siren who calls to us" to confront segregation head-on, and instead ruled on more narrow grounds, finding that segregation on the basis of "Mexican blood . . . of children within one of the great races" was not supported by California law.[78]

As in Texas, a court victory did not necessarily translate into actual desegregation. Despite *Mendez,* the county board of education allowed an all-Anglo section of the El Modena school district to secede in the fall of 1949 so that it could transfer into the all-white Tustin school district, costing El Modena nearly $600,000 in property taxes. Likewise, in 1953 a number of school districts in Orange County were "unified," diluting Mexican American political power, and new schools were built in segregated neighborhoods, to ensure continued separation of schoolchildren. Across the state the practice of segregation continued until the African American civil rights movement brought integration on a wider scale.[79]

In both the jury selection and school desegregation contexts, Mexicans' status as "white" had won them no particular gains in Texas courts in the 1930s and 1940s. Not until 1954 did Mexican Americans win a clear victory using the "other white" strategy. *Hernandez v. Texas,* a jury selection case, was decided by the U.S. Supreme Court just two weeks before *Brown v. Board of Education.* The civil rights litigation team of James DeAnda, Carlos Cadeña, and John Herrera had argued on behalf of Pete Hernandez that the exclusion of Mexican Americans from juries in Jackson County violated the Fourteenth Amendment, a claim rejected by the lower court. As it had so many times before, the court pointed out that white people sat on the jury. The plaintiffs' lawyers responded as they had many times before, but in even more pointed language, that "for all practical purposes, about the only time that so-called Mexicans—many of them Texans for seven generations—are covered with the Caucasian cloak is when the use of that protective mantle serves the ends of those who would shamelessly deny to this large segment of the Texas population the fundamental right to serve as jury commissioners, grand jurors, or petit jurors."[80]

But this time the court accepted that argument. Yes, the court agreed, Mexicans were *treated as* nonwhite by Anglos despite the fact that they were actually white. Particularly poignant was the testimony of John Herrera—as a witness in the case, not an attorney—about the bathrooms in the Jackson County Courthouse, one unmarked and the other with two signs, "Colored Men" and "Hombres Aqui." With such telling evidence, the litigation team was able to show that "persons of Mexican descent were actually treated as a 'race,' class, or group apart from all other persons," and on the basis of that treatment, they were entitled to the protection of the Fourteenth Amendment.[81]

In that sense *Hernandez* was in fact the beginning of Mexican American litigators' strategic use of whiteness claims to fight Jim Crow. Although the "we're white too" argument already sounded old in 1954 because of its extensive use in the political realm, it was new as a courtroom strategy. Before 1954 Mexican whiteness was a cynical trump card used by courts to dismiss equal protection suits based on the litigators' complaints of racial discrimination against Mexican Americans. After 1954 Mexican American activists were finally able to claim whiteness *and* racial discrimination in the courtroom—with remarkable success.

The litigation team of DeAnda, Herrera, and Cadeña went on to invoke Mexican whiteness successfully in a series of school desegregation cases, building on the *Hernandez* precedent. In the 1957 case of *Hernandez v. Driscoll,* for example, DeAnda and several other lawyers prepared a pretrial memorandum arguing, on the basis of *Mendez* and *In re Hernandez,* that "Mexicans" were "members of the Caucasian or Caucasoid race," and therefore segregating them from whites was illegal "even before [the U.S. Supreme Court] held (e.g. Brown v. Bd.) that segregation of children based on race . . . violated the [Fourteenth] Amendment." Therefore, DeAnda and his team argued, "the instant cases do not raise the problems present in the Negro cases. There is present in these cases no question of segregation because of *race.*"[82]

Because of the contradictory nature of their racial identity claims, Mexican American lawyers proceeded cautiously with regard to alliances with other civil rights organizations. Despite the enormous help they had received from amicus organizations in the *Mendez* case, they were wary of any perceived "common cause." When Jack Greenberg wrote on behalf of the NAACP Legal Defense Fund to Pete Tijerina, one of a new younger generation of civil rights lawyers, in January 1967, for example, offering to "extend its services to Mexican-Americans who are experiencing the same kind of discrimination problems which Negroes have experienced in the South," Tijerina opted instead to form a parallel organization, which became the Mexican American Legal Defense Fund, or MALDEF. Likewise, the educator and civil rights advocate George Sanchez commended Tijerina on his "efforts to form a council of Mexican-American lawyers" but warned that he himself was "lukewarm" about "contacts with the NAACP Legal Defense Fund":

> Though we should make common cause with the Negroes from time to time, we should not blend their issues with ours. Don't misunderstand, I was a pioneer among the champions for Negro rights—and I am still on their side. However, while the effects of discrimination against Negro and "Mexican" are essentially the same, the causes, the history, and the remedies differ broadly. Put bluntly, the Negro is mistreated because he is black and was a slave. The bases for mistreatment of the *Mexicano* are much more varied and very different. Their blanket cases are based on "race," ours on "class apart."[83]

This cautious approach to alliance with African Americans reflected Mexican American leaders' recognition of the contradictions in the courts' treatment of Mexicans as a "class apart" but not a "race," that is, the objects of racial discrimination without being the subjects of racial difference. Because courts saw "race" as a natural category rather than one produced by racist practice, they "could not help but be perplexed by Mexican American identity."[84]

Mexican Americans' claims to be white took on a new twist in the 1960s, when many school districts cynically employed Mexican Americans' status as "white" to "desegregate" black schools by integrating them with Mexican Americans—much as courts in the 1940s had cynically relied on Mexicans' "whiteness" to deny their civil rights claims. Only then did Mexican American litigators shift their focus, abandoning the "other white" strategy in the 1970 case of *Cisneros v. Corpus Christi Independent School District*. In that case MALDEF lawyers argued that Mexican Americans, like blacks, were deserving of Fourteenth Amendment protection. The Texas district court agreed, defining Mexican Americans as a "disadvantaged minority group" worthy of protected status under the Fourteenth Amendment, which led the court to rule that Corpus Christi was operating a de jure segregated school system by separating Mexican Americans and blacks from Anglos. Perhaps "white" Mexican Americans were being integrated with black students, but the schools remained segregated nonetheless.[85]

Why did Mexican Americans hold on to whiteness claims for as long as they did? Perhaps the "other white" strategy can be explained by legal pragmatism, as well as the material and psychological benefits of distancing themselves from African Americans. It is difficult to disentangle legal strategy from cultural trend, yet the fact that the "other white" strategy was itself relatively new in 1954 does suggest a more instrumental interpretation rather than a deep psychological need to identify as white.[86]

The shift in legal strategy from "other white" to "brown" came about only at the end of the 1960s, years after *Brown v. Board of Education*, during a time of cultural revolution in ethnic pride. The new identification of Mexican Americans with other "minority groups" in litigation agendas coincided with the racial pride of a new political movement. Mexican Americans who identified as "Chicanos" and "La Raza" rejected outright the strategy of claiming whiteness, proudly proclaiming Chicanos as a nonwhite mestizo race.

A profusion of new Chicano organizations reoriented the discussion of Mexican American identity. The Centro de Acción Social Autonomo (CASA), founded in 1968, began to speak of Mexican Americans as "La Raza"—"the race"—a term popularized by the leaders of the 1910 Mexican Revolution but not used widely in the United States until the 1960s. CASA defined "La Raza" to include "all people of LA RAZA, north, south, and/or Latin America and Antilles, and those individuals who feel culturally as LA RAZA." Thus Chicano pride included a racial element, but also a cultural and pan–Latin American element, as well as a more militant politics opposed to racism in all forms. The Mexican American Political Association (MAPA) and La Raza Unida Party, formed in California to register and mobilize Chicano voters, laid out a "program for Chicano political action." In describing this program, Ysidro Ramón Macías, a MAPA leader, wrote: "One of the most pressing problems for a person of Mexican descent in the United States is that of identity . . . [H]ere is a person who is officially classified as white (Spanish surname) by the Census Bureau of this country, yet because the shade of his skin generally is darker than the Anglos', he is effectively designated as a minority . . . [and] discriminated against because of his desire to retain the Spanish language and some of the customs and traditions of Mexico . . . Every Mexican-American is a potential Chicano." Self-identified Chicanos claimed a positive and politically radical nonwhite identity. As the "Plan Espiritual de Aztlán," written by Chicano activists in 1969, declared, "We are a Bronze People with a Bronze Culture." And Ruben Salazar, the Chicano journalist, asked in the *Los Angeles Times*, "Who Is a Chicano?" and answered his own question, "A Chicano is a Mexican-American with a non-Anglo image of himself."[87]

This shift from claiming whiteness to affirming "brown" and "mestizo" identity had remarkable consequences for both life and law in places that had been extremely resistant to change in the decades before the 1960s. In Del Rio, Texas, for example, the site of the first school desegregation litigation, activists wrote the Del Rio Mexican-American Manifesto, extolling the spirit of La Raza: "La Raza is the affirmation of the most basic ingredient of our personality, the brownhood of our Aztec and Mayan heritage . . . As children of La Raza, we are heirs of a spiritual and biological miracle wherein family blood ties unite the darkest and the fairest." This assertion of racial pride was a far cry from the thinking that had led litigators in *Del Rio* to assert that Mexican children were white and for that reason should go to white schools.[88]

By the late 1960s the public political position of Chicano activists had become one of fierce pride in the newly celebrated mestizo aspect of their identity (though *mestizaje* had been part of Mexican culture for most of the twentieth century) and a consequent rejection of the whiteness strategy. Yet many ordinary Mexican Americans in Texas and California continued to feel conflicted about claiming a white identity, and their understandings of race remain more consciously political and cultural than biological. For example, in New Mexico, where both Spanish and Indian identification have been higher among Latinos than elsewhere in the United States, identification as "Spanish American" or "Hispano" in the first decades of the twentieth century gave way to "Chicano" in the 1960s as part of a radical political mobilization. "Hispanic" became popular in the late 1970s and 1980s in part as a way for ethnic political leaders to draw diverse groups together around a liberal political agenda while avoiding divisive questions of cultural heritage, as well as distancing themselves from "more confrontational, Chicano politics." "Mexican American" never took hold because its connotations of foreignness were resisted by "New Mexican citizens" whose families' residence predated statehood.[89]

In the 1980 U.S. Census, when "Hispanic" became an ethnic category separate from the question of racial identity, 40 percent of Latino respondents checked "other" in response to the "race" question. Ethnographers suggest that they did so because they considered themselves to be non-white, according to a definition of whiteness that encompassed both "race" and "culture." This understanding of racial identity likely came about partly in reaction to changes in legal classification and partly because changing political sensibilities influenced legal transformations. As Neil Foley has argued, "the legal and cultural confusion over Mexican American identity stems in part from the fact that the United States has repudiated the idea of racial hybridity for most of its history and consequently has no cultural or legal context for understanding the racial place of mestizo peoples." In other words, it is not so much whether Latinos believe themselves to be a separate race or not, but that they do not share the Anglo understanding of what "race" means.[90]

The history of Mexican American whiteness in law and culture suggests that there is some complexity in the way Mexican whiteness and *mestizaje* have been deployed for strategic ends—but also that calling attention to Mexican Americans' *cultural* difference has historically been a way to disguise racism in acceptable terms. If, in fact, Mexicans' legal whiteness was used instrumentally by both advocates and judges (for different ends), did the legal regime of whiteness have any larger cultural significance? It certainly had lasting effects on the ability of Mexican Americans and African Americans to work together to combat Anglo racism, and it did little to undermine the equation of whiteness with moral and civic superiority. But the real tragedy of *Hernandez* and its aftermath has been the consistent refusal of state courts and the Supreme Court to acknowledge its central insight that race is produced by practices of subordination, and that racial discrimination can be disguised as discrimination on the basis of culture or language.

More than four decades after *Hernandez v. Texas,* in 1991 the Supreme Court decided another case involving the exclusion of Latinos from a jury, *Hernandez v. New York.* In that case the Court approved the prosecutor's use of peremptory challenges to strike Latinos from the jury, on the basis of the "race-neutral" explanation that Spanish speakers would not accept the translator's version of the trial testimony. Therefore, although no Latinos sat on the jury, discrimination against Spanish speakers did not violate the Fourteenth Amendment ban on racial discrimination. While the Supreme Court did not reach the question of whether "language ability without more" would have sufficed as a "race-neutral" basis for peremptory strikes, later courts have extended *Hernandez v. New York* to the situation in which a prosecutor strikes jurors solely because they speak Spanish, without questioning them at all about their ability to follow the official court translation. In *Pemberthy v. Beyer,* a New Jersey district court held that language ability was a proxy for race in the prosecutor's use of peremptory strikes against Latinos; the Third Circuit, in an opinion by Judge—and future Supreme Court justice—Samuel Alito, overturned the decision, finding that the prosecutor *could have* been concerned about translation issues in striking Spanish speakers from the jury. Despite an important line of precedent from the 1970s and 1980s holding that "race" should be applied broadly, that Latinos are a recognizable group for equal protection purposes, and that language ability can be a proxy for race, courts are increasingly finding discrimination against Spanish speakers to be permissible, whether in the context of jury exclusion, tracking in school, or English-only policies in the workplace. All of these discriminatory practices have their origins in the Jim Crow regime of the twentieth-century Southwest.[91]

What stands out most about the depressing series of pronouncements from Texas courts justifying the second-class treatment of Mexican American schoolchildren and criminal defendants based on a litany of unsubstantiated stereotypes is the continuing respectability of cultural racism. For as long as we equate race with biology and racism with the crudest forms of racial pseudoscience, as American courts have done, discrimination on the basis of cultural and linguistic difference will appear neutral and respectable, and racial hierarchy will continue to flourish.

Conclusion:

The Common Sense of Race Today

THE MID-TWENTIETH CENTURY saw the elimination of formal racial distinctions in U.S. law. In 1952 Congress removed the requirement that individuals eligible for naturalization to citizenship be "white persons." Two years later the U.S. Supreme Court struck down the Jim Crow laws segregating public schools on the basis of race. The mass movement to integrate public institutions and to demand voting rights for African Americans and Mexican Americans in the South culminated in the passage of the Civil Rights Act of 1964 and the Voting Rights Act of 1965 a decade later. U.S. courts began to interpret the equal protection clause of the Fourteenth Amendment as an absolute bar against racial discrimination, and to resurrect Reconstruction-era civil rights statutes prohibiting discrimination in housing, education, and public accommodations. In 1967, when the U.S. Supreme Court struck down Virginia's law against interracial marriage, the last formal discrimination on the basis of race ended, eliminating the need to judicially determine individuals' racial identity for most purposes.[1]

The last racial identity suit to be appealed to a state court took place in 1983 in Louisiana, when Susie Phipps disputed the racial designation on her birth certificate as "black" because she had always "lived white"; the Louisiana courts found her black according to a "1/32 degree of African blood" statute, and the legislature promptly repealed the statute. The Phipps case was the exception to prove the rule; courts rarely litigate racial identity explicitly today.[2]

Yet legal institutions continue to determine racial identities when they need to do so (primarily by asking people to self-identify), even as courts continue to shape narratives about the meaning of racial identity and its connections to citizenship. It is in these cases that we can see the echoes and legacies of earlier racial identity trials.

Since the advent of the civil rights movement, some judges have adopted a more liberal view of race as a condition of political subordination and have sought to use that understanding to create a more equal society. By contrast, some conservative judges combine a definition of race as merely skin color with an assumption about race as culture that supports acceptance of racial stratification as unremarkable and predictable.

The equation of whiteness with citizenship is still with us today in the figure of the Latino or Muslim "alien" and the African American felon, put outside America's civic boundaries. The trials that established this equation—making whiteness a prerequisite for citizenship and identifying civic acts as the proof of whiteness—no longer take place today, but their legacy is ingrained in our thought, our legal system, our cultural practice, and our racial common sense. We continue to reproduce racial hierarchy through seemingly neutral practices that perpetuate established patterns of power and privilege. Race still orders not just the life chances of Americans and their status in society but even our perceptions of events. And although many of us across the political spectrum aspire to be colorblind—or at least claim that we do—we cannot so easily undo our past.

The history of the role of law in creating and reinforcing racial hierarchy through the policing of racial boundaries is the stuff of tragedy, despite the appearance of farce. Racial categories, particularly as they have been understood and practiced in four centuries of U.S. history, are illogical, and they have led to untold misery for people of all national and ethnic backgrounds. The tragedy of this history is not that law did not work because of its logical failures but that it worked too well. Law as it was practiced from the first arrival of African slaves and the first seizure of Indian lands was not attempting to establish a just society based on racial equality but rather upholding and protecting the will of political and economic hierarchies of power and privilege. The racial categories it created and recreated, shaped and reshaped, now appear so natural to us that virtually every American's identity is understood—consciously or not—as at least partially a function of race. Our sense of entitlement to U.S. citizenship— or our sense that such entitlement is precarious—is always to some extent determined by our understanding of how close or far we are from the notion of "whiteness" that was so laboriously created, refined, and re-created throughout American history. Law gave meaning and content to our racial "common sense," creating experts at every level, from scientists and scholars to the ordinary citizens living in local communities. Slaveholders and poor whites, physicians and lawyers, Indians, Mexicans, Asians, and blacks were all called upon to testify, at one time or another, about their racial knowledge, drawing upon their understanding of individuals' appearance, reputation, civic and social performances, and associations. By regulating citizenship according to racial categories while simultaneously producing those racial categories through the performance of citizenship, law helped to establish race.

Yet if we expect "race" to mean only one thing throughout U.S. history, we will have missed the point. Over the course of two centuries, "race" has been a moving target. From the earliest days of colonial history throughout the early republic, the antebellum era, the days of Jim Crow, and the civil rights movement, individuals, groups, and nationalities have moved in and out of racial identities, and the word "race" itself has meant different things at different times. Even in the heyday of scientific racism, in the mid-nineteenth century, courts never relied on racial science alone to determine an individual's racial identity, but always invoked some combination of reputation, performance, and association as well.

Contrary to what we might expect, however, the changing nature of racism has made it harder, not easier, to undo racial hierarchy. If slavery's intimate domination is undone, the segregation of Jim Crow takes its place. If biological racism is discredited, it is replaced by cultural racism. If a binary opposition between "black" and "white" is challenged by massive immigration, some nationalities are deemed "colored" while others are considered "white." The notion that race and whiteness are—and should be—central to U.S. citizenship remains a powerful force in American life, even if the basis for that racism and the definition of that whiteness have frequently changed. Far from being an "error"—the quaint relic of a less scientifically minded time—it remains an integral part of a system of hierarchy and privilege. Whether in the form of slavery, Jim Crow, or institutional racism (often justified by cultural arguments), people recognized as white enjoy political and economic privilege that those deemed nonwhite are denied.

The story of racial identity on trial reveals the persistence of the idea of racial "performance"—that civic acts and displays of moral and social character equated with racial identity can and should determine one's place in the social hierarchy. In a variety of ways the discourse of racial perfor-mance, and especially the connection between racial identity and fitness for citizenship, remains potent today in discussions about culture, af-firmative action, and "the end of racism." Furthermore, the "common sense" of race—the notion that as incoherent a category as it may be, we know it when we see it—is surprisingly durable.

The history of racial identity trials makes clear that race is neither an in-evitable fact of nature nor an accident. Rather, racial categories were en-shrined in law only after a great deal of ideological and legal work. Draw-ing the line between black and white helped to strengthen the institution of slavery by making slavery ever more congruent with race and encourag-ing poor and middling whites' identification with white elites. Drawing the line between black and Indian, and reducing Indians from nations to races, helped to break up multiracial alliances while justifying the expro-priation of Indian lands. Drawing the line between whites and immigrants from Asia and Mexico helped to make the United States a white nation, again ensuring that both immigrant and native-born "whites" would ally themselves with white elites rather than with their fellow workers and small farmers of "foreign" and allegedly inassimilable "races."

This is not to say that law imposed racial meanings on unwilling com-munities; it could never have worked so well if it had. Instead local courts elevated community racial knowledge into the most important evidence of race—even as that community knowledge was itself partially created by the racial categories and systems enshrined in law. For example, colonial law distinguished African slaves from European indentured servants, cre-ating racial categories that then took on a life of their own. As a new gen-eration of colonial Americans grew up in a racially divided society, so was a new body of racial common sense created—and that common sense was in turn made part of a legal system as ordinary citizens were invited to testify about their understanding of race.

Many scholars portray the history of race in the United States as the rise of the "one drop of blood" rule—the legal and cultural norm that any Afri-can ancestry makes a person black. Yet while the history I have told cer-tainly demonstrates how important it was to distance oneself from black-ness in order to claim citizenship, it also suggests that we have made too much of the "hypodescent" rule. It was not the one-drop rule that kept the edifice of Jim Crow strong. Racism could work through many different rules about ancestry, mutating to fit the form of the law. And degree-of-blood rules did not in fact make it impossible for people to cross racial lines. Indeed, in racial identity litigation, juries often seemed to reward people who "passed" successfully into whiteness for doing such a good job at performing as whites. Racial categories were paradoxically reinforced by their flexibility, so that the boundaries of whiteness expanded at times to include people of some African ancestry who nevertheless performed whiteness, while contracting at other times to exclude even well-assimilated immigrants who violated common sense notions of whiteness. This flexibility served to strengthen the overall system of racial identification, and particularly the identification of whiteness with full legal and social citizenship.

The persistence of racially ambiguous individuals and communities, and of the "race mixing" that produced them, reveals that race was a dynamic force. Racial identities were not always rigid or fixed. They were often permeable and thus difficult to police. Despite the ideology that claimed "race mixing" was impossible or repugnant to right-thinking whites, for example, interracial sexual liaisons persisted. Despite the belief that whites and blacks could never socialize, many racial identity trials revealed a rich history of interracial balls, corn-shuckings, and even family dinners. Despite the certainty that Mexicans and Asians were "colored," courts and local communities alike faltered in the face of landowners, professionals, and other manifestly dark-skinned individuals who successfully performed whiteness and, indeed, played integral roles in their local communities. Racial ideologies never accurately reflected the world they described—though they were not necessarily any less potent as a result.

Nor did the persistence of people who for a long time defied or eluded categorization mean that racial hierarchy withered away. Sometimes today it is suggested that racial mixing, especially marriage or sexual intimacy between people of different races, holds the promise of decreasing the salience of race in American life and diminishing racial inequality. Yet both "race mixing" and inequality have marked American society from its beginnings. Intermediate and indeterminate groups had various statuses, and followed various strategies to survive. For so long as blackness has been denigrated, the existence of these groups has not helped to eliminate racial hierarchy.

Today our policies reflect this long and persistent history of making race a central part of U.S. law and citizenship. If we want to undo the world race made, we cannot pretend that our current situation of racial inequality happened naturally. Yet each of the dominant approaches to race that contemporary courts and scholars have taken risks just such a fallacy. It is tempting to read the history of racial identity trials as a fable about the folly of using law to put people in meaningless or nonsensical boxes, or of asking law to determine something it cannot do properly. And so, many legal scholars and political commentators argue that the correct response to such a fable is to eliminate all racial classification in the law; to end all positive remedial uses of race such as affirmative action in employment and education; to make ourselves officially blind to race.

The advocates of "colorblindness" believe that if we refuse to recognize race—particularly now that the Fourteenth Amendment and other legal innovations have removed whiteness as a formal requirement for citizenship—race will automatically cease being an informal prerequisite to the enjoyment of full civic participation as well. In other words, as soon as the law becomes officially colorblind, American society will follow suit. This view assumes that racism is simply the human error of identifying individuals by their race and judging them accordingly. Now that we are wise enough to recognize our error, they argue that all we have to do to correct it is to refuse to continue recognizing those categories.

The U.S. Supreme Court and some federal courts advocate this "colorblind" solution, treating race solely as a formal category and defining it not as a system of hierarchy but merely as "skin color," an irrelevant "morphological accident." For example, Justice Antonin Scalia, in a 1995 case restricting affirmative action in government contracts, conflates "blood" and "skin color" as biological facts that are socially, culturally, politically, and legally irrelevant. He argues that the Constitution rejects "dispositions based on race . . . or based on blood . . . To pursue the concept of racial entitlement—even for the most admirable and benign purposes—is to reinforce and preserve for future mischief the way of thinking that produced race slavery, race privilege, and race hatred. In the eyes of the government, we are just one race here. It is American." By characterizing the harm as "dispositions based on race," Scalia creates a parallel between affirmative action and slavery—between an institution designed to redress the harms of slavery, and slavery itself. The bad "thinking," in his view, is thinking about race at all; seeing race at all, he claims, will lead inevitably to race hatred.[3]

Yet the advocates of colorblindness are less explicit about what they think the result will be if their approach is adopted. Mid-twentieth-century racial liberals, such as Ashley Montagu, Franz Boas's student, who wanted to eliminate the category of race, believed that when the races disappeared, so too would racial hierarchy. As blacks, Jews, and immigrants were assimilated into U.S. society, they would cease to be blacks, Jews, and immigrants, achieving similar levels of wealth, education, and success as whites.[4]

The current advocates of colorblindness seem to harbor no such optimistic beliefs. Instead their opinions seem premised on the assumption, shared with commentators like Dinesh D'Souza, that existing racial hierarchies are inevitable results of cultural difference, not to mention wholly reasonable cultural discrimination. For example, the Fourth Circuit Court of Appeals, when it struck down affirmative action in Texas universities, at times referred to race only as skin color, insisting that it represented no meaningful human difference. But when arguing against using state action to remedy past discrimination, the *Hopwood* court often treated race as a "cultural phenomenon . . . explain[ing] racial status as a product of the cultural resources various groups bring to the task of assimilating the norms of the dominant culture." Courts like the Fourth Circuit begin from the premise that absent state action, there might still be a disproportionate number of people of color at the bottom of the socioeconomic scale—but unlike the mid-century advocates of colorblindness, they feel that such an outcome is acceptable so long as the people at the bottom are not there by virtue of explicit racial classifications imposed by the state. Once colorblindness is in place, blacks and Latinos may well be worse off—but their misfortune will be due to their inferior cultural, moral, and civic attributes, not to race, and so will require neither intervention from the state nor remedy from the society at large.[5]

As a result, conservative courts have severely constricted the ability of states and private actors to restructure racial hierarchy and undo the effects of past discrimination. In so doing they have sanctioned ongoing injustice, rationalizing it with the implicit assumption that racial stratification reflects only cultural difference. To their minds, black people are still poorer than whites and have significantly worse life chances not because of the effects of past racism or continuing racial discrimination but rather because of an implicitly inferior culture. Colorblindness thus becomes an extremely effective rationale for allowing racial hierarchies to continue.

Another response to the continuing salience of race in our society is a defiant politics of identity, asserting racial identities with pride and basing claims to political participation and other benefits on the basis of those identities. This is a tempting, perhaps inevitable reaction to the experience of racial discrimination and the desire of minorities to band together in solidarity, as well as to preserve the institutions and traditions of communities under pressure to assimilate. Politically as well, even sophisticated antiracists who recognize the contingency of existing identities call for "strategic essentialism," building political coalitions around racial identities when it is strategically useful to do so.[6]

Identity politics can sometimes devolve into the idea that there is only one way to *be* black, Latino, Asian, or Native American. The increasing emphasis on "diversity" in the workplace and on campus has lent growing weight to the idea that there is a distinctive "voice of color"—that African Americans or Latinos perform their identities, or should perform their identities, in particular ways. Occasionally the diversity rationale feeds into a "difference discourse" that celebrates the same stereotypes as those promoted by racial bigots. Identity politics focuses not on the need to undo the ongoing effects of past racial hierarchies or to oppose the pernicious effect of present ones. Rather this approach suggests that blacks, whites, and other cultural or racial groups inevitably bring different perspectives and experiences into the classroom or workplace.

To some extent the reliance on the "racial diversity" justification for affirmative action results not from identity politics per se but rather from the constraints on affirmative action presented by the current legal and constitutional environment. In the *Bakke* decision in 1976, Justice Lewis Powell's concurring opinion gave the fifth vote to strike down the University of California–Davis Medical School's use of numerical quotas for admission of African American students, but also suggested that the diversity rationale could justify affirmative action, provided that it was implemented through an individualized inquiry into each student's merits, taking race into account as one of many factors. Since then the Supreme Court's colorblind constitutionalism has closed off many avenues for redressing racial harms. It is impossible under the Court's narrow interpretation of the Fourteenth Amendment to justify any affirmative action program as a remedy for past societal discrimination, or even as a positive effort to restructure society in a nonhierarchical way. "Racial diversity" is now the only legitimate argument for affirmative action programs in education. Furthermore, the "diversity" argument has the merit of being forward-looking, and it does not *necessarily* equate an individual's racial identity with her cultural performances; in fact, some advocates, like Justice Stevens, justify the goal of diversity in terms of the breaking down of cultural stereotypes by exposure to people of different races. In its best expressions, the diversity argument emphasizes the benefits of integration. And identity politics remains a vital expression in many communities because it reflects the genuine need to preserve the political and cultural communities that have developed over decades of oppression.[7]

Yet because identity politics, even strategically deployed, depends on the assumption that race is real, this approach cannot truly combat the work that law has done. The diversity argument for affirmative action works in the margins to carve out some small areas where courts will recognize race—but in such a limited way that it will never be able to redress the enormous harms done over the last three centuries. And identity politics continue to be problematic, not only because of the tendency to enshrine damaging stereotypes of people of color in our consciousness and in law by making them appear to be essential attributes binding people of one race together, but also because they can be balkanizing, masking the shared interests of class, for example, by separating people along racial lines.

Legal scholars have struggled with the right way to respond to each of these inadequate approaches: colorblindness, the cultural racism that is sometimes behind colorblindness, and identity politics. Richard Ford, coming from a left legal perspective, forcefully argues that the only way we can recognize race for what it is—an insidious practice of subordination—is to disaggregate race from culture in the law. Some of Ford's proposals offer a welcome corrective to the dangers of identity politics. In applying his "race-neutral" argument to civil rights law, however, he argues that cultural discrimination should be allowed because it is distinct from racial discrimination. This means that everything from bans on cornrowed hair to "English only" laws should be permissible.[8]

This approach is particularly concerned with the power of law and the ways that courts can coerce racial performances by reinforcing stereotypes about "racial" behavior. For example, suppose a court holds that employers cannot discriminate against people with cornrows on the grounds that such a ban violates the Fourteenth Amendment. In effect, the court would be teaching us that cornrows are an essential attribute of black womanhood—a pernicious stereotype that we must resist, even if, in fact, numerous black women are fired because of their refusal to abandon their cornrows; even if, at the same time, no white women are fired for that reason. In this view, avoiding any legal regime that seeks to equate racial identity with particular stereotyped performances is of such paramount importance that we should accept racially motivated laws so long as they discriminate only on the basis of culture and not on the basis of race per se, even if some actual people of color suffer in the process.

There is no doubt that basing our definitions of race on performance and common sense can be just as damaging as basing our definitions on bogus science. But employers and governments can use their power to co-erce racial performances—to force people of color to perform white-ness—in order to gain access to political institutions or employment. The possibility of this kind of coercion seems much greater than coercion by courts.

Because racial subordination in the United States has historically been based on both racial science and racial performance, racism in the United States has conflated race and culture: "black" culture is considered inferior because it is black, Spanish speakers are considered uneducated because they do not speak English, and so on. Because racism has expressed itself in cultural terms, race and culture cannot be disaggregated without ignor-ing vast realms of reinforcement of racial hierarchy.

If employers really were acting in a racially neutral, rational manner— banning cornrows only out of concern for "neatness," or Spanish language only out of concern for ease of communication—perhaps they might be entitled to discriminate on cultural grounds, and the attempt to distin-guish between racial and cultural discrimination would be justified. But no matter what arguments the employers themselves might offer, cornrows are banned not because they are inherently less neat or professionally ap-propriate but rather because performances of whiteness are considered essential to achieving professional status. Likewise, "English only" laws, language tracking in schools, and other forms of discrimination against Spanish speakers are not mere practical tools to improve communica-tion but rather have been used as extremely effective mechanisms of racial discrimination against Mexican Americans in the Southwest. When em-ployers and governments mask their creation of racial hierarchies through bans on cultural practices, it is a means of allowing racism to enter through the back door of culture.

If colorblindness, identity politics/diversity, and disaggregation of race and culture are unsatisfactory ways of dismantling racial hierarchy, what kind of law might serve an antiracist agenda? As a number of commentators have begun to argue in the context of gender and sexual orientation as well as race, employers today are more likely to discriminate on the basis of the way people perform their identities than to exclude individuals solely on the basis of their membership in a group. Workplaces as well as current legal doctrines enforce assimilationist norms, or what one commentator has called "covering" of identity. That is, employers are willing to hire women who act like men and conform to male standards in the workplace, and blacks who don't act too "black," but they are not willing to hire people who fall outside the white, male norms of the workplace. To the greatest extent possible, we should formulate antidiscrimination law to encompass discrimination not only on the basis of race understood as "skin color" but on the basis of racial performances as well.[9]

The most promising precedents for this kind of legal doctrine have taken place in the area of gender, in a series of cases about "sex stereotyping." In these cases courts have recognized that reinforcing gender stereotypes is a form of gender discrimination. For example, in *Price Waterhouse v. Hopkins* (1987), the U.S. Supreme Court held that Ann Hopkins had been passed over for promotion not because she was a woman but because of the way she "acted like . . . a woman"—or did not act enough like a woman. Her employers found Hopkins too aggressive and pushy, insufficiently ladylike. By finding for Ann Hopkins, the Court recognized that it is sex discrimination to evaluate people for the way they perform their gender. Likewise, it should be actionable race discrimination to require people to perform their racial identity in certain ways, such as to wear only "white" hairstyles or speak in a certain accent.[10]

Courts need to recognize not only that "race" is a historical construction but also that courts themselves have participated in, and continue to participate in, its making. Courts do have transformative power, but their "nonrecognition" of race does not make it disappear; it simply shapes "race" in particular ways. If law acts to leave in place, or is indifferent to, continuing racial hierarchy outside the courtroom, then its neutrality in fact reinforces cultural racism because it assumes that if "blood" has not led to the resulting "differences," culture must have done so. It sends the message that these continuing differences are acceptable, or that there is nothing that can be done about them.

Perhaps the case in which the U.S. Supreme Court came closest to articulating a political definition of race was *Saint Francis College v. Al-*

Khazraji, in 1987, in which the Court found that a professor identified as an "Arab" could seek statutory damages from the college, which denied him tenure on the basis of race discrimination even though Arabs were considered "Caucasian." The first part of Justice Byron White's opinion was relatively conservative. He found for the plaintiff on the basis of legislative intent, concluding that in the mid-nineteenth century, Congress would have considered "Arabs" a race even if we would not today. "Such discrimination is racial discrimination that Congress intended [in the 1875 statute] to forbid, whether or not it would be classified as racial in terms of modern scientific theory." Yet White went on to hold that racial categories have *no* scientific basis, modern or otherwise, and that the real test of whether a group is a "race" is whether it has suffered racial discrimination—whether it has been "racialized," as the academics would say. White noted that "some, but not all, scientists . . . conclude that racial classifications are for the most part sociopolitical, rather than biological, in nature."[11]

Today racial hierarchy both is and is not alive and well. By some measures the gulf between whites and nonwhites in the United States has never been greater. Most African Americans and Latinos attend schools with few whites or none at all and live in extremely segregated communities. African Americans make up 12 percent of the U.S. population but own only 0.5 percent of the nation's wealth. African American income is only 60 percent of whites' income, and a black child is nearly three times as likely as a white child to grow up in poverty. Black-white residential segregation is remarkably persistent, and this neighborhood segregation, according to researchers, explains even more of the gap in SAT scores between white and black students than is explained by school segregation. While racial intermarriage is on the upswing, especially between whites and Asians and between blacks and Latinos, whites continue to be extremely unlikely to marry blacks.[12]

Yet in other ways law has contributed to remarkable changes in our society since Alexina Morrison's time. In part her story is so gripping to us because of its foreignness, because of how far we have come from a time when a woman of color could be stripped to her waist in an open courtroom and poked and prodded by strangers under sanction of law. At key moments in American history—Bacon's Rebellion in the seventeenth century, Reconstruction in the nineteenth century, the civil rights movement in the twentieth—surprising interracial alliances took the reins of history to challenge an entrenched racial order. In those periods of upheaval, people forced great legal and constitutional changes, and those changes in law transformed people's lives and their views of the world. Ironically, we know best what a difference those periods made because of how much energy and work was needed to retrench afterwards.

If we can derive one lesson from this history, it is that law is not made from above. Ordinary people confronted the state in local courts and administrative hearings, and those confrontations shaped the law. Race did not just happen, and law was not imposed on us. We made race, through legal institutions, and we continue to make it every day; we can also unmake it.

But we cannot unmake it by pretending race does not exist. We must speak through our legislatures, courts, and elected officials to confront racial hierarchies as they exist now, head-on, using racial categories to affirmatively undo the exclusion of people of color from positions of power in employment, education, and politics. Racial groups are groups that have been racialized: Latinos are a race because they are *treated as* a race, and that is a working definition of race. Census categories should reflect historical discrimination, not personal expression. And courts and legislatures should recognize Indian tribes as political entities that can be multiracial nations, and that owe as much of an obligation to the descendants of former slaves as does the United States.

Change will not come overnight. But we will know it when we see it.

Notes

Acknowledgments

Index

Notes

Introduction

1. Transcript of Trial, *Morrison v. White*, No. 442 (interrogatories to Benjamin F. Danby, Christopher C. Danby, Josiah Gildes, Andre Hutt, and John T. Trigg; petition for change of venue of James White and grant of petition), 14, 63–64 (La. New Orleans Dist. Ct. Sept. 1858) (collection of Earl K. Long Library, Special Collections and Archives, University of New Orleans, Supreme Court Records; hereafter UNO-SCR), rev'd, 16 La. Ann. 100 (1861). I have discussed this case at greater length in "Litigating Whiteness: Trials of Racial Determination in the Nineteenth-Century South," *Yale Law Journal* 108 (October 1998): 171–176. See also Walter Johnson, "The Slave Trader, the White Slave, and the Politics of Racial Determination in the 1850s," *Journal of American History* (June 2000), http://www.historycooperative.org/journals/jah/87.1/johnson.html (accessed 15 August 2007).
2. Transcript of Trial, *Morrison v. White*, 24–63.
3. Ibid., 80–170; *Morrison v. White*, 16 La. Ann. 100 (1861).
4. Johnson, "The Slave Trader," pars. 36–40.

1. The Common Sense of Race

1. Nicholas Hudson, "From 'Nation' to 'Race': The Origin of Racial Classification in Eighteenth-Century Thought," *Eighteenth Century Studies* 29 (Spring 1996): 247–264; Gwendolyn Midlo Hall, *Slavery and African Ethnicities in the Americas: Restoring the Links* (Chapel Hill: University of North Carolina Press, 2005), 1.

2. Ira Berlin, *Generations of Captivity: A History of African-American Slaves* (Cambridge, Mass.: Harvard University Press, 2003), 38, 55.

3. Edmund S. Morgan, *American Slavery, American Freedom: The Ordeal of Colonial Virginia* (New York: W. W. Norton and Company, 1975), 297; Helen C. Rountree, *Pocahontas' People: The Powhatan Indians of Virginia through Four Centuries* (Norman: University of Oklahoma Press, 1990), 139.

4. On fornication laws, see Kathleen M. Brown, *Good Wives, Nasty Wenches, and Anxious Patriarchs: Gender, Race, and Power in Colonial Virginia* (Chapel Hill: University of North Carolina Press, 1996), 195–197; George M. Fredrickson, *The Arrogance of Race: Historical Perspectives on Slavery, Racism, and Social Inequality* (Middletown, Conn.: Wesleyan University Press, 1988), 193.

5. Quoted in Peter Wallenstein, "Indian Foremothers: Race, Sex, Slavery, and Freedom in Early Virginia," in *The Devil's Lane: Sex and Race in the Early South,* ed. Catherine Clinton and Michele Gillespie (New York: Oxford University Press, 1997), 57–73.

6. Virginia Easley DeMarce, "'Very Slitly Mixt': Tri-Racial Isolate Families of the Upper South—A Genealogical Study," *National Genealogical Society Quarterly* 80 (March 1992): 5–35; Paul Heinegg, *Free African Americans of North Carolina and Virginia,* foreword by Ira Berlin (Genealogical Publishing, 1999), http://www.freeafricanamericans.com.

7. Gary B. Nash, "The Hidden History of Mestizo America," *Journal of American History* 82 (December 1995): 948; Daniel R. Mandell, "Shifting Boundaries of Race and Ethnicity: Indian-Black Intermarriage in Southern New England, 1760–1880," *Journal of American History* 85 (September 1998): 490–491; Patrick Riordan, "Finding Freedom in Florida: Native Peoples, African Americans, and Colonists, 1670–1816," *Florida Historical Quarterly* 75 (Summer 1996): 1; see generally Kevin Mulroy, *Freedom on the Border: The Seminole Maroons in Florida, the Indian Territory, Coahuila, and Texas* (Lubbock: Texas Tech University Press, 1993).

8. See William S. Willis, "Divide and Rule: Red, White, and Black in the Southeast," *Journal of Negro History* 48 (July 1963); James H. Merrell, "The Racial Education of the Catawba Indians," *Journal of Southern History* 50 (August 1984): 363–384; William G. McLoughlin, "Red Indians, Black Slavery, and White Racism: America's Slaveholding Indians," *American Quarterly* 26 (October 1974): 380–381; Theda Purdue, *Slavery and the Evolution of the Cherokee Society, 1540–1866* (Knoxville: University of Tennessee Press, 1979), 40–49 (chronicling efforts of whites to create antagonism between blacks and Cherokees and gradual acceptance by Cherokees of European model of race); R. Halliburton Jr., *Red over Black: Black Slavery among the Cherokee Indians* (New York: Greenwood Press, 1977);

Kathryn E. H. Braund, "The Creek Indians, Blacks, and Slavery," *Journal of Southern History* 57 (November 1991): 603.

9. See Hudson, "From 'Nation' to 'Race.'"

10. Benjamin Franklin to Peter Collinson, Philadelphia, May 9, 1753, and "Remarks Concerning the Savages of North-America" (1783), both in *Franklin: Writings,* ed. J. A. Leo Lemay (New York: Library of America, 1987), 470–471, 969–974.

11. Thomas Jefferson, *Notes on the State of Virginia,* ed. William Peden (Chapel Hill: University of North Carolina Press, 1982), 140; Robert F. Berkhofer, *The White Man's Indian: Images of the American Indian from Columbus to the Present* (New York: Vintage Books, 1979), 42.

12. *Cherokee Nation v. Ga.,* 30 U.S. 1, 2 (1831); *Dred Scott v. Sandford,* 60 U.S. 393, 403, 409, 483 (1856); *Johnson v. McIntosh,* 21 U.S. 543 (1823).

13. 11 Va. (1 Hen. & M.) 134 (1806).

14. Ibid., 134.

15. Ibid.

16. *Gregory v. Baugh,* 4 Rand. 611, 667–670 (Va. 1827).

17. Ibid., 669, 687–691.

18. Thomas E. Partlow, *Wilson County, Tennessee, Deed Books C–M, 1793–1823* (Easley, S.C.: Southern Historical Press, 1984), 353; Thomas E. Partlow, *Wilson County, Tennessee, Deed Books N–Z, 1829–1853* (Easley, S.C.: Southern Historical Press, 1984), 105; Thomas E. Partlow, *Wilson County, Tennessee, Miscellaneous Records, 1800–1875* (Easley, S.C.: Southern Historical Press, 1982), 95–100, 151, 159; Transcript of Trial, *Butcher v. Vaughan,* No. 5626 (Tenn. Sumner County Cir. Ct. August 1823), Roll A-5083 (Tenn. State Library and Archives), appealed in *Vaughn v. Phebe,* 8 Tenn. 4 (1827) (hereafter Transcript of Trial, *Butcher v. Vaughan*).

19. Transcript of Trial, *Butcher v. Vaughan* (depositions of Joseph Davenport, Nancy Davenport, and Rachel Bowers); Partlow, *Wilson County Deed Books C–M,* 329; Partlow, *Wilson County Miscellaneous Records,* 147.

20. Transcript of Trial, *Butcher v. Vaughan* (depositions of Rachel Bowers, Nancy Davenport, and James Weir).

21. Ibid. (depositions of Mary Simon, Martha Jones).

22. Census of 1820 and 1830, Manuscript Population Schedules, Sumner County, Tenn.; *Goodspeed's General History of Tennessee* (Nashville: Goodspeed Publishing Co., 1887), 924; Shirley Wilson, *Sumner County, Tennessee, Bond Book, 1787–1835* (Hendersonville, Tenn., 1994), 14; Carol Wells, *Sumner County, Tenn., Court Minutes, 1787–1805 and 1808–1810* (Bowie, Md.: Heritage Books, 1995), 107; Transcript of Trial, *Butcher v. Vaughan* (depositions of Rachel Bowers, James Weir, Joseph Davenport, Nancy Davenport); Partlow, *Wilson County Deed Books C–M,* 353.

23. Thomas R. R. Cobb, *An Inquiry into the Law of Negro Slavery in the*

United States (1858; reprint, New York: Negro Universities Press, 1968), 51.

24. Ira Berlin, *Slaves without Masters: The Free Negro in the Antebellum South* (New York: Pantheon Books, 1964), 137, 175–176; Joel Williamson, *New People: Miscegenation and Mulattoes in the United States* (New York: Free Press, 1980), 14, 26–27.

25. Berlin, *Slaves without Masters*, 343–380, 374; Thomas D. Morris, *Southern Slavery and the Law, 1619–1860* (Chapel Hill: University of North Carolina Press, 1999), 371–423, 30–36; An Act to Remove the Free Negroes and Mulattoes from This State, 1859 Ark. Acts 175; Peter Wallenstein, "Race, Marriage, and the Law of Freedom: Alabama and Virginia, 1860s–1960s," *Chicago-Kent Law Review* 70 (1994): 371, 373; 1838 Miss. Digest of Laws, ch. 75, §1, at 560; 1857–58 Tenn. Code §§2437, 2445–47, at 481–482; 1870 Tenn. Laws, ch. 39; Peter W. Bardaglio, *Reconstructing the Household: Families, Sex, and the Law in the Nineteenth-Century South* (Chapel Hill: University of North Carolina Press, 1995), 48–64; James Hugo Johnston, *Race Relations in Virginia and Miscegenation in the South, 1776–1860* (Amherst: University of Massachusetts Press, 1970), 165–216.

26. Transcript of Trial, *Guy v. Daniel,* No. 4109 (Ark. Ashley County Cir. Ct. July 1855) (collection of Pulaski County Law Library, Little Rock, Ark. Supreme Court Records and Briefs), rev'd in part, 19 Ark. 121 (1857), aff'd after remand, 23 Ark. 50 (1861) (hereafter Transcript of Trial, *Guy v. Daniel*), petition of Abby Guy, 2–3. Unless otherwise noted, Abby Guy's story comes from the Transcript of Trial.

27. Transcript of Trial, *Morrison v. White*, 63–64, 81 (testimony of P. C. Perret); and Transcript of Trial, *Miller v. Belmonti,* No. 5623 (La. New Orleans Dist. Ct. May 1845) (UNO-SCR), rev'd, 11 Rob. 339 (La. 1845) (testimony of C. Pollock); *State v. Davis,* 18 S.C.L. (2 Bail.) 558, 560 (1831).

28. "Used t'row down Bayou Bartholomew," WPA Life History, Manuscript Division, Library of Congress, taken in Chicago, 1939; Horace Adams, "The Railroad That Never Ran," *Drew County Historical Journal* (1996): 46–49, from *Arkansas Gazette,* March 14, 1937.

29. Census of 1850, Manuscript Population Schedules, Ashley County, Ark., National Archives Microfilm Series M432, Roll 25; see generally Y. W. Etheridge, *History of Ashley County* (Van Buren, Ark.: Press-Argus, 1959); Robert A. Carpenter Sr. and Mary Imogene Noble Carpenter, comps., *Reflections of Ashley County, Including History of Ashley County by Y. W. Etheridge* (Dallas: Curtis Media Corporation, 1988); John Hallum, *Biographical and Pictorial History of Arkansas,* vol. 1 (Albany: Weed, Parsons, 1887).

30. Transcript of Trial, *Guy v. Daniel.*

31. *Daniel v. Guy,* 19 Ark. 121, 137 (1857).

32. Transcript of Trial, *Guy v. Daniel,* 20 (testimony of Richard Stanley, bill of exceptions); Census of 1850.

33. Etheridge, *History of Ashley County,* 90.

34. Census of 1850.

35. Transcript of Trial, *Guy v. Daniel,* 4–5 (Judge's order, January 28, 1855).

36. Ibid., 2–3 (petition of Abby Guy).

37. William Craft and Ellen Craft, *Running a Thousand Miles for Freedom; or, the Escape of William and Ellen Craft from Slavery* (1860; reprint, New York: Arno Press, 1969), 3; "White Slavery in Connecticut," *Arkansas State Gazette and Democrat,* September 12, 1857.

38. "Suit for Freedom Decided," *Arkansas State Gazette and Democrat,* May 30, 1851; Etheridge, *History of Ashley County,* 93.

39. *Bryan v. Walton,* 33 Ga. 11, 24 (Supp. 1864).

40. Transcript of Trial, *Guy v. Daniel,* 20.

41. Ibid., 23–24; Etheridge, *History of Ashley County,* 84, 85.

42. 19 Ark. 121, 124 (1857) (misspells sheriff's name as "Ducker").

43. Transcript of Trial, *Guy v. Daniel,* 20–24 (bill of exceptions); Etheridge, *History of Ashley County,* 84–85.

44. Ariela Gross, "Pandora's Box: Slave Character on Trial in the Antebellum Deep South," *Yale Journal of Law and the Humanities* 7 (1995): 292–294.

45. Transcript of Trial, *Guy v. Daniel,* 31 (bill of exceptions).

46. Transcript of Trial, *State v. Jacobs,* No. 7915 (N.C. Brunswick County Super. Ct. 1859) (collection of N.C. Department of Archives and History, Raleigh, Supreme Court Records; hereafter NCDAH-SCR), aff'd, 51 N.C. 284 (1859).

47. Testimony of G. H. Lyon, Transcript of Trial, *Morrison v. White,* 24–25; 25 (testimony of J. B. Clauson); 26–27 (testimony of S. N. Cannon); 28–29 (testimony of J. H. Breaux); 29 (testimony of B. Preston).

48. Ibid., 24–25, 28, 29, 87–88 (testimony of Seaman Hopkins).

49. Ibid., 80–81 (testimony of P. C. Perret).

50. Transcript of Trial, *Guy v. Daniel,* 21; *Garvin v. State,* 52 Miss. 207, 208–209 (1876).

51. *Warlick v. White,* 76 N.C. 175, 179 (1877); see, e.g., Transcript of Trial, *Chancellor v. Milly* (Ky. Mason County Cir. Ct. Fall 1838) (collection of Kentucky State Archives, Lexington, Supreme Court Files), rev'd, 39 Ky. (9 Dana) 23 (1839); Transcript of Trial, *State v. Chavers,* No. 7249 (N.C. Brunswick County Super. Ct. 1857) (NCDAH-SCR), rev'd, 50 N.C. (5 Jones) 11 (1857) (hereafter Transcript of Trial, *State v. Chavers*); Transcript of Trial, *Williamson v. Norton,* 48–50, 54–59, No. 2427 (La. New Orleans Dist. Ct. 1850) (UNO-SCR), *aff'd in part and rev'd in part,* 7 La. Ann. 393

(1852) (depositions of Rufus Blanchard and Lyman Cole) (hereafter Transcript of Trial, *Williamson v. Norton*); Transcript of Trial, *State v. Jacobs*, No. 7915 (N.C. Brunswick County Super. Ct. March 1859) (NCDAH-SCR), *aff'd*, 51 N.C. (6 Jones) 284 (1859).

52. Transcript of Trial, *Guy v. Daniel*, 65–67 (answer of William Daniel).

53. *Daniel v. Guy*, 19 Ark. 121, 125–126 (1857); Transcript of Trial, *Daniel v. Guy*, 25, 28 (bill of exceptions).

54. Transcript of Trial, *Guy v. Daniel*, 27–29 (bill of exceptions, testimony of James Barnett), emphasis added.

55. Transcript of Trial, *Guy v. Daniel*, 3 (petition of Abby Guy).

56. *Daniel*, 19 Ark. at 129.

57. Transcript of Trial, *Guy v. Daniel*, 16; Census of 1850.

58. See William E. Nelson, *Americanization of the Common Law: The Impact of Legal Change on Massachusetts Society, 1760–1830* (Cambridge, Mass: Harvard University Press, 1975), 20–30; Stephan Landsman, "The Civil Jury in America: Scenes from an Unappreciated History," *Hastings Law Journal* 44 (1993): 579; Alan Scheflin and Jon Van Dyke, "Jury Nullification: The Contours of a Controversy," *Law and Contemporary Problems* 43 (Autumn 1980): 51, 54.

59. Rebecca DeArmond-Huskey, *Old Times Not Forgotten: A History of Drew County* (Little Rock: Rose Publishing Co., 1980), 38, 40, 126; *Goodspeed's Drew County, Arkansas, Biographical and Historical Memoirs*, reprint (Signal Mountain, Tenn.: Mountain Press, 2004), chap. 32, 928.

60. *Daniel v. Guy*, 23 Ark. at 51–52, 54–55.

61. Ibid., 50–51, 54–55.

62. Ariela J. Gross, "Litigating Whiteness: Trials of Racial Determination in the Nineteenth-Century South," *Yale Law Journal* 108 (October 1998): 186–188 (Appendix).

63. Census of 1850; Transcript of Trial, *Daniel v. Guy* (petition of Abby Guy); *Daniel v. Roper*, 24 Ark. 131 (1863).

2. Performing Whiteness

1. I have written at greater length about the idea of "performance" of identity in Ariela J. Gross, "Litigating Whiteness: Trials of Racial Determination in the Nineteenth-Century South," *Yale Law Journal* 108 (October 1998): 171–176. See generally Judith Butler, *Bodies That Matter: On The Discursive Limits of Sex* (New York: Thomson Publishing Group, 1993), 1–23, 167–242; Eve Kosofsky Sedgwick, "Queer Performativity: Henry James's *The Art of the Novel*," *Gay and Lesbian Quarterly* 1 (1993): 1–16; Elin Diamond, ed., *Performance and Cultural Politics* (New York: Routledge, 1996).

2. See George M. Fredrickson, "Aristocracy and Democracy in the Southern Tradition: A Perennial Debate among Historians," in *The Arrogance of Race: Historical Perspectives on Slavery, Racism, and Social Inequality* (Middletown: Wesleyan University Press, 1988), 134, 138–141; W. J. Cash, *The Mind of the South* (New York: Alfred A. Knopf, 1941).

3. See Transcript of Trial, *Bryan v. Walton*, No. A-1154 (Ga. Houston County Super. Ct. April 1853) (collection of Georgia Department of Archives and History, Atlanta, Supreme Court, Case F, Box 17), *rev'd*, 14 Ga. 185 (1853) (hereafter Transcript of Trial, *Bryan I*); Transcript of Trial, *Bryan v. Watson* [sic], No. A-1836 (Ga. Houston County Super. Ct. April 1856) (collection of Georgia Department of Archives and History, Supreme Court, Case F, Box 21), *rev'd*, 20 Ga. 480 (1856) (hereafter Transcript of Trial, *Bryan II*); Transcript of Trial, *Bryan v. Walton*, No. A-3737 (Ga. Houston County Super. Ct. April 1859) (collection of Georgia Department of Archives and History, Supreme Court, Case F, Box 46), *aff'd*, 33 Ga. 11 (Supp. 1864) (hereafter Transcript of Trial, *Bryan III*).

4. *Bryan v. Walton*, 14 Ga. 185, 198–199, 202 (1853) (hereafter *Bryan I*).

5. Transcript of Trial, *Bryan I*, 21a–25; *Bryan I*, 198.

6. *Bryan II* (testimony of Mary Rogers).

7. Ibid., 491–492, 494.

8. Ibid., 492, 494.

9. Ibid., 492, 494, 496.

10. Ibid., 494; see also Martha Hodes, *White Women, Black Men: Illicit Sex in the Nineteenth-Century South* (New Haven: Yale University Press, 1997), 100–103 (discussing the contradictory testimony in the first Nunez trial).

11. *Bryan II*, 498.

12. Ibid., 498, 500, 501.

13. Transcript of Trial, *Bryan III*, 17 (exhibit B).

14. Ibid., 18.

15. Ibid., 18–19.

16. Ibid., 19–21 (testimony of Dr. Green B. Powell, Fielding Stephens, James T. McNowell).

17. Ibid.

18. *Bryan III*, 23–27 (Supp. 1864).

19. Jacob Rader Marcus, *United States Jewry, 1776–1985* (Detroit: Wayne State University Press, 1989), 34, 44, 108.

20. *State v. Cantey*, 20 S.C.L. (2 Hill) 614, 614–616 (1835).

21. Transcript of Trial, *Johnson v. Boon* (Walterborough Cir. Ct. Spring 1842) (collection of South Carolina Department of Archives and History, Columbia, Court of Appeals Loose Opinions, 1843, Box 7), *aff'd*, 29 S.C.L. (1 Spears) 268, 269 (1842).

22. *White v. Tax Collector*, 37 S.C.L. (3 Rich.) 136, 137–139 (1846).

23. *Raby v. Batiste,* 27 Miss. 731, 732 (1854); *Dean v. Commonwealth,* 42 Va. (4 Gratt.) 541, 541 (1847); see also *White v. Clements,* 39 Ga. 232 (1869).

24. *Cantey,* 20 S.C.L. (2 Hill) 615–616.

25. Devon W. Carbado, "(E)racing the Fourth Amendment," *Michigan Law Review* 100 (2002): 947–964.

26. All of the material following, unless otherwise noted, comes from the Transcript of Trial, *Miller v. Belmonti,* 11 Rob. 339, 341–42 (La. 1845), including notes by plaintiff's counsel on the rule for a new trial. All emphasis in original.

27. See "District Court," *New Orleans Daily Picayune,* April 9, 1844; "District Court," *New Orleans Daily Picayune,* May 25, 1844.

28. John Miller, "To the Public," *New Orleans Daily Picayune,* May 31, 1844; John Miller, "To the Public," *New Orleans Bee,* June 1, 1844.

29. James Kinney, *Amalgamation! Race, Sex, and Rhetoric in the Nineteenth-Century American Novel* (Westport, Conn.: Greenwood Press, 1985), 63, 65.

30. All quotations are from William Wells Brown, *Clotel or the President's Daughter: A Narrative of Slave Life in the United States* (Armonk: M. E. Sharpe, 1996), 87–90.

31. William Craft and Ellen Craft, *Running a Thousand Miles for Freedom; or, the Escape of William and Ellen Craft from Slavery* (1860; reprint, New York: Arno Press, 1969), 3, 5–6.

32. Ibid., 2, 3–6.

33. *Miller v. Belmonti,* 339, 341–342.

34. For origins stories, see, e.g., N. Brent Kennedy, *The Melungeons: The Resurrection of a Proud People* (Macon, Ga.: Mercer University Press, 1997); Bonnie Ball, *The Melungeons* (Johnson City, Tenn.: Overmountain Press, 1992); Mattie Ruth Johnson, *My Melungeon Heritage: A Story of Life on Newman's Ridge* (Johnson City, Tenn.: Overmountain Press, 1992). Virginia Easley DeMarce, "Looking at Legends—Lumbee and Melungeon: Applied Genealogy and the Origins of Tri-racial Isolate Settlements," *National Genealogical Society Quarterly* 81 (March 1993): 24–45, provides persuasive data on likely origins.

35. Manuel Mira, *The Portuguese Making of America: Melungeons and Early Settlers of America* (Franklin, N.C.: P.A.H.R. Foundation, 2001); Territorial Act of 1794, ch. 1, sec. 32, Tennessee Public Acts of 1831, ch. 102, Constitution of 1834; see also *Jones v. State,* 19 Tenn. 120, *State v. Claiborne,* 19 Tenn. 331; *State v. Solomon, Ezekial, Levi, Andrew, Wiatt, Vardy Collins, Zachariah, Lewis Minor,* January 25, 1846, and September 29, 1846, Hawkins County Circuit Court Minute Book (1842–1848), Hawkins County Circuit Court, Hawkins County Courthouse, Boxes 31, 32; see also Jack H. Goins, *Melungeons and Other Pioneer Families* (Blountville, Tenn.: Continuity Press, 2000).

36. *Jacob F. Perkins v. John R. White,* Carter County, Tennessee (July 1855), Abstract of Depositions, T. A. R. Nelson Papers, McClung Collection, East Tennessee University, Knoxville.

37. Ibid., unnumbered page beginning, "White said . . ."

38. Ibid., 1 (testimony of Sarah Kennick); 2 (testimony of Elizabeth Cook, Nancy Young); 3 (testimony of Mary Wilson); 5 (testimony of Bedent [?] Beard); 6 (testimony of Daniel Stout).

39. Ibid., 10.

40. Ibid., 7.

41. Ibid., 8–9 (testimony of Jane Griffey, Dr. John E. Copen, Nancy Lipps).

42. Ibid. (testimony of John Moody).

43. Ibid., unmarked page.

44. Frank Merritt, *Early History of Carter County, 1760–1861* (Knoxville: East Tennessee Historical Society, 1950); *Perkins,* Abstract of Depositions.

45. *Perkins,* Abstract of Depositions.

46. Ibid.

47. Ibid.

48. *Goins v. Mayser,* East Tennessee Supreme Court Files, Box 1840 (July 26, 1858), Tennessee State Archives, Nashville.

49. Ibid.

50. Will T. Hale and Dixon L. Merritt, *A History of Tennessee and Tennesseans; the Leaders and Representative Men in Commerce, Industry and Modern Activities* (Chicago: Lewis Publishing Co., 1913), 180 ("the Melungeons were finally restored to citizenship through the efforts of Col. John Netherland, of Hawkins County, the witty and eloquent opponent of Isham G. Harris for the governorship in 1859"); Henry H. Ingersoll, "Biographical Sketch of Colonel John Netherland," in *Tennessee Bar Association Proceedings,* vol. 9 (Nashville: Marshall & Bruce Co., 1890), 233–252; McClung Collection, Biography Folder 4–30, T. A. R. Nelson Papers, Knox County Public Library, Knoxville, Tenn.; "Facts from the Record! Col. Netherland as a Legislator, Democratic State Central Committee Pamphlet 51 of 78 pamphlets bound by T. A. R. Nelson as Speeches, Documents, etc." (1848–1860), vol. 4, McClung Collection, Knox County Public Library, Knoxville, Tenn.

3. Race as Association

1. See Monique Gillory, "Under One Roof: The Sins and Sanctity of the New Orleans Quadroon Balls," in *Race Consciousness,* ed. Judith Jackson Fossett and Jeffrey A. Tucker (New York: New York University Press, 1997), 80–89.

2. 18 Stat. 335 (1875); *The Civil Rights Cases,* 109 U.S. 3 (1883).

3. Transcript of Trial, *Jack v. Foust,* No. 1431 (Chancery Court of Hamilton

County November 1877), East Tennessee Supreme Court Records, Box 1789 (hereafter Transcript of Trial, *Jack v. Foust*), available at Tennessee State Archives, Nashville (hereafter TSA). This trial record was found by an archivist in an uncatalogued box; the date of the trial was several years later than Lewis Shepherd had remembered it, and Betsy Bolton, the heir, was not named as a litigant; hence the difficulty finding the case in the Hamilton County files. Lewis Shepherd, *Personal Memoirs of Lewis Shepherd* (Chattanooga, Tennessee: privately printed, 1915).

4. Shepherd, *Personal Memoirs*, 85, 87.

5. Zella Armstrong, *The History of Hamilton County and Chattanooga, Tennessee*, vol. 1 (Johnston City, Tenn.: Overmountain Press, 1931), 61, 224–225.

6. Transcript of Trial, *Jack v. Foust*, 39–46 (deposition of Hiram Davis); 71 (deposition of Samuel Williams); 83–84 (deposition of James and Elizabeth Jack).

7. Shepherd, *Personal Memoirs*, 83; Transcript of Trial, *Jack v. Foust*, 111 (deposition of Benjamin Clark).

8. See, e.g., Transcript of Trial, *Jack v. Foust*, 116–117 (deposition of John Godsey: discusses "spells" and "shrewd" trading); 121–122 (deposition of James Warren, also on behalf of Martha); 139–140 (deposition of S. G. Thomas on behalf of Jacks); 152–153 (deposition of William Rogers, also on behalf of Jacks).

9. Ibid., 51, 54–55 (deposition of Lucinda Davis).

10. Ibid., 90–92 (deposition of Arch Brown).

11. Ibid., 93–94, 96–97 (deposition of Wm. J. Standifer).

12. Ibid., 258–264 (deposition of Mrs. Malinda White).

13. Ibid., 259 (deposition of Mrs. Malinda White).

14. Ibid., 266–269 (deposition of A. Kelley).

15. Ibid., 315, 318 (deposition of Rev. D. D. Scruggs).

16. Ibid., 307 (deposition of Wm. L. Dugger).

17. Ibid., 311–313 (deposition of Jefferson Simmerman).

18. Ibid., 329–331 (deposition of Kittie Williams).

19. Ibid., 344–346 (deposition of John Godsey).

20. Ibid., 365 (deposition of John Divine).

21. Ibid., 156 (deposition of William Rogers); 236–237 (deposition of Augustus Evans).

22. Ibid., 353 (deposition of Jack Williams); 379–380 (deposition of Charley Carroll).

23. Ibid., 381 (deposition of Jack Williams).

24. Ibid., 174–176 (deposition of A. B. Beeson).

25. Ibid., 174–176 (deposition of A. B. Beeson); 402–403 (deposition of William McGill).

26. Ibid., 324–336; Shepherd, *Personal Memoirs*, 83.
27. Shepherd, *Personal Memoirs*, 87.
28. Ibid., 87–88.
29. *Bolton v. Foust*, Hamilton County Court Records, available at Hamilton County Courthouse, Chattanooga, Tenn. (1872).
30. See Transcript of Trial, *Warlick v. White*, No. 11, 775, Supreme Court Files, NCDAH-SCR, 76 N.C. 175 (1877).
31. Ibid., 4.
32. Transcript of Trial, *Dillon v. Dillon*, Supreme Court Case A-09813, Georgia Department of Archives and History, Br. 113, Box 2, 60 Ga. 204 (1878) 4–5 (testimony of David Dillon).
33. Ibid. (testimony of James B. Read, Dr. J. D. Fish, Dr. John A. Mayer).
34. *Dillon*, 60 Ga. at 205.
35. Ibid., 207.
36. *Marre v. Marre*, 168 S.W. 636, 639–640 (Mo. Ct. App. 1914).
37. Ibid., 640.
38. *Theophanis v. Theophanis*, 244 Ky. 689, 691–92 (1932).
39. *Ferrall v. Ferrall*, No. 151, NCDAH-SCR, 69 S.E. 60, 62 (N.C. 1910) (Clark, J., concurring). I am indebted to Adrienne Davis for this point.
40. *Warner v. Warner*, 85 N.E. 630, 637 (Ill. 1908).
41. Transcript of Trial, *Warner v. Warner*, Illinois State Archives, Record Group 901.000, Supreme Court Case Files, 298–300.
42. Ibid., 322, 324–325, 338–339.
43. *Warner*, 85 N.E. at 637.
44. See generally Earl Lewis and Heidi Ardizzone, *Love on Trial: An American Scandal in Black and White* (New York: W. W. Norton & Co., 2001).
45. Ibid., 36–38.
46. Ibid., 162.
47. Ibid., 160.
48. Ibid., 160–161.
49. Ibid., 203, 232.
50. Ibid., 228, 231.
51. *State v. Cantey*, 20 S.C.L. (2 Hill) 614, 616 (1835).
52. *McGoodwin v. Shelby*, 206 S.W. 625 (Ky. 1918).
53. *Ferrall*, 69 S.E. at 60–61.
54. Transcript of Trial, *Hopkins v. Bowers*, No. 16,598, NCDAH-SCR, 12 S.E. 984 (N.C. 1891) 20–21.
55. Ibid., 20–23.
56. Ibid., 24–25; see *Hopkins v. Bowers*, 12 S.E. 984 (N.C. 1891).
57. *Weaver v. State*, 116 So. 893, 895 (Ala. Ct. App. 1928).
58. *Wilson v. State*, 101 So. 417, 419 (Ala. Ct. App. 1924).

59. *Wilson v. State,* Transcript of Trial, available at Alabama Department of Archives and History, 12–13.

60. *Wilson,* 101 So. at 421; see also *State v. Miller,* No. 289, 1940–1981, NCDAH-SCR,, 29 S.E.2d 751 (N.C. 1944).

61. Transcript of Trial, *Medlin v. County Bd. of Educ. of Wake,* No. 256, NCDAH-SCR, 83 S.E. 483 (N.C. 1914) 16, 19 (testimony of Elmer Maynard, J. R. Medlin).

62. Ibid., 16, 19–20.

63. Ibid., 26, 28–29 (testimony of Thad Ivey, Hardy Bagewell).

64. Ibid., 34 (testimony of A. V. Woodall).

65. Ibid., 52, 55 (judge's charge); see also *Gilliland v. Bd. of Educ.,* 54 S.E. 413 (N.C. 1906) (plaintiff wins by proving "Portugese" reputation and history of voting).

66. Booker T. Washington, *Up from Slavery* (1901; reprint, New York: Doubleday, 1998), 162.

67. J. A. Rogers, *As Nature Leads* (Chicago: M. A. Donohue Co., 1919), 27.

68. Charles W. Chesnutt, *Essays and Speeches,* ed. Joseph R. McElrath Jr. et al. (Stanford: Stanford University Press, 1999), 68; *Southern Workman* (March 1902), reprinted ibid., 176.

69. Frances E. W. Harper, *Iola Leroy, or Shadows Uplifted* (1892; reprint, New York: Oxford University Press, 1988), 39.

4. Citizenship of the "Little Races"

1. *State v. Belmont,* 35 S.C.L. (4 Strob.) 445, 446–452 (1848); the phrase "domestic dependent nations" is from *Cherokee Nation v. Georgia,* 30 U.S. (5 Pet.) 1, 2 (1832); *U.S. v. Rogers,* 45 U.S. (4 How.) 567, 572–573; Bethany R. Berger, "'Power over This Unfortunate Race': Race, Politics, and Indian Law in *United States v. Rogers,*" *William and Mary Law Review* 45 (2004): 1957–2052.

2. Quoted in Robert F. Berkhofer Jr., *The White Man's Indian: Images of the American Indian from Columbus to the Present* (New York: Vintage Books, 1979), 151.

3. See Nancy Shoemaker, *A Strange Likeness: Becoming Red and White in Eighteenth-Century North America* (New York: Oxford University Press, 2004).

4. On the "vanishing Indian," see, e.g., Berkhofer, *The White Man's Indian;* Philip J. Deloria, *Playing Indian* (New Haven: Yale University Press, 1998); Fergus M. Bordewich, *Killing the White Man's Indian: Reinventing Native Americans at the End of the Twentieth Century* (New York: Doubleday, 1996); Brian W. Dippie, *The Vanishing American: White Attitudes and U.S. Indian Policy* (Middletown, Conn.: Wesleyan University Press, 1982); Jean

O'Brien-Kehoe, "'Vanishing' Indians in Nineteenth-Century New England: Local Historians' Erasure of Still-Present Indian People," in *New Perspectives on Native North America,* ed. Sergei Kan and Pauline Turner Strong (Lincoln: University of Nebraska Press, 2006), 414–432; Gideon Hawley to Tho. Cushing, Mashpee, June 24, 1776, Gideon Hawley Diaries and Letterbook, 1757–1804, Folder: Typescripts, 1772–1776, Massachusetts Historical Society, Boston (hereafter MHS); letter enclosed in Hawley to Wm. Toogood, Mashpee, July 24, 1787, Gideon Hawley Diaries and Letterbook, 1757–1804, MHS.

5. Gideon Hawley to Governor John Hancock, Plantation of Mashpee, County of Barnstable, July 8, 1791, Gideon Hawley Letters, MHS, 6; Gideon Hawley to Shearjashub Bourne, Mashpee, December 15, 1788, Samuel P. Savage Papers: 1703–1848, Folder: S. P. Savage, 1788–1789, MHS.

6. Ruth Wallis Herndon and Ella Wilcox Sekatau, "The Right to a Name: The Narragansett People and Rhode Island Officials in the Revolutionary Era," *Ethnohistory* 44 (Summer 1997): 444–447; see also Margaret Ellen Newell, "The Changing Nature of Indian Slavery in New England, 1670–1720," in *Reinterpreting New England Indians and the Colonial Experience,* ed. Colin G. Calloway and Neal Salisbury (Boston: Colonial Society of Massachusetts, 2003), 128.

7. Jack D. Forbes, *Africans and Native Americans: The Language of Race and the Evolution of Red-Black Peoples,* 2nd ed. (Urbana: University of Illinois Press, 1993), 195.

8. Ibid., 199, 200.

9. Virginia Easley DeMarce, "'Very Slitly Mixt': Tri-Racial Isolate Families of the Upper South—A Genealogical Study," *National Genealogical Society Quarterly* 80 (March 1992): 5–35; Paul Heinegg, *Free African Americans of North Carolina and Virginia,* foreword by Ira Berlin (Genealogical Publishing Co., 1999), http://www.freeafricanamericans.com; Forbes, *Africans and Native Americans,* 252.

10. See Karen M. Woods, "A 'Wicked and Mischievous Connection': The Origins of Indian-White Miscegenation Law," *Legal Studies Forum* 23 (1999): 54–55, 67; Christian F. Feest, "Pride and Prejudice: The Pocahontas Myth and the Pamunkey," in *The Invented Indian: Cultural Fictions and Government Policies,* ed. James Clifton (New Brunswick, N.J.: Transaction Publishers, 1990), 53–54; see also Helen C. Rountree, *Pocahontas's People: The Powhatan Indians of Virginia through Four Centuries* (Norman: University of Oklahoma Press, 1990), 212.

11. DeMarce, "'Very Slitly Mixt'"; Heinegg, *Free African Americans.*

12. Karen I. Blu, *The Lumbee Problem: The Making of an American Indian People* (Cambridge: Cambridge University Press, 1980), 37–44, 62–65.

13. J. Douglas Smith, "The Campaign for Racial Purity and the Erosion of Pa-

ternalism in Virginia, 1922–1930: 'Nominally White, Biologically Mixed, and Legally Negro,'" *Journal of Southern History* 68 (February 2002): 87; W. A. Plecker, M.D., to Secretary of State, Nashville, Tennessee, August 5, 1942, available at TSA.

14. Mrs. John Trotwood Moore to W. A. Plecker, August 12, 1942, and W. A. Plecker, M.D., to Mrs. John Trotwood Moore, August 20, 1942, both available at TSA. Archivists at the Library of Congress also tried to classify the Melungeons, along with other "Mixed-Blood Racial Islands," in 1946; see William Harlen Gilbert Jr., "Memorandum Concerning the Characteristics of the Larger Mixed-Blood Racial Islands of the Eastern United States," *Social Forces* 24 (May 1946): 438–447.

15. Quoted in Gerald M. Sider, *Lumbee Indian Histories: Race, Ethnicity, and Indian Identity in the Southern United States* (Cambridge: Cambridge University Press, 1993), 164–167; Blu, *The Lumbee Problem,* 57–58.

16. Hamilton McMillan, *Sir Walter Raleigh's Lost Colony: An Historical Sketch of the Attempts of Sir Walter Raleigh to Establish a Colony in Virginia, with the Traditions of an Indian Tribe in North Carolina, Indicating the Fate of the Colony of Englishmen Left on Roanoke Island in 1587* (Raleigh, N.C.: Edwards & Broughton Printing Co., 1888), 41.

17. George E. Butler, *The Croatan Indians of Sampson County: Their Origin and Racial Status; A Plea for Separate Schools* (Durham, N.C.: Seeman Printery, 1916), 31.

18. Transcript of Trial, *McMillan v. School Committee*, No. 16,384, NCDAH-SCR, 2, 10 (complaint of Nathan McMillan). Appeal reported in 12 S.E. 330 (N.C. 1890).

19. Ibid., 26–27 (testimony of J. C. M. Eachin); 109 N.C. 609, 616–617 (1890).

20. Orlando M. McPherson, "Indians of North Carolina: Letter from the Secretary of the Interior" (Washington, D.C.: U.S. Government Printing Office, 1915), Exhibits B1–B8, 36–41 (petition of Croatan Indians; correspondence between Hamilton McMillan and Commissioner of Indian Affairs John Oberley, 1889–90).

21. Blu, *Lumbee Problem,* 78–79.

22. "School for Indians of Robeson County," Hearings before the Committee on Indian Affairs, House of Representatives, February 14, 1913, 17–19.

23. Ibid., 25.

24. McPherson, "Letter from the Secretary," 33, 35 (Report on the Condition and Tribal Rights of the Indians of Robeson).

25. Ibid., 242.

26. Transcript of Trial, *Goins v. Bd. of Trs. of Indian Normal Training School at Pembroke,* N.C. Supreme Court (Fall Term 1915), No. 296, Robeson County, 8, NCDAH-SCR, appeal reported in 169 N.C. 736 (1915).

27. Ibid., 9, 11, 13.

28. Ibid., 15.

29. Ibid., 22–23.

30. *Robesonian,* August 10, 1914, quoted in *The Lumbee Petition* (Pembroke, N.C.: Lumbee River Legal Services, 1987), 133; Sider, *Lumbee Indian Histories,* 79.

31. Quoted in Blu, *Lumbee Problem,* 77.

32. Exhibit 143, Folder 1-1-14, Paul Campbell Research Notes, MSS 369, Series 1, Box 2, Rhode Island State Archives (hereafter PCRN-RISA), Narragansett Indians 43, December 1831 (Resolution Messrs. Dan King and B. B. Thurston, Committee Relative to Indians), 448–450, 465; Letter to the General Assembly (1832), Exhibit 144, Folder 1-1-14, PCRN-RISA, Narragansett Indians 89, January 1832, 478, 484; Report of the Committee on Indian Tribes, Exhibit 342, Folder 1-1-17, PCRN-RISA, October 1852, 1185; Report of the Commissioner on the Narragansett Tribe of Indians, Exhibit 346, PCRN-RISA, January 1858, 1195.

33. Exhibit 658, Folder 1-1-1, Box 3, PCRN-RISA, Bartlett's, Rhode Island Miscellany, the Narragansett Indians, vol. 6, 2214, December 1866, 28.

34. Exhibit 658, Folder 1-1-1, Box 3, PCRN-RISA, 28–29; see also Memorial to the Honorable General Assembly of the State of Rhode Island, January sess. 1867 ("Under the present organization of society, we do not wish to be citizens. For we know we cannot be so in the full acceptation of that term." Samuel Rodman), in Folder 1-1-1, Box 3, PCRN-RISA.

35. Ibid.

36. January 1880 Act to Abolish the Tribal Authority and Tribal Relations of the Narragansett Tribe of Indians, Folder 1-1-2, Box 3, PCRN-RISA; Report of the Committee of Investigation, Folder 1-1-1, Box 3, PCRN-RISA (Providence: Freeman & Co., 1880), 6.

37. Report of the Committee of Investigation, Appendix B: Evidence Taken by the Committee of Investigation, on the Narragansett Tribe of Indians, at three public meetings, held in the town of Charlestown, 1879, First Meeting, 32–34.

38. Ibid., 38.

39. Ibid., 41, 43–44.

40. Ibid., 53.

41. Report of the Commission on the Affairs of the Narragansett Indians, State of Rhode Island and Providence Plantations, January sess., 1881, Appendix B, Second Meeting, PCRN-RISA, 57–59.

42. F. 7, Box 3, PCRN-RISA, "Pow-wows, Narragansett Tribe Incorporates," *Providence Journal,* December 4, 1934; Indian Office File No. 150, PCRN-RISA, Re Location, History, Government, Language Etc. of the Narragansett Indians, 1935.

43. *Reed v. State,* 92 So. 511 (Ala. Ct. App. 1922); Transcript of Trial, Alabama

Department of Archives and History (hereafter ADAH); Transcript of Trial, *State ex rel. Farmer v. Bd. of Sch. Com'rs of Mobile County*, 145 So. 575, 576 (Ala. 1933), ADAH.

44. Transcript of Trial, *Spencer v. Looney*, 82 S.E. 745 (Va. 1914), Virginia State Archives, Richmond. See also Daniel J. Sharfstein, "The Secret History of Race in the United States," *Yale Law Journal* 112 (2003): 1473–1509.

45. *Spencer v. Looney*, 82 S.E. 745, 746.

46. Hannibal Albert Compton, *Looking Back One Hundred Years: A Brief Story of Buchanan County and Its People* (Grundy, Va.: Buchanan County Chamber of Commerce, 1958), 45.

47. Transcript of Trial, *Spencer v. Looney*, 70, 127, 145.

48. Ibid., 66.

49. Ibid., 60–69, 76.

50. Ibid., 111, 113.

51. Ibid., 119–133.

52. Ibid., 137.

53. 116 Va. 767, 780.

54. *State v. Knight,* Transcript of Trial, Supreme Court Case File No. 37205, 5, 7–8 (testimony of Mrs. Hannon Graves), 55–56 (testimony of Wiley Mc-Henry), 102–103 (testimony of Ella Knight), Mississippi Department of Archives and History, Jackson; see also Victoria E. Bynum, *The Free State of Jones: Mississippi's Longest Civil War* (Chapel Hill: University of North Carolina Press, 2003), 184; *Knight v. State*, 42 So. 2d 747 (Miss. 1949); and Sovereignty Commission Files, Mississippi Department of Archives and History, Jackson.

55. Sovereignty Commission Online Archives, http://mdah.state.ms.us/arlib/, ID No. 3-81-0-9-3-1-1.

56. Ibid., ID No. 3-81-0-11-7-1-1; Bynum, *The Free State of Jones*, 187.

5. Black Indian Identity in the Allotment Era

1. "Indian Country: The State of the Nations," *Newsday*, December 22, 2003.

2. Merrill E. Gates, quoted in Frederick E. Hoxie, *Talking Back to Civilization: Indian Voices from the Progressive Era* (New York: Bedford/St. Martin's Press, 2001), 10.

3. Patrick Riordan, "Finding Freedom in Florida: Native Peoples, African Americans, and Colonists, 1670–1816," *Florida Historical Quarterly* 75 (1996): 1, 3.

4. Kenneth W. Porter, *The Black Seminoles: History of a Freedom-Seeking People* (Gainesville: University Press of Florida, 1996), 5; Kevin Mulroy,

Freedom on the Border: The Seminole Maroons in Florida, the Indian Territory, Coahuila, and Texas (Lubbock: Texas Tech University Press, 1993), 17–18; see also Rebecca B. Bateman, "We're Still Here: History, Kinship, and Group Identity among the Seminole Freedmen of Oklahoma" (Ph.D. diss., Johns Hopkins University, 1990); Thomas A. Britten, *A Brief History of the Seminole-Negro Indian Scouts* (Lewiston, N.Y.: Edwin Mellen Press, 1999); Daniel F. Littlefield Jr., *Africans and Seminoles: From Removal to Emancipation* (Westport, Conn.: Greenwood Press, 1977); William Loren Katz, *Black Indians: A Hidden Heritage* (New York: Atheneum, 1986); Laurence Foster, "Negro-Indian Relationships in the Southeast" (Ph.D. diss., University of Pennsylvania, 1935); Celia E. Naylor-Ojurongbe, "'More at Home with the Indians': African-American Slaves and Freedpeople in the Cherokee Nation, Indian Territory, 1838–1907" (Ph.D. diss., Duke University, 2001), 49–70.

5. Mulroy, *Freedom on the Border,* 26–29.

6. William G. McLoughlin, "Red Indians, Black Slavery, and White Racism: America's Slaveholding Indians," *American Quarterly* 26 (October 1974): 380; Claudio Saunt, "Taking Account of Property: Stratification among the Creek Indians in the Early Nineteenth Century," *William and Mary Quarterly* 57 (October 2000): 733–760; Barbara Krauthamer, "Blacks on the Borders: African-Americans' Transition from Slavery to Freedom in Texas and the Indian Territory, 1836–1907" (Ph.D. diss., Princeton University, 2000); Rudyard Haliburton Jr., *Red over Black: Black Slavery among the Cherokee Indians* (Westport, Conn.: Greenwood Press, 1977); Theda Perdue, *Slavery and the Evolution of Cherokee Society, 1540–1866,* (Knoxville: University of Tennessee Press, 1979); Kathryn E. Holland Braund, "The Creek Indians, Blacks, and Slavery," *Journal of Southern History* 57 (November 1991): 601–636; Littlefield, *Africans and Seminoles;* Daniel F. Littlefield, *The Cherokee Freedmen: From Emancipation to American Citizenship* (Westport, Conn.: Greenwood Press, 1978); Britten, *The Seminole-Negro Indian Scouts,* 5; Karen M. Woods, "'A Wicked and Mischievous Connection': The Origins of Indian-White Miscegenation Laws," *Legal Studies Forum* 23 (1999): 62, 65–66; John Phillip Reid, *A Law of Blood: The Primitive Law of the Cherokee Nation* (New York: New York University Press, 1970); Tiya Miles, *Ties That Bind: The Story of an Afro-Cherokee Family in Slavery and Freedom* (Berkeley: University of California Press, 2005); *Laws of the Cherokee Nation* (New York: Legal Classics Library, 1852), November 11, 1824, 10; Law 20, Laws of the Creek Nation; Cherokee Constitution of 1829, art. 3, §§4–7, 120–121.

7. Littlefield, *Africans and Seminoles,* 15–16; William G. McLoughlin, *After*

the Trail of Tears: The Cherokees' Struggle for Sovereignty, 1839–1880 (Chapel Hill: University of North Carolina Press, 1993), 125; Naylor-Ojurongbe, "More at Home with the Indians."

8. Murray R. Wickett, *Contested Territory: Whites, Native Americans, and African Americans in Oklahoma, 1865–1907* (Baton Rouge: Louisiana State University Press, 2000), 52–53.

9. General John Sanborn to Secretary of Interior, January 5, 1866, in *Report of the Secretary of the Interior* (Washington, D.C.: U.S. Government Printing Office, 1866), 285; Wickett, *Contested Territory*, 9; Eugene Current-Garcia and Dorothy B. Hatfield, eds., *Shem, Ham and Japheth: The Papers of W. O. Tuggle, Comprising His Indian Diary, Sketches and Observations, Myths and Washington Journal in the Territory and at the Capital, 1879–1882* (Athens: University of Georgia Press, 1973), 34, 37, 158.

10. John A. Garrett to Captain H. D. B. Cutler, Fort Gibson, Cherokee Nation, July 22, 1865, quoted in Annie Heloise Abel, *The American Indian under Reconstruction* (Cleveland: Arthur H. Clark, 1925), 273; *Report of the Commissioner of Indian Affairs* (Washington, D.C.: U.S. Government Printing Office, 1874), 70; Report of Commission to the Five Civilized Tribes, 1894, Exhibit A, 26, 31–32; Walt Willson, "Freedmen in Indian Territory during Reconstruction," *Chronicles of Oklahoma* 49 (Summer 1971), Freedmen Vertical File, Oklahoma Historical Society Library, Oklahoma City (hereafter OHS); *United States v. Choctaw Nation*, 193 U.S. 115 (1904); Daniel F. Littlefield Jr., *The Chickasaw Freedmen: A People without a Country* (Westport, Conn.: Greenwood Press, 1980), xi.

11. Memorial of the Delegates of the Cherokee, Creek, and Choctaw Nation of Indians, Misc. Doc. no. 143, Senate, 41st Cong., 2d sess., May 23, 1870, 1.

12. "Editorial on Lewis Downing," *Cherokee Advocate*, December 9, 1871, Cherokee Nation papers, Roll 49, Box 175, Folder 7448, Cherokee Nation Papers (hereafter CNP), Western History Collections, University of Oklahoma, Norman (hereafter WHC-OU).

13. Louis Rough to President Grant, 1872, quoted in McLoughlin, *After the Trail of Tears*, 254.

14. Wickett, *Contested Territory*, 31.

15. Roy Gittinger, *Formation of the State of Oklahoma, 1803–1906* (Berkeley: University of California Press, 1917), 98, 175–177, 187–188; Donald A. Grinde Jr. and Quintard Taylor, "Red vs. Black: Conflict and Accommodation in the Post Civil War Indian Territory, 1865–1907," *American Indian Quarterly* (Summer 1984): 217; Charles F. Meserve, *The Dawes Commission and the Five Civilized Tribes of Indian Territory* (Philadelphia: Office of the Indian Rights Association, 1896), 12, 14–15.

16. David Chang, "From Indian Territory to White Man's Country: Race, Na-

tion, and the Politics of Land Ownership in Eastern Oklahoma, 1889–1940"
(Ph.D. diss., University of Wisconsin, 2002), 192.

17. Interview by Robert L. Miller with Primus Dean, Non-Indian, June 28, 1968, Indian Pioneer Papers, Doris Duke Oral History Collection (hereafter IPP-DDOHC), OHS, T-280, 15, 21; Naylor-Ojurongbe, "More at Home with the Indians," 211–212, 219.

18. Interview by Robert L. Miller with Dave McIntosh, Non-Indian, October 10, 1967, IPP-DDOHC, T-210, 1; Interview by Robert L. Miller with Dave McIntosh, Non-Indian, September 28, 1967, ibid., T-211, 22; Art Gallaher, "A Survey of the Seminole Freedmen" (master's thesis, University of Oklahoma, 1951), 92.

19. Interview by Robert L. Miller with Primus Dean, Non-Indian, June 28, 1968, IPP-DDOHC, T-280, 12; Interview by Robert L. Miller with Charlie Johnson, Seminole, November 21, 1968, ibid., T-337, 6.

20. *Report of the Commission to the Five Civilized Tribes* (Washington, D.C.: U.S. Government Printing Office, 1911), 84.

21. Curtis Act, Act for the Protection of the People of the Indian Territory, reprinted in *Annual Report of the Commission to the Five Civilized Tribes* (Washington, D.C.: U.S. Government Printing Office, 1898), 23–24; *Sixth Annual Report of the Commission to the Five Civilized Tribes* (Washington, D.C.: U.S. Government Printing Office, 1899), 13.

22. J. W. Howell, *Report on Enrollment from the Indian Office of Five Civilized Tribes* (Washington, D.C.: U.S. Government Printing Office, 1909), 93; Kent Carter, *The Dawes Commission and the Allotment of the Five Civilized Tribes, 1893–1914* (Salt Lake City: Ancestry Publishing, 1999), 16.

23. *Sixth Annual Report of the Commission to the Five Civilized Tribes* (Washington, D.C.: U.S. Government Printing Office, 1899), 10; *Whitmire (Trustee for the Freedmen) v. Cherokee Nation*, F. 302 (1895), CNP, Roll 3, Box 11.

24. Instructions relating to the enrollment of Cherokee Freedmen, 1900, 3, File 4040, in Collection 31, Letters Received, location A-4-90-5, National Archives and Records Administration, Southwest Branch, Fort Worth, Texas (hereafter NARA-SW); Report of the Commission to the Five Civilized Tribes, 1904, Department of the Interior, Appendix 5, 141; see also Report of the Commission to the Five Civilized Tribes, Department of the Interior 1896; H. L. Dawes to the Secretary of the Interior, July 9, 1897, Cherokee Correspondence (regarding Cherokee Nation complaints about rolls); CNP, WHC-OU, Roll 5, Box 14, Folder 441 (3,271 were enrolled; 2,883 doubtful; 375 rejected; 98 injunction cases). *Buffington v. Bixby*, reprinted in Report of the Commission to the Five Civilized Tribes, Department of the Interior, 1904, Appendix 6, 144–165; see also "Editorial,"

Holdenville Times, October 31, 1901, Cherokee Nation Papers, Roll 51, Box 178, Folder 7976 (discussing *Buffington v. Bixby*), CNP, WHC-OU.

25. Carter, *The Dawes Commission,* 71.

26. Application for the Enrollment of Bill Colbert, Commissioner to the Five Civilized Tribes, Department of the Interior, February 14, 1907, Entry 90C, Box 1, Folder 1, 3, 13–14, NARA-SW.

27. Ibid., 5, 7, 17–18.

28. Application for the Enrollment of Parlee Clark et al., Commissioner to the Five Civilized Tribes, Department of the Interior, July 23, 1906, Entry 90C, Box 4, Folder 77, 9, NARA-SW; Petition of Josie Brown et al. for the Correction of the Enrollment Records, Commissioner to the Five Civilized Tribes, Department of the Interior, February 13, 1906, Entry 90C, Box 2, Folder 29, 10–11, NARA-SW.

29. Application for the Transfer of Susan Brashears et al., Commissioner to the Five Civilized Tribes, Department of the Interior, February 13, 1906, Entry 90C, Box 1, Folder 5, 9–10, NARA-SW.

30. Report of the Select Committee to Investigate Matters Connected with Affairs in the Indian Territory with Hearings, November 11, 1906–January 9, 1907, Senate Report No. 5013, pt. 1, vol. 1, 97; Sarah Deutsch, "Being American in Boley, Oklahoma," in *Beyond Black and White: Race, Ethnicity, and Gender in the United States South and Southwest,* ed. Stephanie Cole and Alison Parker (Fort Worth: Texas A&M University Press, 2004), 35.

31. Thomas Biolsi, "The Birth of the Reservation: Making the Modern Individual among the Lakota," *American Ethnologist* 22 (February 1995): 41; Act of Congress, April 21, 1904, c. 1402, 33 Stat. 2040; Act of Congress, May 27, 1908, Sess. I, c. 199, 35 Stat. 312.

32. Howell, Report on Enrollment, 145.

33. Application for the Transfer of Frank Eastman et al., Commissioner to the Five Civilized Tribes, Department of the Interior, March 5, 1906, Entry 90C, Box 1, Folder 2, 10–11, NARA-SW.

34. "Choctaw and Chickasaw Indians," Hearings before the United States Senate Committee on Indian Affairs, Senate Doc. No. 257, 59th Cong. 2d sess., January 23, 1907, 1, 10, 15.

35. Ibid., 10, 19, emphasis added.

36. Ibid., 34–36.

37. Ibid., 40.

38. Ibid., 75.

39. Howell, Report on Enrollment, 148.

40. Dawes Commission Records, DC 72, Memorandum Relative to HR Bill 5976 and Changes Suggested Therein, OHS; Violet P. Crain to Secretary of the Interior, May 8, 1906, DC 72, Frames 432–434, OHS; Witty Cudjoe to

Secretary of the Interior, April 18, 1906, DC 72, Records of Commission to Five Civilized Tribes, Frames 426–427, OHS.

41. *Rowe v. Sartain,* 230 P. 919, 920 (Okla. 1924).
42. Ibid., 923.
43. Transcript of Trial, *Rowe v. Sartain,* 162, No. 13211, Supreme Court Files, Oklahoma State Archives, Oklahoma City.
44. Ibid., 208–209.
45. Ibid., 210.
46. Ibid., 214–215.
47. *Whitmire (Trustee for the Freedmen) v. Cherokee Nation,* Cherokee Nation Papers, Roll 3, Box 11, F. 302 (1895); see Samuel Shellabarger, Attorney at Law, to C. J. Harris and E. C. Boudinot, Esq., Tahlequah, November 22, 1895, CNP, Roll 3, Box 11, Folder 299 (regarding appeal in Whitmire case), WHC-OU; proposal for settlement of Whitmire case, using Wallace Roll, CNP, Roll 36, Box 102, Folder 3510, WHC-OU; Agreement between Samuel Mayes, Principal Chief of the Cherokee Nation, and Robert H. Kern, Attorney for Freedmen, January 28, 1896, CNP, Roll 36, Box 102, Folder 3511 (agreeing to substitute for the Wallace Roll a new roll made by a commission approved by the Court of Claims), WHC-OU.
48. *Cherokee Nation v. Whitmire,* 223 U.S. 108 (1912); Transcript of Trial, *Cherokee Freedmen v. United States,* Claim no. 123 before Indian Claims Commission, November 14–15, 1960, collection of Cherokee Nation Historical Society, Earl Boyd Pierce Collection, Cherokee Heritage Center, Tahlequah, Okla. (hereafter CNHS-EBPC), Box 74, Folder 590 (hereafter Transcript of Trial, *Cherokee Freedmen v. United States*).
49. Transcript of Trial, *Cherokee Freedmen v. United States,* 19–20.
50. Ibid.
51. Motion for Summary Judgment, Cherokee Freedmen, Plaintiffs in No. 123 and Intervenors in No. 173-A, CNHS-EBPC, Box 75, Folder 597. In 1963 the U.S. Court of Claims affirmed the freedmen's loss in Docket No. 123 but left an opening for their intervention in Docket No. 173-A, the remainder of the Cherokee Outlet case. The freedmen lost that case in 1971; see Circe Sturm, "Blood Politics, Racial Classification, and Cherokee National Identity: The Trials and Tribulations of the Cherokee Freedmen," *American Indian Quarterly* 22 (Winter–Spring 1998): 230–258 (providing a detailed discussion of the Cherokee Freedmen cases); Sturm, *Blood Politics: Race, Culture, and Identity in the Cherokee Nation of Oklahoma* (Berkeley: University of California Press, 2002).
52. Art. 3, §1, Constitution of 1975 of the Cherokee Nation; *Nero v. Cherokee Nation of Okla.,* 892 F.2d 1457 (Okla. 1989); *Riggs v. Ummerteske,* Cherokee Nation Judicial Appeals Tribunal 97–03-K (2001); 11 C.N.C.A. §12.
53. *Vann v. Kempthorne,* 467 F. Supp. 2d 56 (2006); *Allen v. Cherokee Nation*

Tribal Council, JAT-04-09 (March 4, 2006). Ron Jackson, "Blacks with Indian Blood Seek Tribes' Recognition," *Daily Oklahoman,* August 17, 2003,
13A.

54. *Seminole Nation of Okla. v. Norton,* 206 F.R.D. 1 (D.D.C. 2001); *Seminole
Nation of Okla. v. Norton,* 223 F. Supp. 2d 122 (D.D.C. 2002); Megan K.
Stack, "The Nation; Tribal Rift Is a Matter of Blood," *Los Angeles Times,*
May 16, 2002; *Davis v. United States,* 199 F. Supp. 2d 1164 (W.D. Okla.
2002), *aff'd,* 343 F.3d 1282 (10th Cir. 2003); *Daily Oklahoman,* August 17,
2003.

55. Memorandum from the Commissioner of Indian Affairs to Eastern Area
Director, Muskogee Area Director, November 26, 1976, appearing as Ex-
hibit A to Plaintiffs' Memorandum of Law in Opposition to Defendants'
Motion to Dismiss for Failure to Join an Indispensable Party, *Davis v.
United States,* filed February 14, 2000, 4, 10–11.

56. Hearings before the Select Committee on Indian Affairs, U.S. Senate,
101st Cong., 1st sess., September 15, 1989, 30, 40.

57. Memorandum from Tim Vollmann, Regional Solicitor of the United States
Office of the Solicitor, to Area Director, Muskogee Area Office, Bureau of
Indian Affairs, August 30, 1991, 9–10.

58. Memorandum from Rosella C. Garbow, Tribal Operations Officer, to Muskogee Area Director, Bureau of Indian Affairs, September 10, 1990, 1.

59. *Davis v. United States,* 192 F.3d 951 (10th Cir. 1999); Kevin Gover, Assistant Secretary, Indian Affairs, to Chief Jerry Haney, September 29, 2000.

60. Stack, "The Nation; Tribal Rift Is a Matter of Blood"; *Seminole Nation,* 206
F.R.D.; *Seminole Nation,* 223 F. Supp. 2d; *Davis,* 199 F. Supp. 2d.

61. Grounds Papers, Seminole Nation Museum, Wewoka, Okla. (hereafter
SNM). The source quoted for this definition was the *Bouvier Law Dictionary,* as well as the case *Frazee v. Spokane County,* 69 P. 779 (Wash. 1902);
see, e.g., letter to W. O. Roberts, Area Director, Indian Office, Muskogee,
Oklahoma, March 18, 1853, No. 94.16.8.10A, Grounds Papers, SNM.

62. Bateman, "We're Still Here," 272–273.

63. Andrew Metz, "A Nation Divided; Seminole Rift More Than a Black-and-
White Issue," *Newsday,* December 22, 2003.

64. Stack, "The Nation; Tribal Rift Is a Matter of Blood".

65. Karen I. Blu, *The Lumbee Problem: The Making of an American Indian
People* (Cambridge: Cambridge University Press, 1980), 77.

6. From Nation to Race in Hawai'i

1. *Rice v. Cayetano,* 528 U.S. 495, 514–515 (2000).

2. J. Kehaulani Kauanui, "Rehabilitating the Native: Hawaiian Blood Quan-

tum and the Politics of Race, Citizenship, and Entitlement" (Ph.D. diss., University of California, Santa Cruz, 2000), 11, 16; see *Naone v. Thurston*, 1 Haw. 220 (1856), and *Rex v. Booth*, 2 Haw. 616 (1863).

3. Sumner J. La Croix and James Roumasset, "The Evolution of Private Property in Nineteenth-Century Hawaii," *Journal of Economic History* 50 (December 1990): 829.

4. Stuart Banner, "Preparing to Be Colonized: Land Tenure and Legal Strategy in Nineteenth-Century Hawaii," *Law and Society Review* 39 (June 2005): 273–314.

5. Ibid., 288–291.

6. Ibid., 292–293.

7. Sally Engle Merry, *Colonizing Hawaii: The Cultural Power of Law* (Princeton: Princeton University Press, 2000), 93–94. The Land Commission received approximately 13,500 claims by the 1848 deadline; it granted 9,300, rejected 1,500, deemed another 1,500 duplicates, and called 1,200 abandoned. Twelve thousand were filed by commoners (out of 72,000 total); Banner, "Preparing to Be Colonized," 22.

8. Marylynn M. Vause, "The Hawaiian Homes Commission Act, 1920: History and Analysis" (M.A. thesis, University of Hawaii, Honolulu, 1962), 19.

9. "Jonah Kuhio Kalanianaole, Late a Delegate from Hawaii," memorial addresses delivered in Congress, 67th Cong., January 7, 1923 (Washington, D.C.: Government Printing Office, 1924); Jonah Kuhio Kalanianaole, "The Complaint against the Administration of Hon. Walter F. Frear, Governor of Hawaii" (Washington, D.C., 1911), 2; Davianna Pomaika'i McGregor, "Aina Ho'opulapula: Hawaiian Homesteading," *Hawaiian Journal of History* 24 (1990): 1–6.

10. "Hawaiians Launch Society to Awaken Spirit of Their Race," *Pacific Commercial Advertiser,* February 13, 1918.

11. *House Journal,* 10th Legislature, Regular Session (1919), 734.

12. Statement of the Legislative Commission of Hawaii in Support of a Bill Providing for the Setting apart of Portions of the Public Lands of the Territory of Hawaii for Use by Hawaiian Citizens of Hawaiian Blood (January 1, 1920), available in the Judd Files, Territorial Department Archives, Honolulu.

13. Vause, "Hawaiian Homes Commission Act," 42.

14. McGregor, "Aina Ho'opulapula," 9.

15. Proposed Amendments to the Organic Act of the Territory of Hawaii, Hearings before the Committee on the Territories, U.S. House of Representatives, 66th Cong., 2d sess., February 1920, 30 (hereafter Proposed Amendments).

16. Ibid., 32, 39, 45; see Kauanui, "Rehabilitating the Native," 120–123.

17. Proposed Amendments, 33.

18. Ibid., 121, 170; Kauanui, "Rehabilitating the Native," 125.

19. Proposed Amendments, 30; McGregor, "Aina Ho'opulapula," 12–13.

20. *Pacific Commercial Advertiser,* March 28, 1920; Vause, "Hawaiian Homes Commission Act," 63.

21. "Still More about Public Lands," *Honolulu Star-Bulletin,* July 22, 1920.

22. Ibid.

23. Thornton Hardy, "New Race Group of Island Born Lends Vigor to Hawaiians," *Honolulu Star-Bulletin,* March 19, 1921; *Daily Post-Herald,* October 5, 1920; see also Louis R. Sullivan and Clark Wissler, "Observations on Hawaiian Somatology," *Memoirs of the Bernice P. Bishop Museum* (1927): 9. For the view that Hawai'ians were dying out, see W. P. Elkin, "An Inquiry into the Causes of the Decrease of the Hawaiian People," *American Journal of Sociology* 8 (1903): 411 ("The Hawaiians—not because of lack of natural ability, for physically they are extremely vigorous and mentally they are remarkably active; but because industrially and commercially they are yet undeveloped—are unable at present to compete successfully with Asiatics in the lower walks of life, and with Americans and Europeans in the higher"); Vaughan MacCaughey, "The Physique of the Ancient Hawaiians," *Scientific Monthly* 5 (August 1917): 166–174; William W. Goodale, "The Hawaiian as an Unskilled Laborer," *Journal of Race Development* (1914–15): 416–437.

24. Sidney L. Gulick, *Mixing the Races in Hawaii: A New Study of the Coming Neo-Hawaiian American Race* (Honolulu: Hawaiian Board Book Rooms, 1937), 43–44, 46–47; Stanley D. Porteus and Marjorie E. Babcock, *Temperament and Race* (Boston: Gorham Press, 1926), 29–31.

25. "Hawaiians Launch Society to Awaken Spirit of Their Race," *Pacific Commercial Advertiser,* February 13, 1918.

26. Akaiko Akana, *The Sinews for Racial Development* (Honolulu, 1918), 8, 41.

27. Quoted in Vause, "Hawaiian Homes Commission Act," 72.

28. Hearings before the Senate Committee on Territories, Hawaiian Homes Commission Act, U.S. Senate, 66th Cong., 2d sess., December 1920 (testimony of A. G. M. Robertson), 14–16 (hereafter Hearings); Kauanui, "Rehabilitating the Native," 136–138.

29. Hearings, 22–23; Kauanui, "Rehabilitating the Native," 139, 141–142.

30. Hearings, 30–31; Kauanui, "Rehabilitating the Native," 151.

31. Hearings, 30–31.

32. Ibid., 78 (testimony of Hon. J. Kuhio Kalanianaole).

33. Ibid., 38 (testimony of W. B. Pittman).

34. Ibid., 48 (testimony of Rev. Akaiko Akana).

35. Ibid., 48, 50, 57–58.

36. Ibid., 112–113, 139 (testimony of George McClellan, Hon. J. Kuhio Kalanianaole).

37. A. G. M. Robertson to Hon. Reed Smoot, January 10, 1921, Box 4, Folder 41, Prince Kuhio Kalanianaole Papers, M474, Hawaii State Archives, Honolulu (hereafter PKKP-HSA), emphasis added.

38. Amendments to Hawaiian Rehabilitation Bill proposed by W. B. Pittman, Box 4, Folder 41, PKKP-HSA, 2–3; W. B. Pittman to Hon. Reed Smoot, January 10, 1921, Box 4, Folder 41, PKKP-HSA; Harry S. New to Prince Kuhio Kalanianaole, February 23, 1921, Box 4, Folder 41, PKKP-HSA.

39. Prince Kuhio Kalanianaole to Hon. Reed Smoot, Box 4, Folder 41, PKKP-HSA.

40. Jonah Kuhio Kalanianaole, Report to the Senate, 12–13, Box 4, Folder 41, PKKP-HSA.

41. Jonah Kuhio Kalanianaole to Governor McCarthy, March 7, 1921, Box 7, F. 80, PKKP-HSA, 2–3; *Honolulu Star-Bulletin,* January 31, 1921.

42. Proposed Amendments to the Organic Act, Hearings before the Committee on the Territories, U.S. House of Representatives, June 1921, 79–80, 140; "Senate Shows Land Bill Is Sure to Pass," *Honolulu Star-Bulletin,* April 18, 1921.

43. Kauanui, "Rehabilitating the Native," 173–174, 177.

44. McGregor, "Aina Ho'opulapula," 31; "From Mauka to Makai: The River of Justice Must Flow Freely," Report on the Reconciliation Process between the Federal Government and Native Hawaiians (Department of the Interior and Department of Justice, October 23, 2000), 32, 36, 39–40; Kauanui, "Rehabilitating the Native," 186; Haunani-Kay Trask, *From a Native Daughter: Colonialism and Sovereignty in Hawaii* (Honolulu: University of Hawai'i Press, 1993), 25–64.

45. Proceedings of the Constitutional Convention, Hawai'i, Debates in the Committee of the Whole, September 2, 1978, 647, defining "Hawai'ian" as "any descendant of the races inhabiting the Hawaiian Islands, previous to 1778." Because of a technicality in the ratification process, this definitional section was invalidated in *Kahalekai v. Doi,* 590 P.2d 543 (Haw. 1979); constitutional amendments, Hawaii Const. Art. 12, §5–6 (Supp. 1984); *Hoohuli v. Ariyoshi,* 631 F. Supp. 1153 (D. Haw. 1986); *Arakaki v. Cayetano,* 324 F.3d 1078 (9th Cir. 2003).

46. See, e.g., Native Hawaiian Claims Bill, HR 19448, 94th Cong., 1974; *Pub. Access Shoreline Haw. v. Haw. County Planning Comm'n,* 903 P.2d 1246, 1270 (Haw. 1995); "Inclusion of Native Hawaiians in Certain Indian Acts and Programs," Hearings before the Select Committee on Indian Affairs, U.S. Senate, 95th Cong., 2d sess., February 13–15, 1978.

47. "Overthrow of Hawaii," S.J. Res. 19, 103rd Cong., 1993.

48. "Kame'eleihiwa Statement," quoted in "Reconciliation at a Crossroads: The Implications of the Apology Resolution and *Rice v. Cayetano* for Federal and State Programs Benefiting Native Hawaiians," Hawaii Advisory Com-

mittee to the U.S. Commission on Civil Rights, http://www.usccr.gov/pubs/
sac/hi0601/report.htm, 10; Emmett Lee Loy, quoted ibid.

49. In *Morton v. Mancari*, 417 U.S. 535 (1974), the Supreme Court upheld an
employment preference for Indians at the Bureau of Indian Affairs, finding
the preference to be "political rather than racial in nature." Ibid., 553 n. 24.
Although the Court was interpreting the Indian Reorganization Act of
1934, which contained no definition of Indian identity, *Mancari* set the
stage for the current dichotomizing between "racial" and "political," relying
on Bureau of Indian Affairs rules that limited the preference to members of
federally recognized tribes and equating tribal membership with a political
status, despite the fact that the BIA also had a "blood quantum" requirement. *Rice v. Cayetano*, 528 U.S. 495, 514–515 (2000).

50. Chris K. Iijima, "Race over *Rice*: Binary Analytical Boxes and a Twenty-
First Century Endorsement of Nineteenth Century Imperialism in *Rice v.
Cayetano*," *Rutgers Law Review* 53 (2000): 91–125; Carole Goldberg, "De-
scent into Race," *UCLA Law Review* 49 (2002): 1373–94; Aviam Soifer,
"Descent," *Florida State University Law Review* 29 (2001): 269–276; Jon
M. Van Dyke, "The Political Status of the Native Hawaiian People," *Yale
Law and Policy Review* 17 (1988): 95–147; Neil Milner and Jonathan
Goldberg-Hiller, "Rights as Excess: Understanding the Politics of Special
Rights," *Law and Social Inquiry* 28 (2003): 1075–1118. On implications
for mainland Native Americans, see David C. Williams, "The Borders of
the Equal Protection Clause: Indians as Peoples," *UCLA Law Review* 38
(1991): 759–870; Carole E. Goldberg-Ambrose, "Not 'Strictly' Racial: A
Response to 'Indians as Peoples,'" *UCLA Law Review* 39 (1991): 169–190;
Stuart M. Benjamin, "Equal Protection and the Special Relationship: The
Case of Native Hawaiians," *Yale Law Journal* 106 (1996): 537–612; Carole
Goldberg, "Members Only: Designing Citizenship Requirements for In-
dian Nations," *Kansas Law Review* 50 (2002): 437–471; Christine Metteer,
"The Trust Doctrine, Sovereignty and Membership: Determining Who Is
Indian," *Rutgers Race and the Law Review* 5 (2003): 53–92. On the Con-
federate Flatheads, see Hector Tobar, "A Battle Over Who Is Indian," *Los
Angeles Times,* January 4, 2001.

51. *Doe v. Kamehameha Schools/Bernice Pauahi Bishop Estate,* 470 F.3d 827
(2006), cert. denied, 127 S. Ct. 2160 (2007).

52. S. 344, 108th Cong., 2d sess., §3(8), 7(b).

53. Jon Van Dyke, "Revised Akaka Bill Would Help Protect Existing Hawaiian Programs and Allow Pursuit of Additional Claims," http://www
.nativehawaiians.com/VanDykeAkaka.htm; Hawaii Advisory Committee to
the U.S. Commission on Civil Rights, 43, 47.

54. Anna Keala Kelly, "From Native Hawaiian to Native American?"

Hawai'i Island Journal, http://www.hawaiiislandjournal.com/stories/8a03a.html; http://stopakaka.com/2003/prob.htm.

55. http://www.angelfire.com/hi2/hawaiiansovereignty/AkakaKanakaOp; J. Kehaulani Kauanui, "The Dangers of Federal Recognition," *Hawai'i Island Journal*, February 16–29, 2004.

56. Alani Apio, "Kanaka Lament: Once a Proud Nation, Hawaiians Today Are Defined as Just a Race," *Honolulu Advertiser*, March 25, 2001. "Kanaka" means native Hawai'ian.

57. H. William Burgess, "Federal Recognition Will Result in Legal Apartheid," *Honolulu Advertiser*, October 1, 2000, http://thehonoluluadvertiser.com/2000/Oct/01/101opinion14.html, 3–4.

58. Hawaii Advisory Committee to the U.S. Commission on Civil Rights, 38–39.

59. Native Hawaiian Federal Recognition, Hearings before the Committee on Indian Affairs, U.S. Senate, 166th Cong., 2d sess., September 14, 2000, 58–59, 102.

60. Ibid., 108 (testimony of Keohokui Kauihama), 112 (testimony of Kawika Cuther), 89 (testimony of Beadie Kanahele Dawson).

7. Racial Science, Immigration, and the "White Races"

1. Bhaghat Singh Thind's Statement Regarding His Race, Exhibit "A," trial record, *In re Thind*, 268 F. 683 (Or. 1920), 37, available in Supreme Court Records, National Archives, Washington, D.C. For an excellent discussion of the *Thind* case, and the naturalization cases involving race more generally, see Ian F. Haney Lopez, *White by Law: The Legal Construction of Race* (New York: New York University Press, 1996).

2. Toni Morrison, "On the Backs of Blacks," *Time*, December 2, 1993; Thomas A. Guglielmo, *White on Arrival: Italians, Race, Color, and Power in Chicago, 1890–1945* (New York: Oxford University Press, 2003).

3. *Dred Scott v. Sandford*, 60 U.S. 393, 407 (1856).

4. Lucy E. Salyer, "Laws Harsh as Tigers: Chinese Immigrants and the Shaping of Modern Immigration Law," *American Journal of Legal History* (January 1997): 41; *People v. Hall*, 4 Cal. 399, 405 (1854).

5. *Plessy v. Ferguson*, 163 U.S. 537, 561 (1896) (Harlan, J., dissenting); Gabriel J. Chin, "The *Plessy* Myth: Justice Harlan and the Chinese Cases," *Iowa Law Review* 82 (1996): 151–182.

6. Roger Daniels, *Guarding the Golden Door: American Immigration Policy and Immigrants since 1882* (New York: Hill & Wang, 2003), 31.

7. 22 Stat. 58 (1882).

8. Tomas Almaguer, *Racial Fault Lines: The Historical Origins of White Su-*

premacy in California (Berkeley: University of California Press, 1994), 184–185, 191.

9. Editorial, *New York Times,* October 28, 1929; Mae M. Ngai, *Impossible Subjects: Illegal Aliens and the Making of Modern America* (Princeton: Princeton University Press, 2004), 109; Carey McWilliams, "Exit the Filipino," *The Nation,* September 4, 1935, 265.

10. George W. Missemer, "Why the Californians Mob the Filipinos," *China Weekly Review,* February 8, 1930, in Some Materials Re Migrant Labor–Federal Writers Project, collection of Bancroft Library, University of California, Berkeley (hereafter BL-UCB), Box 16, unnumbered folder labeled "Filipinos," 352; C. M. Goethe, "Filipino Immigration Viewed as a Peril," *Current History* (June 1931): 353–354.

11. E. S. Bogardus, "Anti-Filipino Race Riots: A Report Made to the Ingram Institute of Social Science," May 15, 1930, BL-UCB; Bruno Lasker, *Filipino Immigration to Continental United States and to Hawaii* (Chicago: University of Chicago Press, 1931), 18–19.

12. A. H. Keane, *The World's Peoples: A Popular Account of Their Bodily and Mental Characters, Beliefs, Traditions, Political and Social Institutions* (New York: Putnam, 1908), 1, 12–13.

13. Dillingham Commission, "Dictionary of Races or Peoples," 61st Cong., 3d sess., Doc. No. 662 (Washington, D.C.: Government Printing Office, 1911), 97.

14. Alfred P. Schultz, *Race or Mongrel* (Boston: L. C. Page & Co., 1908), 7, 261; Madison Grant, *The Passing of the Great Race; or the Racial Basis of European History* (New York: Charles Scribner's Sons, 1916), 15.

15. Grant, *The Passing of the Great Race,* 15–16, 47, 228.

16. Eliot G. Mears, "California's Attitude towards the Oriental," *Annals of the American Academy* 122 (1925): 206.

17. See generally Peggy Pascoe, "Miscegenation Law, Court Cases, and Ideologies of 'Race' in Twentieth-Century America," in *Sex, Love, Race: Crossing Boundaries in North American History,* ed. Martha Hodes (New York: New York University Press, 1999), 469–476.

18. Ibid., 470–472.

19. Guglielmo, *White on Arrival,* 8–9.

20. Ibid.

21. See Lopez, *White by Law.*

22. Franz Boas, *The Mind of Primitive Man* (New York: Macmillan, 1911), 260–262.

23. Quoted in George W. Stocking Jr., *Race, Culture, and Evolution: Essays in the History of Anthropology* (Chicago: University of Chicago Press, 1982), 213; Boas quoted in Kamala Visweswaran, "Race and the Culture of Anthropology," *American Anthropologist* 100 (March 1998): 71.

24. Stocking, *Race, Culture, and Evolution*, 272, 275–276.

25. Robert Ezra Park, *Race and Culture* (New York: Free Press, 1950), 17, 191, 380–381, 384, 398; Edward B. Reuter, *The Mulatto in the United States* (Boston: Richard G. Badger, 1918), 396–397; Melville Herskovits, "Race Mixture," in *Encyclopedia of the Social Sciences*, vol. 12 (New York: Macmillan, 1934), 43.

26. *Rollins v. State*, 18 Ala. App. 354 (1922); Matthew Frye Jacobson, *Whiteness of a Different Color: European Immigrants and the Alchemy of Race* (Cambridge, Mass.: Harvard University Press, 1998).

27. Guglielmo, *White on Arrival*, 21–30.

28. *Ex parte Shahid*, 205 F. 812, 813 (1913).

29. *In re Ellis*, 179 F. 1002, 1002–3 (D. Or. 1910).

30. Ibid., 1003.

31. *In re Halladjian*, 174 F. 834, 835, 837 (C.C.D. Mass. 1909).

32. Ibid., 837.

33. Ibid., 838–840; see also *In re Mudarri*, 176 F. 465 (C.C.D. Mass. 1910) (finds Syrians white; relies on science). For a list of all the naturalization cases involving whiteness, see Lopez, *White by Law*, appendix.

34. *In re Halladjian*, 843.

35. *Ex parte Shahid*, 205 F. 812, 816 (E.D.S.C. 1913).

36. Ibid., 815.

37. *United States v. Cartozian*, 6 F.2d 919, 920–922 (D.C. Or. 1925).

38. See Guglielmo, *White on Arrival*, 6 ("We must admit of a system of 'difference' by which one might be both white *and* racially distinct from other whites").

39. 180 F. 694, 695 (C.C.S.D.N.Y. 1910).

40. Ibid., 696.

41. Petition of Mohan Singh, *In re Mohan Singh*, RG 21 (Records of the District Courts of the United States), Central District of California, Los Angeles, Naturalization Petitions, F. 3278, Box 17, National Archives and Records Administration, Laguna Niguel (hereafter NARA-LN); *In re Mohan Singh*, 257 F. 209, 212 (S.D. Cal. 1919).

42. *In re Sadar Bhagwab Singh*, 246 F. 496, 497–498 (E.D. Pa. 1917).

43. Ibid., 498.

44. Answer, *United States v. Deir Chand*, Box 126, Folder G103–105, Equity Case No. G105, RG 21, Southern District of California, Central Division, 1929–1938, NARA-LN; Defendant's Reply Brief in Support of His Motion to Dismiss, *United States v. Akhay Kumar Mozumdar*, RG 21, Box 134, H-5-J, 2, NARA-LN.

45. *In re Young*, 198 F. 715, 716–717 (N.D. Wash. 1912).

46. Brief for Petitioner, *United States v. Ozawa*, 42, 60–61, available at National Archives and Records Administration, Washington, D.C. (hereafter NARA).

47. Ibid., 60–61, 63–64.
48. Amicus Brief, Attorney General of the State of California, *United States v. Ozawa,* 3, 40, 83.
49. Brief of the United States, *United States v. Ozawa,* 9, 32.
50. *Ozawa v. United States,* 260 U.S. 178, 189 (1922).
51. Ibid., 197–198.
52. *In re Bhagat Singh Thind,* 268 F. 683, 683 (D. Or. 1920); Brief for the United States, *In re Bhagat Singh Thind,* 8, 15, NARA.
53. Brief for the United States, *In re Bhagat Singh Thind,* 18–19.
54. *United States v. Bhagat Singh Thind,* 261 U.S. 204, 208–209 (1923).
55. Petition for Cancellation of Naturalization, *United States v. Sakharam Ganesh Pandit,* No. G111, June 23, 1923, Folder G109–111[1/2], Equity Case Files, Box 126, RG 21, NARA-LN; Answer, ibid., No. G-111-T, Box 25, Folder 63, 8, RG 21, NARA-LN.
56. Answer, ibid., 7.
57. Deposition of Doctor Grafton Elliott Smith, July 24, 1924, ibid., 5, 7, 12.
58. Notice of Motion, April 28, 1926, ibid., 1, 7, 9.
59. Objections Made and Amendments Proposed to Plaintiff-Appellant's Statement of Testimony, ibid., 34.
60. Emory S. Bogardus, "What Race Are Filipinos?" *Sociology and Social Research* 16 (1931–32): 275–279.
61. Alfonso Santos, "A Filipino Race in the Making," 160.
62. Nellie Foster, "Legal Status of Filipino Intermarriages in California," *Sociology and Social Research* 16 (1932): 444–445.
63. Ibid., 445.
64. Ibid.
65. Ibid., 446.
66. Ibid.
67. Ibid., 447–448.
68. *Stella F. Robinson v. L. E. Lampton,* No. 2496504, Los Angeles County Superior Court Records, March 1930; *Visco v. Los Angeles County,* No. 319408, Los Angeles County Superior Court Records, June 3, 1931, both available at California State Archives, Sacramento; Foster, "Legal Status of Filipino Intermarriages in California," 449.
69. Complaint, *Murillo v. Murillo,* No. D-97715, Los Angeles Superior Court Records, October 11, 1931, 1, available at California State Archives, Sacramento.
70. Opinion, ibid.
71. Transcript on Appeal, *Roldan v. L.A. County,* Civil No. 8455, 18 P.2d 706 (Cal. Dist. Ct. App. 1933), District Court of Appeal, Second Appellate District, May 20, 1932, 14, 16 (bill of exceptions), available at California State Archives, Sacramento.

72. Ibid., 17–18.

73. Respondent's Brief, *Roldan v. L.A. County*, August 1, 1932, 4, 9.

74. Amicus Brief, U.S. Attorney General, *Roldan v. L.A. County*, July 27, 1932, 4–5.

75. Amicus Brief, Attorney General of the State of California, *Roldan v. L.A. County*, March 11, 1933, 19.

76. Ibid., 4, 9, 5, 13; Opinion, *Roldan v. L.A. County*, January 27, 1933.

77. Pascoe, "Miscegenation Law," 468.

8. Mexican Americans and the "Caucasian Cloak"

1. *Brown v. Board of Education*, 347 U.S. 483 (1954); *Hernandez v. Texas*, 347 U.S. 475 (1954); Appellant's Brief at 17, *Hernandez v. Texas*, 251 S.W.2d 531 (Tex. Crim. App. 1952), No. 24, 816 (collection of Texas State Library and Archives Commission, Austin, Archives and Information Services Division, hereafter TSLAC-AISD).

2. Statement of Facts, *Ramirez v. State*, 40 S.W.2d 138, 139 (Tex. Crim. App. 1931), Texas Court of Criminal Appeals No. 13,789, TSLAC-AISD, 11; Gustavo Garcia, "An Informal Report to the People," in *A Cotton Picker Finds Justice! The Saga of the Hernandez Case*, comp. Ruben Munguia (1954), available at http://www.law.uh.edu/Hernandez50/saga.pdf.

3. Neil Foley, *The White Scourge: Mexicans, Blacks, and Poor Whites in Texas Cotton Culture* (Berkeley: University of California Press, 1997), 19–20, 24–25, 41–42; David Montejano, *Anglos and Mexicans in the Making of Texas, 1836–1986* (Austin: University of Texas Press, 1987), 252; Richard Griswold Del Castillo, *The Los Angeles Barrio, 1850–1890: A Social History* (Berkeley: University of California Press, 1979).

4. Foley, *White Scourge*, 19, 61.

5. Ibid., 19, 24, 28–29, 42, 61; Montejano, *Anglos and Mexicans*, 235–252.

6. Neil Foley, "Straddling the Color Line: The Legal Construction of Hispanic Identity in Texas," in *Not Just Black and White: Historical and Contemporary Perspectives on Immigration, Race, and Ethnicity in the United States*, ed. Nancy Foner and George M. Fredrickson (New York: Russell Sage Foundation, 2004), 341–357.

7. Ibid., 342–343; *In re Rodriguez*, 81 F. 337 (W.D. Tex. 1897).

8. *In re Rodriguez*, 81 F. at 337–338.

9. Ibid., 344–345.

10. Ibid., 346–347.

11. *Flores v. State*, Slip Opinion, No. 727 (Tex. Crim. App. June 22, 1910), Texas Court of Criminal Appeals, TSLAC-AISD, 1.

12. Transcript of Trial, *State v. Flores*, No. 3020 (Dist. Ct. Tex., December 5, 1909), 1–2.

13. Ibid.

14. Ibid., 3–4, 14.

15. Ibid., 9–11.

16. Ibid., 11.

17. Charge of the Court, *State v. Flores*, No. 3020 (Dist. Ct. Tex. November 24, 1909); *Flores*, Slip Opinion, No. 727, 1.

18. 206 P. 405 (Ariz. 1922); Appellant's Abstract of Record, *Kirby v. Kirby*, No. 1,970 (Supreme Court of Arizona Records, Arizona State Archives, Phoenix, hereafter SCAR-ASA), 1–2, 12–15; see also Peggy Pascoe, "Miscegenation Law, Court Cases, and Ideologies of 'Race' in Twentieth-Century America," in *Sex, Love, Race: Crossing Boundaries in North American History*, ed. Martha Hodes (New York: New York University Press, 1999), 464–465.

19. Appellant's Abstract of Record, *Kirby v. Kirby*, 14–15.

20. Ibid., 15

21. Ibid., 16–17.

22. Ibid., 19; Pascoe, "Miscegenation Law," 468.

23. *State v. Pass*, 121 P.2d 882 (Ariz. 1942).

24. Ibid., 882–883.

25. Transcript of Trial, *State v. Pass*, No. 16,267, May 22, 1941, SCAR-ASA, 286, 289, 293–294; *Pass*, 121 P.2d at 883–884.

26. Christopher Arriola, "Knocking on the Schoolhouse Door: *Mendez v. Westminster*: Equal Protection, Public Education, and Mexican Americans in the 1940s," *La Raza Law Journal* 166 (1995): 170; David G. Gutiérrez, *Walls and Mirrors: Mexican Americans, Mexican Immigrants, and the Politics of Ethnicity* (Berkeley: University of California Press, 1995), 40–41.

27. Gutiérrez, *Walls and Mirrors*, 52–53, 69–72.

28. Montejano, *Anglos and Mexicans*, 160; Foley, *White Scourge*, 122; Index to Segregatory Incidents, collection of University of Texas at Austin, Austin, Benson Latin American Collection, LULAC (League of United Latin American Citizens) Archives (hereafter UT-BLAC), Manuel C. Gonzales Collection, Folder 2, 1–6.

29. Manuel Ruiz Jr. to Office of War Information, July 19, 1944, collection of Stanford University Libraries, Palo Alto, Special Collections and University Archives (hereafter SUL-SCUA), Manuel Ruiz Papers, 1931–1986, Box 2, Folder 15; Manuel Ruiz Jr. to Captain Harry Lawrenson, May 9, 1945, SUL-SCUA, Ruiz Papers, Box 3, Folder 12; *People v. Whipple*, 279 P. 1008 (Cal. Dist. Ct. App. 1929); Statements of the Court, *In re* a Minor, No. XXXX (crim. no. 1805), Ruiz Papers, Box 3, Folder 12 (Sup. Ct. Cal. September 2, 1969), SUL-SCUA.

30. *Westminster Sch. Dist. v. Mendez*, 161 F.2d 774, 780 (9th Cir. 1947); "He-

gira of Mexicans Bothers California," *New York Times,* April 19, 1931, in Source Material Gathered by the Federal Writers Project on Migratory Labor, Bancroft Library, University of California, Berkeley (hereafter BL-UCB), Carton 16, Folder 704.

31. Manuel Ruiz, untitled news report from Los Angeles, Associated Press, April 30, 1945, SUL-SCUA, Manuel Ruiz Papers, Box 16, Folder 3; see also National Origins Council of America to Senator Slater, Chairman, Education Committee, California State Senate, May 15, 1945, ibid.; Carey McWilliams, "Is Your Name Gonzales?" *The Nation,* March 15, 1947, 302.

32. United States Department of Commerce, Bureau of the Census, *200 Years of U.S. Census Taking: Population and Housing Questions, 1790–1990* (Bountiful, Utah: Heritage Quest, 2000), 60, 65, 69, 90; University of Virginia, Geospatial and Statistical Data Center, Historical Census Browser, State Level Results for 1930, http:// fisher.lib.virginia.edu/collections/stats/histcensus/index.html (accessed December 22, 2006); Margarita B. Melville, "Hispanics: Race, Class, or Ethnicity?" *Journal of Ethnic Studies* 16 (Spring 1988): 67, 70; Julian Samora and Patricia Vandel Simon, *A History of the Mexican-American People,* rev. ed. (1993), available at http:// www.jsri.msu.edu/museum/pubs/MexAmHist/chapter2.html.

33. Index to Segregatory Incidents, 9; Texas State Department of Health, Form No. M911, Tuberculosis Record, attached to Albert Armendariz to Henry Holle, August 26, 1954; Texas State Department of Health, Form No. M9101, Morbidity–General Medical Record; and Henry Holle, M.D., to Albert Armendariz, September 3, 1954, all TSLAC-AISD, Records, Texas Good Neighbor Commission (hereafter TGNC), Box 1989/59-42, Folder marked "LULAC's 1955–56."

34. Joe Belden, "Minority of Texans Favors Separation for Latin Students," *Austin American-Statesman,* June 9, 1950, TSLAC-AISD, Records, TGNC, Box 1989/59-18; J. G. Riser to Allan Shivers, August 24, 1953, TSLAC-AISD, Records, TGNC, Box 1989/59-17, Folder 11.

35. Ian F. Haney Lopez, "Race, Ethnicity, Erasure: The Salience of Race to LatCrit Theory," *California Law Review* 85 (1997): 1164–65.

36. Objects and Aims of the United Latin American Citizens, 1929, UT-BLAC, Oliver Douglas Weeks Collection, 1922–1932, Box 1, Folder 5, 6.

37. Alonso S. Perales, "The Unification of the Mexican-Americans," *La Prensa,* September 4, 1929, UT-BLAC, Weeks Collection, 1922–1932, Box 1, Folder 13; application for LULAC membership, ibid., Folder 3; LULAC Resolution, "On the Question of the Hyphen," adopted June 6, 1936, reprinted in LULAC, "50 Years of Serving Hispanics, Golden Anniversary, 1929–1979," ibid., Folder 3; Perales, "The Unification of the Mexican-Americans III," *La Prensa,* September 6, 1929, ibid., Folder 13; Perales,

"The Unification of the Mexican-Americans VI," *La Prensa*, September 10, 1929, ibid., Folder 13.

38. "Latin-U.S. Group Form Service Body; Organization's Purpose Is to Gain Equal Rights for All Citizens Here," *Brownsville Herald*, September 22, 1929, UT-BLAC, Weeks Collection, 1922–1932, Box 1, Folder 11; Thomas A. Guglielmo, "Fighting for Caucasian Rights: Mexicans, Mexican Americans, and the Transnational Struggle for Civil Rights in World War II Texas," *Journal of American History* 92 (March 2006): 1212, 1221–22.

39. Neil Foley, "Partly Colored or Other White: Mexican Americans and Their Problem with the Color Line," in *Beyond Black and White: Race, Ethnicity, and Gender in the U.S. South and Southwest,* ed. Stephanie Cole and Alison M. Parker (College Station: Texas A&M University Press, 2004), 123–144, 131.

40. Ibid., 136; Gutiérrez, *Walls and Mirrors,* 154, 163–164.

41. Joe A. Real to Mrs. Pauline Kibee, March 6, 1945, TSLAC-AISD, Records, TGNC, Box 1989/59-42, folder marked: GI Forum, general, 1945–1948; José M. Rodriguez to Coordinator of Inter-American Affairs, June 5, 1944, ibid.; see also John F. Mendez to Manuel Ruiz, November 11, 1943, SUL-SCUA, Ruiz Papers, Box 2, Folder 16 (calling exclusions from theaters an "insult to the entire Mexican race").

42. Quoted in Benjamin H. Johnson, *Revolution in Texas: How a Forgotten Rebellion and Its Bloody Suppression Turned Mexicans into Americans* (New Haven: Yale University Press, 2003), 193–194.

43. State of Texas, Department of Public Welfare, Notice of Investigation to New Applicant, Corpus Christi, certified March 9, 1950, TSLAC-AISD, Records, TGNC, Box 1989/59-18, Discrimination Files, folder marked: Discrimination, correspondence, 1949–1950; Philip M. Hauser to Hector Garcia, February 23, 1950, ibid.; Lauro Izaguirre to Watson Wise, August 20, 1958, TSLAC-AISD; William D. Bonilla to Frank H. Kelley, May 1, 1963, and Frank H. Kelley to Ritchey's River Bend Camp, May 23, 1963, TSLAC-AISD, Records, TGNC, Box 1989/59-17, Discrimination Files, folder marked: Discrimination—General File, 1961–1968.

44. J. Conrad Dunagan to Glenn E. Garrett, February 15, 1960, quoting Wesley Martin, School Superintendent, Monahans, Texas, to J. Conrad Dunagan, TSLAC-AISD, Records, Texas GNC, Box 1989/59-16, Discrimination Files, folder marked: Black-list and discrimination, 1958–1961, 6.

45. Ibid.; Benjamin Heber Johnson, "The Cosmic Race in Texas: Intermarriage, White Supremacy, and Civil Rights Politics" (unpublished ms. on file with author), 8; press release, Mexican-American National Association, "A General Statement on the Founding and Perspectives of the Mexican-American National Association," March 1969, BL-UCB, Carey McWilliams Papers, Carton 21, Folder 6, 2–3.

46. "Mexican-Americans Favor Negro School Integration," *American G.I. Forum News Bulletin* (September–October 1955), TSLAC-AISD, Records, TGNC, Box 1989/59-42, folder marked: American G.I. Forum, 1; Manuel Avila to Ed Idar, State Chairman, American G.I. Forum, February 7, 1956, quoted in Foley, "Partly Colored or Other White," 137.

47. Manuel Ruiz to Jack Busch, June 12, 1945, SUL-SCUA, Ruiz Papers, 1931–1986, Box 2, Folder 16; Johnson, *Revolution in Texas,* 194.

48. J. Luz Saenz, "I Am an American," May 1941, José de la Luz Sáenz Papers, Box 3, Folder 3, UT-BLAC; Johnson, "The Cosmic Race in Texas," 7.

49. Foley, "Partly Colored or Other White," 138; Johnson, *Revolution in Texas,* 51.

50. *Indep. Sch. Dist. v. Salvatierra,* 33 S.W.2d 790, 792–793 (Tex. Civ. App. 1930); "Del Rio Segregating Case Up to High Court," unidentified news clipping, UT-BLAC, Weeks Collection, 1922–1932, Box 1, Folder 19.

51. *Salvatierra,* 33 S.W.2d at 792, 796.

52. Brief for Appellants, *Indep. Sch. Dist. v. Salvatierra,* No. 8,515, Court of Civil Appeals, TSLCA-AISD, 10–11; Appellee's Motion for Rehearing, *Indep. Sch. Dist. v. Salvatierra,* ibid., 5, 7, 21.

53. 40 S.W. 2d 138, 139 (Tex. Crim. App. 1931); Petition for Writ of Certiorari, Statement of Facts, *Ramirez v. State,* Court of Criminal Appeals No. 13,789, TSLAC-AISD, 10–11.

54. *Ramirez,* 40 S.W.2d at 138, 139.

55. Appellant's Motion for Rehearing, *Ramirez v. State,* No. 13,789, Court of Criminal Appeals, TSLAC-AISD; Transcript of Trial, *State v. Ramirez,* No. 932 (Dist. Ct. Tex. April 9, 1930), TSLAC-AISD, 7.

56. 95 S.W.2d 433, 434 (Tex. Crim. App. 1936); 124 S.W.2d 344, 348 (Tex. Crim. App. 1939).

57. Bureau of the Census, *200 Years of U.S. Census Taking,* 60, 65, 69.

58. Statement of Facts and Bills of Exception, *State v. Sanchez,* No. 117 (Dist. Ct. Tex. Oct. 25, 1943) (Bill of Exception No. 1), 54–55.

59. Ibid., 56–57.

60. Ibid. (Bill of Exception No. 6).

61. *Sanchez v. State,* 181 S.W.2d 87, 90–91 (Tex. Crim. App. 1944); Brief for Appellee, *Sanchez v. State,* No. 22,856, Texas Court of Criminal Appeals, TSLAC-AISD, 8.

62. 193 S.W.2d 211 (Tex. Crim. App. 1946); 213 S.W.2d 837 (Tex. Crim. App. 1948); 236 S.W.2d 141 (Tex. Crim. App. 1951); Manuel C. Gonzales to Dr. George I. Sanchez, May 21, 1946, UT-BLAC, Sanchez Papers, Box 28, Folder 5.

63. Gonzales to Sanchez, May 21, 1946.

64. 243 S.W.2d 700, 701 (Tex. Crim. App. 1951); Brief for Appellant, *Sanchez v. State,* No. 25,496, Texas Court of Criminal Appeals, TSLAC-AISD, 8–9.

65. *Sanchez*, 243 S.W.2d at 701.

66. Defendant's Motion to Quash and Statement of Facts, *State v. Sanchez*, No. 7103 (Dist. Ct. Tex. June 22, 1951) (collection of Texas State Archives, Austin), 5–7.

67. George I. Sanchez to M. C. Gonzales, April 25, 1945, UT-BLAC, Sanchez Papers, Box 48, Folder 10, 2; M. C. Gonzales to Dr. George I. Sanchez, April 26, 1945, ibid.

68. Plaintiffs' Memorandum in Opposition to Motion to Dismiss of Defendant State Board of Education and Members Thereof, *Delgado v. Bastrop Indep. Sch. Dist.*, No. 388 (W.D. Tex. June 15, 1948), UT-BLAC, Sanchez Papers, Box 48, Folder 5, 12; untitled report on the condition of Bastrop Schools, UT-BLAC, Sanchez Papers, Box 48, Folder 4, 7; 161 F.2d 774 (9th Cir. 1947); Memorandum of Points and Authorities in Support of Plaintiffs' Application for Injunction Pendente Lite, *Delgado v. Bastrop*, No. 388 (W.D. Tex. June 15, 1948), UT-BLAC, Sanchez Papers, Box 48, Folder 5, 3.

69. Instructions and Regulations from State Superintendent of Public Instruction to All School Officers of County, City, Town and School Districts, UT-BLAC, Sanchez Papers, Box 47, Folder 6; "A Monthly Summary of Significant Events Pertaining to Anglo-Latin Relations in Texas," *Border Trends*, Southwest Area Office, Unitarian Service Committee, McAllen, Texas, April 1948, BL-UCB, Carey McWilliams Papers, Carton 21, Folder 4.

70. Hector Garcia, School Inspection Report on Fourteen Schools, TSLAC-AISD, Records, TGNC, Box 1989/59-16, folder marked: Discrim. Gen. [general file, 1946–1951], 1; Transcript of Meeting with School Board, Edcouch-Elsa High School, January 10, 1949, ibid., 2.

71. Interviews by C. P. Aldrete with Del Rio school officials, May–December 1948, UT-BLAC, George I. Sanchez Papers, 1919–1986, Box 24, Folder 3.

72. Interview by Christopher Arriola, Boalt Hall School of Law, with Marge and J. D. Gobbel, in El Modena, California, August 15, 1991, SUL-SCUA, 10; Interview by Christopher Arriola, Boalt Hall School of Law, with Esther and Ralph Danker, in El Modena, California, August 29, 1991, SUL-SCUA, 5.

73. Transcript of Trial, *Mendez v. Westminster Sch. Dist.*, 64 F. Supp. 544, No. 4292 (S.D. Cal. 1946), National Archives and Records Administration, Pacific Southwest Region, 267, 279, 291, 294.

74. McWilliams, "Is Your Name Gonzales?" 303.

75. Appellee's Reply Brief, *Westminster Sch. Dist. v. Mendez*, 161 F.2d 774, No. 11310 (9th Cir. 1947), SUL-SCUA, Box 4, Folder 8, 33.

76. Arriola, "Knocking on the Schoolhouse Door," 193 (quoting Appellee's Reply Brief, *Westminster Sch. Dist. v. Mendez*), 37; Appellee's Reply Brief,

Westminster Sch. Dist. v. Mendez, 32–35 (quoting *Hirabayashi v. United States,* 320 U.S. 81, 110–111 [1943] [Murphy, J., dissenting]).

77. Arriola, "Knocking on the Schoolhouse Door," 198; *Mendez v. Westminster Sch. Dist.,* 64 F. Supp. 544, 549–550 (S.D. Cal. 1946).

78. Arriola, "Knocking on the Schoolhouse Door," 196 (citing Brief for the American Jewish Congress, *Mendez,* 161 F.2d 774, No. 11310); *Westminster Sch. Dist. v. Mendez,* 161 F.2d 774, 780 (9th Cir. 1947).

79. Arriola, "Knocking on the Schoolhouse Door," 201; see W. Henry Cooke, "The Segregation of Mexican-American School Children in Southern California," *School and Society* 417 (June 5, 1948), BL-UCB, Carey McWilliams Papers, Carton 21, Folder 4.

80. Appellant's Brief, *Hernandez v. Texas,* 251 S.W.2d 531, No. 24,816 (Tex. Crim. App. 1952), TSLAC-AISD, Texas Court of Criminal Appeals, 17; see Foley, "Straddling the Color Line," 347.

81. Garcia, "Informal Report."

82. Plaintiffs' Pre-trial Memorandum, *Hernandez v. Driscoll,* S.D. Tex. January 11, 1957 (Civ. No. 1384), UT-BLAC, Sanchez Papers, Box 47, Folder 8.

83. Jack Greenberg to Pete Tijerina, Esq., January 23, 1967, UT-BLAC, Sanchez Papers, Box 33, Folder 1; George I. Sanchez to Pete Tijerina, February 28, 1967, ibid.

84. Ian F. Haney Lopez, "Retaining Race: LatCrit Theory and Mexican American Identity in *Hernandez v. Texas,*" *Harvard Latino Law Review* 2 (1997): 287, 291.

85. 324 F. Supp. 599, 620 (S.D. Tex. 1970).

86. Clare Sheridan, "'Another White Race': Mexican Americans and the Paradox of Whiteness in Jury Selection," *Law and History Review* 21 (Spring 2003): 109–144; Steven H. Wilson, "Brown over 'Other White': Mexican Americans' Legal Arguments and Litigation Strategy in School Desegregation Lawsuits," *Law and History Review* 21 (Spring 2003): 145–194.

87. La Raza Unida Party, State of California Resolutions, April 8–9, July 1–2, 1972, SUL-SCUA, Manuscripts Division, Centro de Acción Social Autonomo Papers, 1963–1978, Box 26, Folder 6, 2; Ysidro Ramón Macías, "Evolution of the Mind and a Plan for Political Action," May 1969, SUL-SCUA, Centro de Acción Social Autonomo Papers, 1963–1978, Box 26, Folder 8, 1, 3; George Azcarate Macias, "Mexican, Mexican-American, Chicano," SUL-SCUA, Ernesto Galarza Papers, 1936–1984, Box 54, Folder 9; Additions and Expansions of the Program of El Plan Espiritual de Aztlán, March 1969, BL-UCB, Carey McWilliams Papers, Carton 21, Folder 9, 1; Ruben Salazar, "Who Is a Chicano? And What Is It the Chicanos Want?" *Los Angeles Times,* February 5, 1970, SUL-SCUA, Ernesto Galarza Papers, Box 54, Folder 9.

88. Del Rio Mexican-American Manifesto, SUL-SCUA, Ernesto Galarza Papers, Box 54, Folder 9.

89. Melville, "Hispanics: Race, Class, or Ethnicity?" 70; Laura E. Gómez, "The Birth of the 'Hispanic' Generation: Attitudes of Mexican-American Political Elites toward the Hispanic Label," *Latin American Perspectives* 19 (Fall 1992): 55; Phillip B. Gonzales, "The Political Construction of Latino Nomenclatures in Twentieth-Century New Mexico," *Journal of the Southwest* 35 (1993): 158–172.

90. Clara E. Rodriguez, "Race, Culture, and Latino 'Otherness' in the 1980 Census," *Social Science Quarterly* 73 (1992): 930–937; see also Rodriguez et al., "Latino Racial Identity: In the Eye of the Beholder?" *Latino Studies Journal* 2 (September 1991): 33–48; Foley, "Straddling the Color Line," 353.

91. *Hernandez v. New York,* 500 U.S. 352 (1991); *Pemberthy v. Beyer,* 800 F.Supp. 144 (D.N.J. 1992), *rev'd,* 19 F.3d 857 (3d Cir. 1994); see also *Garcia v. Spun Steak Co.,* 998 F.2d 1480 (9th Cir. 1993), and *Garcia v. Gloor,* 618 F.2d 264 (5th Cir. 1980) (upholding English-only workplace policies).

Conclusion

1. Immigration and Nationality Act, ch. 477, 66 Stat. 163 (1952); *Loving v. Virginia,* 388 U.S. 1 (1967).

2. *Doe v. State,* 479 So.2d 369 (1985).

3. *Adarand Constructors, Inc. v. Pena,* 515 U.S. 200 (1995).

4. Ashley Montagu, *Man's Most Dangerous Myth: The Fallacy of Race* (New York: Columbia University Press, 1942).

5. *Hopwood v. Texas,* 78 F.3d 932 (5th Cir. 1996); Reva B. Siegel, "Discrimination in the Eyes of the Law: How 'Color Blindness' Discourse Disrupts and Rationalizes Social Stratification," *California Law Review* 88 (2000): 77–118; Dinesh D'Souza, *The End of Racism: Principles for a Multiracial Society* (New York: Free Press, 1995).

6. "Strategic essentialism" was first theorized by Gayatri Spivak in *The Post-Colonial Critic: Interviews, Strategies, Dialogues* (New York: Routledge, 1990).

7. *Regents of the University of California v. Bakke,* 438 U.S. 265 (1976); see, e.g., *Adarand,* Justice Stevens dissenting.

8. Richard Thompson Ford, *Racial Culture: A Critique* (Princeton: Princeton University Press, 2004).

9. See, e.g., Devon Carbado and Mitu Gulati, "Working Identity," *Cornell Law Review* 85 (2000): 1259–1308; Camille Gear Rich, "Performing Racial and Ethnic Identity: Discrimination by Proxy and the Future of Title VII,"

New York University Law Review 79 (2004): 1134–1270; Kenji Yoshino, *Covering: The Hidden Assault on Our Civil Rights* (New York: Random House, 2006).

10. *Price Waterhouse v. Hopkins,* 490 U.S. 228 (1989).
11. 481 US 604, 613, 610 n. 4 (1987).
12. U.S. Census Bureau, 2007 Statistical Abstract, available at http://www .census.gov.

Acknowledgments

I began this project more than eleven years ago, and I have incurred many, many debts along the way, to colleagues, archivists, students, research assistants, deans, editors, and funding organizations. In fact I have been working on it for so long that I am almost certain to have forgotten to mention somebody. I have been lucky enough to be part of two supportive and inspiring reading and writing groups, the members of whom have read numerous chapters of this book in draft, some of them multiple times. The wonderful women of my manuscript writing group from graduate school—Renee Romano, Wendy Wall, Karen Dunn-Haley, Wendy Lynch, Alice Yang, and Leslie Harris—have all challenged me to rethink my ideas about race and history, and have given me many practical suggestions, pep talks, and much love and laughter along the way. In Los Angeles, our law and humanities reading group has also read carefully many iterations of this work: Nomi Stolzenberg, Hilary Schor, Clyde Spillenger, Stuart Banner, Catherine Fisk, Daria Roithmayr, Cliff Ando, Gary Rowe, and David Cruz. Their fellowship and good cheer have made this effort worth continuing.

Several friends and colleagues have read and given me helpful comments on the entire manuscript: Leslie Harris, Laura Kalman, Stuart Banner, Robert Gordon, and Jon Goldman. In addition, numerous colleagues commented on conference papers or chapter drafts, and their suggestions and criticisms helped enormously to shape the work. They include Tiya Miles, Peggy Pascoe, Willy Forbath, Joseph Singer, Sally Gordon, Greg Keating, Naomi Mezey, Tom Green, Dirk Hartog, Bill Nelson, Barry Friedman, Rick Pildes, Tom Holt, Martha Jones, Patricia Williams, Dan Hulsebosch, Terry Fisher, Janet Halley, Kevin Mulroy, Sally Deutsch, Laura Edwards, Walter Johnson, Scott Altman, Adrienne Davis, Eric Talley, Chris Waldrep, Harry Elam, Mary Dudziak, Rebecca Scott, Theda Perdue, Virginia Dominguez, Erika Bsumek, Bethany Berger, Kenji Yoshino, Ben Johnson, Chris Tomlins, Katherine Franke, Anne Dailey, Judith

349

Jackson Fossett, Michelle Aronowitz, and no doubt others I have neglected to name. Their fingerprints can be found on all of the good ideas in this book.

The opportunity to present my work at seminars or colloquia for law and history faculty has immeasurably improved the book. I would like to thank for their comments and criticisms those who participated in workshops at USC, UCLA, NYU, Harvard, Rutgers-Newark Law School, Tel Aviv University, Haifa University, the École des Hautes Études en Sciences Sociales, the University of Utah Tanner Humanities Center, Michigan, Texas, Colorado, Boston College, Cardozo, Emory, Penn, Chicago, UC Santa Barbara, Boston University, UC Davis, Loyola, the American Bar Foundation, and the National Humanities Center, as well as in conference presentations at the annual meetings of the Law and Society Association, the American Society for Legal History, the American Studies Association, the Organization of American Historians, the Southern Historical Association, and the Association for the Study of Law, Culture, and Humanities.

Numerous archivists and librarians, many of whom I do not know by name, helped me with this work. I thank in particular Charles Miller, Laura Cadra, Corrin Gee, Brian Raphael, and Paul Moorman of the USC Law Library; Charles Sherrill of the Tennessee State Archives; Norwood Kerr of the Alabama Department of Archives and History; Marie Windell of the Earl K. Long Library at the University of New Orleans; Nicky Sherman of the Pulaski County, Arkansas, Law Library; Ann Webster of the Mississippi Department of Archives and History; Mark Stone of the Kentucky State Archives; Lisa Gezelter of the National Archives and Records Administration (NARA) Pacific Region; Kent Carter of the NARA Southwest Region; and the archivists at the Oklahoma State Archives, the Cherokee National Historical Society, the Seminole National Museum, the Texas State Archives, the Bancroft Library, and the University of Texas Library, all of whom went out of their way to help me.

Over the years I have had valuable research assistance from many USC law students who are now lawyers out in the wide world. In particular, Bill D'Angelo helped me get this project off the ground. Sharla Manley provided invaluable assistance on Hawai'i, and Natalie Ganz on Melungeons. I also thank Sonya Springer, Karin Lewicki, Debra Mayfield, Rebecca Wolff, Lori Martinez, Shanaira Udwadia, Marisol Haro, Ryan Fife, Ilana Cristofar, Jamila Berridge, Lennox Ketner, Eli Palomares, Tom Kearney, William Watkins, Riaz Tejani, and Pete Brejcha. Sam Erman of the University of Michigan helped me obtain materials from the Michigan State Archives.

Two terrific editors, in different ways, helped me to shape a coherent narrative out of the many stories in this book. I want to thank Rachel Kranz for our long conversations and the ways she pushed me to articulate my argument more clearly. She helped me turn a set of stories into the rough draft of a book. Joyce Seltzer, with amazing efficiency, intelligence, and an eagle eye, helped me turn a rough draft into a final version. I am also grateful to Todd Shuster, my agent, for going far beyond the call of duty on behalf of this book. He is everything one could want an agent to be—intelligent reader, incisive editor, cheerleader, salesman. The manuscript also benefited from the swift and skillful copyediting of Amanda Heller.

Four USC deans and one associate dean supported my research. I thank Scott Bice, Scott Altman, Matt Spitzer, and Ed McCaffery for their generosity in funding research travel and leaves. In addition, a John Simon Guggenheim Memorial Fellowship, a Frederick Burkhardt Fellowship from the American Council of Learned Societies, and a National Endowment for the Humanities Long-Term Fellowship at the Huntington Library allowed me a full year in an office overlooking lovely gardens to work on this book. I especially thank Roy Ritchie for making that year possible. I also received a generous grant from the USC Zumberge Research and Innovation Fund.

Several chapters of this book appeared in earlier forms as articles. The article that began this project, "Litigating Whiteness: Trials of Racial Determination in the Nineteenth Century South," was published in the *Yale Law Journal* 108 (1998): 109–188. Portions of that article appear in Chapters 1 and 2. A version of Chapter 4 was published as "'Of Portuguese Origin': Litigating Identity and Citizenship among the 'Little Races' in Nineteenth-Century America," *Law and History Review* 25 (2007): 467–512, and a version of Chapter 8 was published as "'The Caucasian Cloak': Mexican Americans and the Politics of Whiteness in the Twentieth-Century Southwest," *Georgetown Law Journal* 95 (2007): 337–392. I thank the editors of those journals for their hard work as well.

As is customary, I have left the most important people for last. My family has not only put up with me for all the years of this project's existence but also shaped my thinking about race in ways big and small. I still remember the first time my daughter Rafi called attention to race in my presence: "Look, Mom," she whispered to me. "That man is so white!" She and her sister Sophia have continued to encourage me to look at American society through different lenses. Jon Goldman has been my "interlocutor," as the academics say, for two decades, always pushing me to articulate my ideas in a way that will make sense to people beyond the ivory tower. He has overcome my bad moods with his humor and supported me through every frustration. My mother, Shulamith Gross, read the entire manuscript more than once, and has been a consistent cheerleader for the book, as with every other part of my life. In so many ways, she has made my career possible. My father, David Gross, and my sister and her husband, Sheva and Yun Woo, along with my entire extended family of academics and other assorted thinkers, helped to create the atmosphere of intellectual exchange that makes this enterprise worth doing. My love and thanks to all of you.

Index